Blue Windows

Barbara Wilson

Blue Windows

A Christian Science Childhood

PICADOR USA ❧ NEW YORK

FOR MY BROTHER, BRUCE

Picador® is a U.S. registered trademark and is used by St. Martin's Press under license from Pan Books Limited.

Design by Pei Koay

Library of Congress Cataloging-in-Publication Data

Wilson, Barbara.
    Blue windows : a memoir / by Barbara Wilson.—1st ed.
      p. cm.
    ISBN 0-312-15066-0
    1. Wilson, Barbara, 1950–   —Childhood and youth. 2. Women authors, American—20th century—Biography. 3. Christian Scientists—California—Biography. 4. California—Social life and customs. 5. Family—California. 6. Spiritual life. I. Title.
PS3573.I45678Z465   1997
289.5'092—dc20
[B]
                                       96-30517
                                         CIP

First Picador USA Edition: March 1997

10 9 8 7 6 5 4 3 2 1

Contents

Acknowledgments

This book has been a long time in the making. I owe great thanks to three people in particular who actively encouraged me to write it and who read my tentative early drafts: my longtime friends Chas Hansen and Wendy Smith, and my London therapist "Deborah," who opened up a safe space for me to begin to remember.

I want to thank my father for all the hours he spent telling and retelling me the stories from my childhood, and for giving me the scrapbooks of his orphan years, for me to study and to ponder. My brother I want to thank for reading the manuscript, and for being my companion throughout so many hard years. Special thanks to "Sally" for believing me and for setting me on the journey to Ireland long ago, and to my new Irish family, the Lanes of West Cork.

I have changed the names of all the Christian Scientists from Long Beach and Battle Creek in my book. I am so grateful to "Viv" and "Edyth" for their loving memories of my mother and my childhood, and to the kind group of friends in Battle Creek for making my grandparents come alive to me.

My school years were not always happy ones. Since I may never have another opportunity, I would like to thank some of my teachers for their kindness and belief in me: Mrs. Franken, Miss Swanson, Mr. Mac, and Mrs. Black, my sophomore English teacher. Thank you, too, to Jane Freeman, who opened her home to me in high school and passed on a sense of the importance of history and politics.

My essay-writing group in the late eighties was where a few pieces of this story first saw light. Thank you to Hollis Giamatteo, Ginny NiCarthy, and Marilyn Stablein for listening. For early support in investigating the memoir form, many thanks to Judith Barrington and to Louise Wisechild, whose own brave memoirs have been an inspiration. Thank you to Ruth Gundle for her warm, thoughtful response to the final manuscript, and to Leah Kosik for introducing me to the Buddhist idea that "Your worst enemy is your most precious jewel." Thank you to Rebecca Brown for encouragement at the beginning, and to Katherine Hanson for loaning me her blissfully quiet office at the end.

Regula Noetzli's steady support was a blessing during the time my manuscript took to find a home. Many thanks to George Witte, my editor, for believing in the book, and to Amity Gaige, for keeping me on track with such warmth.

My greatest thanks go to my partner Tere Carranza for her humor, compassion, and endless interest in the mysterious world of the Christian Scientists. At every step of the way she's stood by me and cracked a joke or held my hand as necessary.

And, finally, I want to thank my youngest friend, Eleanor Roach, age ten, for giving me the great gift of her natural exuberance, and reminding me what a joy it is to be alive.

Introduction

*"How long has it been
since you've been home?"*

*M*idway across the Irish Sea, a tremendous gale blew up.
The ferry tilted crazily from side to side. In the bar, glasses slid and
smashed. After throwing up the lunch I'd just eaten, I went out on deck
and sucked on a butterscotch, while my companion Kath found a corner inside and tried to read. It would be ironic, I thought miserably,
clinging to the rail and watching the heaving gray waves, if the ship
were to sink off the coast of the country my grandfather had tried so
hard to escape. Even more ironic, given that the reason for my voyage, that spring of 1987, was to reclaim my heritage and become an
Irish citizen.

Of course, the reason I wanted an Irish passport had little to do with
family at that point. Expediency pushed me to it. I was traveling regularly back and forth between Seattle and London, and thinking about
settling in England. To do so, I needed to be legal. When I happened
to read an article in the *Seattle Times* about Americans who hoped to
avoid trouble abroad—these were the years of Libyan bombings and
hijackings—by using the passports of other countries, I immediately
took notice. Anyone whose parents or grandparents had been born in

Ireland was eligible for Irish citizenship the article noted. Thousands of people in Boston were said to be busily tracking their ancestors at this very moment.

It had only been in the last few years that I'd learned from a relative that my grandfather, John Lane, had been born in County Cork and had left Ireland for Boston when he was fourteen. "He had an Irish accent till the end of his days, but he could never bear to speak of his childhood in Ireland; it was that poor and hard." My grandfather had died when I was very young and I had few memories of him. I'd stored his Irishness away with the rest of the very few things I knew about my family. John Lane was only another ghost in a family tree with more spirits than living relatives.

I called the Irish Embassy in London and a Mr. Anderson told me what I would need to apply for citizenship. Since I was tracing my heritage through my mother, I would require my grandfather's birth certificate, his marriage license, my mother's birth certificate, my parents' marriage certificate, and my own birth certificate. I set to work. In the very beginning, my search for roots seemed to me to be an adventure, a kind of scavenger hunt, rather than a serious effort to find out who my people were and where I'd come from. I was someone who almost never talked about my family and rarely wrote fiction about them. When I did, the only characters were me, my younger brother, and my father, surfacing from the wreckage of death, stunned survivors who couldn't even frame their loss in words. There was a dead mother who exerted an unseen influence on these fictional characters, but she was only discussed in choked, broken phrases, though her absence permeated everything. When I did write about my childhood I never mentioned that I'd grown up a member of a small religious sect called Christian Science, or that it was my mother's religion, the one that failed her.

I didn't connect the search for my family's documents with my tentative work in therapy. I didn't do much connecting at all in those days; disconnecting was more like it. I wrote my relative and discovered that John Lane came from a town called Dunmanway, in West Cork. "Let's go," I said to Kath. "We'll start with him, find his grave, get his birth certificate, then we can drive around and see some of the country."

I had never been to Ireland before, though I'd been almost everywhere else in Europe. I didn't want to be like the hordes of Irish-Americans who came over every summer with their genealogical charts, buying the locals a Guinness at the pub, and stocking up on tweeds and Aran sweaters. If I identified with any part of my ethnic heritage it was with the Scandinavian. My father's mother, Edith, had been born in Stockholm, and I strongly resembled her in the one photo from her short life. All Ireland was to me then was picturesque farms in the south, violence in the north, pretty postcards and political slogans, and nothing much to do with my life at all.

"John Lane?" said the elderly woman who rented rooms in her large old house. She shook her head. "There's the Lanes that run the butcher shop. You go along and ask them."

Dunmanway is a small town, with little to recommend it. There are twenty-three pubs, an enormous Catholic church, and heavy unemployment. Around the town are crumbling farms and houses, with chickens and a cow or two in the yard and squares of peat in neat piles near the walls. It's a landscape that manages to be both green and bleak. Here and there, sometimes side by side with the collapsed roofs of barns and broken walls, are stucco California-style ranch houses, constructed by those who've returned to Ireland after a lifetime of working in another country. Dunmanway has little that is charming to the tourist. It's an honest town, one that would be hardworking if it could be.

At the butcher shop a gregarious woman behind the counter told us that Lane was her husband's name, but that she didn't know of a John Lane who'd been born in Dunmanway. After some thought she recalled another Lane family who lived in Ballineen, not very far away at all. There was a young Dan Lane; if we wanted to meet him, all we had to do was turn up at a car sweepstakes outside a pub along the Dunmanway Road later that night after Mass. There we'd find him, along with everybody else.

We thanked her and went off to read tombstones. First we looked in the Protestant cemetery, because Lane had never seemed an obviously Irish name (later I discovered that it may come from Laine or Lehane, or even McLaine). But there were no Lanes among the Protestants, and most of the tombstones were from the nineteenth century, the era of the Anglo-Irish aristocrats. We crossed over the road to the big Catholic church with the graveyard right in front, and went up and down the rows. No Lanes appeared among the Celtic crosses. I was ready to give up at that point and wait until we'd found Dan Lane, but Kath had an idea. Having been raised Catholic, she knew that around

3

the back of the church would be the houses of the church workers and parish priests. We knocked on a couple of doors until we found a priest who didn't seem at all surprised to see us (I'm sure, in fact, that Americans looking for relatives turned up frequently on his doorstep), and who said, "You'll be wanting the parish register then. Well, now, before Mass tonight you ask for Mr. Burke and he'll help find it for you. You *are* going to Mass, aren't you?"

Kath looked petrified, and we nodded our thanks and went off. "I am *not* going to Mass," she said.

We turned up at the church again at six-thirty and asked for Mr. Burke, a crotchety old man who knew exactly what we wanted and felt impatient with it. I had guessed at my grandfather's age and said I thought his birth date might be between 1880 and 1890. I was tentative and not very hopeful. Around us the acolytes were rushing about in a flurry of satin embroidery and golden chalices. I could feel Mr. Burke's irritation with me ("You don't know the date?") and Kath's uneasiness at being inside a Catholic church after all these years.

I paged through the tall pages of the register with its neat spidery handwriting that recorded baptisms in the parish and, suddenly, there it was under 1888: "April 18th. John Lane. Father, Jeremiah Lane. Mother, Ellen Lane, formerly Crowley."

"Ellen Lane," I said. "But that's my mother's name."

I realized that, through all the preparations for this trip, and all my lively chatter about becoming Irish, I had not really expected to find anything.

Mr. Burke said, "That's him, is it?" and quickly began to write out the Certificate of Baptism in a practiced way. He grabbed the priest to get a signature and stamped the little piece of paper with a seal.

"Mass is about to start," he told us, as we scuttled out, only to find that Kath's car had been blocked in, surrounded in the parking lot by those of Saturday night Mass goers.

"It might be interesting to sit through the service," I proposed.

"It would be horrible!"

We waited it out in a small pub with a handful of nonbelievers. Later that night we drove along a dark road to the car sweepstakes.

At a crossroads in the countryside stood a pub teeming with people inside and out. A stage had been constructed from a semi-truck with its side flaps rolled up, and the drawing for a red Ford Fiesta was about to take place. The wind was howling in the dark of the March night, and most people wore heavy jackets and caps pulled down over their ears.

I asked if anyone knew a Dan Lane, and someone pointed him out, a handsome fellow in his early thirties. His eyes were glued to the red Ford Fiesta that gleamed in a pool of light by the side of the makeshift stage.

"Are you Dan Lane?" I asked. "I'm from America. I think we're related."

His eyes flickered over me in a friendly way and then turned back to the stage, where a young woman wound in scarves against the chill was rummaging around in a box someone held out to her. "Are you now?" he said. "Let's just wait till they've had the drawing."

She pulled a slip from the box and called the winning number. A cheer went up. "Patrick, me boy, don't forget our long years of friendship!"

Dan sighed and turned back to me. He looked a great deal like photographs of my grandfather when young, and like my mother and uncle too. "From America you are then?" he asked. "How long has it been since you've been home?"

Over the next year or so I slowly pursued my Irish citizenship. Every bit of correspondence seemed to take months. From Dublin I managed to get a birth certificate for my grandfather based on the baptismal certificate from the Dunmanway parish church. I also obtained the marriage certificates from my grandparents' and my parents' marriages, both of which had taken place in Battle Creek, Michigan, one in 1918 and the other in 1947. From my grandparents' marriage license I found reassuring proof that my grandfather had indeed been born in Ireland, and that his parents were Jeremiah and Ellen.

The only thing I couldn't get was my mother's birth certificate. My father had told me she was born in Brooklyn, but after months of waiting, I finally heard from the New York Department of Health saying that they had no record of a Margaret Ellen Lane born in that state in 1920. I contacted Mr. Anderson, who had been working with my files at the Irish Embassy, and asked if there was a way around my mother. It seemed to have been a question I'd been asking for years.

"You'll be needing your mother," he said patiently. "If not her birth certificate, then her death certificate."

Once again I wrote to an agency of vital statistics, this time in California, and one day, about a year after Kath and I had been to Ireland, the death certificate came in the mail. I looked at it quickly, then forwarded it on to Mr. Anderson, trying not to remember what I'd seen.

Under "Cause of Death" it read what I had not known: "Carcinoma, right breast, with axillary and supraclavicular metastases." And under "Other Significant Conditions to Death But Not Related to the Terminal Disease Condition Given in Part I," it read what I had always known, though not in those words: "Psychotic depressive reaction."

My mother developed cancer when I was nine and died when I was twelve. Just before she died, my father told me it was cancer, but I knew so little about illness that it never occurred to me to ask where the cancer was located. At the time she was actually sick and dying, cancer seemed the least of her problems. Far more obvious, though also undiscussed, was the mental breakdown that had driven her to make a suicide attempt, an attempt that disfigured her face. Far more obvious than any mere tumor was her emotional fragility, her withdrawals, her other suicide attempts. The cancer had come to seem secondary, though it was what killed her in the end.

My father was not a Christian Scientist, but he felt as bitter against the church as if he had been. In his shame at having been duped by a religion that based its premise on healing and in his suffering, he kept silent about what was happening. What was wrong with my mother was never talked about at all, and after she died, she was almost never referred to by anyone again. I had memories, yes, but I distanced myself as much from them as possible. When people asked me about my childhood, I said only, "My mother died," as if that summed it up. Occasionally I alluded to unhappy times all through adolescence in my stepmother's house. I rarely mentioned my stepbrother, never my uncle. Most people assumed that my pain was around the death of my mother.

I let them assume that. It was certainly true.

My few stories of childhood were often warm, but always selective. Sometimes, when asked what my religion had been growing up, I said, "We were Christian Scientists." Inevitably someone said, "Isn't that the religion where you don't go to doctors?"

"Yes," I said, and then I either told a brief, funny story about the religion's oddities, or changed the subject. Mostly I changed the subject. It would have been too easy for anyone to make the connection: Your mother died, and you belonged to a religion that forbids doctors—did she die because she didn't go to the doctor?

Yes, and no. It's very likely that my mother would have died of breast cancer anyway in 1963. It's also possible that she could have been healed, either through medicine or prayer. The issue is more complicated than that. My mother, raised in the Christian Science church by devoted Christian Science parents, suffered a crisis of faith. It is also possible she was predisposed to madness. Her brother has spent most of his life in mental institutions, diagnosed as paranoid-schizophrenic.

I didn't want to talk about what had happened to my mother because I was ashamed and frightened to remember. I didn't want to talk about Christian Science, either. It wasn't that I had turned violently against it, as my father had, or that I particularly blamed anyone connected with it. Indeed, it was a religion that still secretly intrigued me, if only because of how completely different its world view was than almost anything I'd come across since. I may have only understood it with a child's understanding, but I knew that it was more than just about going or not going to the doctor. It was a far stranger, far more complex system of beliefs that turned reality on its head, that said that only spirit existed, not matter; that there was only good in the world, not evil. It was a belief system that based its power to heal on keeping the mind fixed firmly on God, who was all-powerful and all-loving. It was about choosing to see only beauty and happiness, no matter what, about choosing, as a children's story I remembered once described it, to look at life through the rose windows, not the blue windows.

Its metaphysics are an amalgam of mystical Eastern thought and primitive Christianity, with its emphasis on healing, updated with nineteenth-century notions of Science as pure and all-powerful. It blends the concept of the material world as unreal, the Maya of the Bhavagad-Gita (via New England Transcendentalism) with the idea of Christ as a "Scientist," and healing as a "Science" that can be "demonstrated." It is quintessentially American in both its spiritualism and its pragmatism. It is the religion of "healthy-mindedness" that William James wrote about; it is the forerunner to the vein of positive thinking that darts like fool's gold through American history. Founded by Mary Baker Eddy in the 1870s, this religion never existed in a historical vacuum. It came out of the popular health movement of the nineteenth century, the struggle over women's roles as healers, and the revolt against New England Puritanism. While its heyday is long over, its churches half-deserted, and its authority over its children's health attacked in the courts, the tenets of the religion live on eerily in the pronouncements of popular New Age gurus like Marianne Williamson, Louise Hay, and Deepak Chopra. Although none of them mention Mrs. Eddy, her teachings, down to the exact wording, filter through their books and speeches.

I know a number of people who pursue alternative forms of medicine, and many who believe in the connection between mind and body, though they may not have put it to the test. But I've met very few people outside the Christian Science church itself who know much about it, and few people who were raised the way I was. Some years ago I did know a woman who had gone to Christian Science Sunday School. She absolutely loathed the religion, and would pinch together her mouth to show the prissy expression her mother got when she was expounding Mrs. Eddy's principles. I never dared talk about Christian Science with her. She had clearly never believed a word of it; she had never been fooled like me, or like my mother.

My friend mocked Christian Science, and, indeed, it lends itself easily to satire. Mark Twain set the tone early on by writing an entire book devoted to debunking Mary Baker Eddy, and writers since then, from V. S. Pritchett to Wendy Kaminer (who quotes liberally from Twain in *I'm Dysfunctional, You're Dysfunctional*) to Harold Bloom have followed it. There is and always has been something ridiculous about Christian Science. All religions can be mocked, but a religion that adamantly insists that reality does not exist is particularly easy to poke fun at. I have laughed at it myself, have even wondered occasionally if my strong sense of the comic did not come indirectly from the church's teachings. Yet I was uncomfortable with others who looked only superficially at Christian Science and who found it irrational and absurd. For I knew that even irrational and absurd doctrines have both dignity and consequences. I might recall some of my experiences in the church as peculiar or foolish, but many other memories were tied up with my love for my mother and my absolute loyalty to her. I wanted to be able to joke about Christian Science, but I knew that what had happened to my family as a result of taking this religion seriously was hardly a joking matter.

I lived much of my life in a double bind that was created for me by family secrets and silence. If I told the true story of my mother's faith, illness, and mental breakdown, I risked subjecting her to ridicule and further shame. If I said nothing, I stayed stuck in my own shame, unable to tell the story of a childhood steeped in religion and love. Cancer is a stigma, and so is mental illness, but disease that is untreated and psychosis set in motion by a religious crisis must be even more stigmatized. How to tell about those things? How to write them?

I wanted to talk more openly about my life, my childhood, my mother, but the habits of silence had begun so early and had taken such a firm hold that I never got started. I could not explain the circumstances of my childhood without resorting to explaining Christian Science, but since Christian Science made people shake their heads in wonder or laugh skeptically, how could I explain it? I didn't understand its doctrines well enough myself. I had stopped attending church at thirteen. Yet I knew that my story would be as incomprehensible to others as it was sometimes to me if I couldn't set it in the context of Christian Science.

My Irish passport finally arrived just at the time I decided to return to the States for good. Over the next six years, I pursued the story about what had happened to my mother in a variety of ways, in the interstices of my other writing and editing, on travels, sometimes intently and sometimes trying not to notice what I was doing. I wrote in ink, on sheets of lined blue paper, sheets I bundled into folders or threw into drawers almost immediately and often didn't look at again for months or years. I wrote on trips to foreign countries, in tiny rooms in apartments or hotels where no one knew me. In Mexico one dry and dusty autumn, I spent two weeks in a sublet apartment bent over an old typewriter, listening to and transcribing a taped interview I'd made with my father about his life. When I emerged from the apartment all I saw were sugar skeletons and orange marigolds, preparations for the Days of the Dead. I wrote down everything I remembered about my father during those two weeks and then dumped the pages in a drawer. A year and a half later in Crete I wrote about my stepbrother and stepmother with tears running down my face. I walked in the hills above Chania and saw the wildflowers, celebrated Easter with red-dyed eggs and spring lamb. After a week of writing day and night I tossed forty pages in a folder and didn't even bother transcribing them to a computer disk. I wrote in great concentration, often followed by amnesia. I told the truth, then forgot I told, wrote down what I remembered, and forgot again. Only the fact that I dated my scribbles shows me that I kept writing the same words over and over.

Scribbles first and then a kind of haunting of places that had been familiar to me or my family. I went back to Long Beach, California, where I'd grown up. I drove up and down the streets of the city, stood in front of schools I'd attended. I looked up friends of my mother's. My journey took me back twice to Battle Creek, Michigan, where my grandmother had lived most of her life, and to the Christian Science community that remained. I began to read books on Mary Baker Eddy and her church, on nineteenth-century medicine and spirituality, on women in religion. I read dozens of books on mind/body healing and spirituality, whose messages were similar to what I'd known as a child. I became absorbed, as a feminist who has grappled with issues of power and creativity in my own life, in the complicated career of Mary Baker Eddy, so unpromising, so paranoid, so successful in the end. I became fascinated in the odd theories and metaphysics of Christian Science, fascinated and disturbed by what it had meant, both for me and for my mother, to grow up in a religion that apparently espouses only light, not shadow; spirituality, not matter; goodness, not evil. I also began to realize from my reading that Christian Science did have a shadow side that I had been mostly unaware of when I was growing up, called Malicious Animal Magnetism. M.A.M., based on Eddy's paranoid conviction that other mental healers were trying to get at her and destroy her, was a more prominent part of early Christian Science than I'd ever known. It reassured me, oddly, that my mother's mental illness didn't come out of nowhere. It was the same repressed madness that such a cheerful religion grows like a cancer.

Originally this was meant to be a book about my mother and what happened to her, but in the end, there was only so much I could piece together of my mother's life. My father always assumes a distant look when he speaks of her, except when he recounts the story of her breakdown. My younger brother has tried as much as possible to put the past out of his mind. My mother's friends, most of whom were also Christian Scientists, were less informative than I'd hoped. By the time I began the work of remembering, some had died and others had put her safely away, idealized or disturbing, in the recesses of their minds. When I began I had only a few things to go on: a baby book my grandmother had kept, a "scribble" book from a summer at Girl Scout camp, a half-dozen children's books my mother passed on to me, a ragged red French grammar, the 1941 yearbook from my mother's junior year at Western State Teacher's College in Kalamazoo, Michigan, and photographs from her childhood through the years of her marriage.

There were many reasons it was difficult for me to write about my mother, however, and not all of them had to do with a scarcity of facts. I have the basic outline of her life, and I have, from my earliest years, a store of emotional connection that often takes the place of facts and even images. It will never be possible to create the kind of richly detailed anecdotal portrait of my mother that I would like; it has been far easier to conjure up the spirit of my mother in fiction. But the spirit of her is only part of the truth. And much of the truth remains unknowable. I will never really know what happened to her, why she did what she did. Part of the reason I cannot see my mother before her breakdown, is that *seeing* came later; *seeing* was shocked by difference. In my early memories I cannot differentiate between me and her; later on, the difference was all-important. It was one of the ways I defined myself as I grew—she was crazy, I was not (maybe); she was sick, I would never be; she was dead, I was alive.

Somewhere in the writing, the scribbles and fragments became a memoir, not of my mother's life, but of mine as her daughter, and of a religion that shaped us both. For a memoir that tells the story of lives consecrated to a single ideology must necessarily come to terms with that ideology. Although Christian Science is a fascinating subject in its own right, it has not been merely to satisfy my curiosity that I have investigated it and written about it here. It is that there is no telling my family's history without explaining the hold this religion had on some of us. Tragedies and losses happen in every family, but what happened in my family was intimately linked to the religion that I grew up in.

Ninety or a hundred years ago, when Christian Science was much more visible in American society, I would perhaps not have had to explain so much. The force of Mrs. Eddy's personality was still evident— she was seen as a threat and as a powerful religious leader. Her church excited interest as well as skepticism, and there were frequent newspaper articles, constant lawsuits, and both negative and positive publicity about Mrs. Eddy. Most educated readers knew a little something about the mind-cure movement that seized the imagination of the country at the turn of the century. Now I cannot rely on any general knowledge of Christian Science, and it is for that reason I have intertwined the story of Mrs. Eddy and her church with that of my own early years. Part One, in particular, is a two-tiered project, in which I explore the origins of Christian Science and its effect on American culture, as well as on the three generations of my family who believed in its teachings. In the course of my research I found how much Christian Science is part of many contemporary discourses: on women's spirituality, on mind/body healing, and on the presence of the shadow, or evil, in our lives.

I struggled for a long time with the idea that, after all these years of evading and ignoring it, that this religion was to be my subject. But how could it not be? As a child, this religion was my life. It is impossible for me to deny that it contributed to making me the woman I am today. And since I knew from very early on that I wanted to become a writer, this memoir is also the story of words in my life, of reading and of listening, and of learning what could be written about and what needed to be hidden, of being told to tell the truth and yet instructed in what that truth could be. As a religion that did not acknowledge suffering or the shadow side of life, that did not admit the existence of disease, madness, abuse, cruelty, or evil—all of which I experienced, indeed, knew well, before the age of fourteen—Christian Science gave me, who had so much to tell, little autobiographical to write about. It was only by breaking its spell over me that I forced my lips to tell the truth, that I allowed my pen to write the story of what really happened.

Like anyone who sets out to write a memoir, I struggled with how I would tell family secrets, and whether I was betraying people, some long dead, others still living and close to me. I also struggled how I would survive the ridicule and disapproval of becoming once again the Christian Science child, not so much ostracized as always different, always having to defend an existence that was not like anyone else's. I struggled especially hard with what it meant to remember the horror of what I'd seen, the shame of it. Telling the story meant to some extent reliving it, and going against the silence that surrounded it. Witnessing another's suffering is painful the first time around; could I bear to remember and repeat it? Did I have the right to tell my mother's secrets? I foundered for a long while before I knew what I wanted to write about, and could write about, was my life. The secrets I wanted to tell were my secrets, not hers. The life I wanted to acknowledge and bear witness to was my own.

Every journey has a beginning; mine began when I applied for an Irish passport. It wasn't Ireland that I wanted to get to in the end, it was an understanding of my own past. That's why I've never really used the passport when I travel. I keep it in a drawer with other documents, and sometimes I look at its unmarked pages, and I remember the day I stood in the Dunmanway parish church and said, "Ellen Lane. But that's my mother's name."

There is a taste of Heaven in perfect health

and a taste of Hell in sickness.

—C.W. Post, 1893

Part One

A
Taste
of
Heaven

Chapter 1

Absent Treatment

*O*ne of our next-door neighbors, when I was a child, had a model railway in his garage, and occasionally he invited me and my brother and other kids over to see it run. Mr. Bear put on his striped engineer cap and pulled the sheet off the big plywood table resting on sawhorses. The garage door was always kept closed, the car parked in the driveway, and the darkness of the garage, thick with the scent of grease and metal, with boxes of newspapers and old clothes mildewing in shadowy corners, made the scene before us, lit only by an uncovered light bulb or two, as dramatic as a theater stage before the play begins. Engineer Bear blew his tin whistle, switched a gear, and the miniature train began its journey, bringing everything to life. Circling in an endless figure-eight, the locomotive and the flatcars piled with logs and tiny chunks of coal (barbecue charcoal), the boxcars with Santa Fe and Burlington Northern lettered on the sides, the passenger car with a tiny blue-uniformed conductor visible at one end, passed over bridges and through tunnels, by groves of matchstick trees and along blue-painted streams the width of a ribbon. Around and around the train chugged, humming electrically, occasionally tooting, sometimes stopping at the station to take on or let off minuscule passengers, sometimes steaming straight through the small village to the railroad yard, where cars could be hitched and unhitched.

We kids would watch the train looping around for fifteen minutes or so and then, depending on our age and attention span, get bored and wander off. If we'd had leave to run the trains ourselves, we would have turned the speed up high and crashed the trains as they went round the curve, or put two trains on the track and watched them smash headfirst into each other. We would have put a plastic cow on the crossroads and shrieked, "Get out of the way, you stupid cow. Whoops! Hamburger!" But disasters were something Mr. Bear would never allow, and we never thought of asking permission to wreck everything for the fun of it. His railroad existed only to maintain the status quo, and he was the only person who never got bored with it. He was always planning a new row of houses for his village or increasing the number of barnyard animals in the outlying farms. The endless looping for him was predictable poetry, the closed system a safe place where imagination, of a cozy and limited kind, could flourish.

I think of Mr. Bear and his miniature train when I try to explain Christian Science, and how it was to be raised in a small religious sect. From the outside all sects seem to be closed systems, the same ideas traveling like boxcars pulled by the locomotive of revealed truth along the same routes, circling and recircling in a figure-eight that admits no outside influence and that never deviates, speeds, or crashes. From the inside, of course, it feels completely different. A sect creates a safe haven, a world where the trains run at stable speeds and are always on time, where the streets are swept and no breeze dislodges even a leaf, where barnyard animals neither defecate nor procreate, and where people do nothing but get on and off a train that takes them round and round the same familiar landscape.

When I was growing up, the place that was most like the miniature railroad world of Mr. Bear was Battle Creek, Michigan, the small town where my grandparents lived and where my mother was born. We used to go there for weeks at a time in the Fifties, traveling from Southern California by train or plane, always in the summer, the high summer when the Midwestern sky was an enormous heavy blue with forceful white clouds blustering across it. When the humid air vibrated slowly with the hum of insects and shadows hovered, dark without being cool, under the thick elm trees that broke the sidewalk with their roots.

When the thick sweet smell of cherry and apple pies cooling on the white-painted kitchen counter mingled with the underground cellar fragrance of wash going through the old-fashioned wringer. When it was thunderstorm weather, lightning and wind driving my younger brother Bruce and me inside to play with our uncle's old Lincoln logs or tin soldiers in the attic. When the rain barely relieved the tension in the air and immediately rose in steam from the red brick street in front of the house, a fizzy locomotive of a noise.

We lived in Long Beach, California, where summer meant going to the ocean and spending hours building sandcastles and letting the waves hurl us up and down and back and forth. In Michigan the water was in lakes and in the rain of those hot midafternoon and early-evening storms. Summer in the Midwest meant swimming in those lakes with their oozy mud and plants that grabbed. Summer in Battle Creek was a wet smell of lake water and mildew, and washing and thunderstorms. But there was something toasted about it too. Day and night trains ran through Cereal City, long lines of boxcars bringing corn and wheat and oats from silos in the prairie states. During the day the trains were full of importance, hurtling through town, stopping traffic, making everybody stare and sometimes wave to the engineer, who gave a friendly and powerful wave back. Yet in the middle of the night, it seemed as if the trains called out lonely and aching in the dark. Raisin Bran came from Battle Creek, and Special K and Kellogg's Corn Flakes and Frosted Flakes. When we visited the Kellogg factory we could hear the pinging and spronging of grain roasting in the big metal vats, hear the cascade of millions of tiny particles cascading through chutes, and breathe in the vast swelling warm scent of toasted grain. Facts were thrown at us as we filed along gangways suspended above the huge stainless-steel machinery, facts to do with numbers of ears of corn, and how many acres of grapevines went into how many boxes of Raisin Bran, and how Tony the Tiger got his name. At the end of every visit we were treated to a bowl of vanilla ice cream sprinkled with Cocoa Puffs and given a six-pack of individual-sized cereal boxes.

Other than going to the Kellogg factory there was not much to do in Battle Creek. My brother Bruce and I would run from the cellar to the attic until they made us go outside; we'd play in the backyard and try to climb the cherry trees; we'd walk slowly to Willard Library to get more books, down streets of roomy old houses, saying to each other, "Look at all those stories. Look, there's a three-story and a four-story.

There's a turret and a balcony." The houses seemed to us old-fashioned and romantic, for in California we lived in a flat-roofed bungalow that looked like thousands of others in the spreading subdivisions of the L.A. Basin. These often-shabby Battle Creek Victorians had belonged to wealthy families once; now they were being turned into rooming houses and apartments. The boom days of Battle Creek were over, even though the downtown still bustled during the week and on Saturdays. By the late Sixties that bustle would be gone, too.

On Sundays we all went to the Christian Science church that was set firmly on Church Street along with all the other massive edifices that served Presbyterians, Methodists, and Episcopalians. Bruce and I wriggled on the hard wooden pews, surrounded by ladies in flowery dresses and white gloves. Afterwards we wriggled even more through a Sunday afternoon in Grandma's tiny parlor, its fireplace mantle lined with photographs and the small piano that no one was allowed to play because of the noise, and where Grandma's lady friends, buxom or withered, brooches at their necks, pocketbooks on their laps, hats with tiny veils skewered firmly to their upswept hair, sat on the horsehair furniture and visited over a plate of cookies or slices of cherry pie. Lace doilies were pinned all over the scratchy sofa and chairs, like so many chloroformed white moths. It was ancient Auntie Grace who made those doilies. She lived a block away and, whenever we went to see her, pressed crocheted items into our hands.

Life in Battle Creek revolved around the Christian Science church even more than it did in Long Beach. Much as my mother tried to keep our world at home small and closed, it was clear that, while Christian Science was the best way—the right way—not every single person believed in it. There was no one else on our street and no one else in my school who went to Christian Science Sunday School. My father didn't go to any church at all. He stayed home every Sunday morning and reveled in his privacy. Wearing his old red flannel bathrobe, he cooked himself strange breakfasts—scrambled eggs with left-over spaghetti—which he ate with powdery white "donettes." Sometimes he'd leave a few in the box for us, and sometimes he just had to eat all twelve. He was a stout man then, with wavy brown hair, bright blue eyes, and a cleft chin. He had a hearty laugh and an easy way that belied an inner carefulness and sense of being set apart, of having been, as an orphan, set apart his whole life. He and my mother never discussed religion, even to agree to disagree. He said simply and often, "I respect the Christian Scientists," but that was as far as it went. To him, they were just a bunch of nice, deluded but well-meaning people, going about their church affairs in a harmless and quiet manner. It didn't concern him very much at all.

But in Battle Creek we moved inside a Platonic world where every daily thing reflected a larger truth, where every day was structured around reading and studying the Lesson for the week, and where there was much talk of healing. My grandparents were both practitioners, which meant that they not only earned a living from healing the sick and distressed, but that they were influential and respected in their church. My grandfather had an office in the Post Building, and my grandmother worked from a glassed-in sun porch off the parlor. Sometimes I could hear her talking firmly to people on the rounded black phone, telling them they *were* well, if they could only see it. And sometimes, running by the sun porch on the way outside to see if any more cherries had fallen to the ground, I saw my grandmother through the glass door hung with Auntie Grace's creamy tatted curtains, her white head bent in prayer, her face thoughtful and absorbed. I knew then that she was engaged in the private ritual of absent treatment, of working on the problems, physical and spiritual, of people who were somewhere else, across town or even across the state.

Many years after my first childhood visits to Battle Creek, I walked into Willard Library again. It was now a large new building with an entire downstairs, the Michigan Room, devoted to local and state history. I sat there for several hours one day and then another, at a maple table piled with books, both scholarly and lively, and there I began to trace the history of my grandmother's people, the Lipscombs, and of Battle Creek itself.

My great-grandparents, Allen and Margaret Aldrich Lipscomb, whose own parents had been pioneers on what had been the wild Michigan frontier—north of Detroit—had settled in Battle Creek in 1875, just after they were married. The town was about thirty years old then, and flourishing, with a population of approximately 5,000. Into this boom town came Allen Lipscomb, a carpenter and self-taught architect, who designed and constructed many of the local buildings, including the Maple Methodist Episcopal Church, which still stands. Later he went to work for Nichols and Shepard, one of Battle Creek's largest employers, makers of the famous Vibrator Thresher, as foreman of their woodworking department.

Yes, Battle Creek was a flourishing town, an ordinary Midwestern town, but already one with a peculiar hospitality to eccentric ideas, particularly those centering on health and spirituality, and to the eccentrics and their followers who espoused them. One of the first free-thinking sects was the Alphadelphia Society, an experiment in socialist living which was, like Brook Farm and many other utopian groups, based on the principles of Joseph Fourier, who believed that society should be broken down into units called phalanxes. The community of 300 managed to exist about as long as most utopian colonies, that is three or four years, from 1844 to 1848, just west of Battle Creek. There the members constructed a tabernacle, a school, and a communal dwelling place, and published religious journals, *The Alphadelphia Tocsin* and *The Primitive Expounder*; there they quarreled, disbanded and moved back into Battle Creek. The Swedenborgians also gravitated to Battle Creek in the 1840s, where they built the New Jerusalem Church, and the Spiritualists came along soon after. Battle Creek became a hotbed of Spiritualism; in fact, the movement that had begun with the Fox sisters in Rochester, New York, in 1848 and that focused on occult communication with the dead via spiritual mediums, Ouija boards, table tippings, and slate writing, was so pervasive in Battle Creek that even the Quakers who had arrived there in the 1850s found themselves experimenting with séances and mediums. In 1855 a group of these Quakers bought land six miles from Battle Creek and platted out a settlement called Harmonia, where Sojourner Truth lived for about ten years before getting fed up and moving back into town. More than six feet tall, in Quaker dress, smoking a pipe, the riveting speaker was a familiar figure in Battle Creek for twenty-five years. She's buried in Oak Creek Cemetery, with a monument right next to that of C.W. Post, the cereal magnate.

The deranged and visionary continued to come to Battle Creek. One of the most colorful was James M. Peebles, who arrived in 1856 as a self-proclaimed "spiritual pilgrim," and who lectured on spiritualism, temperance, and morality. He had his own church for a time, and on the side assisted stage mediums who came through town. In order to cure his own ill health he found a way to contact the spirit of Chief Powhatan, of colonial Virginia, who instructed him in the art of picking wild herbs and pounding them into medicine. Peebles wrote great numbers of books, from *Who Are the Spiritualists and What is Spiritualism*, to *Hell Revised, Modernized and Made More Comfortable*.

In the 1860s Peebles left Battle Creek to wander in California and New Jersey. Amazingly enough, he was appointed United States Consul to Trebizond, a Turkish Black Sea port, and after he left that post he traveled three times around the world studying occult forces and chronic diseases. In 1876 he procured a diploma from the medically suspect Philadelphia University of Medicine and Surgery and set up psychic healing institutes all over the U.S. Finally back in Battle Creek at the age of 73, in 1896, he set up Dr. Peebles Institute, a business that specialized in mail-order diagnosis. "Hundreds of patients who have been speedily cured," Peebles wrote in his circulars, "have never seen the doctors who treated them."

My Great-Aunt Shirley, who married my grandmother's brother Guy Lipscomb, was Dr. Peebles's stenographer for many years. It was she who sent out the promotional circulars that claimed he had extraordinary powers of curing, even that he could restore life, claims that brought him an indictment for fraudulent medicine in 1901. As a reporter described his court appearance:

> District Attorney Gordon bellowed at Peebles on the stand: "Do you, before this jury of God-fearing men, now claim, under oath, that you have the powers of our Lord and Savior Jesus Christ, to heal the sick and restore the dead to Life?"
>
> Peebles rose from the chair to his full height of six feet four and raised his fist above his head. He looked like Moses in a Cecil de Mille supercolossal epic. "I do!" he cried in a rich baritone voice that reverberated through the old court chambers. "I do! And may God strike me dead on this spot if I am not possessed of such power! He gave it to me. Speak, O God, and give this jury the proof! The proof!"
>
> The jury and I waited for divine action. The air was tense . . . Peebles stood there with his arm still high, waiting, waiting, waiting. For about a minute he stood, then relaxed. He turned to the jury in a soft purring voice and said: "Gentlemen, you see for yourself."

He was convicted anyway, but that only made him shift into the mail-order patent medicine business, marketing a preparation called the Peebles Epilepsy Cure. When the Pure Food and Drug Act chemists analyzed his "brain restorative" and "nerve tonic," they found the first to be an alcoholic tincture flavored with bitter almonds and the other a solution of vegetable products. Peebles left Battle Creek for California in 1915 and died just short of his one-hundredth birthday.

Battle Creek's reputation as a mecca for both crackpots and more serious seekers and purveyors of health continued to grow. The Seventh-Day Adventists had been in Battle Creek since 1855 when they transferred their operations from New England and upstate New York. They took their teachings from the apocalyptic Millerites and from the visions of Sister Ellen White. The Adventists were wildly opposed to the Battle Creek Spiritualists and one of the ways they proselytized was through the printed word. Their printing plants were all located in Battle Creek; by 1878 a hundred printers ran seven presses to print thousands of books and periodicals, and ten years later there were 262 employees printing 5,000 volumes a day.

In addition to the printing plants, the Adventists established the Western Health Reform Institute in 1868, which focused on hydropathy and diet. One of the Institute's doctors was John Harvey Kellogg, who eventually took it over from the Adventists and called it the Battle Creek Sanitarium. The "San," as it was nicknamed, became more than just a hospital and nurse's teaching school. It was a way of life for thousands of people around the country who referred to themselves as "Battle Freaks" and who flocked there for the latest hydropathic treatments and dietary reforms under Dr. Kellogg's direct supervision. Kellogg was obsessed with the digestive tract and wrote more than a score of books inveighing against the dangers of meat, condiments, and stimulants, and recommending celibacy, vegetarianism, and enemas. At the Sanitarium patients could undergo dozens of water treatments, including sitz baths, dripping sheet baths, cataract douches, plunge baths, and electrical baths, as well as an array of enemas (Kellogg believed that the bowels should be emptied at least twice a day, preferably three or four times). Meals at the San included plenty of stewed prunes, as well as grains and meat substitutes such as "nut roast," "nuttolene," and sliced "protose."

One of the chronic invalids who came to Battle Creek in 1891 looking for help was Charles William Post. After nine months at the Sanitarium his dyspepsia had not improved and Kellogg told him he probably would not live much longer. Instead he moved into the house of a Christian Science practitioner, Mrs. Gregory, where, according to

Post's biographer, he was instantaneously healed and began eating pork chops soon afterwards. In gratitude, Mrs. Post, his wife, helped fund the building of the first Christian Science church in Battle Creek in 1906. Neither of the Posts became Christian Scientist members, however. Instead, Post went into the health business in rivalry with Dr. Kellogg, practicing a mix of positive thinking and "mental negation." He opened a clinic which he called "La Vita Inn" and published a book in 1893 entitled *I Am Well,* in which he wrote that human emotions consisted of negative and positive currents and which owes much to Mrs. Eddy's metaphysics. "The negative currents are thoughts of anger, hate, grief, anxiety, jealousy, apprehension, sensuality, disease, etc. These negative currents are disease producing and tend to destroy and throw out through the pores and other excretory channels the valuable parts or elements in the nerve centers, and deplete and exhaust the battery, so to speak."

To wean his guests off caffeine Post also introduced them to a grain beverage very similar to what he'd been served in the Sanitarium; he called it Postum. A brilliant advertiser, Post coined phrases like "It makes red blood," and by 1900, with the addition of another product, Grape Nuts (which he first tried to sell as a beverage and only later as a breakfast cereal), he had become a millionaire. Post's turn-of-the-century success spawned a mania in Battle Creek for producing breakfast cereals. Soon there were dozens of different brands competing in the market, all based in Battle Creek, cereals with gimmicky names like Grain-O, Malt-Too, Per-fo, Certo-Fruto, Mapl-Flakes. Most of the products failed, but several survived, including one invented by J. H. Kellogg and brilliantly marketed by his brother, William Keith Kellogg—Corn Flakes.

Meanwhile the Christian Science church thrived in Battle Creek, recruiting converts from those the Sanitarium couldn't cure, and helping local practitioners to build substantial practices. By the early years of the twentieth century, Christian Science was a well-established religion, with thousands of members and an aura of middle-class respectability. Although Dr. Kellogg railed against all mind cures in general and Christian Science in particular in his newspaper *The Battle Creek Idea,* calling it a "quagmire of irrational thought," he did find some good in it. "The philosophy is bad—absurd, unbelievable, incredible to the intelligent individual; but it is true that thousands have found relief, comfort, health in it. There is unquestionably something in it that practically is good. The good element in Christian Science is faith. The man who buys a gold brick is happy so long as he thinks he has the real thing and just as happy as though he were the possessor of a lot of gold. So the believer in Christian Science may be helped, not by Christian Science, but by his own faith."

Faith Lipscomb's parents were Methodists, but the Battle Creek that Faith was born into in 1890 was well populated with religious and health faddists, so it's no surprise that she would be drawn into a lifelong preoccupation with health and spirituality. She had left high school after her sophomore year to enter the Battle Creek Sanitarium's nursing school, where she trained from 1907 to 1910. According to the school's yearbook, the students not only studied a curriculum that was comparable to the best hospital training-schools, but in addition took courses in hydrotherapy, electrotherapy, and medical dietetics. Afterwards she nursed for a year or two on a Navaho reservation in Arizona before moving to Detroit to work in a hospital there. That was where she met John Lane, the Irish immigrant, who when he was fourteen had come to Boston, then run away from relatives there to join the U.S. Cavalry in Oregon. In the tantalizing way of family narratives, there are only hints and guesses about my grandfather. At any rate, he somehow ended up in Detroit, where he took up cooking and restaurant management, his line of work until he became a practitioner. He went to France during World War I as a cook, and afterwards he and Faith moved to Brooklyn, where he managed an automat and my grandmother continued nursing.

Perhaps it was in the course of her hospital work that my grandmother witnessed some miraculous healing, or perhaps she saw how often people did not improve through surgery and drugs. Years later a friend of hers told me, "She worked for the Red Cross during the war, while John was in France, and she told me that at times she despaired over material healing, and at those times she would go into a utility closet at the hospital and correct her thinking." They used to say in those days that Christian Scientists were recruited, not from other churches, but from the graveyards. These two typical testimonies of healing in the Twenties are from the book A Century of Christian Science Healing:

Five years ago, I had just spent my last dollar on a bottle of medicine for my wife, when an angel of God's presence caused me to tell a friend my tale of woe. He was a student of Christian Science, about which I had never heard. I told him I was about at the end of my row, as I had been spending all I could rake and scrape up for medicine for my wife, and the doctors said she could not be healed of pellagra, which she had had for years. My friend told me to have no fear, but have my wife read the *Sentinel,* which he gave me. Inside of a week or two she was well and out in the field helping me, completely healed.

A few years ago my baby boy had infantile paralysis; and nine doctors passed the death sentence. Two of the doctors, after taking an X-ray picture, confirmed the sentence. I had help from a Christian Science practitioner, and the baby was healed at once. When I went to pay the doctor for taking the X-ray picture, he said, "I am awfully sorry for you, George; I know the child is dead." I told him that Christian Science had healed him, and that he was playing around, happy as a lark.

In 1929, when my mother was nine years old and my uncle was a baby, my grandparents moved back to Battle Creek, where they lived in the Lipscomb house with Faith's parents and her unmarried sister Grace. For the first year my grandfather ran a small diner called Lane's Restaurant. Someone who used to eat there at the time recalls him serving "typical Depression fare: frankfurters and beans, beef stew, everything costing less than a quarter." However, within a few years he'd become a full-time Christian Science practitioner, able to support his family.

Becoming a practitioner is nothing anyone does overnight, I've learned from reading "The Socioreligious Role of the Christian Science Practitioner", an article by Margery Fox. It's not a case of going to school and getting a degree; there is some instruction, but it is minimal and consists of an intensive ten-day course by a Christian Science teacher, who has in turn been instructed at a week-long course given every three years at the main Christian Science church, the Mother Church in Boston. But formal recognition comes slowly. The practitioner begins to get a small, local reputation as someone you can talk to, someone who understands and can explain the ideas in *Science and*

Health, Mrs. Eddy's main work, someone who can heal his or her family and friends. Later, gaining confidence, the practitioner answers informal calls from other members of the church, calls that may concern health, but might just as well deal with questions of employment and schooling, business problems, even some theological confusion. It is recognized in Christian Science that everyone is capable of healing themselves, but that it is given to relatively few people to be able to heal others. Practitioners are self-selected through their success in healing others, not through ambition. They become spiritual leaders, because others recognize that they have the power to heal. In the absence of a trained clergy, Christian Science practitioners take on a role in their community of introducing people to the main ideas of the religion, helping people through crises, and generally keeping everyone's faith strong and clear. Eventually a practitioner will take the final step of becoming "*Journal*-listed," which involves submitting evidence of three "physical" healings to the church's governing body, the Board of Directors, who will approve the application and allow the practitioner to be listed in the *Christian Science Journal* and thus to formally set up shop as a healer.

Christian Science practitioners work through prayer, but much of what that involves is keeping one's thought clear in order to "handle the claim of illness." It means reading and studying the Bible and Mrs. Eddy's works and keeping a focus on the patient as a perfect being. While many of the problems patients exhibit have less to do with major physical diseases than with niggling ailments like hay fever and rashes, and with the general wear and tear of being human, practitioners are not meant to probe and psychoanalyze their patients. In fact, they are not supposed to pay much attention at all to patients' recounting of their symptoms, physical or mental. In some cases they do their work at the patient's side, but in many cases they work over the phone or without any contact at all. It is even considered preferable to do absent treatment, which simply means that the practitioner endeavors very hard to bring his or her own mind, as well as the mind of the patient, into accord with spiritual law.

Among the people who had known my grandparents, I found memories of two very distinct ways of healing. My grandmother was vigorous and no-nonsense. One friend said, "Faith used to tell me, 'Hazel, you need to unscrew your head and pour some starch down your spine.' "

Another friend, Verna, laughed. "She was exuberant when I first knew her, full of joy, both feet on the ground. She made you *want* to be well."

"That's right," Ed agreed. "Oh, she was strong-willed. She used to say, 'Snap out of it. Pull yourself together.' And I would. She was like a drink of cold water."

"One thing I remember about Faith," Ronald added, "if she undertook to work for you, you had to do your share."

My grandfather was different, they said. He was gentle and kind. "That's what you remembered about him. How kind he was. That and how beautifully he dressed. He had that Irish accent, you know, and he was always in pinstripes and lovely white shirts with cufflinks. When he was First Reader in the church he wore a cutaway suit; now that was something."

The six of us were sitting in a restaurant called the Country Kitchen eating loin of pork and mashed potatoes with gravy at noon on a Sunday. I had appeared at the service that morning and had gone up to one of the ushers. I had only to say my name when she knew me again: "Faith's granddaughter!" And she had invited me to Sunday dinner with her husband and friends, all of whom had known my grandparents.

Now Ronald, a sweet-faced, rotund man in his sixties, was speaking: "I'll tell you a story of how your grandfather healed me once. He healed me several times over the years of various things; when I came back from World War II, for instance, and had been stuck on a ship in the Pacific and couldn't get off for about a year or more, and when I got back home I was pretty low and didn't want to go out of the house. Mr. Lane helped me with that and soon I was able to go back to work and everything was all right. But the time I'm talking about, it was earlier. I was about seventeen or eighteen and for some time I'd been afflicted with boils in my throat. It was some kind of infection that kept coming back, my whole throat inside would be covered with these boils and of course I couldn't eat, had a lot of trouble swallowing food. These boils would go away and then they'd come back again, and I was in my first year of college and, I can tell you, it was an annoying thing to have to deal with. Plus I was losing weight. So I went to Mr. Lane's office in the Post Building, where he used to have it, and I told him about my problem, and he asked me, kind as kind, if I thought I had the boils now. I said yes, and he said, 'Please stand up. Stand up and look at me.' And he stood too, behind his desk, and very quietly said, 'You are healed.'

"And at that very moment, the boils burst and blood came spurting out of my mouth, it sprayed across the desk, over all the books and papers and things, and right onto him, over his beautiful white shirt. But he didn't care. And the boils never came back."

The friends concur: "They were very different, the two of them, but they were happy together. Your grandfather used to say, 'I had a little bit of Faith when I got married—but in a few years I had a whole lot more.' That was because your grandma got stout. She was a little bit of a thing when they married."

I remember my grandmother's toughness and strong will, and also her skepticism about human nature. Underneath the metaphysical mists she had a solid bedrock of common sense. There's a story that one of Mrs. Eddy's followers, trying to ingratiate himself with her, said tentatively, "This lemonade *appears* to be good." To which Mrs. Eddy replied, "It *is* good. Why don't you drink it?" Like Mrs. Eddy, Grandma Lane didn't suffer fools gladly. Although she thought that Man was Good, she didn't necessarily think that people were always to be trusted.

My father used to think it hypocritical that my grandmother regularly renewed her RN license, even after thirty years of self-employment as a Christian Science practitioner. To me it only suggests my grandmother's conservative nature; it also suggests that her religion was a choice for her, albeit one that she made over and over. That is the difference between those who come to a religion and those who are born into it. For my mother, and consequently for me, Christian Science had nothing to do with choice. It was the truth of the universe, and if you didn't choose truth you chose lies. For my grandmother it was also about the high-minded metaphysics of truth and lies, reality and unreality, but I suspect that it also had a lot to do with stubbornness and will, with imposing her vision on an imperfect world. I was especially struck by another story that Ronald told that day in the Country Kitchen. He'd been treated by Faith Lane some thirty years ago and he still recalled her technique perfectly:

"I came home from work and wasn't feeling too well. I felt hot all over, hot and feverish. I called your grandmother and asked her to come over. She said, 'I will come over. I'm making dinner, but I'll turn off the stove and I'll come over. But, Ronald, I want you to be well by the time I get there.'

"Well, I got nervous then, because I'd interrupted your grandmother at her cooking and she only lived ten minutes away and how was I going to feel better by the time she got here? So I got in bed and lay down. And I noticed that all of sudden my feet felt very hot, burning hot, and just when I thought I couldn't stand it, the heat moved up my legs and hotter and hotter moved into my chest, and, I tell you, I was just burning up, and the heat went through my chest, and my neck into my face, and then—it was like an explosion, it burst out the top of my head. All that heat, it went right out of me. It was gone. And then the doorbell rang and my wife let Mrs. Lane in, and she stood there and said, 'Ronald, are you well?'

"And I said, 'Yes, I am, Mrs. Lane, yes I am.' "

When I was very young I saw my grandmother as strict but not solemn. She liked a good joke, and didn't mind if it was at her expense. I recall a story she told of her early housekeeping days, when she just couldn't be bothered to do the dishes, and she put them in the oven instead. A friend dropped in with a new acquaintance. "Faith's kitchen is always sparkling," bragged the friend, and before Grandma could stop her, she flung open the oven. "After that," said Grandma, "I thought I'd better live up to my reputation."

My grandmother was in her sixties and seventies when I knew her. She smelled of talcum powder and had false teeth, which she removed at night. Her thin white hair was knotted in a bun at her neck; she wore glasses on a chain around her neck. Whenever she went out she dressed up, in her rayon "stroller" dress with the coral cameo at the neck, her stockings with the brown seam up the back, her freshly polished white shoes, her white gloves, her pillbox felt hat with the stiff little veil. She frequently told me to keep my voice down, but *her* voice pushed at the walls with conviction. She said, "I know my own mind. I have always known it." Sometimes she would look at me, as if surprised, and say, "You're like me, aren't you?" Sensing in me even then an absolute stubbornness, some quality that would not let go.

In those early days of visiting Battle Creek, I thought of my grandmother as basically kindly, someone who made us cherry pies and gave us pocket money, but someone who was also stronger and more force-ful than my mother, more powerful than anyone I'd ever met except Dolores Bear, our next-door neighbor, who once sprayed her husband Barney with the garden hose. One visit, when I was five or six, and my grandfather lay upstairs dying in the walnut marriage bed, his thick white head of hair continually sinking deeper into the ever-plumped pillows, his dark eyes fading, his voice hardly audible, my grandmother had had enough of me tearing around the house. Because of a heavy storm, Bruce and I had been inside all afternoon. Over my mother's meek protests, Grandma put me in her study on the narrow daybed "to think things over." What I was supposed to think about was how to be nice and quiet and good, qualities I never really dwelt much on at home where my mother let me rampage around the neighborhood on my bike and skates, and where my voice was never too loud.

Left alone on the daybed in the sun porch to "calm down" and to "think about how to be quieter," I did no such thing. I looked around the little room and decided it was like a ship of glass and that the rain that streamed against the panes was the Pacific Ocean in an uproar. I held the hard embroidered pillow like a wheel and steered; I rocked the daybed like a raft. "What are you doing in there?" demanded Grandma, sticking her head in after five minutes. "You're supposed to be thinking." "I know." I sighed and looked around for some other means of escaping reality. The study, which I had never been in by my-self before, was really more like a library, I decided. There was a shabby wingback chair with a bookshelf next to it; on the shelves were a few very small, very thick calfskin volumes of Dickens and Thackeray. The pages were the strangest thing I had ever seen, thin as butterfly wings, hundreds of them crammed together with not a single picture, only lines and lines of tiny black type. More familiar on the shelves were stacks of recent *Monitors* and *Sentinels*. I crept over to take some *Monitors* to look at the pictures and photographs on the Children's Page. That took about three minutes.

I yawned and sank deeper into the dull richness of the afternoon, which stretched, because I had so little sense of time, on into infinity. I put away the *Monitors*, lay flat on my back watching the rain slide in sheets along the glass walls and imagined I was a fish in an aquarium. Another two minutes. If only I had my picture books, my fairy-tale books. Again, desperately, I looked at the bookshelf, and found a small thin volume called *The Book of Baby Mine*. The cloth cover had once been blue, but had turned almost black, and it had the familiar stiffness of all the books in this house, which had been so often damp then dry. Inside were pastel designs and illustrations and verses like "In the Sleepsin Garden behind the Moon / That drowsy garden with poppies strewn, / We babies wait till we come to earth, / And the moon flowers shape us for our birth." There were also advertisements for carriages, florists, pastry shops ("Give your time to Baby / And let us do your Baking!") and the Peoria Life Insurance Company. It was the baby book Grandma had kept of her daughter and first child, Margaret Ellen Lane, born July 31, 1920, and it was full of photographs and of Grandma's writing: "About three days before we left Battle Creek you started to sing a little song when you were rocked and you kept it up until you were four months old, then stopped abruptly. It was dearest thing your mother ever heard a tiny baby do!" Under a photograph of my mother at a few months, Grandma wrote: "When you were sober, you were sober. Ditto smiling!"

Later on, in Brooklyn, Grandma kept up the record. "Mother took you to New York and had another photo of you taken. The winter has been so dark it has been impossible to get Kodak pictures. You are climbing on your little red chair. You say "hello"—"cocoa"—"all right"—"here we go"—"who's that?" You sit down and read a book or newspaper—sing a song—and dance some. You frown at me when I frown at you. . . ."

Of course I could read none of this at the time. I looked only at the photos, which astounded me. My mother had never been a storyteller and I had no sense of her childhood. But now it occurred to me that these pictures had not been taken in Battle Creek, in this house, but somewhere else, somewhere she'd never mentioned. And these people—her parents—I could hardly recognize them. Her father—my Grandpa—looked so young and prosperous, dignified in a bowler and topcoat. There were many photographs of him with his little girl, who was also well-dressed in a fur-trimmed coat. They stood in front of a brownstone in the snow and in Prospect Park. There was even a photograph of my mother in an old-fashioned bathing suit at a beach with Model-Ts in the background. And the little girl grew in the photographs to something like my age. She was long-limbed, with fluffy brown hair and a cheerful wide smile.

Then, once again, I grew bored. All these photos of a baby and a little girl couldn't hold my interest for long (though it had been a good ten minutes). I wanted a toy, a game, a picture, even a doll, though I didn't care much for them. But all I had was my mind. I heard frequently that Mind was everything. But I couldn't visualize it. Not like Spirit, which I confused with Sprite and saw fizzing out of a glass bottle like a genie, or Principle, which was one of Christian Science's main synonyms for God and was clearly like Mrs. Peech, the principal of my elementary school, a big, bosomy lady with a slight mustache.

There was no spread on the daybed, only a thin yellow wool blanket that scratched my cheek. The rain was the strange hot rain of the Midwest, which never cooled things down, but made you feel that you were in a teakettle, unable to get out. I had a sudden, intense realization that the weather at home was *not* like this. If only I could be back in Long Beach, where the heat was dry and separate from the wet. You lay in the sun on the sand or the grass and became very warm, and then you jumped into the wading pool or ran into the ocean to cool off. *Here* the heat and wet ran together, and made everything feel damp and sticky and made everything smell like the underside of a rock. I wanted to be home! Grandma had said that when she prayed she ceased to be in one spot and could be anywhere she wished. I pictured her corseted up tight in her stroller dress, hat firmly in place, white gloves gleaming like just-peeled potatoes, sending her mind over the rooftops of Broad Street across the little park at the end of the block, down Church Street past Willard Library, across the river and over one of the little lakes. I imagined her firm, loud voice popping into someone's head— someone who lay flat in bed, groaning—and saying, "Rise up, Gertrude. And eat your breakfast."

This was Absent Treatment. It was like magic. It was one of those phrases I understood only in my own way, as a kind of mental flying. You didn't need a telephone. You didn't need an airplane. It didn't take a few days on the train or a week in an old automobile. It was instantaneous. It was spiritual travel.

Something came over me then. Now I might call it homesickness, but that's a very weak word. It was a terrible sweet longing for home, a desire that depended for its existence on the knowledge of two places, one designated as familiar, the other to be called new or different or strange. I sent my mind back over half the country that we had crossed, and was instantaneously in the blue Pacific ocean. I saw a wave coming fast at me, felt it crash over my sturdy brown body, staggered on the sand that sucked under my feet, heard a roar echoing deep inside my ears, saw globules of salt water, rounded, perfect as transparent pearls, rolling off my brown arm. When I was *there* the longing—the homesickness—was less. And yet I was not *there,* not quite. I was there for seconds, the roar of the ocean was in my ears, the salt water was crusting on my skin, and then I was back *here,* in this hot glassed-in room with its comfortable, even luxurious scent of mold and age.

In my mind, I sailed back and forth between the two places, consciously tasting, for the first time, a knowledge of how place mattered, how place had a mood, and a smell and a sound and a look. I felt though I couldn't have said, then, what the difference between Long Beach and Battle Creek was. The first was edgy, expansive, brash, wide-open, loud, and bright. The second was solid, predictable, hardworking, frugal, and complacent. In the Midwest talk turned naturally to farming and religion and olden times; people sat on their porches at night and fanned themselves and the moon shone through the heavy elm trees on the glasses of cool lemonade and the swarms of bugs that circled those glasses. In California the talk was of the present and the future, and people said, "Have you seen the new shopping mall, the new school, the new park?" Trees were small, houses were flat and without attics or cellars, backyards had barbecues and redwood picnic tables, not shabby old chicken coops and garden sheds. In California everybody was young; in the Midwest everybody was old. Youth smelled like suntan lotion and salt water and orange groves and expectations. Age smelled like a musty attic full of old tin soldiers and dog-eared copies of *Treasure Island,* and a cellar full of damp clothes, and an old man lying in his marriage bed, saying good-bye to his daughter and his wife and all of us who stood around him, but of course not really saying good-bye, because Christian Scientists did not believe in death.

I lay on the daybed and perhaps by this time I was already asleep; certainly I was as quiet as my grandmother could have wished. Once I think she opened the door slightly and looked at me; once I think I realized that the rain had stopped and my brother was running out the door to play. But I wasn't there. I was in a place that I'd just discovered, a place you could say I've lived in ever since—an imaginary space carved out, created between two real or perhaps also imaginary cities or states or countries. One place is always home—there needs to be a home—and one place is always strange. I leave home precisely in order to long for it, a longing I don't understand. I could be at home so easily. Why don't I stay there? But it's out of the longing that language comes. Language is a sort of absent treatment. You don't have to be there to write about a place. It's better, often, to live somewhere else than the place you want to write about, to live, perhaps, in that incessantly poignant moment that is neither *here* nor *there*.

Eventually my mother came in and sat beside me on the daybed. She had suffered to see me punished, for she always had an excuse for me and my wild spirits. But there was something else. She was sad. She had been crying.

"I hope you didn't think we'd forgotten about you," she said. "We were upstairs, with Grandpa. We were praying for him."

I wanted to be a good daughter. I thought of the girl in the photographs with the man in the bowler hat. "I gave him absent treatment from here," I said.

It was the kind of thing that made my mother think sometimes I had a religious vocation, but of course it was, as usual, made up. I hadn't been thinking much about my grandfather at all, but about swimming in the sea in Long Beach. I hardly knew my grandfather in some ways. Grandma was always so much more prominent.

The afternoon shadows were lengthening. There was sadness in the room. From across town came the haunting whistle of the train, as lonely as a nighttime wail. My mother hugged me close. "Oh, sweetheart," she said, as if acknowledging something she shouldn't. "He was always so good to me. I'm going to miss him."

Her freckled arms went around me, warm and familiar with the scent of mother. I had never known anyone to die. I had just learned that you can miss a place. I didn't yet know that you can long for a person in the same way.

More than thirty years later I stood at the wide picture window of the Battle Creek Stouffer Hotel, on the eighth floor, staring out at the sunset over the railroad tracks a block away. It was April, and had been a warm Sunday. I had spent the day with the Christian Scientists, hearing stories about my grandparents, of their healings as well as what a large role they had played in the life of the town and the church, how well liked and respected they were. We'd laughed a lot. I had forgotten that Christian Scientists laughed a great deal, at least the ones I'd known. They'd told stories, these kind Midwestern people, of mispronouncing Mrs. Eddy's long words during readings. "I saw the world *sepulchre* coming and couldn't for the life of me figure out how I was going to manage to get through it!" They had embraced me when we parted. None of them had known my mother well. I would always be John and Faith's granddaughter to them.

I had walked around town for a while after leaving them. So much had changed. Old Willard Library stood, but the books were in a modern building next to it. Battle Creek Central High Schol was still there, as were all the imposing, half-deserted churches on Church Street. On the edge of town was the glorious old Sanitarium, now a federal building. Downtown, almost everything was closed up; it was not a town that had preserved its past, and if it hadn't been for the determined efforts of the Kellogg Foundation to pump money into it, the whole town center would have vanished long ago into mildew and dust. Standing there at the window, seeing the light slip away, I felt wrung out, homeless, and full of longing. Neither Long Beach nor Battle Creek was home now, and they had not been for a very long time. From the west came the long, drawn-out sound of a train coming, wailing in the way of trains with news of its arrival. It was one of those that didn't stop in town. Not so many trains stopped now. This one hurtled through, shrieking in the dying light, and then it was gone, gone east, I guess. I felt its leaving, the sound of it disappearing. Trains had no home either. That must be why they called out so sadly as they traveled through.

Chapter 2

Mother Church

In divine Science we have not as much authority for considering God masculine, as we have for considering Him feminine, for Love imparts the clearest idea of Deity.

—Science and Health

Where you cast your glance, the dead awake, the sick arise; The bewildered, beholding your face, find the right way.

—Song to Ishtar

*A*sked to draw a picture of God, most of the children Robert Coles interviewed for his book *The Spiritual Life of Children* came up with some version of a face. Swedish children might give him blue eyes and Latino children brown, but in every case the face seems to have been masculine, a fact so obvious that Coles does not bother to point it out. But in the Christian Science world that I grew up in, God was our Father-Mother, and most of the religious people I saw around me were women. I would not have drawn God as a woman, of course; like the children of Islam, I knew that you didn't draw images of God. The other kids on our block might come home from Sunday school with coloring books full of blond Jesuses surrounded by little lambs, and of bearded patriarchs up in the sky with angels all around, but I was instructed in a loftier metaphysical view. God was Spirit, God was Mind, God was Divine Principle, all-seeing, all-knowing, all-loving. God was not just up in the sky, but present in everything, in a flower, in a blade of grass, present daily and forever in a gorgeously mysterious universe pulsating with love.

All the same, if I had been pressed as a young child to picture the face of God, it would have been female. Not Mary in turquoise blues and golds, or female martyrs going up in flames, transparent eyelids over suffering eyes. No, I would have pictured the face of an elderly white-haired woman, calm and proud, with a penetrating gaze and a stern expression. It would have been the face of Mrs. Eddy, Mary Baker Eddy, the Founder and Discoverer of Christian Science, a face with some resemblance to my grandmother's.

When I was very young I believed that Grandma and Mrs. Eddy were the same person. Later I thought of them as just good friends. It had something to do with my grandmother being called Faith and knowing that what she did was faith healing. But it also had to do with the way Mrs. Eddy was constantly invoked in our house and in my mother's circle, which made it seem that she was as alive as Grandma. Although Eddy had died in 1910, she never seemed dead. It wasn't only that Christian Scientists never quite acknowledged death, it was that Mrs. Eddy's spirit was still so present, in her writing, in the memories, of course now fading, of those who had known her, and particularly in the bureaucratic structure of her church. She had created this organization, which she called the Mother Church, just as one might put together a perpetual clock, one that would run forever once you turned the key, neither too quickly nor too slowly, but with a measured tick-tock, always telling the correct time, the completely correct time.

The Mrs. Eddy I was introduced to as a child was not a complex woman, driven alternately by spiritual intensity and the desire for worldly power. She had been sanitized and sentimentalized, the dubious, confusing, real incidents of her life expunged or recast. No hint of scandal darkened the pages of *A Child's Life of Mary Baker Eddy*, a book by Ella Hay that claimed to be "a simple record of a life that was beautiful from childhood."

In reality Mary Baker Eddy was a spoiled and sickly child, self-willed and given to tantrums and paroxysmal fits if she did not get her way. But *A Child's Life* cast her as a model girl: peaceable, generous, kind, and courageous. If she collected nuts, it was to give them to other children. If she found people quarreling, she tried to help them sort out their argument. She stood up for what she believed, and she was fearless. *A Child's Life* included stories like this:

"Once she faced an insane man who entered the yard of the academy she was attending. He was swinging a large club, and the children ran away terrified, all but Mary. She spoke to the sick man gently, asking him to leave the yard. He became quiet at once."

Ella Hay, who was only following the hagiographic convention of Mrs. Eddy's approved biographers, made every attempt to show that Mary had been spiritual from a young age, and that she realized her destiny early on. When asked what she would do when she grew up, Mary replied, "I will write a book."

I found it hard to imagine Mary Baker Eddy as a child, and, in any case, I disliked model children. But like most of us, I was easily able to ignore the prescriptive moral element of what I read and to take to heart the lessons I really could use. The life of a girl could be dramatic and visionary. A girl could stand up for what was right. She could be strong in the face of danger. She could decide that she wanted to write a book. She could grow up to be a powerful woman.

I once had my own copy of *A Child's Life of Mary Baker Eddy*, given to me by my grandmother, but that copy has long since vanished. The one I own now, squarish, bound in red cloth, illustrated with line drawings, comes from a used book shop. There are many copies of Christian Science books now in used book shops. I've collected much of my research library among the dusty religion sections of such stores. The volumes go for a few dollars and the booksellers always take my money gratefully. The books must have been on the shelves for years. I picture the relatives of deceased Christian Scientists coming with boxes to these stores now, and being turned away.

Of course, not all books about Mrs. Eddy are so easy to find. Probably the best one ever written has been out of print most of this century. It was an investigative report first serialized in *McClure's Magazine*, and then published as a biography in 1909. The book appeared under Georgine Milmine's name, but most of the writing is now attributed to Willa Cather, McClure's editor at the time. I have a paperback copy now, reissued only a few years ago. The used books I have on my shelf at home have titles such as *A Christian Science Way of Life*, and *Twelve Years with Mary Baker Eddy*, and *A Century of Christian Science Healing*. They bump covers with books that psychoanalyze Mrs. Eddy, that take a sociological look at sects in America, that tell stories of people harmed by the religion's doctrines. Another shelf, which grows ever more crowded, is taken up with books about women in religion: histories and anthologies and academic surveys, books on goddess worship in ancient civilizations, studies of women saints, memoirs of contemporary women struggling to make sense of religion in their lives.

As I read and take copious notes, on women in religion and Mrs. Eddy in particular, who she was and how she became what she was grows more and more fascinating to me, more fascinating and more complicated than I ever imagined, or was taught, as a child.

Mary Baker was born in New England, in Bow, New Hampshire, in 1821. Her father was a moderately well off farmer with a stern Calvinist outlook. Mary was the youngest child; strong-willed, but unable to face her harsh father directly, she resorted to fits and fainting spells and long bouts of vague illnesses. These illnesses were encouraged and coddled by her mother, who liked to think of her baby girl as delicate. Mary's delicacy became her main—approved—form of self-expression. It kept her out of school for long periods, and, in fact, Mary was badly educated, something that did not stop her from writing long, ill-spelt letters, poetry, and articles as she grew into womanhood, and of dreaming of herself as a writer. Although *A Child's Life* says that "She always knew a great many words. She used eighteen thousand in her writings on Christian Science. This unusual number places her second only to the great poet Shakespeare in the number of words used by those who have written in the English language," the truth was that Mary's grammar and spelling would always be shaky.

At the age of twenty-one, Mary Baker married George Washington Glover and moved to South Carolina. Within six months she was a widow; her son George was born three months later. She returned to the family farm, where she lived first with her parents, and then, after her mother died and her father remarried, with her older sister Abigail, who had married a wealthy mill owner. During all this time Mary suffered from physical ailments and nervous complaints, which made her unable or unwilling to take on the care of her child, and she gave him over to the care of a nurse, a temporary situation that became permanent.

Mary's second marriage, to Dr. Patterson, an itinerant dentist, was marked by poverty and frequent moves. While Mary still dreamed of becoming someone important and still wrote verse, she had few outlets for her energy and intellect. Her chronic ill health, diagnosed at different times as "dyspepsia," "neurasthenia," and "spinal inflammation," led her to an interest in Spiritualism and the physical and mental therapies of her time. It was while taking a water cure that she heard of a healer called Phineas Quimby, who was practicing a form of mesmerism in Portland, Maine. When she sought him out, she experienced an immediate healing of her symptoms; her amazed gratitude kept her coming back to him for several years. Opinion is split on how much of Mary Baker Eddy's theology of healing stems from Quimby. In later years, Eddy was at pains to disassociate herself and her church from any taint of mesmerism or the occult, and to show that her primary example of a healer came from Jesus. Nevertheless it was with Quimby, who first coined the phrases "Science of Health," "scientific healing," and "Christian Science," that she first began the process of putting down ideas on the nature of healing and, more specifically, of trying to understand how that knowledge could be codified and taught to others.

In 1866, only two weeks after Quimby had died, Mrs. Eddy suffered unspecified injuries after slipping on an icy sidewalk near her home in Lynn, Massachusetts. In the 1890s journalists trying to debunk the myth of Mrs. Eddy's miraculous healing interviewed witnesses to the fall. Some said it was just a bump on the head, others that Mrs. Eddy had been left for dead. The important thing is how she retold the story later. She said that while lying in bed, sure that she would never walk again, she had turned to the Bible and reread the passages in the New Testament in which Jesus heals the sick and makes the lame to walk. And, reading, she'd had a revelation: she need not depend on anything—water cures, patent medicines, mesmerism; or anybody— Quimby—to heal her. She could heal herself. It was a revelation she was to build her church on.

Eddy spent the next few years studying the Bible and writing down the ideas—a hodgepodge of thoughts on the nature of reality, on God and on healing—that later turned into her book *Science and Health.* In the process, although she was hardly independent, having no real means of sustaining herself financially and being frequently ejected from boardinghouses, Mary Baker Eddy transformed herself from a frail, clinging invalid into a strong, purposeful teacher and leader, convinced of her authority to speak for God. Her husband deserted and divorced her; she took up with a succession of younger men, not as lover, but as mentor. She taught them the principles of healing and they, in turn, at least until she quarreled bitterly with them, gave over a percentage of their income to her. Eventually she married for a third time, a mild-mannered student of hers named Asa Gilbert Eddy.

In 1875 the first edition of *Science and Health* was published. It abounded in grammatical errors and muddled thinking, and was not exactly an overnight success. Yet more and more people began to come to be taught to heal. She first formed the Church of Christ, Scientist in 1879 and made herself president. Three years later she founded the Massachusetts Metaphysical College in Boston, a state-chartered school that taught her new church's doctrines and methods of healing. In the beginning the movement attracted a number of fringe characters who had been involved in other alternative health and spiritual fads around Boston, and who eagerly embraced Christian Science. For some it was a user-friendly religion that seemed to promise a beneficent Christianity without hellfire or Jehovah's wrath, which explained away suffering and illness and gave you the tools to heal yourself; for others, setting up as a mental healer seemed like a good way to make money. But Christian Science, from the beginning, was neither eclectic nor easygoing, and most of Eddy's early followers found her far too authoritarian. Some of them split off to form rival mind-cure groups, while others returned to the Protestant fold, where the local clergy denounced Eddy as a charlatan and a "Petticoat Pope." Still, by the 1890s, in spite of great opposition, Christian Science was well established in Boston, New York, and Chicago, with branch churches springing up in other parts of the country. Eventually, in spite of its mysterious beginnings and radical ideas, it achieved recognition as a genuine religion, even a respectable one.

As I read about Mrs. Eddy and her climb from obscurity to renown, a whiff of the nineteenth century, with its sentimentality and idealism, its vigor and sham, blows off the page. I sit surrounded by my books, underlining sentences, making notes. And I remember another woman reading. A woman in a short-sleeved cotton blouse that shows the freckles on her chest, a woman curled up, in a skirt that hikes up slightly, revealing her bare tanned legs, on her favorite blue armchair. A woman with books and newspapers and magazines all around her. A woman studying, carefully underscoring the lines of type on the onionskin paper of her copy of *Science and Health*, with erasable blue chalk. Thirty years later, my mother's strokes of blue still remain in that book, which is mine now, unerased and now permanent, bracketing earnest paragraphs on spiritual remedies as opposed to material, on Truth as opposed to error.

Christian Science is the religion of readers, of incessant studiers. You see their Reading Rooms everywhere, in every large city, in most smaller ones. In suburbs, in shopping malls, in the heart of downtown. There is one in the San Francisco airport. Although few people but Christian Scientists ever go in them, they're nice quiet places to sit, beautifully maintained, with large wooden tables displaying the literature and cozy upholstered chairs to sit in. The meek and gentle, often elderly people who staff them are not there to proselytize or convert, but to answer questions if asked and to sell the books and periodicals. They are extremely reluctant to appear pushy. At the most they will hold up a copy of *Science and Health,* remarking, as if they expect to be challenged, "This says it all."

It's a reader's religion, but not a scholarly one. Its texts are not cryptic in the way of the Talmud or the Tao. Mrs. Eddy said clearly—as clearly as she could—what she meant. What Christian Scientists have done for the hundred years since is parrot and rehash those thoughts. The endless reading and studying is not meant to be a starting place for brilliant additional commentary. It's more like mass hypnosis, a means of keeping the faithful under Mrs. Eddy's spell. For although reading—deep reading, endless study—is exalted, wide reading is not. The basic canon is the Bible, *Science and Health,* Eddy's autobiography, *Retrospection and Introspection,* and her miscellaneous writings. There are a few approved biographies and a handful of books of collected testimonies. In addition there are piles of periodicals to read: the daily *Christian Science Monitor,* the weekly *Sentinel,* the monthly *Journal,* and four times a year the *Christian Science Quarterly.* The tone of all the periodicals, except the *Monitor,* which has excellent journalistic standards, is the undeviating tone of Mrs. Eddy herself, updated regularly in an old-fashioned kind of way, but still using plenty of the original arcane language, only jolted by the constant insertion of truly moving and startling phrases from the Bible.

The Mother Church created a mother tongue, one that my mother passed on to me. She'd lift me onto the blue armchair and search in the Bible for stories to read aloud, or sometimes just give herself over to the pleasure of reading the Psalms. She had a light, firm voice and easily lost herself in the stories and the words. Close to her freckled breast, breathing in her warm cotton and vanilla scent, I could be close to her for hours, letting the words of the Bible roll through my body like waves in the deepest ocean.

As I grew older and thought about what I heard, my mother found herself having to translate the King James Version into ordinary language, because when the stories were read aloud, the vocabulary, rich as candied citron and almonds in fruitcake, made the meaning hard to absorb. It wasn't only names like "A-has-u-é-rus" and "Mor-de-cai," which were at least broken up in syllables so they could even be pronounced, but words like "pestilence" and "vexed" and "chaff" and "loins," which had to be explained if the story were to make sense, and not only explained with other words, but explained according to the convoluted appearance-vs.-reality abstractions of Christian Science ("Pestilence is when it seemed that rats were biting people and causing mortal error.") and explained with modesty ("Loins—well, what they are is—sort of your legs and things.").

But perhaps it's not true that I asked for explanations. Certainly later on, as the language of the King James Version became more familiar to me, the meaning became embedded in the cadence—in the "walketh" and "sitteths," in the italicized *is* and *art* for emphasis, in the strong, precise choice of words, often verbs, that got right to the point of the human condition. People wept, they cried out, they departed, they trembled, they sowed, and they reaped. I loved to hear sentences like, "And he shall be like a tree planted by the rivers of water, that bringeth forth his fruit in his season; his leaf also shall not wither; and whatsoever he doeth shall prosper." The world of the Bible was one of gardens and deserts, of thunderstorms and battles and great feasts where wine and water flowed and lambs lay down with wolves. The words were a feast in themselves, meals of delicious and sustaining dishes with a hundred different fragrances and tastes.

Mrs. Eddy's language, on the other hand, was like cotton candy that vanished in your mouth as soon as you took a bite; it was like mashed potatoes whipped with too much air. The words in *Science and Health* weren't proper words, they were metaphysical concepts, abstractions with no teeth, no elbows or legs. The only way I could remember her words was to turn them into pictures of something else or look for a root syllable that was like a real thing. Thus "divine" had something to do with grapes. "Omnipotent" was praying on your knees in a tent made of blankets.

When Mrs. Eddy began to explicate Genesis line by line in *Science and Health,* the magic and vividness of the biblical language vanished. The bold simplicity of "And God said, Let there be light; and there was light," became in her torturous exegesis: "Immortal and divine Mind presents the idea of God: *first,* in light; *second,* in reflection; *third,* in spiritual and immortal forms of beauty and goodness. But this Mind creates no element nor symbol of discord and decay. God creates neither erring thought, mortal life, mutable truth, nor variable love."

Science and Health is an infinitely repetitious book. The central ideas are stated and restated in different variations chapter after chapter. By the time my mother was in her early thirties, she must have read every word of it hundreds of times. Yet every day she sat down and read and meditated on some part of it again. And this is how I realized that there was such a thing as a sacred text, that the limp, onionskin, blue-chalked pages of *Science and Health* held a kind of wisdom for my mother that sustained and guided her. It wasn't like asking to hear the story of Pinocchio night after night; it wasn't even like my staring at my picture books for hours on end, finding endless new degrees of meaning in the illustrations. *Science and Health* was the word of Mrs. Eddy. It *was* Mrs. Eddy, in all her grand authority. *Science and Health* existed to provide reassurance not inspiration. It existed as a manual for how to correct your thinking. It existed, in all its idiosyncrasy, as a book that could always be turned to, a source of wisdom and love that would, like the perfect mother, always provide.

I was seven before I learned to read at all well. Throughout first grade I struggled in the slow readers' group to turn the words on the page into pictures in my head. I'm not sure whether I had a slight learning disability that prevented me from putting letters together (even today I still transpose letters and find it almost impossible to transcribe the phone numbers that people rattle off on my answering machine), or whether the subject matter was just too boring. All I know is that for two or three years there was an unbridgeable gap between the complicated vocabularies of Mrs. Eddy and the Bible and the words that appeared on the page of the school reader in front of me.

"Sound it out, Barbara," urged the special reading teacher who came in to work with those of us who were behind. Oh, the painfulness of being seen to be stupid and slow. At home I was a storyteller and a famous actor/director. I had a hundred plagiarized and invented plots in my head, which ranged from Bruce and Jamie (my little brother's best friend) in the Lion's Den (our cat Ginger reluctantly standing in for the lion) to Sleeping Beauty and the Four Dwarves on the Moon, plots that recklessly amalgamated characters and scenes from many sources and were thick with dramatic incident and Old Testament language. Some smiting usually went on, and fleeing, usually accompanied by crying out.

What an outrage to sit in a circle with other stupid children, with so many dazzling words in my head and all kinds of ingenious and marvelous stories waiting to have me bring them to life, and have to stagger slowly through a sentence that said only, "See Spot run." But there was no help for it. For a long time, until Mrs. Franken took me in hand in the second grade, there was no connection between my ears and my eyes.

A woman reading. Women reading. Women in the living room drinking Sanka and telling stories. Some of the stories were funny, and a few were sober, but all had a different tone to them than chat between my mother and the neighborhood women. When my mother talked with Dolores next door or Betty Mortensen down the street, she never used terms like mortal error or demonstration, but in the company of Christian Science friends, like Viv and Edyth, the words cropped up naturally. You couldn't tell the story of your daily temptations, struggles, and successes in any other way than through the vocabulary of Mrs. Eddy. Although they tried to be matter-of-fact, these modern women who had given up their jobs to stay home and raise children in the Fifties way, who wore their dark hair mid-length, curled and fluffy, who had red lipstick and powdered noses and earrings, a sort of thrill would rise sometimes in their voices as they recounted healings and understandings. Edyth, a solidly built, emotional woman with a big voice that could sink down to a whisper, was always the most dramatic. Her son Ken had had polio or something very like it, but he was cured. When she talked about that healing, tears came to her eyes, no matter how many times she told it. "And I had the practitioner on the phone, telling her Vern says I have to take him to the hospital, and Mrs. Armitrage said, 'Did Mrs. Eddy go to the hospital when she lay on her bed after falling on the ice?' That simple question was all it took. I put down the phone on the stand without hanging up, so I could still be connected to her, and I walked over to Ken. 'Son, stand up and walk,' I said. And he said, 'Mother I can't.' 'You can and you will,' I said."

The two other women leaned towards her eyes shining. "And he stood up," said Viv. "And he walked," said my mother. Edyth basked in their radiant attention. Then they sipped their Sanka, and tried to act as if healing was just a normal thing, no big deal, and Edyth produced the familiar ending, the Christian Science punchline. "So Vern said, 'Well it couldn't have really been anything. It must have been all in his head.' "

"All in his head," laughed Viv, putting her cup down.

"Well I should think *so*," said my mother.

Both Viv and Edyth had daughters my age; Christine and Carrie and I were all born within a month of each other in the fall of 1950. Christine was thin, sweet-faced, with straight dark bangs cut over her eyes and a ponytail, the most feminine of us all. Carrie was blond, sturdier, athletic; she wore straight skirts and cardigan sweaters with a circle pin. I was the roundest and the loudest, only intermittently feminine, as when my mother curled my limp blond hair, put a dress on me, and admonished me to behave like a girl. I tried, and if I were surrounded by adults I could put on a passable imitation of girlness. But in a group of kids my high spirits always seemed to get the better of me. I had many ideas, many bad ideas, on how to have fun. Once Christine and I broke her bed by jumping on it, pretending it was a circus trampoline; another time I urged her to give her dolls a haircut for a dramatic production that required a boy chorus; I tore her pretty chiffon dress grabbing and tugging at her during Pin-the-Tail-on-the-Donkey. There was no end to it. I used to like going over to Viv's house—she always made us grilled cheese sandwiches for lunch, a dish more mysterious and elaborate than my mother could manage—but I knew that Viv saw me go into Christine's pink and white ruffled bedroom with trepidation. It was not the first and definitely not the last time someone's mother would say anxiously to me and her daughter, "Now girls—Barbara—please play *nicely*."

When our mothers got together the subject of raising children often came up. My mother always took refuge in pointing out how creative I was, even if I was " . . . energetic." She would pull out my latest drawings—a series of dancing ostriches inspired by *Fantasia*—or the small, stapled books I made with stories about animals and elves with my own crayon illustrations. Once, very proudly, she showed Viv and Edyth a poem I'd written, one rhymed stanza about a duck with waterproof feet. Edyth gently pointed out that this same poem had appeared in the *Monitor* a few months before, on the Children's Page. They were not as convinced of my originality and imagination as my mother.

Viv's husband George was a Member of the Church, but Edyth's husband Vern, a milkman, felt the same about Christian Science as my father: indifferent. Sometimes I saw Vern drive by early in the morning in his white truck with the open doors. He wore a jaunty white uniform and carried a tray of milk bottles so white they looked as if they had nothing to do with cows. It didn't surprise me that fathers didn't go to church. The service was something I believed that mainly women attended. There were some boys in my Sunday School class, but the teachers were always women: gentle young women, firm older women, women who told us Bible stories and explained how being Daniel in the Lion's Den or David up against Goliath with only a slingshot was a lot like being a Christian Scientist. Our Lions were school nurses who wanted to give us shots, our Goliaths were neighborhood bullies who challenged our faith by tripping us as we flew by on our roller skates. I never thought about the fact that David and Daniel were boys. The Bible, our teachers told us, speaks in metaphor, and David and Daniel were symbols of divine Mind and how it helps us overcome adversity.

In spite of stories of boys and slingshots and lions, there was something mild and middle-class and ladylike about this church at mid-century. It was not a church of anguish and yearning, of declamation and drama, of sin and redemption. The members all had individual stories of illness and healing, but they spoke about them quietly and confidently, as if there were no question of the outcome. The services lacked a theatrical element; they were endlessly predictable. Indeed, that was the point. Mrs. Eddy had dispensed (some say because her father was too much of a Calvinist haranguer, in church and at the table) with the need for a thundering or cajoling preacher who might usurp her power or distort her ideas. Instead the Church Manual provided for two Readers, one male and one female, one to read selections from the Bible and the other to read "corresponding" passages from *Science and Health*. The selections came as no surprise on Sunday; they had been chosen by the Board of Directors and printed up in booklets that were issued quarterly. There were twenty-six topics to be covered twice a year, including such subjects as "Are Sin, Disease and Death Real?," "Unreality," and (one of my favorites as a child, though I had no idea what it meant) "Ancient and Modern Necromancy *Alias* Mesmerism and Hypnotism, Denounced." The Sunday service began with a few announcements, then the Lord's Prayer, a silent prayer (another rebuke to Mark Baker's endless speechifying perhaps), and then the readings. The hymns were standard Protestant fare, except for the ones written by Mrs. Eddy. There was one soloist, in a long, pastel evening dress, and two bouquets on either side of the dais, for color. Other churches have their routines, too, their unchanging liturgies and set patterns of prayer, and there can be something restful in predictability. Restful, but never rousing.

Still, and this is important, I saw something during those orderly services that for years I wouldn't see in any other church: A woman standing in the front of a church on a dais, her voice filling the room, her gaze steady and true, a woman who knew her connection to the divine, and who spoke it loud and clear.

I've discovered in my reading that the number of religions created by women are few indeed. Susan Starr Sered cites twelve examples in her excellent study *Priestess, Mother, Sacred Sister: Religions Dominated by Women*. Among them are the ancestral cults of the Black Caribs in contemporary Belize, the indigenous religion of the Ryukyu Islands, the *zar* cult of Northern Africa, the Sande secret society of Sierra Leone, the matrilineal spirit cults of northern Thailand, Korean shamanism, and Afro-Brazilian religions. The United States is unusual among Western countries in having fostered several women-dominated religions: the Shakers, a sect founded in England in the eighteenth century but which came into its own in New England under the leadership of Ann Lee; the cult of Spiritualism, which began when two young girls, the Fox sisters, claimed they heard rappings from the dead—although they later admitted that the rappings emanated from their feet (they were adept at cracking their toe joints), the movement took deep hold in North America and Europe for two decades, and still exists today. Sered also includes the contemporary feminist spirituality and black womanist movements in the United States. And, of course, Christian Science.

If it is true, as Gerda Lerner and other feminist scholars assert, that women's connection to the divine was broken at the beginning of civilization, then the last four thousand years have been a struggle to make that connection again. The ways have been many, from the worship of female goddesses that went on in cultures as diverse as Celtic Ireland and the Middle East, to the cult of the Virgin in Europe, from the thriving convents of the Middle Ages to the persecution of the midwives and witches in Europe and New England. In *The Creation of Feminist Consciousness,* Lerner details the attempts that women have made for a thousand years, usually with no knowledge of the work that women before them have done, to interpret and reinterpret the Bible, and to change it into a text that would not be as harmful to them. *Science and Health,* while hardly the feminist revision of a holy book that Stanton and Gage's irreverent *Women's Bible* is, is definitely a woman's view of the Bible. Eddy makes the bold leap of conceiving of God as androgynous; in fact, in the third edition of *Science and Health* she experimented with substituting She for He in several chapters. From her point of view, a Divine Principle, being omnipotent and omnipresent, would have to include both male and female qualities. Eddy thought that, just as Jesus had embodied God's maleness, her mission was to embody femaleness.

Mary Baker Eddy didn't call herself a suffragist, although she lived through the first wave of the struggle for women's rights that began in the 1840s. There's no evidence that she was much affected by the debate over suffrage or had even read the work of Elizabeth Cady Stanton or Susan B. Anthony. But the change in women's public status from the time of her youth to the 1870s when she began to create her church must have given her confidence. People were more ready to accept a woman as a religious leader by the end of the century than they had been at the beginning, though this should not minimize the enormous difficulties she faced in having her ideas accepted.

Eddy was a theological outsider, certainly because of the peculiarity of some of her concepts, but also because she'd asserted her right as a woman to not only have a deep religious experience, but to base a religion on it. Other women throughout recorded history had been mystics and heretics, and a few, a very few, such as Hildegard of Bingen and St. Teresa of Avila, had assumed positions of leadership. But their power had always been subject to the greater power of the Pope and his male hierarchy.

Although in the beginning Eddy believed that her principles of healing would be an idea acceptable to mainstream Christianity, it was clear relatively soon that she would need to found her own organization, and after that a church, in order for her ideas to survive her. By 1895 when the Mother Church building was completed in Boston, the Church of Christ, Scientist had grown from its twenty-six original members in 1879 to two hundred thousand nationwide. The new church was capable of holding fifteen hundred people and on the day of its dedication held four services. Ten years later work was begun on an extension to the church, at a cost of two million dollars. The extension seated five thousand. There were twenty-five thousand people present at the dedication, and six services. The *Boston Post* covered the event and noted:

> The temporary increase of the population of Boston has been apparent to the most casual observer. And so, we think, must be the characteristics of this crowd of visitors. It is a pleasant, congenial, quietly happy, well-to-do, intellectual and cheerfully contented multitude that has invaded the town. . . . We congratulate these comfortable acquaintances upon the fact that they have their costly church fully paid for, and we feel that Boston is to be congratulated upon the acquisition of an edifice so handsome architecturally.

From the start Christian Science was attractive to women. Not only was the founder a woman and the theology based on the notion of an androgynous god, but in a practical sense Christian Science offered employment as healers for women who had been barred by men from their traditional occupations as midwives and doctors. At the founding of the church, the ratio of women to men practitioners was five to one. In 1926, a study showed that while 55.7 percent of the membership of all churches was female, in Christian Science the percentage was 75 percent. In the 1950s, 87.7 percent of all Christian Science practitioners were women, and most recently a study showed a ratio of only one male practitioner for every eight women.* One of the possible appeals of Christian Science to women lies in the fact that it's a religion that stresses self-help, not helplessness. Just as Eddy transformed herself from a pathetic invalid into a determined organizer and leader, so could any woman.

*(*Priestess, Mother, Sacred Sister,* p 23–24, Susan Starr Sered, Oxford University Press, New York, 1994.)

Eddy herself, while creating a structure that did not discriminate against women, was sometimes ambivalent about them. She considered herself their mother as well as their leader and, as long as they were dutiful daughters, she cherished and helped them, often sending them out across the country to found branch churches, or calling them back to Boston to assist her in her work. But her maternal feelings could turn to rage and fear when her daughters disobeyed or seemed to disobey her.

In the early days of her teaching, Eddy had managed to quarrel with almost all her students and with anyone who challenged her, and throughout the 1870s she was often in court accusing one male student after another of betraying her. In one of the more bizarre cases, she accused a former colleague, Edward Arens, of "mentally poisoning" her third husband Asa Gilbert Eddy in 1882. (To be fair, many of the accusations and lawsuits of this period were in response to lawsuits against *her* for malicious mesmerism). However, in later years it tended to be women who were her primary rivals. A former student, Mrs. Hopkins, went to Chicago and set up shop there, while Mrs. Plunkett, whom the newspapers dubbed the "high priestess of Christian Science," started her own organization in New York. When Mrs. Plunkett and her husband divorced, Christian Science became identified with free love. Worse was the case of Mrs. Josephine Woodbury, who though long critical of Eddy, gathered together a number of followers and told them of her closeness to the "Leader." On July 4, 1890, she gave birth to a baby boy, declared it an immaculate conception, and then revealed that Mrs. Eddy was the father.

But it was Mrs. Stetson in New York who was Eddy's most serious rival. Eddy had originally sent her there with instructions to form a church; she hadn't counted on the fact that Stetson would sow discontent among the Christian Scientists already established there by telling them she was Mrs. Eddy's favorite student and heir apparent. Nor had Eddy realized that Mrs. Stetson would prove so popular as a teacher and a leader in her own right. Although Mrs. Stetson wrote Eddy constantly of her love and admiration for her, it's fairly clear that she was also out to build a power base of her own. Mrs. Stetson raised money for and built an enormous Christian Science church, much larger than the one in Boston. In the end, Eddy excommunicated her.

Eddy's fallings out with students and followers were all after a pattern. Up to a point they were her beloved children. Then, as she promoted and encouraged them, she would become aware of their ambition, an ambition she chose to interpret as hostile to her own ideas and plans. Mrs. Eddy persisted in believing that these conflicts were not "personal" and that she was not emotionally involved in them herself. To her mind it was not so much a question of loyalty to her, as to her single Truth. This truth had been revealed to her and her alone, and anyone who doubted it or disagreed with her was an enemy and probably under mesmeric influences. Her supporters, of course, always found reasons to excuse her severity. In *The Cross and the Crown*, Norman Beasley writes about how the students complained of Mrs. Eddy's strictness at the Massachusetts Metaphysical College. "They could not seem to realize that it was not she who was strict. It was spiritual law that was strict."

There was something to that. My mother's morality always seemed to be backed up by something larger. Unlike in many families, that larger shadow behind my mother was not my father. There was no "Just wait until your father gets home." Although my father spanked my brother several times, hard, during Bruce's pyromaniac period, for the most part, he was more likely to give us a brief talking to than to discipline us. Later, during my mother's illness and in his second marriage to my stepmother, he was to become much harsher, but during my first ten years he was content for my mother to bring us up. He'd been beaten frequently by his alcoholic adoptive father, but he didn't reenact that abuse. Nor, in any case, would my mother have let him.

No, it wasn't a father standing behind my mother as she explained what was right and good and true, but a woman or women, the mythic Mrs. Eddy, perhaps joined by her first lieutenant, my grandmother. Hera and Athena, God's wife, Jesus' sister, and with the addition of my mother, a kind of holy female trinity: Mother, Daughter, and Holy Ghost. It was a particularly female kind of authority—neither violent nor warlike, with no hint of the vengeful Yahweh smiting or laying waste. Its hallmark was mild to severe exasperation and reflected pain. My grandmother and Mrs. Eddy were severe; my mother, fortunately, was mild. But she could still be disappointed and puzzled.

Usually I disappointed my mother in the realm of truth-telling. For her, strict honesty was the mark of an honorable child; for me, the mark of a boring one. I didn't so much lie as embroider on reality or more often manage to convince myself that what I made up was real. This was the wall that my mother and I found ourselves on either side of, again and again, for instance, in the matter of the plagiarized duck poem.

I was about eight then and had recently been given a collection of poetry called *Favorite Poems Old and New.* Emily Dickinson and Carl Sandburg were in it as well as limericks by Edward Lear. I went around chanting these poems for the sound of them. Sometimes, when I came across another poem I liked, I copied it and stuck it in the pages of the book. The duck poem was a bad poem, but a "cute" one, the sort an adult trying to be mistaken for a child might write. When my mother found it in my room and asked if I'd written it, she looked so pleased when I said yes that I made myself believe that it had come out of my head, that I *could* have written it. And yes, after a day or two, the words seemed to become mine. I repeated them in my head—"wa-ter—*proofed*"; they were mine; they sounded like me.

But as soon as Edyth pointed out that the poem had been printed on the Children's Page, I snapped back into the knowledge that I had only copied it. My mother was shocked, embarrassed for me. Later she said, "You can't take other people's words and say they're your own. If you want to write, the words have to come from you. It's stealing otherwise."

It made an impact on me, her saying that; in fact every time she told me something important it made an impact. Perhaps it's just that I idealized her after her death, but I think it was more my realization that my mother did not expect me to lie. Other adults did. My teachers did. My grandmother did. Even my father did. They believed that it was the nature of children to try to get away with as much as they could. They were waiting to catch you out, just waiting for you to make a mistake so they could trap you and trick you. But my mother wasn't like that. She knew she couldn't expect me to behave well every minute. She knew that I was too loud and broke things and let my imagination carry me away. But she didn't expect me to lie or to steal. She believed, with little evidence, that I was better than that.

Mrs. Eddy's personality *was* authoritarian and paranoid. But like any woman who goes against the grain, these attributes probably helped her as much as hurt her. Certainly she was constantly having to respond to the profound fears that, as a powerful female leader, she stirred up. Clergymen and doctors, in particular, lashed out at her, using terms like *witch, spider, worm, anaconda.* The clergy called her Satan disguised as a woman, a devil in disguise, "the woman who introduced the corrupting leaven into the pure meal in the Gospel and leavened the whole lump." To the medical profession she was simply neurotic, hysterical, paranoid, and degenerate. Her position as a leader caused male writers to both disparage her as masculine and power-hungry as well as to ridicule her as weak and idiotic (women journalists were also critical, but not with the same degree of fury or patronage). Here is a typical example from Stefan Zweig's book *Mental Healers:*

> But who was Mary Baker Eddy? Mrs. Anybody, unattractive, by no means beautiful, not particularly sincere, rather stupid, one whom it would be a compliment to describe as even half-educated, isolated, unknown, and utterly without position, money friends, or what the Americans call "pull." There was no group or sect for her to appeal to; she had nothing in her hand but a pen, and nothing in her mediocre brain but one solitary idea. Everything was against her: science, religion, the schools, the universities, common sense. . . . In the breadth of her influence, in the swiftness of her success, in the number of her supporters, this old woman, scarcely more than half-witted, always ailing, and of very dubious character, outstripped all the leaders and investigators of our time. Never beneath the eyes of us moderns has spiritual and religious disturbance emanated from any one to the same marvelous extent as from this daughter of an American farmer, this lone being whom her countryman Mark Twain angrily terms "the most daring and masculine and masterful woman that has appeared on earth in centuries."

Today, when church membership is small and shrinking yearly, it's almost unbelievable to read that Mark Twain was terrified of Christian Science overrunning the world. The Standard Oil of Religion he called it, predicting that "It is a reasonably safe guess that in America in 1920 there will be ten million Christian Scientists." Twain, who had tried Christian Science healing himself and turned against it, wrote several articles for the popular press denouncing Christian Science, and then added to them and turned them into a book, which was published in 1907. All of the critical biographies of Mrs. Eddy quote Twain's sarcastic tweaks at the religion of Eddygush, and I was prepared for a hilarious essay on the order of "The Awful German Language." But

Twain's fear of Mrs. Eddy is so vivid that his sense of humor actually deserts him, making for reading about as dull as some of Eddy's own texts.

When it was published, however, it did create a stir among the Christian Scientists, and Mrs. Eddy was especially irritated that Twain mocked her role as "Mother." Sternly she responded by changing it to "Leader." The *Church Manual* was altered to read:

THE TITLE OF MOTHER CHANGED. SECTION I.

In the year eighteen hundred and ninety-five, loyal Christian Scientists had given to the author of their textbook, the Founder of Christian Science, the individual, endearing term of Mother. At first Mrs. Eddy objected to being called thus but afterward consented on the ground that this appellative in the Church meant nothing more than a tender term such as sister or brother. In the year nineteen hundred and three and after owing to the public misunderstanding of this name, it is the duty of Christian Scientists to drop the word *mother* and to substitute Leader, already used in our periodicals.

Although Mrs. Eddy's role as mother was dropped, the concept of motherhood continues in Christian Science, most specifically in the concept of the Mother Church, which is not only the First Church of Christ, Scientist, in Boston but is the home of the governing body, the Board of Trustees, who carry out the task of upholding and enforcing Mrs. Eddy's ideas. There is only one Mother Church; the rest are branch churches. In the branch churches the officers are elected democratically from the congregation, while the Mother Church is administered by a select group, also responsible for publishing the church's periodicals and books by and about Mrs. Eddy.

After the Mother Church was built in Boston, branch churches sprang up across the country. It's been said that these churches resemble banks more than places of worship, and it's true that many of them have a grand and prosperous air. They sit on valuable pieces of real estate in cities all over the United States, half-filled with mainly elderly congregation, big buildings with columns and staircases. Increasingly the churches are being sold off or turned into community centers or recital halls.

Southern California still has one of the largest populations of Christian Scientists, and dozens of churches were built there after World War II to accommodate the growth of suburbs. Downtown Long Beach had had a large church, so popular at one time that, as Edyth told me, "It was so crowded that you had to get a ticket to get inside on Sundays." But when my mother and her young women friends moved out of the center of the city to the new developments being built on the outskirts, they had to start from scratch, a prospect that only invigorated them. Much of my childhood was taken up with this project: the fundraising and construction of the Sixth Church of Christ, Scientist, in Long Beach.

In keeping with the Christian Science practice of raising all the money for the edifice before construction began, the congregation, most of them young women, worshipped for eight years at an American Legion Hall on Woodruff Avenue. All my early memories of Sunday School and church take place in this drab shoebox of a hall filled with cheerful plans for the future and many, many American flags. We arrived at eight thirty and helped arrange the metal chairs in circles for Sunday School; afterwards, everyone raced around, and with a great deal of lively banging, the chairs were dragged into rows for the church service at ten. There was a slapdash energetic feel to the whole endeavor, rather like putting on a circus in a town where you knew you only had two hours before the news of how you'd been forced out of the last town caught up with you. After church the metal chairs were once again folded and stacked along the sides of the church. Everyone worked together and then people stood about, laughing and chatting. In a small room by the door the treasurer counted the week's takings, including the money in envelopes set aside specifically for the building fund.

My mother had been a kindergarten teacher before I was born. Afterwards she was a housewife, not a very devoted one. She had no interest in cooking or cleaning. Meals were on time, and beds were made every day. She didn't go much beyond that. She didn't sew or knit and had no desire to learn. She never tried a new recipe but stuck firmly to cheap cuts of meat, potatoes, and canned vegetables, the Midwestern meals she and my father knew and loved. She liked gardening and filled our yard with flowers. It induced a sort of dreaminess in her, not the energy it arouses in more dedicated gardeners with their seed catalogs and gardening books. No, my mother simply drove periodically to the local nursery, loaded up on annuals and returned to plant them.

Then she mainly watered. I remember her drifting about the yard with her garden hose as if the water she lavished on the plants was satisfying some deep need of her own. The spirit of play was very strong in her. The further she moved away from the Midwest and her mother, the more she could indulge it. In my early childhood we spent hours and hours drawing pictures and making clay figures together. She wasn't impractical, however. The Depression had made her thrifty and she knew the value of money, which was probably how she ended up on the building committee.

In the mid-Fifties the church purchased a site on the corner of Studebaker and Monlaco Avenue. We used to drive out to this weedy spot at least once a week with one or two of the other building committee members. Long before the builders ever set foot on the lot, my mother and her friends had dreamed the whole building into existence dozens of times. They used to trudge around through the dirt and nettles waving their hands: "We'll have a nursery for the babies and toddlers. And rooms for the Readers to prepare. A office, a kitchen. A Sunday School room and an auditorium with"—here they shrieked with laughter—"*comfortable* seats."

One afternoon she and I went to the site alone. The ground had just been broken, the foundation was to be poured the next day. My mother held out the unwieldy blueprint the architect had given her and tried to explain to me how it would look, how vision would become reality. I was seven or eight perhaps. She'd picked me up from school and I was wearing school clothes still. It was autumn and the air had a bite to it. I had to run to keep warm. She was in a tailored blouse and skirt, a yellow sweater thrown over her shoulders. Perhaps she'd just come from a meeting because she had on stockings and fresh bright makeup, the dark red lipstick that made her lightly freckled skin seem pale and her hair very dark. She strode around the edges of the lot, pointing to walls that did not exist yet, to corridors and patios. She was excited the way I was when I made a tent from an old bedspread, but more than that: she was powerful, as if she'd found some part of herself that could make things happen, a part that had been invisible to her before.

"It's going to be a church," she said, exulting and running with me around the edges of the lot. "A real live church!"

I went back to this church a few years ago. Everything was just how they'd dreamed it would be. A nursery—though few young parents attended anymore—rooms for the Readers to prepare, an office and a kitchen. My mother had died a few years after that afternoon at the construction site; she didn't live to see the last section, the auditorium, constructed. In the early days we had to dismantle the Sunday School chairs for church just as in the early American Legion Hall days. The Sixth Church was very modern-looking when it was built—long and low and filled with light from large windows that looked out on to landscaped patios. Now it seems comfortably settled into a mass of greenery that has grown up around it.

I sat through the service with George and Viv, who had invited me. They're retired now, white-haired, good-humored, gentle people who play golf and go on ocean cruises and to whom life has been good. The service was exactly the same as it had been and would be forever. The only thing different was that both Readers were women. "It's often the case now," Viv told me in her matter-of-fact way. "There aren't many men left in the church." I looked around and saw she was right. There were precisely four out of a congregation of about forty or fifty. Two of them were very old and supported on canes; one was George and the fourth had short hair and looked too serious to be only twenty-five.

Even though the women up in front were saying nothing that they'd thought or written themselves, I still felt a kind of thrill watching them up there, I felt how there had always been a thrill for me seeing a woman doing nontraditional work or getting up in front of a crowd of people and saying, "Here I am. I deserve to be up here." I listened and remembered. The reason it all felt so familiar, though I had not been in a Christian Science church for almost thirty years, was that the structure of the service had not changed, nor had the words. Mrs. Eddy had made sure of that. She had the revealed Truth, she and no other, certainly not the upstarts who had once planned to overthrow her. Although early in her career she had inveighed against creeds, after she reorganized the Boston Church so that her power was absolute, she began to set down in her *Church Manual* an inflexible system of rules that she characteristically claimed did not come from her, but from above.

They were not arbitrary opinions nor dictatorial demands, such as one person might impose upon another. They were impelled by a power not one's own, were written at different dates, and as the occasion required. They sprang from necessity, the logic of events, from the immediate demand for them as a help that must be supplied to maintain dignity and defense of our Cause; hence their simple, scientific basis, and detail so requisite to demonstrate genuine Christian Science, and which will do for the race what absolute doctrine destined for future generations might not accomplish.

After Mrs. Eddy had finished spelling everything out in her *Church Manual*, from how many hymns would be sung, to the order of the service down to the twenty-six topics to be discussed each year, she decreed that she and she alone could revise the *Church Manual*. The last time it was revised was 1908, two years before her death. William James has written, in *The Varieties of Religious Experience*, that "Churches, when once established, live at second-hand upon tradition; but the *founders* of every church owed their power originally to the fact of their direct personal communication with the divine." We all live at secondhand upon tradition in the latter days of any movement, remembering how it used to be and trying to re-create that, oftentimes in precisely the wrong way, through mindless repetition, instead of seeking our own connection with the divine.

After the service George and Viv and I met Christine for lunch, in one of those suburban Hofs or Havens in a mallette along a palm-lined boulevard near the church. She was still tall and thin, I was still round. She was a divorced single mother now, a high school math teacher, a woman who would probably not call herself a feminist exactly, but whose life had been changed utterly by the feminist movement. We talked about computers; we ate and drank decaf coffee; we laughed remembering all those grilled cheese sandwiches, those birthday parties and the trips to the beach. Christine and I had been babies together, we had sat in Sunday School together year after year. Viv listened to us laugh and smiled. She didn't mention how Christine and I had destroyed her bed, or her doll collection; I kept hoping Viv didn't remember my loud and careless ways as a child. She didn't seem to. She looked at me with patience and affection. I had told her that I was a writer now, though I was a little vague about my work, so much of which has to do with being a lesbian. "I remember you always wanted to write," she said. "Even as a child. Didn't you once write a poem about a duck?"

We hugged good-bye and while Christine was paying the bill, Viv thanked me for having come to church with them. "Christine stopped going a long time ago," she said. "It's not that she doesn't believe, she says. But she says the service doesn't have enough punch. She says she finds the whole thing just a little too predictable."

I watched them drive off, mother and daughter, with all those complex feelings of loss and envy and freedom that mothers and daughters rouse in me. It could so easily have been my mother and me driving off together in our American sedan down a wide palm-lined suburban boulevard. I might be a teacher, too, living alone with my child after a very brief marriage. I could not imagine myself attending church. But perhaps I would, like Christine, have continued to believe.

Chapter 3

Science

nce, in second grade, I saw something astonishing. It was a calf being born. My class, led by Mrs. Franken, had gone by bus on a field trip to a dairy in Norwalk, which was then part of the fertile California countryside that stretched for miles outside Long Beach. We'd visited the dimly lit milking parlor, had seen the tubular, gleaming steel machines attached to Bossy and Flossy's undersides, had seen, through glass, the pasteurization room, with its white tile floor and walls and its enormous metal vats of milk. And we'd seen waterfalls of white milk funneling into glass bottles gliding down a conveyor belt. Never was there such a contrast—the brown-stewed, pungent, sweet-hayed odor of the cows in their stalls, and the scentless, whiter-than-white brilliance of the transformed milk shooting through mirrorlike surfaces of metal. Now we were on our way to the outdoor picnic area where we'd been told there was a surprise for us. *Fresh* ice cream! we guessed excitedly. White-as-paper vanilla ice cream with thick, dark chocolate swirled through.

We were walking single file along a path between two paddocks. I don't know who saw the spinning cow first, but suddenly we all stopped, even Mrs. Franken, transfixed by the sight of a brown cow with a bony spine and bulging belly turning in circles as if she were trying to catch her tail. There was a wild, intense look in the glaring eyes that rolled so they looked almost white not brown, but that wasn't what made us stop as if our feet had grown into the ground. It was the sight of a large blue balloon emerging from the back of the cow, like a rubbery exhaust cloud from a car. Around and around the cow spun and the blue balloon just kept getting larger and larger until it seemed half as big as the cow itself, heavy and bulging and wet, the color of a pale blue plum. The cow moaned, whirled, bellowed, and the balloon grew bigger, until, with a thick plop, the blue bag, huge as an army duffel, dropped on to the dusty ground. It was as if the cow had turned herself inside out and now looked down at what had been her vital parts.

She looked with exhausted interest and then, to our horror, she began to eat the bag.

Until now, no one had said anything, but when we saw her eating her insides, chomping and licking her big lips, we couldn't help squeaking and squealing in protest. Mrs. Franken, usually so organized and authoritative, stood there stunned and could say nothing except, "Oh, my. Oh, my." But our guide to the dairy, the man in the bright white uniform with his name stitched above his heart, who had gone ahead to put a pile of ice cream cups on the picnic tables, now rushed back to reassure us.

"It's nothing to be worried about. The cow is just having her baby."

And suddenly the picture cleared and it was plain to see that emerging from the viscous blue duffel bag was a baby cow, struggling to find her feet.

"The mystery of life, children," said Mrs. Franken in her normal teacher's voice that also had a touch of relief in it. "Aren't we lucky to have seen the mystery of life? And now come along, your ice cream will be melting."

The mystery of life, the mystery of life. How that phrase lingered in my mind, long after the field trip. I thought of it when my cat Curie had her kittens in my closet and the tiny mewling creatures emerged wet and blind one by one; I thought of it when I found a tiny bird fallen from its nest in the midst of hatching, bits of sky-blue shell still clinging to its featherless, transparent skin. It was still warm when I picked it up. Where had the heartbeat of the bird gone to and what was the mystery that had taken its heartbeat away? The mystery of life was the mystery of flesh and bone and blood, mysteries that I was carefully taught I should know nothing about, because they were mortal lies.

"Man is not matter; he is not made up of brain, blood, bones and other material elements. The Scriptures inform us that man is made in the image and likeness of God. Matter is not that likeness." This was the Scientific Statement of Being, written by Mrs. Eddy and prominent in her writings. It was the basis for healing. We heard it frequently in Sunday School and I heard it even more often from my mother's lips when she was praying for me and my brother. When I read the *Sentinel*'s children's stories the kids in trouble always recited it or their mothers did, as reminders of why they should not believe that there was anything wrong with them. I knew it by heart.

At home and in Sunday School, the statement made a kind of rhythmic and poetic sense, pronounced as it was in such gentle and firm tones and with the confidence born of knowing that it worked. Only Mind existed, there was no life or intelligence in matter. But outside the closed circle of the church the question seemed more vexing. When I asked what matter was, I was told "things" or "everything you look at, touch and hear." Did that mean my favorite brown shoes, rounded at the toe and pleasingly scuffed from kicking my tin lunchbox, the first shoes I ever learned to tie tightly with a neat bow, or my teddy bear, its brown fur ragged down to the cotton batting inside from being chewed on during naps, its once bulging, warm golden brown eyes replaced by two inscrutable black buttons? Was matter the red tricycle I loved with a passion until I got my skates with their special skate key and loved them more? What about our backyard, just planted with trees and grass and roses the year I was born and now, well watered through the hot months, more and more fruited and flowery and fragrant? What about the ocean, its salt and spray, the hugeness behind every crashing wave, the hugeness I wanted to get inside of, once I was big and could leave my little brother splashing alone with the bucket and shovel on the shore? What about the neighborhood houses that I dawdled by on my way to school, and whose lawns I ran through on the way home? And school itself, Patrick Henry Elementary, fresh-plastered stucco, adobe-colored, with its smell of new wood desks, barely scuffed linoleum, chalky green blackboards, tarry black asphalt that stretched for miles from the first-grade rooms to the sixth-grade bungalows. Was that high-decibel playground, all broken into colored lines and circles, surrounded by eucalyptus and pyrocantha bushes, patrolled by teachers who could not see everything, but whose voices sounded as if they could—was this not real?

And what did it mean that my body too was matter and thus had no reality? What did it mean to be inside a body that did not exist, a body that was not made up of brain, blood, and bones? As a baby I'd spent hours staring hypnotized at my toes and hands; as a toddler hours more looking at what went in and what came out of my body: bananas and puréed carrots in one end, pee and poop out the other. And blood? As a young child I was not squeamish, only curious. I loved my blood, that sweet, bright red milk that poured copiously through my skin when I fell on the rough asphalt playground at school and skinned my knees and elbows. I sucked at my wounds and cleaned the sand and dirt from the shreds of skin, the threadlike cobwebs over those crimson hearts of injury. I didn't mind my injuries, not because I was a Christian Scientist, but because I loved the scabs that grew over them.

I loved my scabs. I always had them, thick, tough, black and red little gates across the mystery of the inside of my body. They were doorways to an interior world that otherwise I could never see, a world that opened briefly only when I skinned my knees and elbows. I loved to prize open chinks in the gates and to see the yellow-green pus form and squeeze out, to start the whole thing bleeding again, to keep the scab formation going on as long as possible. My mother taught me not to believe in the material world, but she was observant enough to say, "Don't pick your scabs!" I loved to pick them though, loved that tiny ripping noise as the whole top, crusted and black, lifted off what was so smooth and liquid underneath. What was underneath? Only my little wounds gave me some inkling and some intimacy.

Next to scabs I liked worrying my baby teeth until they fell out. Of course they never fell, they were cajoled and teased and threatened out. Hour after hour in the second and third grades I'd rock the tooth back and forth in its bloody little bed, painstakingly seducing it with my tongue from its clinging roots. Only half my mind was on the lesson; the other half was waiting with complete absorption for the moment when the tooth would let go with a thin inner pop and warm sweet blood would gush up into the well like an oil strike. The blood came from inside; economically I swallowed it, like a cat her cream. There was a secret ecstasy in this; secret to me, anyway. Mrs. Franken must have looked out, during her lessons on the most rudimentary arithmetic, to see blind eyes and rows of tongues busily working their baby teeth back and forth.

I knew that Mind was real and matter was unreal, but it seemed that some aspects of matter were more unreal than others, more objectionable and thus more to be struggled with, and those aspects always had to do with the body. The word "corporeal" was always used negatively in Christian Science; it was often linked with sensuality as in "a corporeal and sensual belief." Evidence that came to us through the "five corporeal senses," as they were sternly called, was always suspect. Like hardened criminals, they lied whenever you put them on the witness stand: "false sense testimony" was the most you could expect from them.

Christian Science, although it split the mind and body like most Western religions, exalting the one and denying the other, did not ask that we mortify the flesh, only dismiss its claims on our attention. We did not have to confess our temptations and our sins; to do so would give matter power, would be to fall into the trap of mortal error. Unlike Catholics, for instance, who saw the body as only too real, too sexual, and too powerful, a worthy opponent to struggle with, we Christian Scientists did not give the body any power at all. We transformed it into allegory and euphemism. In Christian Science every human organ of perception was a metaphor for something else. Eyes were "spiritual discernment—not material but mental." Ears were "not organs of the so-called corporeal senses, but spiritual understanding. Jesus said, referring to spiritual perception, 'Having ears, hear ye not?' "

To have a body—I knew this deeply, without thinking—was to touch and taste and smell your way through a world that was endlessly rich and varied. But in my metaphysical childhood, to have a body was also to have a kind of enemy scout between your mind and Divine Mind, a secret agent whose dispatches from the physical world had to be ignored at all costs. You couldn't have thought this up on your own, not as a child; you couldn't have learned to treat your senses as treacherous. It was a system thought up by an adult, a middle-aged woman who was disappointed in her body and where her body had taken her in the world, a New England woman who felt at home with Transcendental abstractions and Spiritualist testimonies of communications with other worlds, a nineteenth-century woman, reticent about the flesh and lavish with the spirit.

As a child, I knew nothing of Mary Baker Eddy's personality or her historical context. I knew nothing of the sophisticated phenomenological arguments that had been going on for centuries on the exact nature of reality. But I did know, without understanding, that you had to have a thing in front of you to realize it was not really a thing. You had to see a bird to know it wasn't there, hear a rainstorm to know it wasn't happening, touch a rose petal with your tongue to know that its silky delicacy was matter and unreal. You had to have a body so you could act as if it didn't exist. You had to have eyes that you could turn away from the corporeal world.

Once I remember going to a Saturday movie matinee alone with my mother. It wasn't something we did often and I recall that she was dressed up, in a small felt hat over her dark wavy hair, white gloves, and a flowered dress, cinched around her increasingly ample waist with a white leather belt. She had heard something about this movie. It was a foreign film, a French film. She had studied French years ago in college: "They say it's the most beautiful language in the world," she told me. "It's so beautiful you can hardly speak it if you're not born in France." I was six or seven, thrilled to be on this excursion with my mother, to have her to myself, to be grown up and dressed in a plaid dress and my polished brown shoes, to be initiated into the mysteries of the foreign. The movie would be all in French my mother told me; even though I wouldn't understand anything, it would be a good opportunity for me to hear this beautiful way of speaking. I nodded expectantly. I had never heard a foreign language before and didn't even really know what that meant.

The theater was a small one, with red velvet draping everywhere and a dusty scent of popcorn and used perfume. The seats were soft and big, red velvet too, and worn to a thin, silky nap. All around us adults were sitting, talking quietly. I thought they must be French or understand it like my mother. I was the only child. I ate my popcorn quietly, waiting. Then the dark red drapes parted and the film began. It was black-and-white, mostly faces of adults talking. One man had a dark mustache that ran like a pencil line between his mouth and nose. A lady wore a hat like a pancake. There were no pictures of the Eiffel Tower, as I had hoped there would be. I couldn't understand a word they were saying, and even though I'd been told I wouldn't, I had still expected somehow to know what they were talking about. They were talking French but I didn't know if it was beautiful or not. It sounded like gibberish. Below their faces ran long lines of type. I wasn't much of a reader yet. Here and there I recognized a word: *the, and, but*. Once I saw *house* float by, and once a long sentence that had *love* in it three times.

Suddenly a woman opened her blouse onscreen, revealing a black slip. Just as suddenly my mother forced my head down into my lap. I had to stay like that for a few minutes, smelling popcorn and my mother's panic. When I was allowed to come up everything was fine again, everyone was dressed and back to talking. But it happened again—the lady had nothing on now except the slip and she was sitting on a bed smoking a cigarette—and this time my mother wrenched me out of my seat, and pushed me out of the row and up the aisle of the crowded theater, holding my shoulders so I couldn't look back.

If my mother were still alive I could ask her if what I remember is true. I could ask her who taught her that the body is forbidden territory. Was it her own mother? Was this the job of Christian Science mothers, to avert their daughters' eyes? I can't ask her, and so I only remember it the way I do: my mother in hat and gloves and a belted dress that rustled, with her freckled arms and neck, her red lipstick, her powdered nose, dressed up for a French experience, and excited to share it with me. And I see myself, anticipation turning to boredom, not titillated until I knew that what I had seen was forbidden and disturbing. I smell the dry, musty upholstery of the seat, feel my mother's firm, anxious hand on my neck, know that on the flickering screen something strange and fleshy and thrilling is happening.

Something to do with the body. The mystery of life.

When I told my father about the cow being born he launched into glad memories of the various farms in Wisconsin and Illinois where he'd spent his youth. He'd seen plenty of calves being born, and piglets and lambs too. Once he'd even seen a colt come out. He'd raised a calf himself for the 4-H Club. The blue balloon? Perfectly normal. The cow ate it because it was nutritious. Watching animals give birth was fascinating, my father said, remembering his childhood and forgetting mine. Forgetting that he had agreed to let my mother raise me and my brother in the Christian Science church where such things were unreal.

"I saw you being born," he went on. "Not many fathers can say that. They usually keep them out. But your mother was in Shepherd's Nursing Home. It wasn't like a hospital. There were just two rooms, and right after you were born the other lady started her labor and so I had to write out your birth certificate myself."

"Did I come out in a blue balloon?" My mother, whom I'd once pressed for details on the subject, had been vague. "You were a twinkle in your father's eye," she said. "And we're very happy to have you here with us."

"You were all wet," my father said. "Just like a little piglet, but with your eyes wide open. And screaming fit to beat the band."

I was born in 1950, at the beginning of a decade that seems in retrospect to gleam with test-tube glass and stainless steel and to flicker to the sound of a newsreel voice, "Science marches on." Science had never been more powerful nor more revered. Science had won the war for the Allies and had made the United States a superpower, not only able to keep the peace through continued arms production, but to create and fulfill consumer desires worldwide. Science was closing in on infectious diseases, eradicating TB and smallpox, threatening war on polio. Science was sending satellites into orbit and figuring out how to get chimps and men up there too. Science was inventing a new, clean, and cheap source of power, nuclear energy, and creating pesticides that would wipe out crop diseases and increase agricultural yields.

In the Fifties the voice of science was the voice of salvation. So much had been destroyed in the first half of the century—cities bombed, populations left homeless, whole cultures wiped out. But science and technology would make it better. The middle of the century was a fresh start. Talk was of the future, not the past, of a spanking-clean future where everything happened without effort and for our benefit. At Disney's Tomorrowland we glided around on the Monorail and visited modular homes where robots did most of the work. "This is the kind of house I'd like." My mother sighed. She hated housework more than anything.

Science and technology were not just at Disneyland, however; they were all around us, and the lure of the future was something that my parents could not resist, any more than could most of the millions of Americans who had lived through the Depression and the War. My parents had only admiration for the culture springing up around them in Southern California, for the freeways and airports, the malls and parking lots. My mother had spent her Midwestern adolescence laboring in a kitchen garden, canning every summer and having to make thrifty soups and cakes from scratch. Now whatever appeared on the grocery shelf advertising itself as time-saving was soon on our table: instant potatoes, Minute Rice, minute steaks, Reddi-Whip, and a whole freez-erful of flash-frozen Bird's-Eye vegetables.

My father, who'd grown up on a farm where they still used kerosene lamps and washed in a galvanized tub in the kitchen, also sped forward into the future with the rest of his generation. He taught bookkeep-ing and accounting at the Business and Technology Division of Long Beach City College. He'd majored in history and had loved the clas-sics, but now he talked at the dinner table of artificial intelligence and data processing. Machines were on the horizon that would do the grunt work of thinking, leaving humanity to enjoy itself. When we went to his school to visit him, the hum and buzz of the future was evident. In one room former GIs were learning aeronautics, in another algebra and trigonometry. From a metal Quonset hut, recycled from the war, came the flash of welders' arcs. Douglas Aircraft was hiring; they needed skilled engineers and assembly-line workers to build the new passenger planes that would revolutionize travel.

Science was everywhere, in advertisements, in cartoons, in the the-aters. On the movie screen were absentminded scientists and mad sci-entists and evil Russians spies trying to steal our scientific research. The good scientists in these movies were white men with short hair and glasses, wearing white lab coats, looking earnest and assuring us that they could find the answer, fight the plague, save humanity, defeat the Communists. Scientists looked smart, "brainy." To put someone down people said, "He's no Einstein." We took IQ tests in school and after the Russians launched *Sputnik,* parents panicked that the United States was falling behind in the race to the moon. They gave their boys model rockets and chemistry sets, microscopes and telescopes.

My brother and I weren't allowed to have chemistry kits, but we once got a small telescope. My mother was fascinated by everything to do with space, which she called "outer space," from the night sky to the competition between the U.S. and the Soviets. She cut out sto-ries from the *Monitor* about the first *Sputnik* in 1957 and *Sputnik 2* a month later, which carried a space dog, and she put the cuttings in a scrapbook. "We're living in very historic times," she told me. She said, "When you get older you'll be interested to look back on this period. Maybe you'll even be living in outer space. That's the next step you know, men in orbit, men on the moon." We went out to look at the stars and I scared myself by thinking that the enlarged reflection of my eyelashes was a dreadful spider on the moon. "Someday we might all be going up in space," she said. "If it happens soon enough, maybe I'll get there too."

How could my mother be interested in space, in astronomy, when science in general was so forbidden? Was it that the science of the stars seemed somehow less material, more abstract and spiritual? You couldn't smell or taste or hear anything in outer space; it had nothing to do with the body. Tidy in space suits and big plastic helmets, the spacemen would be weightless, practically pure spirit. Astronomy was not a "life" science. It had echoes of the metaphysical. "The scientists who are becoming most convinced of the existence of God are the physicists," my mother told me. "They are beginning to understand what Mrs. Eddy said all along. There is no such thing as matter as we know it."

But what I wanted to know was this: Who did the work of getting those satellites off the earth and keeping them up there, and how could they have managed it without taking any science classes in school?

Twice a week, beginning in the third grade, our heavy, unwieldy science readers, with their chapters on "Weather" and "Pollination" were passed out. I didn't get one. I didn't open one up. I only glimpsed, half in longing, half in firm rejection, the blue-black duotones of cirrus and cumulus clouds, the intriguing diagrams of bees in flight, as the books were opened flat on the wooden desks. That was my signal to get up from my desk and walk across the asphalt playground to the school library, where I spent the next hour reading or making special projects, like shoebox dioramas of the Greek myths.

Some of my classmates envied me for getting out of class, and since I loved to read by then, I, too, tried to feel lucky to have a free hour during the day to lose myself in books and to skip being tested. I preferred to believe that I was lucky than that I was odd or strange. But missing science classes troubled me. It wasn't only because I would hear the other kids talking about the fun they'd had replicating some famous scientific experiments, like using a three-sided prism to refract light into a Newtonian spectrum, or where they'd displaced water (with a lot of splashing) like Archimedes or dropped marbles off the teacher's desk like Galileo. It was because I loved to construct things even more than I liked to read and when I returned to class and saw the "Model Eye" made from a fishbowl or the papier-mâché volcano that could actually erupt, I was fearfully envious. I'd glance covertly over at a shelf by the window and see the desert terrarium with miniature cactus and a real lizard or the wood box with mesh on top and inside some papery larvae in the process of turning into moths, and I wouldn't understand why this world had to be closed to me. I wanted to look through the microscope and see the weird things floating in a drop of tap water; I wanted to hold a fertilized egg up to the light bulb and see the form of the baby chick inside. Why couldn't I?

Sometimes when I returned to class there would still be something written on the board:

What is Science?
Science is obtaining and using knowledge of our physical world. We obtain that knowledge by a special method called **the scientific method.** In a sense, the method is a way of thinking. First, a question is asked. Then facts relating to the question are gathered. From the facts, a tentative answer is formed. Then that answer is tested. The best means to test an answer is by experiment.
Without the experiment, science as we know it would not exist.
The results must be able to be achieved again and again.

If science was only questions and answers, why was it forbidden to me? I wondered about these things on my solitary trek to and from the library. I took my time, scuffing my feet on the asphalt playground, staring at the eucalyptus trees waving high up in the blue sky, listening for the birds. It was part of a deeper problem with Christian Science, this science business, and it went beyond averting my head when somebody brought their Invisible Man model to class. It was an ontological problem. The blackboard asked questions that I wanted to know the answers to: What is the earth made of? What is the sea made of? What is the air made of? Through all the changes they undergo something remains constant. What is it? Mrs. Eddy would say that Divine Mind was the constant. But if Mind was the constant, if Mind was enough, why had all these other things that I touched and tasted and saw been created? Why were they here? Why was I here?

The two librarians, old Mrs. Hatch with her marble-perfect curls, and her younger assistant Miss Beech, who smelled of vanilla and library paste, had discovered that I liked fairy tales and myths and each week there would be a pile of books on the blocky wooden table by the bay window with two palm trees outside. Month after month for four years that's all I remember reading: fables, legends, folklore; Norse myths, Celtic myths, North American Indian myths, Asian myths, and Greek myths. The Greek myths were my favorites. They were violent and bloody and splendid. The Greek gods were jokey, easily offended, quick to anger and to revenge. Cronos ate all his children, one after the next, because it had been prophesied that one of his sons would someday dethrone him. This was Zeus, who was saved from being eaten by his mother Rhea. When Zeus came to power after the battle of the Titans, Cronos threw up all his undigested babies, who promptly became gods too: Demeter, Hades, Poseidon. Zeus ate people too; he ate his wife, Metis, who was pregnant. Zeus's daughter Athena was born from inside him, through his forehead.

If my mother had known what I was reading, the kind of mythological knowledge of the universe that I was absorbing, perhaps she would not have been so eager for me to miss science classes. For while the other children were learning the difference between cumulus and cirrus clouds and what caused rain, I was soaking in shocking tales of sibling rivalries and marital quarrels on Olympus, and punishing stories of humans who fell afoul of these gods. I was soaking in etiologic tales in which I learned that natural phenomena have all been caused by the actions of capricious and dangerous gods and heroes. Why did the earth have ice caps and volcanoes? Because Phaeton, Apollo's son, had insisted on driving the chariot of fire across the sky one day against his father's wishes. Unable to control the horses, he drove the chariot too close to the earth, scorching it, and too far away, freezing it. Where do giraffes and zebras come from? They were Poseidon's mistakes when trying to craft a horse for Demeter.

As for cosmogony, there were a hundred different creation myths. There was a cosmic egg; there was a primordial battle; there was a sky god father and an earth god mother; there was water everywhere and a creature who had to dive into the water to bring up earth to start things going. One of my favorites was from a book on Finnish folk tales. The daughter of the air descended from the sky mansions into the sea where she floated for centuries with a child in her womb, unable to give birth. She was the Water-Mother who became the World-Shaper. A little dirt here, a little sand there. Here a mountain, there a coastline. And finally, when the world was just the way she liked it, she had her baby. In the water.

Did I think these stories true? Not exactly. But I had no other explanations for how the universe was created or maintained except for these myths of arbitrary and restless gods and the tragic humans who had to put up with them. The Bible had a tale of creation of course, but my mother had told me early on that Genesis was just a story, a beautiful story, but just a story nonetheless. A metaphor, she said. The earth was not really created in a week; it had always been here. Mrs. Eddy had no cosmogony. Mind *was*. Spirit *was*. Matter *was not*. Mortal mind *was not*.

I parroted these ideas in Sunday School, but I couldn't think in those terms as a child. Instead, I fell back on myths and stories to keep me company in the unknowable universe, just as if I had been living in a more ancient time.

"If you're a Christian *Scientist*, how come you have to leave class when we study *science?*" It was rarely said sneeringly. I might feel separated, isolated, but my leaving was something everybody was used to, and only a few curious about. But I didn't know the answer. I had struggled countless times with the question myself and had never quite been satisfied by the answer. It was part of belonging to a nineteenth-century religion with a vocabulary that was slightly arcane and erratic even in those days. "When *I* use a word," Mary Baker Eddy might have said with Humpty-Dumpty, "it means just what I choose it to mean." So it was with science. In the lexicon of Christian Science it did not mean biology, chemistry, and physics, but only that we could prove the truth of God's existence and good intentions towards us scientifically through healing.

In the 1820s, when Mary Baker Eddy was born, the world was still described according to the mechanistic model of Newton; by 1910, when she died, Einstein had published his famous paper on relativity. The concept of science underwent many changes in her lifetime, from Darwin's evolutionary theories to the discoveries of Pasteur. But throughout Mrs. Eddy's life, science had the connotation of order and authority, and she came to consider it her task to bring Christianity into the Scientific Age. Her initial understanding of the word *science* was not actually far from the accepted definition—the knowledge or understanding of objective fact and the necessity of verifiable proof to support this knowledge—but her manner of applying scientific methodology and the ends to which she thought it should be applied were highly unusual. She asked, for example, how if "Science compelled the admission that behind every phenonemon was a law, must there not be a still undiscovered law behind the healings of Jesus?"

She did not call herself the *creator* of a new religion, but its *discoverer*. She believed what she had discovered was the law behind the phenomenon of healing, that healing was not random, was not the result of God's momentary mercy, but a practice that could be demonstrated on a regular basis and taught to others. "Demonstration" is an important concept in Christian Science, but it is not so much the culmination of a logical argument as it is the practical proof of Divine Law or Principle. For Mary Baker Eddy, in spite of her metaphysics, was a pragmatist. She insisted that her science was proved by healing, and that healing would be the demonstration of the workings of Divine Law. Robert Peel, her best-known biographer, writes that in Christian Science "a trial of faith has a special significance: it is the theological equivalent of a laboratory test." And as Eddy asserts in *Science and Health*, "If the student adheres strictly to the teachings of Christian Science and ventures not to break its rules, he cannot fail of success in healing."

Originally she called her work Moral Science and, before she decided she must found a church, she seriously considered forming a scientific society. But although she used the scientific words such as "demonstration" and "proof" (she even referred at times to "mental molecules" and "microbes of sin"), her science was the science of mind, not matter. And by mind she meant divine Mind, not mortal mind. She wrote, "To develop the full might of this Science, the discords of corporeal sense must yield to spiritual sense. . . ." She asserted that "matter possesses neither sensation nor life." Error comes into our lives through the "false testimony of false material sense." Thus the only reality is that of divine Mind. Mortal mind causes us to suffer, but it is only the suffering of mortal mind. In Mary Baker Eddy's view, "To material sense, the severance of the jugular vein takes away life, but to spiritual sense and in Science, Life goes on unchanged and being is eternal. Temporal life is a false sense of existence."

Oddly enough, some of Mrs. Eddy's most derided ideas have been proven to be correct, at least theoretically. Today, physicists tell us that there is no such thing as a thing, no such thing as matter; there are only gadzillions of atomic and subatomic particles whizzing around in a quantum field through voids of empty space. Your false sense impressions don't tell you that (they urge you instead to sit down on that chair, to pick up that cup, to say, "What a gorgeous sunset!"), but it's true nonetheless. It's only energy, not matter, that truly exists. As for a temporal sense of existence, ever since Einstein's equation made the news, humanity has known, in theory anyway, that time is only relative.

These ideas will always affront our common sense, but they are concepts that continue to fascinate successive generations of scientists and metaphysicians alike. New Age authors recently realized how the discoveries of quantum mechanics could bolster their claims of a consciousness that is not bound to place or time and that energy, not matter, is the stuff of the universe. "Quantum," in fact, has become a key word in the current crop of mind/body books, many of which now take up space on my bookshelf. Quantum healing is the nebulous term that Deepak Chopra uses to explain why we should neither age nor sicken. Often photographed with a stethoscope discreetly in view, to show he's not a crackpot, and with a biography full of conventional credentials, Chopra supports his theories with the latest scientific research in the burgeoning field of psychoneuroimmunology. Neurologists used to think the mind was in the brain; immunologists once believed that the immune system was autonomous. Now, thanks to new research on neuropeptides and their receptors, scientists know that every cell of our bodies has a mind of its own. The mind is everywhere, and the amount of conversation going on between the brain and the immune system would drown the din of a sports stadium, if it could be amplified.

Although he doesn't mention Christian Science and perhaps doesn't even know of it, many of Chopra's statements remind me of Mrs. Eddy's teachings. He speaks of the physical body as an illusion, like all material objects, and of the "tyranny of the senses." He says we are not our physical bodies; he calls materialism a "superstition." But Chopra differs from Mrs. Eddy in asserting elsewhere (contradicting himself) that the body is intelligent. The body in fact is a "river of intelligence." Combining the best of his Ayurvedic spiritual philosophy with American cognitive therapy, the theory that "We are expressions of eternal unchanging Being" becomes a mandate for changing the perception of ourselves as ill or aging. What Chopra proposes are techniques for how you can make changes in your body at the molecular level and thus prolong your health and your life.

Larry Dossey, also an M.D., though arguably even more of a metaphysician, also uses new developments in immunology and neurology research to prove that the mind is "not confinable to the brain," which he calls its "non-local" nature. Dossey's use of "non-local" reminds me of Eddy's omnipotent divine Mind. Unlike Chopra, who speaks of Eternal Being, Dossey doesn't shy away from words such as prayer and God. He wants to bring Christianity into the Scientific Age (just as Eddy did) and his books are full of case histories and scientific studies, for instance a series of studies that were performed by a group called Spindrift on the calibrated effects of prayer on the growth of rye seeds. As Dossey says, "We need to know just *how* God is working, so we might systematically and more reliably make use of the effort."

When I try to read Dossey and Chopra, just as when I try to read Mrs. Eddy, I grow restive and my brain seems to spin apart into quantum particles. I'm not at home in the upper realms of speculative thought. I have never had a metaphysical mind, not as a child, and not now. I am comfortable with ideas, but ideas that are closer to home, ideas are based on particulars, on specifics. Most of all I like the particulars themselves. I like things I can see and touch, taste and hear and smell. I have always liked them best.

Science, in its simplest definition, is a knowledge of the nature of things. The world is full of things; in order to teach a child to live in the world, you have to teach her language, which is, in large part, the names of things. In order to teach her to make her bed, for example, the word "bed" must be considered to represent a real object. Anything else can only invite argument ("If the bed's not real, why do I have to change the sheets?"). Nor can you stop a child from absorbing the world through her senses. It would be the height of hopelessness to correct her every waking moment ("No, that may look like a rose, but it's really just a symbol."). Life must go on, breakfast eaten, chores done, schoolwork accomplished. Children already ask too many questions; you can't always be engaging in epistemological debates. But what you can do is limit the number of names a child knows for things and deemphasize the power of specific naming, of true naming, of the importance of naming. You can blanket the physical world with a soft comforter of abstractions so that it becomes idealized, sentimentalized, prettified.

Rilke says that things don't exist until the poet gives them names. What would he make of Mrs. Eddy's early poetry, where she writes:

The wild wind's race, the stars which light
their shining lamps on high.

or

Thy smile through tears, as sunshine o'er the sea
Awoke new beauty in the surge's roll.

Thoreau would call such writing "sublimo-slipshod." He despised such poetic attempts that substituted gushing for observation. Nature was not absent from Mrs. Eddy's writing, but it existed only in hackneyed metaphor. Things could never just be themselves—solid, discrete, separate—they could only be representations of some larger Principle. This was not Mrs. Eddy's singular failing as an author. It is typical of the sentimental poetry of the time (and sentimental poetry of all times). It is also typical of the metaphysical mind, the mind that is always trying to see the Ideal behind the apparent and to fix the meaning of nature somewhere else than in the thing itself.

Transcendentalist Emerson, echoing Plato, had written in his well-known essay "Nature" that "every natural fact is a symbol of some spiritual fact." And he'd explained, "When I behold a rich landscape, it is less to my purpose to recite correctly the order and the superposition of the strata, than to know why all thought of multitude is lost in a tranquil sense of unity. I cannot greatly honor minuteness in details, so long as there is no hint to explain the relation between things and thoughts. . . ."

Mary Baker Eddy was familiar with Emerson's writings and possibly with Thoreau's as well. But Thoreau could not have appealed to her. For Thoreau did honor minuteness in details. He kept meticulous observations on the flora and fauna of Concord and most particularly Walden Pond. "He thought that, if waked up from a trance, in this swamp, he could tell by the plants what time of the year it was within two days," Emerson wrote, in his eulogy that veers from admiration to impatience. Thoreau's purpose was not taxonomy, however. Once he discovered a new species of striped bream in Walden Pond, but he shuddered at the idea that the little fish he took to the natural history society would be one more bottled specimen on their shelves and that it was all the same to them that it was bottled and not swimming freely. For although Thoreau was an empiricist, who scorned any other way of apprehending the world than through first-hand observation, he was also a poet and his writing is full of metaphors. He wrote:

> The chub is a soft fish, and tastes like boiled brown paper salted.
> The bluebird carries the sky on his back.
> The tanager flies through the green foliage as if it would ignite the leaves.

Thoreau, as much as Emerson, wanted to find meaning and unity in nature—arguably even *more* than Emerson, for he chided himself, "It is as bad to *study* stars and clouds, as flowers and stones. I must let my sense wander as my thought, my eyes see without looking." But Thoreau did not begin with great questions, as Emerson did ("Three problems are put by nature to the mind: What is matter? Whence is it? And Whereto?"); he began with the information he took in from his senses and from there moved into a description of his relationship to nature and the thoughts and emotions it roused in him.

This is the difference between the metaphysically inclined mind, which is perfectly happy talking all day about divine Mind and Spirit and energy and quantum healing and non-local mind, and using natural metaphors to prove or illustrate a point, and the—what shall I call it?—the empirical-poetic mind, which loves the physical world for its own sake and yet finds in the workings of nature a pathway to something numinous, transcendent, and sacred.

I recall thousands of physical sensations from my childhood, from the exact texture and scent of a ripe apricot exploding in my face during a backyard fruit fight, to what a cold, salty wave felt like when it had me in its implacable grip. I remember how the sprinklers sounded late on a hot summer's night and how my mother's voice rose and fell reading the Bible. I remember the taste of grass and the taste of blood and the taste of rose petals. I remember everything about that dairy trip when I was seven, the dark, hay-sweet, poopy smell of the barns, the way the milk was bright as the stars in the sky, how the big blue balloon poured heavily and mysteriously from the cow's body. What I grew up lacking was not the ability to observe, but to name. While my body was busy recording every sensual detail of my childhood and imprinting it somewhere in my memory, my nascent scientific mind was dulled by dogma and my nascent literary mind was engaged in turning every image and sensation into acceptable metaphor. Like Mrs. Eddy's, my early poems were all about "beauty." There were *trees, sunsets, oceans, flowers*. None of them stood on their own, as a felt picture of anything in the real word: they were all in service of some vaster truth, and were basically interchangeable. Watching a lovely sunrise was the poetic equivalent of watching waves crash on the beach. Since God was good and the world was good, then only things which were also good could be written about. A beautiful sunset was never beautiful on its own; it was beautiful because it was a reflection of God's Love. Everything ugly or bad was shoved like old, ill-fitting, smelly shoes into a cardboard box and left out for the garbage collectors. Ugly represented matter, but matter didn't really exist, so there was nothing really ugly either. And if you did see anything ugly, you could just turn your head away. Or have it pushed down into your lap by a zealously protective Christian Science mother.

If you had pressed me, I would have been able to tell a maple from a palm and a snapdragon from a rose, but I wouldn't have considered it important to be able to do so. A flower was not interesting in and of itself, but because it meant something apart from how it looked or smelled. It was this meaning that I was encouraged to find as a child in my writing, not detailed descriptions. I might be aware of hundreds of differences in the flowers in the backyard; I might be able to distinguish all sorts of weathers, all sorts of seas. I might have an enormous encyclopedia of sense impressions in my memory, but I never realized I could use any of this knowledge in my writing. Even as I matured as a writer, I believed, without considering it overmuch, that flowers were flowers and trees were trees, and if you wanted to fix them in the reader's mind, you came up with striking similes that compared them to something else.

At its best science is more than a dry discipline that quantifies and calibrates; it's far more than nomenclature. It's about observation, about learning to see and to trust your perceptions, about noticing details and their importance. It's about living in the world with open eyes and an open, curious heart. It is about knowing the names of things in the world, but letting those names spark poetry. Allowing metaphor to emerge from observation, not substitute for it. The best nature writers, says Edward Hoagland, "combine rhapsody with science."

A woman who creates a religion that denies the life of the senses has long ago put the life of the senses behind her. For Mary Baker Eddy, corporeal existence—her own body—was a failure. It had only caused her pain; and even constant illness had never sufficiently gotten her the attention and love she craved. It's not surprising that she conceived of a religion where she could transform the memory of pain into a bad dream and dismiss the material world as unreal. Once again, for her it was a choice, and one she made willingly, in revolt against another way of life she had known.

But for me it was never a choice. It was gridlock of thought that kept me, not from experiencing the natural world I loved, but of blurring it, sentimentalizing it, putting it mentally at a distance. At nine, at ten, at eleven, as I walked away from my classroom, across the asphalt playground, I saw the eucalyptus trees, red-streaked, trailing thin streamers of fragrant, olive-tan, thin bark, and I heard the drunken singing of the cedar waxwings in the berry bars of the bursting red pyrocantha bushes. But to me they were only part of the picture I took with my inner eye and stored away forever, and I noticed them with unobservant pleasure as I made my way to the library to read the myths and fairy tales that were always waiting, piled in stacks, on the heavy blond table. The picture of the playground was being spoken in the most beautiful language in the world, but it was almost foreign to me. All I could see and understand were simple words like *birds* and *trees* and *clouds,* floating underneath.

Chapter 4

Health

There is nothing to heal but a false belief.

—Science and Health

$\mathscr{T}$he picture is by Norman Rockwell, or would be, if he'd painted it. A pigtailed little girl, in a flowered nightgown, only slightly pale under her freckles, sits upright in bed, the pillows white and well plumped up behind her, the quilt before her strewn with toys and jig-saw puzzles and books. On the table beside her is a pitcher of water and a glass, a bottle of cough syrup and one of pills. The doctor is call-ing—he has his stethoscope to the girl's chest. Perhaps a thermome-ter is stuck in her mouth. On the other side of the bed, a bit plump under an apron, anxiously bending forward, hands clasped, awaiting the news, is the girl's mother.

In spite of the sickness, there is something cozy in this scene (so dif-ferent a picture from Munch's *The Sick Child* where, in a shadowy brown room, the wasted figure of a bedridden girl stares with unsee-ing and unsettling eyes at something outside the frame). In a moment the doctor will give the girl a friendly clap on the shoulder and tell her mother, "Keep her out of school a day or two, give her lots of fluids and she'll be back to perfect health in no time."

The relieved mother will follow the doctor out of the room and down the stairs and press on him homemade cupcakes or a slice of pie, while up in the suddenly quiet room the pleasures of being ill but not too ill begin: the fever that slows down time, muffling some senses, heightening others, the sense of comfort and floating. Eventually the girl will become bored, will want to get up and play outside, will hear the voices of other children in the house or through the window and feel left out, estranged, and sad. But for now there's only peace, only a sense of comfort, slowed time, love, a chance to stay home from school and spend the day dreaming and sleeping.

These are not my memories, but those of friends who tell such stories of being ill as children. How they read and drew and put together puzzles, how they watched daytime TV or listened to the radio, how they ate their favorite foods, how everyone was nice to them and gave them the attention they sometimes didn't get otherwise. For some of my friends, illness was the only time their mother was kind to them, or more than kind, truly affectionate and solicitous. She looked worried when they coughed and frightened when they wheezed. She didn't yell at them when they were sick; she didn't punish them. Instead she sat by their beds, touched their hot foreheads, asked, "Would you like another bowl of Jell-O, sweetheart?"

No wonder some friends talk about their childhood illnesses with nostalgia and yearning and seek to replicate the experience in adulthood. A day in bed with a cold or the flu is a day off work, a day with the phone unplugged, a slow, stuffed-up, dreaming, chicken-soup kind of day when the world stops and responsibilities slip away. A day, the only sort many of us can allow ourselves, to let go completely. No other excuses are needed. "I'm sick," said with a voluptuous cough or sneeze, is enough. "I'm sick" starts the sympathy flowing.

This can never be so for me. I'm a bad patient, and a reluctant nurse. About others I find myself thinking, He can't really be *that* sick, or She's sick so *often*. I am sympathetic to a point—"A temperature of 104? And what a terrible cough!"—and then the skeptical voice inside whispers, "Let's not overdo it." When I have the flu I hide away glumly, sleeping and reading, sniffling and drinking tea, longing for it to be over. Only when I've been really ill, when I have stood feverish on that far shore of near-delirium, have I glimpsed, for an instant, the pleasures of giving up a hold on health. More often I'm impatient and apologetic about being nursed and get out of bed as soon as possible.

I am not often ill, and I don't like it when I am.

Sickness was not a means of giving or receiving love when I was a child. I have no happy memories of plumped pillows and bedspreads covered with books and toys. No doctor ever came to our house with his black bag. The conditions for illness did not exist at our house and nobody was ill, not my father, not my mother, not Bruce and not me. There was no talk among my mother's Christian Science friends of bugs "going around." There was no expectation that any of us would "catch" anything. My mother's friends didn't trade tips about keeping their children healthy; they didn't spend their time telling anecdotes about Carrie's earaches or Christine's tonsillitis.

Bumps and bruises and unexpected events were another matter. Once my father fell asleep on the beach and burned his legs so badly that he had to use crutches for a few days. Once my mother twisted her ankle jumping off the back porch and was reluctantly persuaded to spend a day or two with her foot up. And my brother and I were always doing something to our bodies. Whenever I was really hurt, shaken from a fall out of a tree or from my bike, pushed over in a quarrel, knocked in the face with a ball, I went running to my mother, shrieking. I threw myself on her lap, let her arms surround me, heard her voice in my ear, felt her hand stroking my hair. Whatever bruise or scrape I'd sustained went unregarded, though with her practiced maternal eye my mother had ascertained it wasn't serious. She didn't touch or kiss it. There was no baby talk, no "Did my baby get a boo-boo? Kiss and make all better now." I heard instead the Lord's Prayer or the Twenty-third Psalm or the Scientific Statement of Being. I heard the comforting circular reasoning of Christian Science: "God loves you. God wouldn't want you to hurt. Therefore, you don't hurt."

I climbed into the stuffed rocking chair with my mother and pressed my face against the V of her blouse where the freckles faded into the shadow between her breasts, and where the smell was strong, of tears and heat and Pond's Cold Cream. My mother had all the time in the world to hold and comfort me, to read to me from the Bible or Mrs. Eddy. For not only was she my mother, not only did she love me, but this was her work on earth, to assert the Truth of God's love for us, to heal us. She had all the time in the world to teach me her belief system, and I learned it deeply, tenderly, and almost irreversibly.

"God loves you. God doesn't want you to hurt." And why shouldn't that be so? For if God's love was like my mother's love for me, warm and strong and smelling of Pond's Cold Cream, if God's love lifted me like my mother's arms and rocked me close, why shouldn't I be healed? A neuroscientist might say that endorphins caused by a conditioned stimulus were flooding my brain and immune system, causing the cessation of pain, the experience of pleasure supplanting it. Like those people in current mind/body studies who show remarkable recovery after being given a placebo at the same time they are handed a rose to smell, a rose they associate with the previous strong drug prescribed them, all I had to smell was Pond's Cold Cream, warm in the V of her neck, to know that I was being healed.

In talking about Christian Science people sometimes use the phrase "mind over matter" in the belief that the religion is mainly one of willpower. Yet there was nothing that felt like force in the view my mother presented to me; it was more like what would be called by today's alternative healers a visualization of perfect health. You did not visualize your T-cells fighting off infection, of course, nor your cancer cells being surrounded and murdered by your healthy cells. That would have admitted the physical evidence of illness, would have given the body some sort of reality. Instead, you visualized God's perfection, realized you were created in God's image and knew that you were perfect too. You prayed, not to be healed, but to have error removed. When something happened to me, all my mother had to do was repeat the words that would trigger my sense of the underlying belief system. All she had to say was "God is love," and "God loves you," for me to begin to feel better.

Christian Science was "discovered" by a woman who had been in ill health and pain much of her life and for whom illness was a metaphor for learned female helplessness. Christian Science appeared at a time when medical care was a highly disputed terrain, the arena for a series of struggles to disempower male and female lay healers in favor of male professionals, to determine the kind of medicine that was legitimate and to disenfranchise different and sometimes more effective cures like homeopathy, herbalism, and hygiene. Without an understanding of the times in which Mary Baker Eddy lived there can be no clear understanding of why the mind-cure movement came into being. And so I turn to books by historians of popular culture and by feminist scholars, books that are full of charlatans like Dr. Peebles of Battle Creek as well as sincere and effective healers like Phineas Quimby, Mrs. Eddy's original mentor. Along with odd characters and strange tales of greed and chicanery, these books are replete with the horrifying facts of the era.

We tend to forget how ignorant and useless the practice of medicine could be a hundred and fifty years ago. The causes and spread of disease were not well understood. There were no antibiotics. There were no X-rays, lab tests, anesthesia, much less ultrasounds, CAT scans, dialysis, the many treatments we've come to take for granted in the late twentieth century. Bloodletting was standard therapy for most complaints until well after the Civil War, and it was not uncommon to "bleed the patient into unconsciousness." Other treatments used in the so-called heroic medicine of the day were blistering, in which a blister was raised on an unaffected part of the body, emetics to induce vomiting, and cathartics to purge the intestines. The 1800s were called the "Poisoning Century," in part for the prevalence of dosing many diseases with calomel, a laxative that broke down in the body and caused mercury poisoning. Louisa May Alcott, for instance, lost her health (and most of her hair) from doses of calomel that she repeatedly took while she was working as a Civil War nurse. These drastic measures were designed in part to show ill patients and their families that the doctor was doing something. However, most people, including almost all working-class sufferers, only called the doctor as the last resort.

Alternatives to heroic medicine ranged from the early home remedies of Colonial women to the success of patent medicines such as Lydia E. Pinkham's Vegetable Compound. Pinkham, born only two years before Mary Baker Eddy, in Lynn, Massachusetts, brewed her tonic in her kitchen and sold it to women suffering from undisclosed female complaints. The marketing strategy that made her face, reproduced on the bottle label, familiar to thousands, was a marvel of advertising. But what really sold the elixir was the same distrust of doctors that made people flock to join such sects as Thomasonianism and Grahamism. Thomasonianism, a "botanical" movement that favored induced vomiting through vegetable emetics, had a following of three million by 1843. Grahamism was equally popular; it attracted a large audience in the 1840s by promoting fresh air and a vegetarian diet, and left us with the perennial Graham cracker. Homeopathy was another movement that won over thousands. Developed by a German physician, Samuel Hahneman, the cure operated on the principle of similars, or that "like is cured by like." Instead of dosing their patients with lethal quantities of dubious medicines, homeopaths of the time used highly diluted, pleasant-tasting tinctures compounded of pharmacological preparations. In the 1860s there were twenty-five hundred homeopathic doctors practicing in the U.S., and the majority of them were women.

Midwives and folk healers, often women, had dominated the medical scene in the United States from the earliest days in Colonial America until the beginning of the nineteenth century. They had no formal training and developed their skills on the job. Often they used folk remedies that they learned from the native Indian communities that their towns and farms were displacing. However, by the early 1800s, the number of male scholar-doctors, trained in England and the Continent to think of themselves as professionals, was growing. Although no one could prove that bleeding patients and inducing them to purge and vomit was any more effective than gentler prescriptions of herbs and instructions for diet and hygiene, by the 1830s the "regulars" had passed medical licensing laws designed to root out the "irregulars."

A new professional class of medical doctors rose up in the United States by mid-century but, in response, so did the Popular Health movement. This struggle coincided with antislavery and the beginnings of the suffragist cause. Women's rights became linked with women's health, as women demanded the right to continue practicing as midwives and lay practitioners. However, as the century progressed, even alternative medical groups such as the homeopaths, which had medical colleges and graduated doctors, were denounced and deregulated. A few women, like Elizabeth Blackwell, were allowed to attend medical school and join the ranks of the "regulars," but most women were forced to stop practicing. As the country became more divided by class, middle- and upper-class women were redefined as patients, particularly of nervous complaints, while working-class women, often immigrants, were accused of spreading disease. After the practice and licensing of midwifery became more difficult, the only profession for women was that of nurse. Eventually the medical profession was almost completely divided by gender: male doctors did the "curing" and received the credit (and the increasingly large fees) and the female nurses did the caretaking and remained invisible.

Not only did Christian Science provide a place for women to make a living at healing, but it offered women a way out of the cult of female invalidism that dominated the second half of the nineteenth century, when middle- and upper-class women had been increasingly defined as weak, hysterical, and at the mercy of their physiology. Mary Baker Eddy had known vague and specifically female debilitation her whole life. Her revelation that God can heal enabled her to stand up and walk not just in a literal sense, but in a metaphoric one. She managed to change the ground rules of the discussion about health and who could heal by relegating both doctoring and nursing to unreality. No university degree was needed to understand the ideas in Science and Health. No expensive medical license was needed to practice the art of spiritual healing.

It began early in elementary school, my knowledge of my rights and my need to stand up for them. It began with my beleaguered relationship with my first-grade teacher, Mrs. Grant, and through extension, with the school nurse at Patrick Henry, Mrs. Pale. Mrs. Pale was a big, soft woman whose puffy white nurse's hat made me think of a mushroom cap and whose heavy white legs were like double mushroom stalks. The first time I was sent to her in first grade, she washed my scraped knee off and put some reddish-orange stinging liquid all over it before attaching an enormous gauze square with thick adhesive tape. I was six then, and even though I knew that there was something wrong with letting Mrs. Pale do this to me, I still couldn't help sneaking admiring glances all the rest of day at the crisp white bandage with the stain of Mercurochrome spreading out like bright orange juice on either side. But when I got home, my mother was indignant. "Who put this on you?"

"The nurse."

"They sent you to the nurse? Who sent you there?"

"Mrs. Grant."

"Mrs. Grant, your teacher? After I explained to her?" My mother peeked under the bandage. "What's this orange stuff?"

"She said it kills the germs."

"There are no such things as germs in God's universe. We have absolutely no need of materia medica," my mother said, and she brought me into the living room and read me the Scientific Statement of Being.

The next day I carried a note from my mother to Mrs. Grant, who read it and pursed her lips.

"And who will be held responsible if anything should happen to you?" she demanded. "That is what I would like to know."

I didn't like this teacher. She was thin and had her dark hair in a bun that sat on a little hump just below her neck. The hump made her head jut forward and her arms hang down to her knees. She looked like a cross between a camel and a monkey. We children knew that her name was Mabel and we had made a chant out of it, out on the playground; "Mabel, Mabel, get your elbows off the table." Somehow that went together with her long dangling arms and the forward thrust of her head, and the glasses that sat on her nose, only to fall off and be caught, like a circus acrobat, by the chain around her neck.

The skirmish between Mrs. Grant and my mother went on all year. It was impossible not to get knocked about on the asphalt, particularly if you were an active little girl who had to wear a short-sleeved dress. Each time Mrs. Grant found me bleeding, she sent me off to Mrs. Pale, who hated to see me coming. It went against all Mrs. Pale's training to merely wash my wound with soap and water and put a conventional Band-Aid over it. She had been, she told me often, a Nurse in Wartime, and she had had to assist surgeons as they cut off the arms and legs of soldiers. "And you can bet your bottom dollar that nobody said he was a Christian Scientist on the operating table."

But even though Mrs. Pale made her peace with soap and water, she had a hard time coming to terms with the fact that my mother was refusing to let me be inoculated against polio with the other first-graders.

Jonas Salk's polio vaccine trials had begun in 1954, at a time of great hysteria over the disease. Although polio had been around for decades (Roosevelt had contracted it in the Twenties; the March of Dimes had been providing children with leg braces and iron lungs for years), the spread of disease had reached epidemic proportions in the late Forties and early Fifties, and 1952 had been the worst year ever. Every summer parents watched helplessly as their children contracted the disease in swimming pools and holiday camps. So when the first mass trials showed the vaccine to be effective, government support was quickly mobilized to ensure adequate supplies. Late in 1954 a million children were vaccinated; by 1955 nine million children had received the shots; and by 1956, the year I was in Mrs. Grant's class, every first-grader in the country was supposed to get the free series of three shots.

My mother said no to the shots, of course, along with the other Christian Science parents all over the country. For although it was the Fifties, although the prestige and authority of medicine had never been higher, the Christian Science church was also strong. Legislation and continued lobbying had secured the right of parents to refuse medical treatment and vaccinations for their children.

But it wasn't my mother who had to give the note to Mrs. Grant. It was me.

She wouldn't accept it. She read it with her glasses up on her nose, tight against her eyes as if she needed their extra magnifying power to take in the message she saw there, and then she let the glasses fall, like a hapless car over a cliff, on to her chest.

"I was afraid of something like this. But it's really the limit. It's one thing if your mother wants to let you run around with dirty scabs all over your legs and arms, but it's another one entirely for you to put other innocent children at risk. Thousands of children have died of polio. And now we have a chance to save these innocent children, and your mother says, 'No, thank you, I'm not interested.' "

Mrs. Grant handed the note back; it was crumpled from the force of her feelings. "Well, you'll just have to give this to Mrs. Pale and the special polio nurse yourself. You can't stay in the room alone while the whole class goes to the nurse's office."

"But Mrs. Grant. . . ."

She turned away, her little hump emphasizing her thorough rejection of me and my note. If only Carrie and Christine had been here, I thought; then I wouldn't have been the only one. Then there would have been three of us little girls, hanging on tight to each other, saying no together. But Carrie and Christine went to another elementary school. At my school I would be the only Christian Scientist until my brother came along.

Mrs. Grant marched us single file out the door and across the playground to the nurse's office. Up in front I could see children from other classes coming away from the office with their sleeves rolled up, Band-Aids on their arms. The hot sun pushed down on my head and the black asphalt reflected heat up into my dress. My soles burned through my shoes. I clutched the note sweatily in my palm. I was speechless. But I did not back down; I stood in line and moved up to the front in my turn. When I came to the top, where Mrs. Pale was waiting, like a large white mushroom with a smaller mushroom beside her, I held out the note.

She sighed and looked at me and then at Mrs. Grant, who was suddenly, accusingly next to me.

"It's really the limit," said Mrs. Grant. "Isn't it? These people don't care about anybody but themselves."

"She's a little Christian Scientist," Mrs. Pale explained to the small mushroom beside her. The young woman's eyes blinked wide. "Oh, dear," she said. "Oh, dear."

"Go on, Barbara," Mrs. Pale said gently, "join the others now."

As I ran back to my classmates, all of whom were peeking under their Band-Aids at their new punctures, I heard Mrs. Pale say to Mrs. Grant, "They have their rights, you know."

Mrs. Grant's voice, in her anger, rang out loud. "Their rights to kill people, you mean."

I never said anything to my mother about this—she didn't ask—but from time to time through that year, feeling Mrs. Grant's accusing eyes on me, I wondered why my mother's notes were so upsetting to her. I had only heard about love and healing in Christian Science, and even though there were stories of people being brought back to life and of run-over dogs standing up again, the real drama of Christian Science was not in physical cures but in the healing of false beliefs. Mrs. Grant had false beliefs that made her act the way she did.

All the same, I didn't like her.

Healers have known for centuries that much of the power of the healer comes from the desire of the sufferer to be healed. Medications play their part and so do ritual trappings, whether those are masks or stethoscopes, but the power of suggestion is, many times, what actually creates the condition for healing. No one knows exactly why suggestion works, or why it works better on some people than others, or why, sometimes, it doesn't work at all. Doctors have been aware of the placebo effect for years, but more recently medical researchers have begun enthusiastically investigating the scientific roots of alternative healing, from Chinese acupuncture, which relies on meridians not known to Western medicine, to the benefits of meditation and biofeedback. A significant number of researchers have been working on aspects of mind/body healing and their research fuels endless self-help books, lectures, and tapes by people who claim that we can heal our bodies either without, or in addition to, conventional medicine.

What came to be called the mind-cure movement in nineteenth-century American had its roots in Paris of the late eighteenth century, when Franz Anton Mesmer attracted crowds of patients and onlookers with his dramatic cures. He had people sit around tubs of dilute sulfuric acid, holding hands, or grasping metal rods protruding from the solution. He was convinced that there was some fluid or vital spirit in the air through which healing transferred from the doctor to the patient. Magnets also seemed to work, and he waved them over or touched them to afflicted parts of a patient's body, and called it "animal magnetism." It wasn't Mesmer, but one of his disciples, who realized that patients were falling into a sort of sleep and during this sleep they were highly suggestible. The technique of putting people into a trance came to be known as Mesmerism, or hypnotism. It soon created a circus atmosphere of somnambulists and helped to destroy Mesmer's credibility as a doctor. But the technique remained and resurfaced about twenty years later in American popular culture, where it was employed equally by traveling performers, by medical charlatans, and by more earnest healers who believed in the power of the mind.

Phineas Quimby, who in 1862 healed Mary Baker Eddy of her numerous complaints and whom she relied on until his death in 1866, was not strictly a charlatan. He was a former clock-maker who learned some of his suggestive techniques from one of Mesmer's disciples, Charles Polyen. At first Quimby, too, used a medium to make a clairvoyant diagnosis. After putting the medium into a hypnotic trance, Quimby would motion the sick person to approach. The medium would declare the nature of the illness and prescribe the correct medication or treatment. Enough sick people were cured to cause Quimby to become famous far beyond the limits of Portland, Maine. But Quimby was curious, as Mesmer had been, about the source of his power to heal. Eventually he decided it had nothing to do with clairvoyance and everything to do with the strength of his own personality and his power to believe in the health of the patient.

Quimby dismissed his medium and gave up any pretense of suggesting medicine or treatment to his patients. What was necessary, he decided, was to destroy the patient's belief in her illness. His method was simple. He would sit next to the patient and, without making a medical exam, would ask for a description of the symptoms in the patient's own words. Then he would explain his theory of disease and healing to the patient, namely that disease proceeded from the imagination and that healing came from removing this error of thought.

Sound familiar? Many people saw the origins of Christian Science in Quimby's theories. Early on Eddy praised Quimby and quoted him; later on she pretended she'd never heard of the man. But whether or not one believes that Eddy plagiarized wholesale from Quimby, it's clear that she was deeply influenced by his ability to heal without medicine or treatment, and that she assimilated his ideas of the power of the mind to cure. In part her desire to disassociate herself from him came from the need to clear Christian Science of any connection to Mesmerism. But it was also necessary for her to reaffirm that Christian Science came to her by revelation, and that *Science and Health* was a wholly original product, not a hodgepodge of Quimby's ideas and convoluted metaphysical thought current in the nineteenth century, ideas that drew from sources as varied as Hindu spirituality, Hegel, and the Popular Health movement with its anti-doctor and pro-take-responsibility-for-your-own-health message.

When I was growing up I was told that there was no other religion like Christian Science. It was part of the sectarian nature of the religion to assert that Mrs. Eddy had known the Truth direct from God's lips (if God had had lips), and that it was a Truth that did not exist outside our church. When I first began my research for this memoir, then, I was confused as I thumbed through self-help books and books on mind/body healing and read sentences that echoed *Science and Health*, all about how illness and unhappiness have mental causes and can be cured through affirmative thinking. I felt a sense of déjà vu when I heard best-selling authors and lecturers talk about how you can create your own reality through simply changing your perception of events. Since none of the books cited *Science and Health*, even in a footnote, as a source, and few who spoke of changing their reality seemed to have heard of Mrs. Eddy, I wondered how these ideas had so thoroughly percolated through American society.

But I found, with deeper reading, that the mind-cure movement that had contributed to the birth of Christian Science had also created younger siblings who followed, albeit more timidly or rebelliously, in the footsteps of their bossy older sister. Other patients of Quimby, the Dressers, had founded a loosely organized school of mental healing and life philosophy called New Thought. Like Mrs. Eddy's teachings, the New Thought movement could be traced back, via Hegel, Hinduism, and the Transcendentalists, to Platonic idealism where ideas are more real than matter. Unlike Christian Scientists, however, New Thought adherents did not accept Mrs. Eddy's interpretation of the scriptures as the final revelation. Nor, although the movement published books such as *Mental Cure* (1869) and *Mental Medicine* (1872) by Warren Evans which explored the ideas of Quimby, did New Thought healers oppose medical science. They stressed optimism and material prosperity and believed that human suffering and illness could be corrected through mental processes.

Another group with roots in the mind-cure movement is Unity, which was founded in Kansas in 1889 by Charles and Myrtle Fillmore. They were influenced by Emma Hopkins, the former follower of Mary Baker Eddy, but their intent was more educational than religious. They formed a service called Silent Unity to counsel people by phone and built a large center, Unity Village, on fourteen hundred acres outside their farm. This village still exists, as well as approximately three hundred Unity centers around the country. Like New Thought, Unity teaches that illness and unhappiness are unnatural and emphasizes spiritual healing and prosperity. In contrast to Christian Science, Unity believes the material world to be real and accepts conventional medical intervention. Finally there is Religious Science, which was founded by Ernest Holmes, the author of *Science of Mind* (1926), which teaches that man and nature are fundamentally good. Religious Science, based in Los Angeles, calls for Affirmative Prayer, or "spiritual mind treatment." The results of such work are called a "demonstration," just as in Christian Science, and Religious Science produces both ministers and practitioners.

One self-help guru who is connected with the church of Religious Science is Louise Hay, author of *You Can Heal Your Life* and many other books and audio tapes. Louise Hay begins with the premise that "The only thing we are ever dealing with is a thought, and a Thought can be changed," and invites the reader to create affirmative thoughts that create "New Thought Patterns." She states that "all disease comes from a state of unforgiveness" and counsels letting go of anger and hatred. Every illness or pain has a specific cause, and that cause is not biologic but mental. She has lists of diseases and how to get rid of them. Most important is to recognize "I am a beloved child of the universe and the universe lovingly takes care of me now and forever more." The concept of God is loosely interpreted by Louise Hay and other New Age authors to mean love or the universe. Although the New Age movement speaks negatively of ego, the focus is very much on self and on the power of the self to control reality. *Your* thoughts make your life. *You* are responsible for your thoughts. Getting sick or being unhappy proves nothing about God. All it proves is that you haven't been aligning your thoughts correctly, that you do not love yourself enough. Love yourself *enough* and all your problems—medical, financial, and romantic—will resolve themselves.

This is not Christian Science; it only sounds like it at times. The stern message of Mrs. Eddy has given way to a mix-and-match spirituality. Today's healing path has many tributaries, as a visit to any New Age bookstore will confirm. There is almost a bazaar-like festivity to such a place, with everything from tantric yoga manuals to tarot cards, from Native American sage bundles for burning to shamanic drums, from Buddhism's most esoteric texts to Natalie Goldberg's cheerful Zen writing manuals. Nor do many New Age prophets believe they have a monopoly on the truth. In *You Can Heal Your Life,* Louise Hay lists a bewildering array of options for further spiritual development: Bach Flower Remedies, Tai-Chi, Rolfing, Biofeedback, Past Life Regression, Astrology, Transcendental Meditation—and metaphysical churches such as Religious Science and Unity.

Christian Science, by contrast, is not eclectic. And that has not served it well in the consumer culture of the late twentieth century. Its Reading Rooms are not boutiques of spiritual sidelines and the books range only from Mrs. Eddy's writings to writings about Mrs. Eddy's writings. Christian Science is exclusive and authoritarian, which also does not sit well (and never sat well) with people who look at alternative healing and spirituality as a chance to experiment and be free of the word "should." ("I believe that should is one of the most damaging words in our language," says Louise Hay). Instead of a wealth of empowering statements, Christian Science has one basic message: God heals. You will be healed if you believe in God. Not if you believe in yourself. Not even if you believe in miracles.

My father and mother had made an agreement that Bruce and I would be raised in the Christian Science church and that we would be raised to follow Mrs. Eddy's teachings. My father had respected that agreement. After all, Christian Science as he understood it wasn't completely unreasonable. It did allow broken bones to be set. It did allow dentist visits. And it did not absolutely prohibit doctors in emergencies. He stood by my mother when she refused to let us have, as babies, the usual inoculations against childhood diseases. His reward was his wife's confidence and his children's radiant health.

And then, when I was five and my brother was two, we came down with whooping cough.

We shouldn't have gotten it. Aside from the matter of God's love, every other child in the neighborhood should have been inoculated against pertussis.

But Bruce and I did get it, and it was bad. All day long we coughed. We coughed until we couldn't breathe. We coughed until our lungs felt as if they were lined with needles, lined with knives. Of course we didn't know they were our lungs, for Christian Science teaching never mentioned parts of the body. All the same the inside of our chests hurt, dreadfully. Hour after hour we lay, I in my bed, Bruce in the crib next to me, coughing and moaning, "Mama, it hurts."

After a day and a night of this, my father could bear it no longer.

"I'm taking them to the doctor tomorrow morning, Ellen. I don't know what's wrong with them but it's not just a cold."

They were in the hall outside our bedroom and their voices were raised. It was late at night but no one was sleeping. I had never heard my parents speak angrily to each other before.

"I've called the practitioner," my mother said. That showed she was serious. Usually she believed that she could "handle the claim of illness" herself. "She's working on it."

"But Ellen, they're really sick!"

"I thought we agreed, that I would decide how to deal with all this kind of thing."

"I go along with you in most things, but now I'm worried. They sound like they're going to burst!"

At that time my brother and I still shared a room. The room was not large. I heard his every labored gasp and he heard every wracking cough of mine. It was like hearing an echo—a competitive echo. He was working at imitating me. I had been interested in my brother since he was born, interested in his babyness as it was and interested in shaping him. He was still at the stage where only I could understand his baby-talk, as it was a language I had only recently given up speaking. "What's he saying, what's he saying?" my parents were always asking.

Now, through my own coughing, I obligingly translated to my parents through the half-open door, "Bruce wants water!"

My mother rushed back into the room, followed by my father. They stood between us, still arguing.

"I can't stand by and watch them suffer, Ellen."

"I know they'll get better. I know they'll be better by tomorrow. I'll stay with them all night. I'll pray very hard. If they're not better by tomorrow, then . . . ," but she could not articulate the words, could not even give the coughing a name and thus a reality in our lives.

All that night my mother sat with us. She did not eat dinner, she did not get into her bathrobe. She sat in a hard wooden chair between my bed and Bruce's crib with the instruments of her faith: the Bible and *Science and Health.* And she prayed. She prayed, over and over, the same prayers. She knew that this was a test of her faith. She knew, too, that God didn't like bargains, didn't like backup arrangements. Every ten minutes she brought us cold washcloths for our foreheads and helped us drink a little water. Sometimes she held my brother on her lap. Once she crawled into the bed with me and hugged me while I hacked breathlessly against her chest. She smelled of Pond's Cold Cream and sweat and fear; her smell didn't do the trick this time, nor did her constant repetition of the mantra of God's love.

Somewhere in the dark of night the practitioner was giving us absent treatment and back in Battle Creek Grandma and Grandpa were also praying hard. I heard my mother on the phone, "Yes, Mother, I *know* he shouldn't take them to a doctor, but Woody says . . . and if you *heard* them . . . I know . . . I'll try harder."

She sat between us all night, never giving up on her mental work. "God loves you," she kept saying, like a mannequin that speaks the same phrase, in the same tone, every time you put another nickel in. "God wouldn't want you to hurt."

In the morning my father bundled us up and took us to his doctor.

"Whooping cough," the doctor said after examining us. "You don't see much of that these days."

"My wife is a Christian Scientist," said my father. "I wanted to bring them in yesterday but we agreed to try. . . ."

"Glad you brought them in," said the doctor jovially. "Prayer can be effective, but it's most effective when combined with medical help. Of course I'm biased, you know."

The room was white and cold. I coughed loudly and at length when the doctor asked me to. I was already a great dramatic actress, and knew you must exaggerate for the full effect. I was beginning to enjoy this strange experience very much, the laughing doctor with his shiny disk on rubber tubes, the glass thermometer in my mouth with its faint stinging taste, the responsibility of being oldest, of translating for my brother.

Then a nurse came in and took me off to the bathroom, explaining that I must go wee-wee in a little tiny cup. She kept the door to the bathroom open with a white shoe. I could hear her talking to another nurse, "Whooping cough, the two of them have whooping cough. It's really a crime. When a vaccine actually exists. It's one thing to believe in crackpot ideas yourself, but to force your little kids to suffer because of them, that's a different story."

"Well, luckily the father has his head screwed on right," said the other nurse. "If he hadn't brought them in, well, who knows?"

"You're right, they could be in the hospital. They could be blind. Whooping cough can cause blindness, you know."

Back in the examination room the doctor was joking with my father. "Here they are again. You did wee-wee, good! They're basically healthy kids, they'll be bright-eyed and bushy-tailed again in a week or two. Meanwhile keep them quiet. Give them aspirin for the fever, cough syrup, some cod liver oil to build them up. And a little candy afterwards to take away the taste. Sound good?" He patted each of us on the back. "I know it hurts," he said, "but you'll be better in a few days."

But in the corridor I heard the doctor say quietly to my father, "If something like this comes up again, Woody, don't hesitate to call. I've always found Christian Scientists to be rather reasonable people."

Nothing like it came up again. We missed measles, mumps, and chicken pox when they went around, and our health was the marvel of the neighborhood. "Remember when we had whooping cough?" Bruce and I asked each other sometimes, but it became the bad dream that Christian Science always said illness was, a dream of fever and raised voices and coughing and our mother's voice, patient, urgent, determined, afraid, saying over and over, "You will be healed. You will be healed."

If Christian Science was never as much out of the American mainstream as I once imagined it to be, I also did not imagine, as a child, how much leeway some members of the church felt in interpreting Mrs. Eddy's instructions regarding the point at which someone could seek medical help, or "go medical" as some contemporary Christian Scientists put it. Mrs. Eddy herself had had recourse, because of painful kidney stones, to morphine injections in the last years of her life, and this was generally known in the church, though not exactly condoned. Still there were passages in *Science and Health* that could be and were construed as "outs," for instance this one: "If from an injury or from any cause, a Christian Scientist were seized with a pain so violent that he could not treat himself mentally—and the Scientists had failed to relieve him—the sufferer could call a surgeon, who would give him a hypodermic injection, then, when the belief of pain was lulled, he could handle his own case mentally." Elsewhere Mrs. Eddy described spiritual healing as something that might not quite have arrived, a situation that would allow for human frailty: "During the sensual ages, absolute Christian Science may not be achieved prior to the change called death, for we have not the power to demonstrate what we do not understand. But the human self must be evangelized. This task God demands us to accept lovingly today, and to abandon so fast as practical the material, and to work out the spiritual which determines the outward and actual."

Since the founding of Christian Science there have been members who have quietly gone off to doctors, and parents who took their children in for inoculations and medical treatment. But for the most part, Christian Science members accept Mrs. Eddy's dictum that "We cannot serve two masters," and that Christian Science's "radical reliance on the truth" means a policy of no compromise on the issue of medical vs. spiritual healing.

Christian Science encourages a vigorous approach to the process of healing. It's not just a matter of sitting around waiting for a miracle to occur. "Demonstrating" the truth is an active process, requiring reading, studying, and keeping one's mind clear of error. Healing isn't seen to be a by-product of faith, but of spiritual understanding. It isn't even about the body, though that's where the site of most healing takes place. But since "Healings are miracles only to mortal science, in Absolute Science there is nothing to heal," as *Science and Health* puts it, it's important to ignore the physical evidence of illness, since that can so easily distract you from the spiritual evidence.

Christian Science, true to its New England origins, has an ethos of hard work. Grace is not bestowed; mercy doesn't fall from on high. Church members and their practitioners are called on to do "mental work" and to "handle the claims" of illness. A great deal of energy often has to go into fighting fear. If God is good and loving, what could there be to fear? The fear tends to be closely linked to incipient disbelief; it's the fear of God being unable or unwilling to come to one's aid. This is the time when most people call practitioners—when the fear escalates and it's impossible to keep a mental image of health in one's mind. The practitioner is thought to be an impersonal force; she works on the fear and seeks to remove it.

For much of this century, Christian Science families lived secure in the belief that the government allowed them to bring their children up as they wished. The Mother Church's lobbyists and lawyers had insured that even in states that had passed laws that made it a crime for parents to neglect the health and well-being of their children (which by the 1970s was every state) that there would be exemptions for parents who belonged to an alternative religious tradition. In the words of the California bill, a parent would be exempted from prosecution who: "provides a minor with treatment by spiritual means through prayer alone in accordance with the tenets and practices of a recognized church or religious denomination, by a duly accredited practitioner thereof."

But in the 1980s, with a new awakening to child abuse, these exemptions began to be challenged in the courts. There were not many cases, but they were treated seriously and received maximum publicity. Parents whose children died without having been treated medically were charged with everything from felony child abuse to manslaughter. Few were convicted, or they were convicted of lesser charges, such as "reckless child endangerment," but the courts were clearly sending a message. In 1989, in Minnesota, an eleven-year-old boy who lived with his Christian Scientist mother and stepfather died of diabetes after being sick for several days. After originally charging his mother and stepfather with manslaughter, the judge dismissed the criminal charges on the grounds that a state statue recognizes prayer as an alternative to medical care; however, the judge then ruled two years later that the boy's biological father could pursue a lawsuit against his former wife and her husband for causing the boy's death, thus opening the gates for a parent to be prosecuted not only by the state for manslaughter, but to be sued by another relative who disagreed with spiritual healing.

An interesting aspect of these cases is the judicial rulings on what the teachings of Mary Baker Eddy actually say about relying on spiritual healing completely. Several judges have pointed out that while Christian Science *claims* to rely only on God, that there are no enforceable laws in the church against seeking medical help for oneself or one's children, and no unforgivable stigma in doing so. Mrs. Eddy herself had given parents the "out" they needed: why hadn't they taken it to heart?

But in the Fifties there were no lawsuits. The struggle was not between the state and my mother; it wasn't even really between my mother and my father. It was between my mother and herself, or perhaps between my mother and my grandmother, who was, in spite of the fact that she had been an RN and still kept her nursing license up to date, the forceful voice of "radical reliance on the Truth." The vigorous personality that Grandma Lane's friends and clients in Battle Creek enjoyed so much came across the nighttime phone lines from Michigan to California as bullying and controlling. In my family there was no other way than to believe completely. Other Christian Scientists might be, as the doctor suggested, "reasonable people," and sneak off to the doctor from time to time; others who had not been raise in the church might see Christian Science as only something to be tried and discarded if it didn't work. But for my mother belief was nonnegotiable. "The practitioner may fail, but Science, never," Mrs. Eddy wrote.

When does belief become obsession? When does a radical reliance mean complete denial? And how do you know that Science is not failing if you are?

"When we had whooping cough," my brother and I say, remembering the cod liver oil followed by the candy corn. For all my vaunted health my lungs have always seemed, perhaps symbolically, the weakest part of my body. During foreign travel, I've had a tendency to pick up colds that have turned to bronchitis and once, in France, to something more serious. That time I caught cold on the plane going from Seattle to London, and the cold had worsened by the time I got to Paris a few days later. I was feverish but that didn't stop me from walking all over the city. I even thought having my nose stuffed up improved my French accent immensely. But in Clermont-Ferrand, visiting a friend, I began to cough and couldn't stop coughing. I should have stayed there and seen a doctor. Instead I insisted on traveling south as I had planned.

It was March; the mistral was blowing all through Provence. I went to Nîmes, to Avignon, to Arles, buying cough syrup at the *pharmacie* and swigging it down in the street. I was reading Katherine Mansfield's short stories and a collection of letters and journals. On February 19, 1918, she wrote to her new husband J. M. Murray from Bandol: "I've got a temperature and I'm not so fat as when I came—and Bogey, this is *not* serious, does *not* keep me in bed, is absolutely easily curable, but I have been spitting a bit of blood."

I didn't spit blood, but I constantly felt as if my cheeks were flushed and my mind went too fast and not deeply enough. I sat in cafés and drank only espresso, wrote intense mood pieces in my notebook. I lost my appetite, I couldn't sleep at night for the cough that rattled my ribcage. One afternoon I lay on top of my bed in the little pension at Arles in a pool of sunlight and fell into a kind of delirium. I couldn't get my breath, my lungs felt like two sacks of wet cement, heaving uselessly inside my chest. *I'm going to die here*, I thought. *I'm very very sick.*

It had been a long time since I prayed to be cured of error and to be healed. Instead I got up and went to a post office where I sent a telegram to friends in Germany asking them to meet me at the station a week earlier than planned. When I got there I collapsed for two weeks. I'd had walking pneumonia and hadn't recognized it. Had not had a clue what name to give my pain, had denied it up until the last.

My brother smokes, has smoked two packs a day for twenty years. Sometimes when I visit him in Atlanta I hear his hacking cough across the hall from the bedroom he shares with his wife. He hacks and hacks, a deep, dry cough that needs no translation. When I say, "You smoke too much; you don't sound good," he answers, "It's really nothing; it's just a little cough."

Chapter 5

Blue Windows

*To prevent the experience of error and its sufferings, keep out of
the minds of your children either sinful or diseased thoughts.*

Science and Health

*I*f, as William James asserts in *The Varieties of Religious Experience*,
the "completest religions would seem to be those in which the pes-
simistic elements are best developed," then Christian Science must be
one of the least complete. A kind of half religion, a comic mask without the usual tragic one next to it, a smiley face of a religion, a cheery
I'm OK, You're OK sort of a faith with a totalitarian insistence on happiness. In fact, though James dismissed Christian Science as a "religion
of healthy-mindedness," the word "optimism" appears only once in
Mrs. Eddy's writing, and the word "happiness" not at all. Wendy
Kaminer, in her book, *I'm Dysfunctional, You're Dysfunctional*, a critique
of the recovery movement, lumps Mary Baker Eddy together with
Norman Vincent Peale *(The Power of Positive Thinking)* and Napoleon
Hill *(Think and Grow Rich)*, but that is a misreading of her work. We
were not enjoined to be happy—or to make money—in Christian Science, but to know the essential nature of reality, which was good, and
to set ourselves free of illusion or error, which made us think we suffered.

Yet Christian Science has a reputation as a religion of optimists, and that has as much to do with its historical and philosophical origins as with the popular impression of Christian Scientists as people who always look on the bright side. Part of the reason for Mrs. Eddy's success at getting her teaching across comes from the fact that Christian Science manages to combine two different but characteristic strands of American thought. One is Transcendentalism, a New England literary movement of the 1830s and '40s that rejected Calvinism and embraced a romantic belief in the essential unity of creation and the innate goodness of man and the universe. The other strand is Pragmatism, which followed on the heels of Transcendentalism and suited the goals of the Gilded Age: expansion, consolidation, accumulation of wealth; in short: results. Pragmatism, as espoused by William James and John Dewey, is a philosophy that cares little for ontological theory, but instead makes practical consequences the test of truth.

This combination of influences accounts for the dual nature of Christian Science, at once dizzyingly *other-worldly*, with its talk of infinite Mind and immortal Truth, its insistence that the material world is unreal and illusory, and, at the same time, efficiently *this-worldly*, with its equally strong insistence that truth can be tested and proved through alleviating physical suffering. Where Christian Science departs from most religions is not so much by denying the reality of the phenomenal world, but in denying the existence of evil. Christian Science insists that the reason evil does not exist is because, if God is good and we as human beings are created in the image of God, then there is no room for anything else. Or, as one of Mrs. Eddy's followers, Dewitt John, put it in typical effusive fashion, "Not a molecule of evil could exist anywhere in the Perfection of Love, for Love could not permit any opposite of itself to exist anywhere in its infinite presence."

But if Being is wholly good, and evil does not exist, how is it possible to have the experience of evil, even the thought of evil, even the *word* for evil? Robert Peel, in his biography of Mrs. Eddy, writes that she "did not simply reclassify evil as good in order to get rid of it; instead, she redefined it as error, demanding correction. The metaphysical logic of Christian Science left no place for evil to operate in the perfectly ordered universe of Spirit. But in the relativities of human life this logic was confronted daily by the empirical evidence of evil. Mrs. Eddy's answer to the riddle was that the false evidence, not the true logic, must go."

When I was a child the word "evil" was rarely mentioned. Instead we heard about "bad thoughts," "error," and "mortal mind." Having bad thoughts meant believing in illusions rather than eternal Truth. It meant falling prey to human cravings and desires; it meant experiencing anger and envy as if they were real. All these things weren't real; we were told so adamantly, over and over. Yet to even talk about them enough to speak of their unreality meant admitting that they existed.

Adults have enough trouble with ideas like these, and everyone who joins the Christian Science church must come to terms with inconsistencies between the "perfectly ordered universe" our spirits dwell in and the "relativities of human life" where we have to go to work and feed the dog, where we have to deal with unpleasantries ranging from irritable bank tellers to scheming coworkers, and serious challenges like being fired and being mugged. Not to mention car accidents and natural catastrophes. But how do you teach children a faith like this, what words do you use, what stories do you tell? How do you explain what evil is without using the word evil? Mrs. Eddy's instructions for teaching are characteristically vague yet grand. She writes in the *Church Manual:* "The Sabbath School children shall be taught the Scriptures, and they shall be instructed according to their understanding or ability to grasp the simpler meanings of the divine Principle that they are taught."

One day a few years ago I sat and paged through bound volumes of *Christian Science Sentinels* from the Fifties in the elegant Reading Room in downtown Seattle. I sat in this tasteful little haven of quietness in the midst of the city and reread the brief stories that came out every two or three weeks and were noted as "Of Special Interest to Children." These stories were designed to help children understand some of the core Christian Science beliefs. Each story gently brought up a problem of everyday life and found a means to explain it, solve it, or dismiss it in terms of Mrs. Eddy's teachings. Although the stories often had different authors, they struck the same note—sentimental and uplifting. Parents, especially mothers, were always at the ready in these tales to offer reasons for why things seemed to be going wrong. Many of the tales were very tame, ranging from the small misfortune of losing a bracelet (later found, of course) to discovering a dead ("an apparently dead") goldfish in the glass bowl, but others dealt with serious issues of illness and healing. Their aim was to show a child grappling with the difference between material appearance and spiritual reality, to bolster her against the claims of sickness, and to give her the tools to help her heal herself, her friends, her family, and her pets.

The imagery of Christian Science is everywhere in these stories. Metaphors abound, especially those of mirrors and reflections. A 1955 story, "Always in the Right Place," describes a rose in a roomful of mirrors: ". . . one reflection cannot decide to be yellow if the real rose is red, nor can another decide to be droopy if the real one is straight and sturdy. It is easy then to see that the reflection of God could not be unhappy or hurt, because God could never be unhappy or hurt."

"Elsie Learns About Illusions," from 1956, takes a light bulb as its central image. At the beginning of the story, Elsie believes she may have been sick. Her friend tells her that "God's child, being His reflection and therefore perfect, could no more be ill than God could be ill." Still, Elsie is a bit doubtful; she really does remember having had a headache and a cough.

But while they've been talking Elsie has noticed that the electric light bulb on the wall is reflected in a glass door, something that makes the light appear to be lying in the center of the stairs. She points this out to her friend, who pretends to think that there really is a light bulb on the stairs.

" 'It is there! I just know that it is! Why, Elsie, I can see it with both of my eyes; so of course I know that it is there.'

"Elsie giggled at this ridiculous thought and insisted she look at the light bulb on the wall. 'That bulb on the stairs is only an illusion.' Then she hesitated. 'Oh, I see, you tried to make me think that you believed there was a light bulb lying on the stairs, just as I believed that I was sick. Now I know what an illusion is. It is something that we seem to see, but it really isn't true.' "

Another key metaphor in these stories is the dream, particularly the act of waking from a bad dream, taken from Eddy's assertion that "Pain, then, is only a belief, a dream. It disappears when we awake to the truth that we are in reality spiritual, safe in the harmony and protection of our Father-Mother, Love." In a story published in 1955, "A Lesson from a Dream," a boy dreams of spilled ink, so vividly he believes it really happened. But his mother sits him down next to his brother and tells them that it is the nature of bad dreams to seem real. "They then remembered that there had been other times when they seemed to be experiencing a bad dream with their eyes wide open.

Once the dream had called itself 'polio' and it seemed that Charles was very sick. Mother and Father and a loved practitioner turned from the dream picture to God in deep and joyous gratitude for His goodness. They recalled that His truth had awakened them from dreams before, and they knew that it could again in this case. Then Charles was lifted completely out of this bad dream instantly and into perfect health."

In another story from 1957, Mark dreams that his parents were unkind. Mark's mother tells him, "Dreams aren't any more real than the stories you make up about your toy set of knights or your set of spacemen."

"You mean I'm dreaming when my eyes are open?" asks Mark.

"You are," says his mother. "When you see yourself or anyone else as a sick, cross, or unhappy mortal, you aren't seeing the real spiritual man that God made any more than you really saw Daddy or me in your dream last night."

"How can I wake up then?" Mark asks.

"Start thinking of the truth. Remember that God is All and that you really are His idea."

Error can be explained in terms of light bulb reflections and dreams; it can also be explained by arithmetic. Rodney, for instance, has just learned that 4 plus 0 or nothing is 4. Later that evening he seems to fall ill. His mother sits beside him and reads a relevant passage from *Science and Health*: "The nothingness of nothing is plain; but we need to understand that error *is* nothing and that its nothing is not saved, but must be demonstrated in order to prove the somethingness—yea, the allness—of Truth."

His mother then goes on to explain to Rodney "that he was God's spiritual idea. Nothing had happened to him, and there was nothing in reality that needed to be healed. Man, made in God's image and likeness, never changes. He is always perfect. She said that evil, being nothing, has not power to attach itself to anybody or to change anything. Four plus nothing remains four."

The stories try to keep to examples that might resonate with children. In "A New Kind of Tool Chest," Barry comes to Sunday School eager to describe the new tool chest he's been given.

" 'I have an idea,' said the teacher. 'Why don't we have a mental tool chest?'

"The teacher explained that they would call their thinking or consciousness the tool chest and that the tools would be the first lessons of Christian Science." Later Barry has cause to use his mental tools to heal himself of a stovetop burn from making popcorn. He reflects that, "Saws and hammers sometimes wear out, but our 'Truth tools' become more valuable each time we use them."

It's not unusual for children in these stories to be called upon—when out of sight of their Christian Science parents—to defend the faith against baby-sitters and teachers who would try to force "material remedies" upon them. "Yes, I know it appears that my arm is broken," says a resolute boy in one story, "but I don't want to go to the school nurse. I think I'll just go home and pray." And Jamie's mother gives him a way to respond to kids on the school bus who have been talking about some disease going around. "Jamie, did you ever see a purple cow with yellow polka dots?"

"Of course not."

"Neither have I. But if I were in some place where people were talking about things I knew positively were not true like a purple cow, then no matter how much they talked, I still wouldn't believe it."

Sometimes you had to work harder to repel error, and some stories, particularly from the early Fifties, contain a surprising number of warlike images. Some of these come directly from the Bible, particularly the popular story of David and Goliath, when an "armor of light" envelopes David. "Good thoughts," Eddy is quoted saying, "are an impervious armor; and therewith you are completely shielded from the attacks of error of every sort." A story called "Watch," written during the anti-Communist hysteria of the Cold War is quite direct. "As soldiers of Christian Science we must be on guard. Our watch, however, is to be kept at the door of thought, and only good thoughts should be allowed to pass. The door must be firmly shut on everything not Godlike. We must be on guard against such enemy thoughts as resentment and impatience."

Watchtowers and fortresses and standing guard are all metaphors that make regular appearances in these stories. In "Angel Thoughts Heal Us," which takes its cue from Eddy's advice in *Science and Health* to "stand porter at the door of thought," Jean's aunt tells her: ". . . we are all porters, guarding the door of our thinking; we must open it only to the good thoughts, or angels, which come from God." As the Fifties continue, however, the fortresses become houses. If you're building a house like the three little pigs in the story, you must make sure that your house is constructed of good thoughts, so it can withstand the huffing and puffing of error. A house, too, needs a porter, as the mother in this story explains. "A porter is one who stands at the door and allows only those who belong in the house to enter. We must watch our thinking very carefully to see that we do not let in any thoughts that are not Godlike."

And a story from 1958, "Be a Good Porter," is even more explicit.

" 'Let's pretend,' said Peggy's mother, 'that someone is knocking at the door of your thinking and you tell me if you are going to let him in.'

"Peggy agreed and her mother began to pretend.

" 'Knock, knock!' she said. 'I am error, and I want to come in and rob you of your happy smile and your comfort and your joy. Let me in! Let me in!'

" 'No, no,' Peggy quickly replied, hardly waiting for her mother to finish. 'You may not come in!'

"Peggy's mother smiled and said, 'Well then, let's see what you do this time.'

" 'Knock, knock!' I am an angel thought which has come to tell you how much God loves you. May I come in?'

" 'Yes! You may come in.' "

The message of these stories is deviously clear: it's a jungle out there, but not really. It *could* be scary, if you thought it was, but you don't have to, and so it's not. But you do have pay attention every minute to keep it as safe and nice as it is. One false step—you're having a bad dream, looking in the wrong mirror, unbarring the gate of your fortress, falling asleep on the watch.

The good news is that you have control; the bad news is that you have to use it all the time.

One of the stories from this period that always stayed with me was not in the *Sentinel,* but in a small illustrated booklet of the sort that the Christian Science Publishing Society issues, regularly updating the pictures to give the children a more contemporary look, and changing the names of children to Matt and Heather as opposed to Harold and Martha. The story as I recall it went something like this:

Two children, a brother and sister, out walking one day, discovered a small empty house on a hillside. The door was unlocked. They went in and each went to a window, where they soon began to disagree about what they saw. The boys maintained that the view from here was splendid. He saw a town in the valley below, filled with cheerful people enjoying themselves. The fields were ripe with grain and scattered with wildflowers. Off in the distance was a sunrise sea where sailboats bobbed and children swam.

The girl was astounded. For what she saw was the very opposite. The town had a dreary twilit look and the people went about their business like automatons. The fields were fallow, and off in the distance a dark storm hung over the sea. It looked like the setting of *The Wizard of Oz* just before the twister hit Dorothy's farm.

They quarreled, each one asserting that what she or he saw was true. And when they left and went home, they quarreled again in front of their mother, who decided that the next day she would return with them to the house.

The next day they found everything the same. The little house stood unlocked on the top of the hill, and the view was exactly what it had been the day before. But this time it was the boy who burst out, "Everyone looks so sad today. What happened?" And it was the girl who said, "The people in town must have had good news today. They seem so happy and carefree."

Their mother went to each window in turn and looked out for a long time. And then she told them that this house had a blue window and a rose window. If they looked out the rose window they would see a glowing warm light that bathed the landscape in joy; if they looked out the blue window all they would see was sadness. For blue was the color of sorrow.

Given the choice, the children resolved always to look out the rose window, which was, as the children's mother assured them, God's window.

Whose window was the blue window then? I wondered. And was blue really such a sorrowful color? Up in our kitchen cupboard, rarely used, was a set of cobalt blue glass plates that my grandmother had given us. When I took one out and held it up to the light, the world took on mystery and magic. Unlike in the Christian Science story, this blue glass didn't make a landscape or interior appear washed-out and gloomy. No, the contrast between light and dark was still marked, perhaps even more so. What was in the shadows grew deeper and more violet; what was sunlit became more crystalline and pure. There was an iciness, a freshness, a clarity to blue; the blue glass filter turned the world into a place you didn't want to walk away from, but into. It was an underwater vision, a dream vision, a fairy-tale vision. Children's librarian Betsy Hearne writes that in picture books magic scenes are often dominated by the color blue. Blue was the underbelly of the whale, the shade the tree threw on the grass, the shadow deep inside the closet. It was also the arch of California sky, what made white clouds look so white, the bougainvillea so red, the grass so green. It was the sea, navy from a distance, aquamarine inside, an enormous wave carrying you high on its shoulder.

Whereas rose. Whereas pink. Well, frankly, I didn't like pink very much. I was not a pink kind of girl. Didn't like to wear it. Didn't like to be given it. Didn't want to have anything to do with it. It was soft and pretty and, a word I hated early on, "sweet." I did not want to be sweet, but to be wild, and yellow was the color I preferred above all others. It blazed, it throbbed, it spun, it flew. It glared like a lighthouse beacon, and buzzed like a yellowjacket.

If the choice had been between looking through a yellow window and a blue window, then I might have been torn. Having everything golden and bright would be splendid—for a while. I thought I would miss blue though. Blue spoke to me like a dream; it made its claim on me like a beloved friend in a thoughtful mood. Blue that was magic, twilight, cool, lunar and deep.

I held the cobalt glass plate up to my eye, between me and the world, and I thought, I wouldn't look out the rose window if I was in that little house. Not always. I would look out the blue window, I thought, the blue window. Which was not God's window.

There were three girls in our child-rich neighborhood and all the rest were boys. One of the girls was too young to play with. One of the girls was too old. And one of them—though our mothers would have liked us to be friends—was too much of a girl for me. I preferred Johnnie Krebs, who lived right next door.

Johnnie's birthday was a few days after mine and I had known him since the moment our two mothers, probably reluctantly, wheeled up to each other with their baby strollers and stopped to chat. Johnnie and I must have looked at each other right then, friendly and curious. All we were, were babies, neither boy nor girl; all we were, were eyes and noses and little mouths without teeth. Yes, it seems as if I remember him that far back, from out of the blur of shrubbery and sky, that familiar scrunched-up expression. From the beginning he had a rubbery face that made him look a little goofy. He was a towhead with two cowlicks, one on his brow and one at the crown. He had brown eyes and a sprinkle of tiny brown freckles on his soft nose. We liked to make faces at each other from our bedroom windows, which were directly opposite.

The Krebses had two boys and the younger, Jamie, was the same age as my brother Bruce. Jamie had good-natured freckles all over his face, and black curly hair and dimples. He was a charmer, and mischievous—one of his habits was setting small fires out of curiosity, a habit he shared with my brother. Another was packing a lunch in a handkerchief and setting off to run away, occasionally with my brother accompanying him.

You didn't see much of their mother, Dot, during the day. She was a night nurse at a nursing home. Sometimes in the morning, if I were up early enough, I saw her coming home from work, walking wearily in her clunky white shoes from the bus stop a couple of blocks away, or pulling up in one of the family jalopies, if any were running at the time. Dot Krebs had a long black ponytail and doughy white skin. Mostly I thought of her as sleeping behind a bedroom door.

Because their mother slept during the day, it wasn't very often that I went inside Johnnie and Jamie's house. The drapes were always drawn and the air had a dusty smell. Their house was the same size as ours, but the furniture was covered in bedspreads and there was no carpet. You had to tiptoe when you went in. We never played games in their bedrooms or ran around in their unkempt backyard. If we did creep inside, all we did was eat peanut butter sandwiches with grape jelly that we made for ourselves in the empty-looking kitchen. There was fear in that house.

Mr. Krebs—Keith—used to beat his boys with a belt. He would kick them, too; I had seen the bruises on Jamie's small legs. Keith was a car mechanic and brought home cars to work on in his driveway. There were usually engine parts spread out on the lawn, and a couple of stripped-down junkers parked on the street. Sometimes he worked late at night, with a spotlight that shone into my bedroom. I fell asleep to mechanical noises, engines trying to turn over: grrr, clunk and silence; grrr, clunk and silence. My parents spoke to him about it, and it would stop for a while; then a new car would appear in the driveway and it would start again.

Our parents did not get along.

Our neighborhood was one of working people, but where they worked was different and made a difference. The longshoreman next door and the union carpenter across the street had the biggest families, the largest houses; after them came the traveling Upjohn salesman, the office manager, the two assembly-line workers, and my father, a bookkeeping teacher at the community college. My mother was middle-class and had been to college; she'd taught kindergarten before stopping work when I was born. She carried the values of her church and class, which were genteel and upward-striving. My father came from nothing, an orphanage in the Midwest during the Depression; but he had worked hard at studying and at getting people to like him, and had managed to put himself through college. He had respect for all working people, but even more respect for education, which could take you out of poverty. He felt uneasy around the blue-collar workers in the neighborhood who had made it, and who made more money, without going to college, and because they were big masculine guys, which he was not. He felt especially uneasy around whip-thin Keith with his snapping black eyes and dislike of authority, Keith who did not play the game and never would.

Johnnie and I were friends from the time we could walk between the two houses, not quite ignorant of our parents' dislike, but indifferent to it. My mother often watched Johnnie for Dot when she was sleeping and that's how Johnnie ended up spending most of his time at our house. I have a dozen photos of us in the wading pool together and running through the sprinklers, and later playing tag with our two brothers. Once when we were four we managed to climb our apricot tree and pick almost all the apricots as a present for my mother; unfortunately, they were still green. He came to my birthday parties and sometimes went with us on brief trips to the store. In summer especially we spent long days, all day, together. Johnnie would throw a pebble at my window, or I'd throw one at his. His sleepy face under the cowlicks would pop up between the curtains. "Hey wake up," I'd stage-whisper, "Johnnie, let's go trash-digging!"

He'd pull on his shorts and shirt and join me out front. Like wild things, we'd leap over hedges and borrow bicycles left out on driveways. On those summer mornings there was still dew on the grass and the flowers were closed up tight; the air was fresh and promising and nobody in the whole neighborhood was up besides us, nobody belonged here like we did, nobody was as young and expectant and delirious as we were.

We collected treasures from people's garbage for our secret hideout in my backyard. This was the place where two fences at the very back of the yard came together to make a corner. Behind a clump of bushes, Johnnie and I had a room big enough for two. We had furnished it with a bald bathroom rug, a wobbly spice rack full of ceramic curios, and a small library. We had pictures from old calendars on our redwood fence walls. Our weapons to defend ourselves, should that ever become necessary, were the legs from a broken stool. Mostly, however, we liked looking through people's trash for the forbidden interest of it. The Mortensens' trash cans were where we found movie magazines and ceramic knickknacks: a spotted fawn with a missing ear, a painted shepherdess holding only the top half of a crook, gingerbread houses with cracked chimneys. Often we also found the broken-off part, and with Elmer's glue stuck it back on again. The Italian-American family across the street had dusty plastic flowers and holy pictures. We put up a saint or two in our hideaway, though I felt guilty knowing Mrs. Eddy's feelings about Roman Catholics. But Johnnie said it was all right, we could just pretend they were movie stars. We found paperback books for our library from the old man down the street. Most of them showed men in battle fatigues storming Pacific islands and beating off the Japanese. There were also a few of ladies in transparent nightgowns. We had two rules about trash digging. One was not to leave a mess and the other was not to go digging in our own trash cans, or each other's.

Once, when we were five or six, we did something that made our families get into an open fight. The Krebses had gotten a dog, a boxer about a year old named Bullet.

Johnnie and I were standing in my backyard and talking to Bullet through the wooden fence that separated our houses. The fence was about six feet high and we couldn't see over it. Johnnie said, "If I called Bullet, he would come."

I said, "No, he wouldn't, the fence is too tall."

"He could jump over. If I called him."

"Could not."

"Bullet! Bullet!"

On the other side of the fence, unseen, Bullet whined and cried.

"See," I said.

"Bullet!" Johnnie increased the urgency in his voice. "Jump, Bullet!"

But instead, with a splintering and a crashing that sounded as if the world were breaking apart, the boxer burst right through the fence. He leaped on Johnnie and knocked him down with love, while I stood there, half in admiration, half in terror, and my mother ran out of the house, crying, "What's going on?"

Through the new gap in the fence, we saw Dot appear, wearing an old quilted bathrobe, her black hair tangled about her face. "Johnnie," she said dangerously, "you know what your father's going to do."

Later that evening my father and Keith got into an argument, each standing on his side of the splintered fence. Keith was in his blue car mechanic's uniform with streaks of oil and grease. His black hair was straight and hung between his eyes. He was smoking, listening to my father say, "Redwood is not that expensive. It's sturdy. It's what we have all around our property."

My father was proud that our corner lot was almost twice as big as anyone else's in the neighborhood. He always called it our property.

"Chain link," said Keith Krebs. "That's the only thing that will stop a dog like Bullet." He sounded proud of Bullet. Earlier in the evening, though, I had heard Bullet whining, just after I heard Johnnie crying in his room.

My father said, "No. No chain link."

At dinner I had begged, "Can't we just leave the hole? Then Johnnie and I could just run back and forth."

"And have that dog in our yard?" said my mother. "His barking is already driving me crazy."

"Besides," said my father. "We don't want to have to look at their yard. We'd lose our privacy."

Now my father said to Keith, "No chain link. It's got to be solid."

"Then you put it up," said Keith, turning away and tossing his cigarette down. "If you've got to have everything your way, you put it up."

In the end my parents had to do it, even though the Krebses paid half.

From early on, Johnnie and I play-acted together. He was my partner in Let's Pretend, my muse, my audience, my collaborator in appropriating and adapting myths and fairy tales. Our sources were picture books first and the Disney films of *Snow White, Cinderella,* and *Pinocchio* and the stories my parents read me and I passed on to Johnnie. Later I began to read collections of Grimm and Andersen and to work my way through the Andrew Lang anthologies of world fairy tales, beginning with the *Red* and the *Blue Fairy Books.* The myths I took from Hawthorne's *Tanglewood Tales* and *The Wonder Book,* which my mother had from her childhood, and of course from my reading during science hour at school.

Play-acting was our private game. Occasionally Johnnie and I pressed our younger brothers into service as footmen, elves, and small animals. But often they had other fish to fry, other fires to set. By common consent neither Johnnie nor I suggested telling the other kids on the block about our plays. We knew, obscurely, that what we were doing was "girl stuff," even though neither of us liked girls that much.

What we played with the boys was cowboys and Indians and Japs and GIs and I always had to struggle not to be cast as the nurse. Not only was it anti–Christian Science to bind up wounds, but it offended my sense of fair play: I wanted to run around and shoot people, not wait for their torn, broken bodies to be delivered to me.

Sometimes Johnnie and I, too, stuck to gender roles. He was King Midas, I was his daughter; he was Hercules, I was a sea nymph; he was Ulysses, I was Circe. My power was to weave spells and ensnare, to dance around and laugh joyfully, to weep and moan. Johnnie was to raise his garbage-can shield and fight off invisible demons with his broom handle. But sometimes I tired of ensnaring and dancing around, and then I became Theseus tracking the Minotaur to his lair and cutting off his head with a single blow. I was Hercules and Johnnie was the giant Antaeus and we rolled on the ground and fought to the death.

What I liked best, though, was to be the monster myself, and one of my favorites was the Gorgon sister, Medusa. I put the mop on my head and groaned in my sleep and flung my snaky locks around, while Johnnie looked in his shield so as not to catch my eye directly and be turned to stone. And I hissed the voices of my snakes and was as terrifying as I knew how to be. Very often we did not play by the rules of the story and chased each other around, the wakeful Medusa brandishing her cotton mop of snakes and shrieking, "You'll be turned to stone. You'll be turned to stone if you look at me!"

But there was pathos in beastliness as well as horror. I became Beauty, rushing back to my Beast who lay dying by the wading pool.

"Oh, Beast," I said. "I'm so sorry I didn't come back sooner. I was shopping and I just forgot, and then the bus didn't come on time and I had to walk. Oh, Beast, will you ever forgive me?"

The Beast in my arms groaned and slapped fitfully at the pool with his paw. "You forgot," he said. "Farewell."

My tears (sprinkled from the pool, not my eyes, but intensely felt all the same) dripped onto the Beast's hairy snout. "Oh, you do care!" he said and jumped up, the perfect image of a relieved prince. "I was hoping I didn't have to stay a beast forever."

It was fun to be a hero or a god in a myth, and more fun to be a giant or monster, but acting out fairy tales was even better. Myths were violent, fairy tales involved more cunning; myths were grim, but fairy tales had happy endings; myths were always the same, but fairy tales allowed for some variation, some embroidery. As long as you had the basic story—the death of the mother, the dark woods, the talking animals, the wicked witch, the tower—you could do what you wanted.

Fairy tales were a mixture of common sense and enchantment, where having both feet on the ground was no guarantee that the next minute you wouldn't be flying through the air. Fairy tales mocked those who stuck up their noses and rewarded those who were canny and quick, but who also had open eyes and open hearts. In fairy tales the hero was crushed only to rise again. She was scorned and rejected only to take her true place in the end. She was abandoned in order to be found. What was required from her was curiosity and stubbornness, flexibility and delight. What was necessary was that no matter how badly she was treated, she did not become bitter. She must instead be generous to those she met on her path, and especially kind to old people, poor people, and animals. When the time came for her reinstatement or elevation she could exact vengeance—but it must be speedy and just: beheading or banishment. She should not let past wrongs take up permanent residence in her heart. And yet, all her pluck, kindness, and good sense was never enough. She needed help. She needed charms and spells. She had to seek out witches and sorcerers. And she often had to do impossibly difficult and even repugnant things in return for their help.

It would not have occurred to me to suggest that Johnnie and I act out stories from the *Sentinel*, even though, next to fairy tales and myths, those Christian Science stories were my models for how children should behave. But the *Sentinel* stories could not be translated into action, because the children in those tales never *did* anything. They were never abandoned in the forest, never had to set off in the dead of night to perform three tasks; they never had to find the witch who would give them the answer, or face the dragon who was hiding the gold. They never returned home to their villages in triumph, never married the prince or princess of their dreams, never ruled wisely and well ever after.

The *Sentinel* children's heroism was of the mental sort. All they were required to do was look at adversity and say, "It doesn't exist," and "No thanks." They always had their wise mothers and their thoughtful fathers to explain things and a kindly practitioner to back those parents up. In fairy tales, healing was magical, but in Christian Science healing was meant to be ordinary, the natural result of correct thinking. The lame might walk, the dead might sit up and ask for a nice bowl of tomato soup, but that was only to be expected. If a boy who had the "bad dream" of polio jumped up out of bed and ran around the block, nobody in the *Sentinel* stories said, "Yow! Way to go, boy!" They simply nodded quietly, in satisfaction, and produced a Christian Science homily.

Fairy tales and myths had plots you could act out over and over. Unlike the Christian Science stories, they had a power and a mystery that reverberated, and although both sorts of stories were alike in having happy endings, the endings of fairy tales were huge and satisfying in a way that Christian Science stories were not. You would think that the tale of a dog who was run over and then, after a night of prayer by his child owners, got up and ate kibble the next morning would be a big deal, but, strangely, it was not. For one thing the outcome was certain: you never read, "So Bob and Nancy read *Science and Health* for twelve hours straight and still little Puggy didn't get up from her bed. In fact little Puggy had begun to smell."

Fairy tales were formulaic too, but the formula managed to suggest mystery, not gloss over it. The meanings were endless and multilayered, like dreams. In Christian Science every symbol used was predictable— a rose was good, of course, and reflected God's true nature. But a rose in a fairy tale was beautiful, was dangerous, was tempting. Beauty's father stole a rose from the Beast's garden and condemned Beauty to live in the Beast's castle; but the rose also led Beauty to realize how much she loved the Beast, and thus the spell was broken. Snow White was pricked by the thorn of a rose and fell into a deep sleep. But when she woke up, she was being kissed by the handsomest prince in the world.

124

But the greatest difference between the two, the difference that could neither be explained nor bridged, was the notion of wickedness. There was no getting around it: in fairy tales there were wicked stepmothers and cruel viziers, nasty trolls, mean-spirited sisters and scheming brothers. They were there to abandon the hero at birth, to kick her out of the house, to throw her into a dungeon or lock her up in a tower, to change her into a bird or a beast, to prevent her from marrying her beloved, to keep her away from her heart's desire. They were there to be tricked and outsmarted and sometimes, but not often, fought with in hand-to-hand combat.

I knew that wickedness meant evil, and that evil was error and had to be kept out of the picture as much as possible. You could not believe wickedness existed or it would exist. You absolutely had to close your eyes against any manifestation of error, which meant selfishness, envy, greediness, and rotten-for-the-heck-of-itness. But just as certainly as I knew that, I also knew that when you were in a certain mood, there was nothing more satisfying than acting out the parts of wicked characters, even though it meant you were always vanquished. Because that was the point of it, the glory and the joy of it. Wickedness was vanquished—always. But in order to know the joy of overcoming wickedness, you had to believe in wickedness. In order to pretend to be the vanquished one, you also had to pretend to be wicked. The only solution was not to name what you were doing, not to use the word wicked. As long as you didn't do that, as long as you didn't admit the existence of evil, you could shriek and snarl and raise a threatening hand or an imaginary wand and chase after the boy hero walking through the forest and pretend you were going to turn him into a toad.

It's not surprising that even though I loved to tell stories and by the age of eight already dreamed of becoming a writer someday, most of my storytelling took place in the backyard or the garage, out of the sight of my mother. For the stories that I wrote down had to tame the wild magic of fairy tales and make dramatic and shocking events somehow congruent with the teachings of Christian Science. I had to tread carefully the line of what was allowable. I knew that I could imagine more things than I could put down on paper, just as I could read things, in fairy tales, that would make Mrs. Eddy shudder.

Every Sunday I stared up at the biblical quote painted in large letters on the wall of the Christian Science church: "Ye shall know the Truth and the Truth shall make you free." What I understood by Truth with a capital T was the large Truth of Christian Science—that we were created in God's image and if we remembered that all the time, we'd be just fine. The opposite of this Truth was everything bad and unreal: sickness, misery, material error, etc. But there was also uncapitalized, everyday truth, and the opposite of this truth was lying. More often it was called fibbing. It involved moral values as opposed to ontological issues, and these values were pretty clear: You weren't supposed to say you didn't take your brother's Lincoln logs and make a raft which then got sucked down a storm drain during a winter rainstorm. When confronted by a direct question—spurred by a direct accusation (from your brother): "Did you take the Lincoln logs?," you gulped and said, "Yes."

But there was another whole area—not gray, for it was gorgeous and multicolored—between Truth and truth. An area, a world, of exaggeration and invention, of magic and imagination. And this was the world of storytelling, particularly the world of fairy tales and myths. This world of pretend, of make-believe, of sheer fantasy was from the beginning the world I wanted to live in. Long before fantasy became a defense mechanism and a necessary escape, it was the greatest pleasure of my childhood. I was not allowed to see horror films or read ghost stories, and anything to do with the supernatural was firmly discouraged. But my appetite for fairy tales was allowed to rampage unchecked. Perhaps, like most adults, my mother had forgotten the brutal, down-to-earth nature of fairy tales as well as the wisdom they contained.

The stories that I wrote under my mother's guidance were not quite as insipid as those I read in the *Sentinel*, but they had cheerful characters, easily resolved problems, and happy endings. The action was condensed to a line or two under a picture. *"What are you doing?" she asked the frog." "Jumping," said the frog.* The point of the little books I stapled together and illustrated was to make something that my mother would like, that would make her smile and say, "You're so talented." And I did love the permanency of books, that you could hold them in your hands and read them over and over. But, from the beginning, I could not tell the complicated, violent, heartrending stories that I needed to on the page. I could not tell stories of wickedness and wickedness revenged. My mother would have shaken her head and been alarmed. I knew that already. I knew she didn't know about my secret world and that she wouldn't want to know. To tell my true, uncensored stories I needed privacy and complicity, an intense friendship with a boy who knew nothing about Christian Science and whose imagination was as vivid and boundless as my own. I needed play-acting to explain my inner life to me, and fairy tales to prepare me for the great wickedness I knew, already, was in the world.

Johnnie and I played together until we were almost ten, but more and more often it was in the company of the other kids and more and more often we played softball and race-car driver, which involved running in circles around someone's lawn until we crashed into each other. One morning on trash day, I threw a pebble against Johnnie's window and his head didn't pop up. Because I was mad at Johnnie I did something I wasn't supposed to: I looked through the Krebses' trash. I found a bunch of used Kotex, empty peanut butter and jelly jars, and vacuum cleaner dust. Mrs. Krebs saw me on her way home from work, and she told my mother. After that I was forbidden to go trash-digging, with Johnnie or alone. "Oh, it was stupid anyway," Johnnie said. He said things like that more often as we got older. "I don't want to play fairy tales," he said. But what he meant was, "I don't want to play with you."

It wasn't fair. Our brothers kept playing together, as close as twins. They lit a fire under the Krebses' house once and practically burned it down. It was my mother who found out about it. Bruce came racing home with news that they couldn't put it out and Dot was too asleep to know. My mother called the fire department and later that evening Keith beat Jamie to within an inch of his life. My father spanked my brother too, and for a while they were forbidden to see each other. But that was different than not wanting to see each other.

"Go play with the girls," the boys on the block sometimes said to me.

What girls was I supposed to play with? Terry next door who was already in high school and had pimples? Beth who was three years younger than me and played with dolls? Or the girl down the street, just my age, who wore matching dresses with her mother and had her own sewing machine?

Now it was the start of summer. School had been out two weeks and I hadn't seen Johnnie alone, not once. He had either been playing with the boys or helping his father work on cars. I could see them from my bedroom window in the late afternoons and evenings, Keith under the car, making clanking noises, Johnnie standing nearby, handing him tools, never looking at my window.

I had been rereading one of my favorite fairy tales, the one that reminded me of Johnnie. It was the *Snow Queen*. Gerda and Kay were neighbors, not brother and sister, but as close as if they really were. Only Kay got something in his eye and wasn't nice to Gerda anymore. One snowy day, he hitched his sled to a huge white sleigh traveling through the city and he couldn't untie it again. The sleigh was driven by the Snow Queen, who drove him far away to her ice palace in Lapland. And Gerda had to go after him. First she was delayed, in a house with red and blue windows and a garden all around, by a kind old woman who wanted her to stay forever. Then she met a prince and princess, a crow, a robber girl, a reindeer who took her far north. Finally she came to the ice palace of the Snow Queen, where she found Kay blue with cold. Gerda cried to see him; the tears melted his frozen heart, and when he cried, the splinter that had gotten into his eye was washed out too.

That evening, because I'd been reading this fairy tale and because I thought that if Johnnie just knew I missed him, he might change back into how he used to be, and because I was lonely, I went over to Johnnie's driveway.

"Hi," I said.

"Hi," said Johnnie. He had been growing, and his pants looked too short. They were covered with grease. His face looked different too; it didn't move as much. It didn't look goofy anymore, but leaner, harder.

"You want to play?" I asked him. He knew what I meant. Fairy tales. He shook his head. He looked embarrassed.

"No, come on," I said. I was desperate, now it seemed I was losing him. "It will be fun."

"John's helping me," said his father, head over the engine. "He doesn't want to play with you any more."

And then, I still don't know why Johnnie did it, he walked over to me and kicked me, right between my legs, hard, so his shoe rammed against the bone.

He didn't say anything. I didn't say anything, but I remember the feeling of eggs breaking: my eyes, cracking and sliding down my face.

Keith stuck his head out from under the hood and laughed. "That's good, boy," he said. "Show her you've had enough of being pussy-whipped."

Johnnie backed up behind the car and hid. Once I would have slugged him, once I would have risen up like Athena to cut him to pieces, like Medusa to turn him to stone, but I was too hurt, and too ashamed. Keith laughed right in my face. "Run away, crybaby. Leave us men alone."

I didn't tell my parents what Johnnie had done or, almost worse, what Keith had said. I ran away to the hideout and in the summer twilight I took all the knickknacks we had painstakingly pieced and glued together over the years, and I smashed them up again, hard, on the redwood fence.

What makes a writer? What tools is she given and which ones is she forced to invent? What shapes the desire to write? What is her subject? What is forbidden? What stories does she tell and which ones does she keep locked within her heart? How did the Christian Science emphasis on Truth fit with the storyteller's art of telling many untruths in order to tell a greater, more enduring truth? How could I write about wickedness, how could I tell about it? How could I tell what really happened to me?

I believed in happy endings, I believed in rose windows, I believed in courage and being valiant and persevering. I believed in God. I didn't believe in mortal error. I believed that good would win out. I believed that God loved me. I believed that my parents loved me. I believed in a good world where not one molecule of evil could exist. I believed in healing. I believed in telling the truth. I believed that I lived in a safe and happy world where nothing bad ever happened.

But I also believed in blue windows, in fantasy, in wickedness and retribution, in using my wits, in the dark wood of the soul, in the consolation of fairy tales, in the wicked stepmother and the good witch, in the cruelty of giants and the heartlessness of people you used to think were your friends.

Because for everything that I believed, I also, deep down, knew the opposite. I knew that courage did not help you in many circumstances. I knew that there was plenty of lying and hiding and pretending. I knew that mirrors could break; they could splinter and crack, and the shards could fly straight into your heart.

Chapter 6

Splinters

"Once there was a wicked demon—one of the worst: it was the Devil. He was very pleased with himself because he had made a mirror that had a strange power. Anything good and beautiful reflected in it shriveled away, while everything bad and ugly swelled up. The loveliest countryside looked like boiled spinach; the prettiest people looked horrible, and seemed to be standing on their heads or to have no stomachs at all. As for faces, the mirror twisted them so that you couldn't even recognize yourself.

"If a good thought went through anyone's mind while he was looking in the mirror, it pulled a face at him. The Devil had a good laugh at that, too. All the pupils at his school for demons said it was a miracle. This is the real world, they said; this mirror shows what people are really like. And they ran around with it until there wasn't anyone or anyplace that hadn't been twisted by it.

"Then the demons wanted to fly up to heaven, to make fun of the angels and even of God himself. The higher they flew, the more the mirror grinned like a gargoyle. They could scarcely hold it still. The mirror shook and grinned, and grinned and shook, till they dropped it, and it fell straight down here to earth and broke into a million billion splinters.

"That was only the start of the trouble. Some of the splinters were scarcely the size of a grain of sand, and they blew everywhere, getting into people's eyes and making them see everything ugly and twisted. Some splinters even got into people's hearts, and that was awful, because their hearts became like blocks of ice.

"Some of the pieces of glass were big enough to use as windowpanes, but it didn't do to look at your friends through that sort of window. Others were made into spectacles, and the people who wore them never could see things straight. The Devil laughed so much he nearly split his sides. And he's laughing still, because there are plenty of those splinters flying about right now, as you will hear."

—Hans Christian Andersen, *The Snow Queen*

A few miles outside Battle Creek, not far from where the utopian community of Harmonia was replaced, first by Fort Custer and then by an industrial park, stands a huge complex of red brick buildings. This is the Veterans Administration Hospital. They have a psychiatric floor and that's where my Uncle Andrew lives now, on a locked ward. He has spent many years, though not all of his adult life, here in this hospital. At times he has been lucid and able to live on his own; he has been married twice and has a son. His diagnoses have ranged from schizophrenic to manic-depressive and back to paranoid schizophrenic again. A couple of years ago he told a visitor that the doctors thought he had as many as five separate personalities. "He seemed proud of that," said the visitor wonderingly, and added, "He's not in a good state. There's something violent about him. I don't think you'd want to see him the way he is now."

No, I wouldn't want to see him. I haven't been inside the grounds or the buildings of this V.A. Hospital since I was fourteen. Yet twice now in the last few years, I've pulled off the highway in my rental car and into the parking lot. I've gotten out and stared at the administration building, walked up to it and then retreated. Vets from Korea and Vietnam, amputees, paraplegics, pass me in their wheelchairs. Some of them live here, and others are just getting checkups or their meds.

I think about going in, not to see my uncle, but talk to his doctors. How crazy is he? I want to ask. How long has he been crazy? Was his craziness why he did what he did to me? I stand in the parking lot and imagine him somewhere inside, behind a locked door.

I don't go in. Even the buildings frighten me.

If you read between the lines of any of the *Sentinel* stories, you can easily recognize that Christian Science has a shadow side. *Something* lies outside the boundaries of the sunny world we supposedly inhabit. *Something* is trying to get inside that watchtower where we must constantly be on guard. *Something* is always threatening us. Like Bullet the boxer on the other side of the fence, *something* is always trying to break through the barriers we set up. And sometimes, in spite of our constant vigilance, it smashes through.

That something is not exactly evil or even mortal error, though error is what it's called in the *Sentinel* stories. For evil in Christian Science, considered as a theological problem, has a logical solution. If God is all-powerful and God is good, then evil cannot exist. Evil or error is a bad dream that can be forgotten, a carpet stain that can be removed. Yet even after error has been removed, and evil has been defined out of existence, there is, inexplicably, something that remains.

That something in Christian Science goes by several names: mental malpractice, mesmerism, animal magnetism, and, more specifically, Malicious Animal Magnetism. It is a concept that sprang originally from Mrs. Eddy's authoritarian personality—her fear that, having helped introduce mental healing to the naive and ignorant, she had lost control of some of her students and had thus unleashed a negative force into the world. She saw them turning their backs on the correct manner of healing, that is the spiritual, hands-off manner, and she named their insistence on head-rubbing and passes over the body "mesmerism."

Although Mrs. Eddy herself had once used physical manipulation in her healing, she had discontinued it as she grew more convinced of the spiritual nature of her work. So it became increasingly disturbing to her that one of her original students, Richard Kennedy, continued to touch and wave his hands over patients during his healing work. Their falling-out came in 1872, as Mrs. Eddy was beginning to write *Science and Health.* With Kennedy in mind, she defined a mental malpracticer as one who relied on touch to control the patient. She saw it as a form of seduction and manipulation, not as healing. She worried that, as the malpractitioner grew more powerful, the hypnotized subjects could carry out his will into the community. "Unrestrained by Christian Science," she wrote in *Science and Health,* "a false practitioner will work mischief. . . ."

Mary Baker Eddy turned her personal conflict with Kennedy into a larger moral issue, not the first and certainly not the last time this would happen. Obviously she was concerned that, in trying to launch her new movement, not yet then a church, but very much a Christian organization, that she would be identified with mesmerists and other performers and charlatans. She also saw the real danger of a healer using mind control for his or her own benefit in order to manipulate the subject. However, the charge of mesmerism against Kennedy was also one of the first outbursts in what was to become a familiar pattern. Mrs. Eddy's anxieties about her students, her fears of betrayal and defection, took shape as accusations of mesmerism and mental malpractice and then, more graphically and hysterically, as claims of "malicious mesmerism" and "mental poisoning." These terms finally became institutionalized in Christian Science as Malicious Animal Magnetism, or M.A.M. If thoughts could heal, then it seemed to follow that thoughts could also harm. In the beginning Mrs. Eddy believed that these powerfully disturbing thoughts were directed solely at her by rivals and enemies who wished to undermine her spiritual work; eventually her paranoia would infect the wider circle of her followers and the very structure of her emerging religion.

By 1878, she had begun to find troublesome another of her previously favored students, Daniel Spofford (one biographer suggests it was because she was emotionally attracted to him). Another student, Edward Arens, accused Spofford in court of harmful mesmerism and in turn Spofford brought a lawsuit against Arens and Gilbert Eddy, Mrs. Eddy's husband, accusing them of trying to kill him through mental means. These lawsuits generated unfavorable publicity for Mrs. Eddy, but that did not stop her from responding to them. In 1882, when Gilbert Eddy died in his sleep, she accused Arens of murdering him, and gave the story to a reporter from the *Boston Globe.* She demanded an autopsy, which proved only that Gilbert Eddy had died of degenerative heart failure, exactly what a medical doctor had once diagnosed him with. But Mrs. Eddy would not accept this; she called a press conference to assert that her husband had been "mentally poisoned."

It's not surprising that Mary Baker Eddy felt persecuted and abandoned during this period, for the truth was that she *was* mocked by the newspapers of the time, railed at from the pulpits of churches, frequently deserted by students whom she had once trusted, and embroiled in controversies not of her choosing. Her paranoia, however, went far beyond a sensitivity to rejection and a hysterical projection of her own feelings on to her enemies. Disenchanted former students and colleagues talked in later years about how two-thirds of Mrs. Eddy's lectures on Christian Science during the 1880s and '90s were filled with discussions of how best to protect herself and her church from mesmeric influences. Students were directed to repel these influences by turning the malicious thoughts of ill-wishers around, so that they would instead attack the perpetrator. Believing that she was under mesmeric attack, Mrs. Eddy called for constant prayer watches that would form a kind of shield between her and evil wishers. Nor were her students immune from M.A.M. For a while they were instructed to mail their letters secretly, in distant parts of town, so that mesmerists working for the U.S. Post Office might not get at them.

The stories of Mrs. Eddy's frantic precautions against harmful or evil intent against her have an almost ludicrous side. There is something quite ridiculous in the picture of Mrs. Eddy's well-meaning followers running around Boston like secret agents with their unmailed letters. There is something amusing to me in the image of Bostonians in sober dress sitting outside Mrs. Eddy's bedroom door in relays so that they could repel mental attacks.

Once again I find myself caught between the absurdity of this religion and my knowledge that such paranoia had consequences in my life. And so I turn from the biographies of Mrs. Eddy to another story of a woman's life, a woman named Mary Collson, whose experience of M.A.M. was far from silly. Mary Collson left a record of her thirty troubled years as a Christian Science practitioner in an unpublished autobiography which became the basis for Cynthia Grant Tucker's study, *Healer in Harm's Way*. Collson was an early feminist who had previously studied to be a Unitarian minister and who had been employed at Jane Addams's Hull House as a social worker. The stress of her work there brought her to the edge of a nervous collapse, and when conventional medical help did no good, she sought out a Christian Science practitioner.

Like other independent women of her time, Mary Collson was attracted to Christian Science by the fact that it had been founded by a woman and seemed to promote gender equality. She also saw in it the possibility of work for herself and other women, the possibility of earning a good living while contributing to society. In order to study, she moved to Boston in 1904 and set herself up in practice. But Collson's high hopes for Christian Science were soon challenged. She had heard almost nothing of M.A.M. before beginning to treat new patients who were experiencing an almost primitive fear of being swamped by this powerful force of evil. And to Mary Collson's surprise and dislike, when she took further Christian Science instruction in Boston, her teacher, Alfred Farlow, focused almost exclusively in his lessons on the necessity of self-defense against mental malpractice. "I was bold to complain," she wrote later in her autobiography. "I said, 'This is the worst form of evil that I have yet encountered.' I added, 'You have talked this thing up until I am . . . actually getting scared.' He laughed and replied, 'I have talked it up to teach you to talk it down.' "

But even though Mary Collson did become a practitioner, she remained disturbed by the concept of M.A.M. and confused and demoralized by the way Farlow and other church members used it to try to keep her in line. "On one occasion she found herself asking him if he thought it safe for her to go out to dinner with some friends. She was warned against it. Farlow said he himself had not gone out socially for years, and he simply could not protect his students from animal magnetism if they refused to exercise the same prudence."

After some years of vainly trying to free herself from Farlow's influence, she revolted against "such superstition and truly devilish doctrine," and left the church. Within a year she was back again, however, for financial as well as spiritual reasons. She set up a new practice in New York, only to find herself again in thrall to the insidious power of M.A.M. For even though she wanted not to believe in it, she seemed to have lost sight of a world outside Christian Science: "the monotonous repetition of statements which I employed to ward off the evil influences of my teacher soon put me into a superstitious anticipation. . . ." It was this "superstitious anticipation" that brought her near to existential paralysis one day when she found herself frozen to her bus seat, unable to get off and go to her office in Manhattan.

"Since I seemed unable to make the effort to get off the bus at this point, I decided that if I rode around the loop, perhaps I could make it on my return. The result was that I spent hours repeating this trip, for every time I caught sight of my office building I felt glued to my seat.

"I said the Lord's Prayer and the 'scientific statement of being' over and over. I repeated the 'definition of God' and everything else that I could think of as statements of Truth with power to exorcise animal magnetism. I declared that this experience was unreal, that it was a dream, and I repeated these declarations until, as in a dream, the bus began to appear to be floating along, rather than rolling over the pavement. It was almost like a phantom bus, and with the Ancient Mariner I could easily have said that Death and Death-in-Life were casting dice for my soul."

Collson was so unnerved by this vision that she held tightly to the railing in front of her and began to assert the reality of the material world around her. "In detail I declared the buildings were real—made of real brick and real stones—and the people about me were real human beings, right-minded, sensible people going about reasonable tasks in a sane and normal manner." Although she continued her work as a mental healer, from that point on she worked mainly outside the church structure. Finally, in 1932, Collson came to the conclusion that, "All the years I was a successful Christian Science practitioner, I wrestled in vain with the treatment; for no human being was ever transfigured into a 'child of God' in my sight."

Mary Baker Eddy had toned down her public rhetoric about M.A.M. as her church became more successful and well known. She was persuaded to omit from later versions of *Science and Health* a chapter from the third version titled "Demonology" in which she detailed the mental crimes and lawsuits of Arens and Spofford. The current sentences in *Science and Health* that deal with the problem of M.A.M. are strongly worded, but rather brief. "As named in Christian Science, animal magnetism or hypnotism is the specific term for error, or mortal mind. It is the false belief that mind is in matter, and is both evil and good; that evil is as real as good and more powerful."

After Eddy's death in 1910, the Board of Directors moved quickly to downplay an aspect of their religion that had been misunderstood by the outside world and by many members as well. The monthly column in the *Christian Science Journal* devoted enthusiastically to the notion of M.A.M. and how to combat it was discontinued, and serious discussion of mesmerism was limited to those who went on to study Christian Science in depth. The appeal of Christian Science to the industrious middle class lay in its cheerful optimism. What then was this concept of Malicious Animal Magnetism, some wondered, and what role did it play in a faith that stressed mind over matter and belief above all? As the case of Mary Collson shows, there were those who were drawn to Christian Science because they had been healed and because they saw the effects of healing, but who were surprised or shocked to discover this tendency to superstition in such an apparently rational, "scientific" religion. Many, no doubt, would have been happy to see M.A.M. disappear. But since Christian Science is structured so that Mrs. Eddy's writings are the only text, it is difficult to expunge the many references to mesmerism, mental poisoning, and animal magnetism.

It would also be wrong to say that, even with a more benevolent outlook and a greater emphasis on good and not evil, Christian Science does not have a place for M.A.M. The concept, originally framed as emanating from the minds of Mrs. Eddy's enemies, was refined so that malicious magnetism became a more general term for those thoughts which seemed to control one's mind and which seemed to prevent healing from taking place. For as Christian Science received more and more publicity, as the claims of the church to be based on its members' ability to heal themselves and to be healed grew, then something needed to be invented to explain why healing didn't always work. M.A.M. provided the answer. It gave practitioners a way of explaining their failure to heal, and individuals a reason to accept that failure.

William James speaks of religions as having either monistic or pluralistic views of the world. The monistic view holds that there is a no room for evil; but the pluralistic mode sees evil as separate, and independent. On the surface, and in most of its teachings, Christian Science is a monistic religion, asserting that God is good and that evil is an error or a lie. But M.A.M. puts Christian Science in the pluralistic camp. It makes room for something that is not part of God and with a power that comes from some other source. What source? Christian Science doesn't say. Beginning as a clumsy but effective means of assigning blame, a way for Mrs. Eddy to explain her own failures and the animosity that her authoritarianism fostered, M.A.M. grew to be an essential aspect of Christian Science, little discussed in Sunday Schools and churches, but crucial in the instruction of teachers and practitioners and, in this way, kept alive.

In some ways Christian Science, which presents such a benign face today, perhaps was healthier when Mrs. Eddy was struggling openly with her reputed mental poisoners and those who sought to maliciously magnetize her, when she required her followers to demonize whoever she decided was the enemy. Because after her death, when M.A.M. began to be downplayed in favor of a consistently cheerful and optimistic face that could be presented to the world, the notion of evil became a secret teaching, a kind of Christian Science Gnosticism. M.A.M. became the repressed, the shadow side of the religion, the side it ignored and couldn't see clearly, the side that was more apt to flare up uncontrollably.

Growing up, my mother was a good girl, quiet and well-behaved. At Willard Library in Battle Creek, I discover her high school yearbook and pulled it off the shelf to read about her. I find Ellen Lane on the staff of the school newspaper, *The Key*, involved in something called Daughters of Liberty, and a member of the Usher Club, which provided ushers for lectures and concerts at Kellogg Auditorium. In her senior year at Battle Creek Central, in 1938, a page in the *Paean* titled "Goofily Grabbed Grads" lists students along with their "Characteristic"; "Apparent Aim"; and "Pet Peeve." Inez de Moss, for instance, is described like this: "Blonde; Art; Soft Eggs." Elaine Jones is "Being nice; Home maker; Snooty People," while Maxine Snyder is "Conscientiousness; Cooking; Crooked Seams."

My mother is "Studious; Studying; Not Studying."

Then I take out another yearbook, from 1946, the year my uncle Andrew was in his senior year. Under his name there is no list of worthy activities, only a single line: "There's a little deviltry in this fellow."

My uncle was born late in my grandparents' lives, when my grandmother was thirty-eight and my grandfather forty. Andrew was eight years younger than my mother, and in all the photographs of them together she has a protective, older-sister look. They're both dark-haired, hazel-eyed beanpoles. When I put their photographs side by side with those of my brother and me, I see a similarity. Not in the looks, for my brother and I took after the Swedish, not the Irish side of the family and were small and blond and blue-eyed, but in the way we have been arranged or arrange ourselves. I, too, have my arm around my brother and already, at four years old, look responsible for him. Although Bruce and I are only two and a half years apart in age, I've always felt much older. I used to think that was because I'd had to learn to care for him during the years of my mother's illness, but now I think that the sense of responsibility began earlier, that it was instilled in me by my mother. She taught me to treat my younger brother in the same way she'd been taught to treat Andrew.

If Bruce and I were chasing each other in the hall and from bedroom to bedroom and Bruce ran into a door, gave himself a black eye and began shrieking for Mama, I'd be the one to get in trouble. "Barbara," she would say, cradling him in her arms, "You know better than that."

"But we were just playing. . . ."

"Yes, but you're the older one, you should be more careful."

If Bruce and I were are running around the backyard and if, in escaping him, I dashed headlong into a bush with a sharp twig that tore my eyelid and made my face bloody, I was still responsible. "But he *made* me run into that bush." "No," said my mother, "You're the older one. You know better."

My brother was physically small and didn't grow much until he was fourteen, when he suddenly shot up to almost six feet. His big eyes were such a dark blue that they verged on navy, unlike my father's bright lapis lazuli and my own green-blue. They were eyes that made people sometimes stop us in the street and say, "What blue eyes that little boy has!" When Bruce was five it became clear that he couldn't see very well and he was taken to be fitted for glasses. The frames sat on his face awkwardly and were constantly falling off and being smashed and bent during play and games with other kids.

Bruce was an angel with a sweet face and dark blue eyes, but he had another side. Fires were part of it, and breaking his glasses in football scrimmages, and experimentally tossing a large rock at a boy and rendering him half-unconscious. Once my mother looked out the window to the backyard where Bruce and Jamie Krebs and another kid were playing cowboy and saw Bruce with one end of a rope over a branch of the apricot tree and the other tied in a noose around his neck, and Jamie just about to kick the chair out from under Bruce's feet. Another time Bruce and I were leaping from a chair to the couch in the living room; he leapt too high, went over the couch and through the large picture window in a shower of glass. Before he even met Jamie he had the fire bug. Once, when he was only three, he tossed a lighted match into the toaster and the toast caught on fire, flaming up one side of the curtain hanging near it and down the other to a pile of clothes to be ironed. It happened very quickly and my brother was dumbly silent with interest and horror. I cried out, "Mama, there's a fire," and she rushed to put it out with a blanket.

Jamie and Bruce also involved the neighborhood in a crisis one afternoon when, aged six or so, they decided to pack up their belongings in pillowcases and hit the road. They were eventually found sitting under a tree half a mile or so away, but not until after dark. I remember it as exciting. The ice cream man was out looking and the bakery truck man was out looking and half the neighbors and our father were driving around in their cars looking. The police were called and my mother was alternately listening for the phone and rushing out on to the porch wringing her hands. When dinnertime came and went and I asked, if we weren't going to have dinner that night, if I could make myself a bowl of Frosted Flakes, my mother turned on me and said, "*How* can you even think of eating at a time like this, when your little brother may have been murdered!"

More troublesome events and near disasters seemed to dog my brother than me, but it was hard to tell if it was because he couldn't see well, or whether, as my father worried, because he was easily influenced, or whether it was just because, as my mother maintained, he was a boy. Invisible forces seemed to pull me back from experiencing physical harm myself and wreaking it on others or on inanimate objects. Was it that my energy got channeled earlier into reading and making things, or that I was more cautious by nature than my brother, or that I never fell under anyone's influence? Or simply that I was a girl, and was not expected to hurt myself or hurt anyone else, seriously, that is.

My mother had always given me room to develop outside the restrictive Fifties' notion of femininity. Still, the specter of being older, of being the older sister and thus a kind of surrogate mother, hung over me. I was meant to instruct in a good way, to take care of him somehow, to make him my responsibility. It seems, when I look at most photographs of myself from childhood, that my brother is always in the picture. There I am, throwing out my arms, posing or mugging or showing how I can balance on the edge of the wading pool, trying to capture all the attention, certain that I deserve it, and there is Bruce, never front and center, but always off to the side, intent on some private pursuit of his own. He may be watching a bug on the water or staring at a patch of sunlight. He has no need to be the subject of the photograph; he doesn't thrust himself forward. It's touching, but oddly embarrassing for me to look at those photographs, to see how much I wanted to fill the frame, to see how easily I pushed him aside.

And yet I know that much of our secret life together was never caught on film; that in real life there was not such a distinction between him and me as the photographs show. I see his small body next to mine in the wading pool or running back and forth with me over the sprinklers. Alone by ourselves, without the tender look of our mother on him, or the more ambivalent one of our father, we didn't always play our role of older sister, younger brother, but became something else, something more chameleon-like and intertwined. What happened to me often happened to him, or so it seems when we talk about the happy times. Perhaps my brother and I preserved our childhood in a kind of double collusion, editing out the hard parts, gilding and enhancing the good times. Perhaps that's why those happy memories of ours have such a mingled quality about them. After the good times were over, as we grew older, we were to tell each other stories about the past, each adding his or her own fragment of pleasurable detail, until the joint memory became larger than each single memory, and yet became something that each of us possessed fully, as if it were solely our own.

Some memories have titles or are entire stories: The time we decided to "escape" out my bedroom window using a braided yarn ladder that tore at the first step; the time our father decided to build us a sandbox and came back from the nursery with a sack of sand that unfortunately was also full of red ants. The sandbox was never used and instead formed a low mountain in a corner of the backyard; it was called the anthill and had a mythological quality. It was where my brother and

I performed strange, ritualistic duels with wet dishtowels. There are memories of vacations and memories of holidays, memories of our obsession with Monopoly, memories of the stories I told my brother about the boy and girl who went down the kitchen drain and had adventures, memories of the game I fell compelled to play and teach my brother when we were at the beach. "Escape from the Mean Uncle" it was called and involved dashing panic-stricken over the sand dunes, desperately looking for the ocean, which would save us.

All I remember hearing about my uncle's childhood is that he liked to slide down the banisters, and that he kept his parents in a constant state of worry through a series of unspecified escapades. My grandmother could never regard him as anything but her baby. He was, of course, raised a Christian Scientist, but he lost interest in it early. The story goes that he ran away from home right after high school and joined the Army. He was stationed in Panama. This would have been in 1946, the same year my mother left Michigan for California. Although one version is that Andrew's mental problems started much later, in the Fifties, I remember when I was twelve reading a letter I found in my mother's little housekeeping desk in the hall. The letter was either from someone in the Army or it quoted an Army physician as saying that Andrew suffered from hallucinations. I didn't know what hallucinations were, exactly. The letter has long since disappeared.

Discharged from the Army, Andrew returned to the Midwest, but not to Battle Creek. He'd decided to become a painter and was accepted at the Chicago Art Institute. I remember when I was six or so seeing paintings of his in my grandmother's basement; sometime later the basement flooded in a storm and the paintings were destroyed. I have no idea whether he was talented or not. He seemed to have the temperament of an artist though—reckless, bold, and energetic. Sometimes in the early Fifties he met and married a woman named Robin. I saw a photograph once of my uncle and a pretty girl cutting a wedding cake. But I never met Robin and the marriage was short-lived. Apparently he'd walked in on Robin and a friend of his in bed. "That just broke me," he told several people. At the time he was under other pressures. Having given up the idea of an artistic career, he was getting a graduate degree in sociology at the University of Chicago, while supporting himself and Robin by driving a cab. His thesis involved interviewing dozens of pregnant black women and hearing the stories of their lives. "The pain of it was too much for me," he said. Still, serious hospitalization didn't come for a few years. In 1957, when my family drove through the Midwest back to California, we stopped overnight in Chicago to see Andrew. I remember a lot of talk about The Loop and how I thought it was a joke about roller coasters because of the way Andrew drove, careening our car around corners and apparently trying to run over pedestrians. Bruce and I thought it was fun; our parents were white-lipped. The following summer Andrew came out to California, possibly for a visit and possibly to get a job and relocate. I was seven.

Many years later I found out that all that summer Andrew had been a problem. My father said, "He said he'd get a job, but he never did. He would take the car and stay out all night. Your mother would be calling the police station. She had no idea where he was." My father paused and went on, "There was a string of murders that summer in Long Beach. They never found who did it. Your mother thought it might be him. It was probably the beginning of her illness."

Her friend Viv confirms this when she talks about when she first noticed that my mother seemed "odd." "She stopped me in the parking lot of the church. She was feeling so guilty. She had sent her brother away and the next thing she knew he'd turned up in a hospital in Indianapolis, with some sort of . . . mental problem. She blamed herself. She was talking wildly. She told me about the serial killings, about her brother being gone so much, her fears. I just listened and then I told her whatever happened to her brother wasn't her fault. I don't think she believed me though."

This is what I remember from my uncle's visit:

Him fumbling with my pajama bottoms in the middle of the night, the feeling of his fingers where no one has ever touched before, like that. The sensation of my stuffed rabbit next to my chin falling away and off the bed, and how that seems to make everything more scary. I want my rabbit, but it's on the floor and I don't know how to get it. If only I had the rabbit, nothing would be as bad.

The backseat of a car, an old-fashioned car whose back window is rounded. I see the light blue sky outside, above, and then, on the floor of the backseat, a pair of black shoes. I am lying on my back, looking at the sky through the window. My uncle has placed a heavy, slightly scratchy, olive-drab Army blanket over my body. It goes over my mouth and I feel a kind of suffocation, as if the Army blanket is in my mouth. On top of me my uncle rubs back and forth. Later, he's in the front seat, driving. I see his neck, remember his neck. How sad it looks, how very sorry somehow.

I see him at the beach with Bruce and me. He has bought a spear gun and plans to hunt in the ocean. Off he goes, in his flippers and snorkel, right into a wave. I wish he would not come out again, and yet I'm afraid he won't and that Bruce and I will be left on the beach alone. I want to run away but I don't know where to go that he won't find me.

I see him exposing himself to me in a green river, his bathing trunks down, his erect penis white in his hand. We have rented a cabin along Oak Creek Canyon in Arizona for a week. Often Uncle Andrew floats me and my brother down the river to a deeper pool of water behind a dark rock. One day I go alone with him. My brother isn't there, just as he isn't in other memories of me and Uncle Andrew. I'm alone with this man, alone with these memories.

The green river, the white skin was the first memory of abuse that came back to me. It waked me from a fitful sleep one night years ago in Mexico. I had gone there alone for two weeks to begin to find words for this memoir, and had been writing down memories every day and feeling pursued by them at night. During the day the memories were often warming as well at painful; at night they were only painful. I woke up from a dream of standing in a long white corridor with several doors. Behind one of them stood "the evil man."

"Open the door," said the dream voice. "You'll know who it is then."

"I don't want to," I said. "I'm not going to."

And I woke up to show I meant to keep control of what I remembered, meant to keep all those doors firmly shut.

But the memory flashed up anyway and immediately I knew that it was true.

Until I had these memories, I used to think that I remembered my childhood from the time I was two and a half. That was when I was taken to someone's house overnight and separated from my parents for the first time. My mother was in the hospital having Bruce. I remember standing in the woman's kitchen and looking at her cupboards, which seemed like perfect small doors for me to enter. And I remember how into a patch of sunlight on the floor stepped a large, glossy black shape that stared at me with interested but wary green eyes.

"That's Blackie, Barbara," said my mother's friend. "She's a cat."

What did my uncle say to me that made me afraid to tell? What made me block this sexual abuse from my memory when I seemed to have remembered other things later on in horrific detail? I'm not different from thousands of other adults who were abused when young and didn't tell and didn't tell, until the not-telling became part of my life and the incidents were forgotten. Our culture has until recently been almost completely silent on the subject of abuse. But I also think now that there was something specific in Christian Science that made it impossible to incorporate acts of sexual aggression into the metaphysical view of the world that was being drummed into me. Being touched down there, being forced to lie there while it happened, was so far out of my experience and the experience of a totally good universe, that I couldn't assimilate it. All my young life I'd heard that evil was a lie, was a bad dream, and that all we had to do was say it didn't exist for it not to exist.

I say I don't remember the abuse until that nightmare in Mexico, but memory leaked through in less conscious ways. In how I used my body and let it be used, in my attraction/repulsion towards the theme of incest in my own writing and in other people's. Years ago I published a short story about a woman remembering having been abused as a little girl by her uncle. Later I wrote a mystery about a teenage girl, abused in early childhood, in thrall to her stepbrother. And I never forgot that childhood game I taught my brother, "Escape from the Mean Uncle," which we played in our backyard and at the beach.

On the surface I felt sorry for my uncle, as I knew I should be. After he left our house that summer, he spent the next ten years at the V.A. Hospital in Battle Creek. He was well enough to work in the laundry there, and came home for visits. He read a great deal, and taught himself languages off records from the library. After my grandmother died, he seemed to improve. He continued to work at the hospital, but he lived at home. He joined a dating service and met a woman. They were married soon afterwards. Those were my uncle's good years. He was relatively stable as long as he took his Thorazine. His wife Sally, a down-to-earth, sympathetic woman who worked in the medical field, truly loved and stood by him. Though she accepted his diagnosis of schizophrenic, she believed his problems were related to the nervous breakdown caused by overwork and the betrayal of his first wife, and by the overbearing nature of Grandma Lane.

Because of Sally, I had more contact with my uncle in those years. There were phone calls and birthday cards. On the phone my uncle's voice was usually slow, slightly slurred, a side effect of the Thorazine. The letters he wrote me were printed in block capitals, their meaning sometimes unclear. Once I asked him what he could tell me about my mother. He said he hardly remembered her, she was so much older.

Sally and my uncle moved away from Michigan to a southern city where Sally had been offered a job. Unexpectedly, they had a child. Andrew began to deteriorate, to refuse to take his medicines, to engage in erratic behavior. His moods became more volatile, his temper more violent. Several times he ran away from Sally and his son, back to the V.A. Hospital, where he felt safe and welcome. Eventually he just stayed there.

Once, a few years ago, I went to the library in downtown Long Beach and scrolled through microfiches of the Long Beach *Press-Telegram* from the summer of 1958. I wanted to read about these unsolved serial murders. I found nothing—oh, a murder or two, yes, but not the headlines I'd expected. Had it been solely a delusion of my mother's, then, that Andrew was a murderer? Had it been the harbinger of her own mental breakdown two years later? She knew that Andrew had been discharged from the Army with hallucinations; she knew he'd had some sort of breakdown after he and Robin divorced. Was she expecting to see signs of mental illness in him? Was she afraid of him? Did she have any inkling of what he was doing to me? Did she think him under the influence of mesmerism and did she try to pray it away? Did she feel M.A.M. directed at her and her family and did she try to repel it? Did she feel the same insidious effects that Mary Collson did, having to spend so much time repeating statements to disapprove the existence of M.A.M.? Was her guilt the price of his hospital commitment? And how could she reconcile his visible and suspected behavior with Christian Science?

Why didn't Christian Science take with my uncle? How was it that my mother in that same strict but loving household grew up permeated with Mrs. Eddy's teachings while my uncle rejected it all? Was Christian Science too quiet and nice for him? Was it that he needed something to rebel against? Or was it that a doctrine that saw no reality in evil or sickness did not jibe with his own inner world?

What was, what is that inner world? Did demons tell him what to do? Did he feel evil himself? Were his evil actions towards me unconscious, involuntary, part of his mental illness, or were they premeditated, born from some anger at his family or mine?

There are folk tales in abundance, especially primitive ones, about people who are taken over by evil powers, who are transformed into something destructive and demonic. Who are possessed. When did my uncle become more than devilish, when did his enchanted wickedness become so great he couldn't control it? Or was he just a man who developed some form of mental illness in his late teens and was never able to live a normal life, even though he yearned to? In fairy tales the wicked don't have excuses or medical explanations; they are simply wicked, and eventually they will be made to pay for their wickedness.

Could I have imagined a worse fate for my uncle than to be locked behind the doors of a psychiatric ward of a hospital, away from anyone who might care about him, drugged heavily and yet still at the mercy of his demons? For so much of my life what I felt for my uncle was a mixture of fear and grudging pity, and guilt because I felt I avoided him and didn't want to think about him, to talk to him, to know about him. When I finally remembered what he had done to me, I felt a cleaner rage, a terrible sorrow. I live, as all survivors of sexual abuse do, with the consequences of his violence and selfishness, and I live it in my body.

It is possible to discuss evil in purely theological terms, to see it as a logical problem for any religion that accepts that God is omnipotent and all good at the same time that evil exists. To see the possible answers as well: God doesn't have the power to stop evil; God could but doesn't want to; God's ways are mysterious and it's better for us not to try to guess at God's intentions. Or, as Christian Science says, There is no evil.

But to look at evil as a theological problem for religion still does not address the issue of what evil *is*. Is evil simply the lack of love or compassion, or is it more active? Is it a sense of dread, a fear of the supernatural, the not-human? Is it cruelty, is it causing pain, is evil using others, denying them their humanity? If acts of cruelty and abuse are not named or acknowledged; if evil is called an error, an illusion; if evil is defined out of existence, where does it go? In Christian Science evil disappeared into the shadows and reemerged as mesmerism, as M.A.M.

Our shadow sides are what we don't see about ourselves. Our

shadow is what we don't consider acceptable. It's not the part of the persona we want to show to the world. It's the disowned part of our personality; it's the part that's not integrated. The shadow makes it possible for us to think and do evil and for that evil to seem separate from us. Societies have shadows, too. Poverty, racism, fear, and neglect. It is not only ignorance of others' suffering, it is indifference to it. It's what we claim not to know and what we condone. Religions also have their shadows. The shadow doesn't come from the obvious splitting up of good and evil, heaven and hell, God and Satan. The shadow has always been what's not discussed: hypocrisy and cruelty, the abuse of children; the punishment of women for being sexual; the lack of charity and compassion; the lack of tolerance for those who believe differently.

The shadow of Christian Science continues to be found in aspects of Mrs. Eddy's personality, in her authoritarianism and paranoia. The authoritarianism is the shadow that is not seen. It is just the way things are run and have always been run in the church. The paranoia that created M.A.M. is the shadow side that is not integrated, that is always projected *out there*. In Mrs. Eddy's view, mesmerism always came from outside. In the *Sentinel* stories it was always beyond the gate we were guarding. There was no suggestion that any negative thoughts were inside us, or that we ourselves harbored negative thoughts, that they were part of our personalities. Necessary parts, perhaps.

Christian Science built its church over a cellar in which disowned emotions like hatred and anger and fear had been shoved, along with their milder cousins, like envy and greed and spitefulness. And then it pretended that it had no cellar. It pretended that the church started from the ground up and was built entirely above ground, in the sunlight. But all those buried things down there in the cellar created a rotting smell, and sometimes, when the wind was right, the smell would drift up, thin but unmistakable.

When I stand outside the V.A. Hospital in Battle Creek and don't go in, I wonder if sexual abuse is evil in the theological sense or merely the result of power imbalances between men and women, adults and children. Can someone be truly wicked who is insane? A part of me has never believed that he was crazy, has never wanted to believe that. Has wanted to hold him accountable, not to pity him. Has feared his mental illness, and hated him. Behind the red brick walls, behind the locked doors with hospital porters standing guard, lives my uncle, my mean uncle, who has been shut away so we don't remember him or have to see him. The brother of my mother. Whom I hate and fear and pity.

Malicious Animal Magnetism is not just error. It is not the evil which has been defined out of existence by Truth and God's love. It is the shadow side of Christian Science, the repressed side that bulges with things that cannot be talked about, looked at, remembered. Its initials spell out a variation of mother: M.A.M., the murky, dread-filled side of the Mother Church.

Part Two

A Taste of Hell

Chapter 7

Warpaint

But put forth thine hand now, and touch his bone and his flesh,
and he will curse thee to thy face.
And the Lord said unto Satan, Behold he is in thine hand; but save
his life.

—Job 2:5,6

*I*t begins in a nightmare, with a scream, a scream in the middle of the night that wakes me and that continues to wake me all these years later. A scream that continues to echo down the hallway from my parents' room into my room, where the night-light no longer shines, because I am ten, but where the door is always open a crack, still. In my nightmare I just lie there in bed, because I know that going down the hall in my bare feet will not make any difference, that the screaming will just go on until I wake up, return to being my own adult age, get up and make myself a cup of herbal tea.

But when I was ten, I did go down the dark hall in my bare feet to my parents' bedroom. I waited a moment outside. There was no more screaming, but instead a kind of wild weeping. The overhead light blazed above like a cold white sun. In the center of the soft double bed with the carved walnut headboard, my mother was sitting up in her pink nylon nightgown with the small capped sleeves. I had never seen her cry like this before, not even when she twisted her ankle in a sprinkler hole and clenched her teeth and had to sit reading *Science and*

Health very hard. Sometimes my mother looked soberly thoughtful and sometimes she was dreamy, but often she was smiling that wide white smile that made me feel so happy. She laughed often and she hummed around the house, doing tasks she didn't like so she could go out into the garden and water the flowers. She wasn't laughing now. Her eyes were terrified. She clutched the sheet to her chest and sobbed, "She's dead. She's dead."

"Who's dead? Who's dead?" I asked, creeping closer to the bed, but my mother couldn't speak. Across the room my father was at the telephone. He was wearing only his printed boxer shorts and a baggy undershirt. He didn't have his glasses on and he was fumbling, almost comically, with the receiver. "Yes, I'll wait," he said.

"Who's dead?" I asked him. "Who's dead?"

"Nobody's dead!" he said. "Your mother just had a bad dream. She dreamed that her teacher Mrs. Arborgast died. I'm trying to get her number from Information just to. . . . Yes, thank you." He dialed the number.

It rang and rang.

I climbed into the bed and tried to put my arms around my mother, to calm her as she would have calmed me. She was shaking and her skin was cold and sour-smelling. Her eyes looked right past me, as if she didn't recognize me. She was listening to the dial tone through my father's head.

"Just because she's not home doesn't mean she's dead," said my father desperately.

Now my mother began to mutter wildly, "It's animal magnetism. I know it's animal magnetism."

Animal magnetism? I'd never heard her talk about that before. What animal?

I wondered if she was upset because a few weeks ago our cat ran behind the car as my mother was pulling out of the garage and was killed.

"Mama," I said tenderly, stroking her freckled arms, her dark wavy hair, her tearful face. "I know you didn't mean to run over Curie."

She stared at me as if she couldn't understand what I was saying, or even who I was. The tears poured down her face.

The next day my father managed to locate Mrs. Arborgast, but by that time my mother had broken irrevocably with her old life and with all of us, and was headed into a landscape of nightmarish climate and vegetation, a country where none of us could follow.

The night my life changed was just after Halloween, that ancient holiday when the veil between the world of the living and the dead is said to be most transparent. It was a few weeks after my tenth birthday. Halloween and my birthday always went together in my mind; when I had a party, the crepe paper covering the table was often orange; the cupcakes were decorated with black arched cats and smiling pumpkin heads. We usually had the party in the backyard, at the redwood table under the apricot tree, where the squash-colored leaves fell in slow arcs around us. By mid-October, the stores were full of fright wigs and skeleton costumes that glowed in the dark. Woolworth's had an aisle that was nothing but masks—Dracula, Frankenstein, witches, and red devils. When we were little we went out trick-or-treating in white sheets with holes cut out for eyes; later I became Cinderella, Tinker Bell and Wendy from *Peter Pan.* My costumes were a combination of store-bought harlequin masks that I painted and flecked with glitter, homemade wands or tiaras, and dresses that my mother rigged up from old petticoats or nightgowns. My brother went as an Indian with a headband of feathers and a bow and arrow, a cowboy, or a little hobo with a bundle on a stick. With our mother in tow, Bruce and I carried our pillowcases up to the lighted porches, rang the bell and screamed, "Trick or Treat." "Why, who's this little Tinker Bell? I don't think I've ever seen her before." "It's me, it's me, *Barbara!*" I shrieked and took my miniature candy bars. Back on the sidewalk where my mother stood chatting with the other mothers, I said proudly, "They didn't even know it was me."

Other children might be Creatures from the Black Lagoon, or ghouls with blackened eyes and blood dripping from their mouths, or witches with pointed hats, broomsticks, and masks speckled with warts and wrinkles. Other children might talk of haunted houses crawling with rats and spiders, of bats flying across the moon and of bony hands scraping on the windowpanes, but in our house Halloween was a cheerful holiday. It was carving a pumpkin with a five-toothed grin. It was making caramel apples. It was dressing up as someone else. The scariest thing we were allowed to do was to buy those sweetened wax lips or vampire teeth, and even so my mother shuddered to see us. I remember chewing on my full red lips and making a distorted frowning mouth or one pulled completely out of shape. The wax lost its elasticity very quickly and became hard and pale pink. "I don't understand why you think it's fun to look like that," said my mother. "But it *is*," I assured her.

Mrs. Eddy did not love the supernatural and neither did my mother. Monsters were deadly physical, matter that had come back to life. One of the credos of the Christian Scientists, "Man is not brain, blood, bones and material elements," held doubly true for ghouls. I was forbidden to see scary movies and had to be content with the distorted versions explained or acted out by friends on the playground: "So there were these pods, see, and the people didn't know, they thought they were just watermelons, so they ate them up and then. . . . Then the people turned into pods!"

Like any child I loved to scare and be scared. Tossed up in the air, bounced on the knee—will they drop me? Peekaboo is underlined with anxiety: Where did Mommy go? Hide 'n' Seek and Tag are all about pounding hearts and fear and cunning. As older sister I loved to scare my brother; even as late as thirteen I was still stepping up from behind a door to surprise him. A certain amount of fright is orchestrated by parents, teachers, and older children, purely for the pleasure of giving relief: See, that wasn't so scary after all, was it? And they drop you off the high dive or give the old bike with balloon tires a last push on your first solo ride. As adults we confide, "I was terrified to do it," before continuing, "But I'm glad I did. It wasn't as bad as I thought it would be." Challenge almost always carries a charge of fear: adrenaline gives us courage, and the sense of having surmounted fear builds our self-confidence.

How can you be a child and not know fear of the unknown, when you come into a world that is still so unfamiliar? In the closet there are bears, if you fall asleep they will eat you. Dark things live in the corners of the yard, they come out at night and bang against the house wanting to get in. Among my many nightmares I had one dream that haunted me for years, but I could not describe it as a child. I said to my mother, "There was a street with sunlight and a pile of oranges. Then something dark fell down. There was music with it." Sometimes

I would hear that music during the day and my breath would almost stop: light broken by shadow; darkness falling over the oranges. I could never explain it. Perhaps it was connected with that unspoken thing, that bad dream: my uncle.

Feeling inexplicable horror was one thing; cultivating it quite another. Yet how can you be a Bluebird or go to a slumber party and not hear ghost stories? Many of them were jokes and puns (I recall one interminable story in which the phrase, "It floats, it floats" kept being repeated in sepulchral tones outside the bedroom door of some terrified soul, till he finally cried out in desperation, "*What* floats?" And was told in matter-of-fact tones, "Why, Ivory Soap, of course."). Others conjured up archetypal emotions of primitive terror about night and death. Ghost stories acknowledged the power of the unknown, while laughter defused the fear. "That's enough giggling now, girls," our leader or someone's mother would say wearily, and we'd settle down deep into our sleeping bags, protected in community, very sure that no monsters would get us as we slept.

In fourth grade someone pointed out to me a row of books in the school library. "Read some of these," she advised. "They're really good and scary." I didn't say immediately, "Oh no, I can't," as I would have to her suggestion that we take in the matinee showing of *The Bride of Frankenstein*. This was something more subtle. "It was in the school library, Mama," I could hear myself explaining innocently. "I didn't know." In the end I succumbed and checked out a few of these books, though I hid them from my mother. They were collections of "eerie" and "supernatural" tales. In one a man met a girl sitting on a tombstone late one night. She was very beautiful in an old-fashioned way. He fell in love with her. The next day he asked everyone in town who she was, but no one had ever seemed to have heard of her. Finally he went back to the cemetery and read the tombstone where she'd been sitting. JENNIFER TAYLOR: 1892–1912. She'd died forty years ago!

Once, and my mother looked serious when she heard about it, a baby-sitter at someone else's house let several of us kids sit up and watch *The Twilight Zone* with Rod Serling. I still remember something of the episode, which concerned a man sitting on a train. He fell asleep and when he woke, something about the train seemed different. The passengers wore old-fashioned dresses, the conductor had a big pocket watch and a funny cap. More disturbing is that when the traveler asked when he'd be arriving at his stop, he was told that no such place ever existed. I may be remembering the story completely wrongly, but I know that—like the mild little ghost stories that I read on the sly at school—it aroused in me strange, unquiet feelings. Of a world different than the one we knew and lived in, of things that happened for no reason you could understand.

"Mama, Mama, won't you stop walking? Mama, please. Are we going to have dinner?"

A woman with my mother's face and body, but with blank, wild eyes and that strange sour smell, was pacing up and down the hall, which had become a kind of force field that separated the living room from the bathrooms and bedrooms. It was after school, a long day in which my stomach churned and my fingers felt like they didn't work. We were studying Colonial America and I was supposed to be making a sampler in class. Never dexterous at the best of times with a needle and thread, I had simply sat staring at my cloth hoop with the letters A, B, C painfully embroidered in. I had told myself all day that last night didn't happen and that when I got home everything would be okay. My mother would be sitting in her blue rocking chair reading the Bible and Mrs. Eddy. After hugging me hello she'd say, "Change your clothes and then have a glass of milk and an apple if you're hungry." She would say I was too big now to sit on her lap, but I could lean against her and she would put her arm around me and kiss my forehead and stroke my hair. And when I asked her about her dream last night, she would laugh and say, "Oh, sweetheart, it was only mortal mind telling me a lie."

"Mama, Mama, it's me and Bruce. Mama, we're home from school now. Mama?"

But the woman with my mother's face, the woman wearing my mother's old white terrycloth bathrobe over the pink nylon nightgown, ignored us. And when I tried to touch her arm, to hold on to her sleeve, she brushed me aside. She didn't look at me or speak to me. Instead she muttered to herself, "Man is not matter; he is not made up of brain, blood, bones and material elements." She reached the end of the hallway and turned back again. "Man is not matter." She clasped her hands urgently together. "Man is *not* matter." She hit the opposite wall and turned. "Man is not matter, not matter, not *matter*, doesn't matter, doesn't matter, doesn't matter."

Behind me my little brother's big blue eyes filled with tears, but he said nothing. Last night he didn't get up with me, didn't go into the bedroom. We hadn't talked about what had happened, but after school we walked home together. I waited for him, which I didn't usually do, now that he was in the second grade and wanted to be more independent. But today I waited, today I didn't want to be alone or have him be alone coming into the house. Other kids on the block had walked with us, had said, "Change your clothes and come back out. We're going to have a softball game."

From outside we heard the sound of shouts and laughter, of a bat cracking. It was a warm November day in California. Jamie called Bruce's name from the porch; the doorbell rang. Our mother didn't notice the door ringing. She was in the Twilight Zone, she was a ghost in a ghost story, she was not herself any longer. And Bruce and I stood there paralyzed, watching our mother walking up and down.

The psychiatric term for animal magnetism might be psychosis, the splitting off of a part of the psyche and believing it means to do one harm. This was how the doctors who saw my mother defined and tried to treat her mental illness, as a recurring psychosis "in which the individual's ability to think, respond emotionally, remember, communicate interpret reality, and behave appropriately is sufficiently impaired so as to interfere grossly with his capacity to meet the ordinary demands of life," as the term is defined in a standard psychiatric glossary. But religious mystics past and present would have understood her madness as a crisis of faith. A madness induced by the belief that God no longer listened to her prayers, that God looked the other way while she suffered, that God knowingly visited pain upon her and then abandoned her to the shame of acknowledging that He would not, though He had the power, heal her of her physical and mental distress.

For since the summer, my mother had been struggling secretly with the knowledge that she had discovered a lump in her breast, and that even her most fervent prayers, even her lifelong belief that such things could not happen in God's perfect world, couldn't seem to change the fact that the lump was growing.

From Buddha to Job to the Christian saints, spiritual literature is filled with accounts of demons and imps who try to tempt the holy off the path of righteousness and who try to plant in her or his mind the sense that God has turned His back or that the forces that rule the universe are cruel and malevolent, not just and kind. Stories of the saints are stories of the lure of madness. The Anchorites wrestled with female temptresses and Satan himself out in the desert. And Job, of course, did not just see trouble everywhere, he experienced it: boils, pestilences, deaths. But in spiritual stories this emotional turmoil, these voices that appear to come from the devil, this sense of torment and forsakenness, was often a precursor to revelation and an increased experience of wholeness and understanding. Anton Boison, in his book *Exploration of the Inner World*, published in the 1930s, maintains that madness and spirituality have similar psychological roots, that they are attempts at emotional and mental reorganization. "When the attempt is successful . . . it is commonly recognized as a religious experience. Where it is unsuccessful or indeterminate, it is commonly spoken of as 'insanity.' "

That first day of her pacing we all stood around and watched. My father came home from teaching; he tried to talk to my mother, he tried to get her out of the hallway, he tried to stop her constant pacing. But she batted him away as if she didn't see him either, as if she didn't recognize him either, and all the time she kept up the muttering and crying. My father made phone calls, but my mother wouldn't talk to Mrs. Arborgast or even to her mother.

My mother kept walking.

We had to go past her to the bathroom and to get to our bedrooms; it was like avoiding a steadily moving submarine in deep waters. She walked through the evening and all through the night. I lay in bed and through the crack of the slightly open door of my bedroom I saw her figure pass one way and then the next. At some point I closed my door, or my father did. When I woke up in the morning she was still pacing.

My father didn't go to City College that morning. A nurse arrived, a Christian Science nurse, they said, something I'd never heard of. She helped get us off to school. She was still there in the afternoon, sitting in an armchair reading *Science and Health*. My mother was still in the hall, though the nurse told my father she'd gotten her to eat something and had her lie down for a little.

This went on for four days.

On the fourth afternoon when we came home from school, no one was there: not my mother, not the nurse, not my father. Terry, the fourteen-year-old girl next door, came over to tell us that an ambulance had come and taken our mother away a few hours ago. It rushed screaming and red down the normally placid street and men in white went in with a stretcher and came out with our mother. Terry hadn't seen this for herself, but someone else told her. Everyone wanted to know what had happened. Terry was there to baby-sit us until our father came home. But he didn't come home that evening, and not that night either.

One night there was a scream, and then there was four days of pacing. And then our mother was gone. We wouldn't see her again for five months.

My father says now, "I blame myself for respecting your mother's religion. Get a Christian Science nurse, your grandmother said! She turned her back! On a woman who was suicidal! She was no nurse! And then she called me at work. She called me before she called the ambulance. She said, 'Your wife has drunk Drano. What should I do?'

"I told her to get off the phone and I'd call an ambulance immediately. I met them at Long Beach Memorial.

"That's when they discovered she had cancer. They saved her life, but they couldn't keep her there. They sent her to L.A. County General. They couldn't handle her in Long Beach. I'll never forget when I got to L.A. County. She was in a padded cell. Like an animal! She didn't recognize me. I'll never forgive the way they treated her there. In a cell, like an animal."

My father and I are sitting in a little park across the street from his apartment. It is 1988 and I have come to visit armed with a notebook and questions about what happened. Most of this I have never heard before. The words strike deep in both of us. I don't write them down. I don't write them down for years, but in my head I hear them over and over, "in a cell, like an animal."

I hear them silently whenever I'm tempted to say, "My mother had a spiritual crisis." My tongue jams fat and useless against my teeth. A spiritual crisis sounds so polite and pale and interesting—an Oxford scholar in the nineteenth century, sitting at a mullioned window with his hand to his brow. My mother had her spiritual crisis in a padded cell, like an animal; and the word given to it was psychotic break.

My father said Grandma was coming, by train, since she didn't like to fly, and at first I was relieved. Grandma would explain what happened, Grandma would take care of things and bring my mother home. But my grandmother was in a terrible state herself—at home she had a schizophrenic son in a hospital and in California her dutiful and well-behaved daughter had snapped, seemingly overnight. There were two grandchildren to be cared for and a son-in-law, whom she'd never really liked, to have to depend on for everything. Grandma quickly established her routines—she studied Mrs. Eddy and the Bible in the mornings after getting us off to school, she cleaned and washed clothes while watching her soap operas in the afternoon, and by the time we came home from school she was again studying her Christian Science lesson. Almost every evening she and my father left us with Terry next door and went off to see my mother.

I still thought it all had something to do with the cat and went over and over the events surrounding Curie's death a few weeks before. We'd always had a cat, usually one that I found and brought home, and something was always happening to them. They disappeared, boxer dogs chewed them up, they were found dead several houses away under a bush. The first one we had was named Ginger, and later on there was a Midnight and a Curie for curious. This cat was Curie.

My mother had been backing the car down the driveway, in a hurry, and the cat was in the way. My brother and I were in the car. Why didn't Curie run away? Cats always move in time. Was my mother going too fast? There was a yowl and a bump, and my mother slammed on the brakes and jumped out. Curie was writhing on the driveway, blood pouring out of her mouth. My mother tried to pick her up, but Curie clawed her and spat. There was no talk of mental healing. "We've got to get her to the vet," my mother said. But suddenly it was all over; with a last, staring-eyed twitch, Curie stiffened and was gone. My mother burst into tears, completely distraught. My brother and I stood staring. It had all happened so fast and had been so awful we couldn't react.

Later my mother calmed down and we buried Curie in the backyard in a large box. My mother got the hose out and tried to wash off the blood from the cement, but a small stain remained. After she was gone, taken away by the ambulance, I used to go out to the driveway and look at the stain. I remembered her sobbing about animal magnetism and how bad she'd felt, and I kept wanting to tell her, "Mama, it wasn't your fault."

There was no Thanksgiving dinner, though I'm sure that we had been invited somewhere. For years we'd celebrated that holiday with my mother's two friends, Georgina and Harriet, sisters from Battle Creek who came out to California with my mother. Georgina was a Christian Scientist too, and Harriet was married to a Swiss man who played the zither. We always had to listen to Hans play on the zither at Thanksgiving. But now Thanksgiving came and went without even a turkey. It was the beginning of holidays that would never be like the past, that would always have something sad and wrong about them. In fact, my grandmother scolded us when we asked about Christmas, "How can you want to have Christmas when your poor mother is away from home!"

I have a photograph from the Christmas before, when I was nine and Bruce was six. It's Christmas morning and we sit under the enormous green tree, heavy with glass bulbs, as well as new decorations we've made at home and at school from construction paper and glitter. Christmas tree lights and tinsel sparkle in the flash of the camera. Bruce and I are in our new pajamas and robes, surrounded by toys. It's the best year ever! Our father in his red plaid bathrobe sits smoking his pipe and reminds us as he does every year that when he was a boy on the farm during the Depression all he got was an orange and two or three English walnuts, and he was happy to get them. We don't care, we love all our presents. There's a new bike for Bruce, and white lace-up rollerskates for me. There are sweaters from my grandmother. There are books and board games, and stockings with small toys and candy. In the lurid color photograph our eyes look sated with pleasure.

The first Christmas of my mother's absence, we had a little blue frosted tree, two feet high, which my father bought at the last minute and which sat forlornly on the dining room table, its trunk wrapped in a white pillow case. My father didn't have time to get the familiar bulbs and strings of lights from a shelf in the garage, so Bruce and I decorated it with a few things we made in school, overglued glittery stars and bells of red and green construction paper that clashed with the pastel blue branches of the tree. Underneath, on the pillowcase, were a few utilitarian presents—a sweater for me, a pair of pajamas for my brother. I realize now that my father, having seen L.A. County General, had made a vow that he would keep my mother in a private hospital, whatever the cost, and that most of his salary and all the extra work he took on would go towards that. At the time it felt like an extra punishment. Noting our disappointment, Grandma said, "How can you expect presents when your poor mother is away from home!"

All Bruce and I knew was that our mother was in the hospital. That's what we said to people when they asked. A couple of kids at school wanted to know, "What for? Is she having a baby?" I didn't know what for. For walking in the hall? For having a nightmare? For not recognizing us anymore?

Whenever we asked, "When can we see her?" my father or grandmother would say, "Not yet. Soon."

The doctors were putting my mother's face back together. They were grafting skin from her thigh onto her mouth and chin. If you want to kill yourself, don't drink Drano, and don't fail. It is pure acid, it will burn your lips and throat and tongue long before it gets to your stomach and kills you. The doctors were doing radiation therapy for her breast cancer, and electroshock therapy for her state of mind, which was fragile, at best. My mother had been moved to a sanitarium where they specialized in people with chronic mental and physical illness. It was where she would spend much of the next two years, and where she would die in March of 1963.

In March of 1961 my father took me and Bruce to visit her there for the first time.

She must have been eager to see us. She was standing at the edge of the parking lot when our car pulled up. She waved and we recognized her from the distance, though she was much thinner and her hair was different. It was almost gray now and it used to be dark brown. Bruce jumped out of the car and ran towards her; I held back, approaching more slowly, almost hiding behind my father. Because the closer I got the more I could see that everything about her was changed.

Her lower face didn't match the upper anymore. From her nose up the skin was still freckled and slightly rough from old adolescent acne. Below the nose the skin was pink and shiny with smooth white patches; it looked new, but not like a baby's skin. It looked sewn together, like a quilt made out of different pieces of pink and white silk. She said hello, but her mouth didn't work very well. The lips had a chawed white look, like wax that had been melted and shaped, but badly, and stuck in two disconnected pieces around the mouth. The tongue was a hard, short thing that couldn't shape the words they wanted to say.

Her eyes were back; they were my mother's eyes; they saw me, her daughter, Barbara, they recognized me. But because they saw, they couldn't help but see my fear and horror. And I saw that hurt her. She knew how she looked.

Monstrous.

I let her hug me with my arms half up but not around her. She smelled odd, not sour as she had in the hallway, but medicinal, like Mrs. Pale's office at the elementary school. Her ribs were sharp in her chest. When I stepped back, she held Bruce close again. He didn't seem as afraid as I was; he was only seven. He pressed against her legs. She said something in a kind of croak; it sounded like, "My little boy." My father took me by the arm and spoke gently, "Ellen, how about giving us the grand tour?" and together the four of us started off across the green lawn towards the buildings that would become so familiar to me.

Compton is now mostly a black and increasingly Latino city and known mainly for its poverty and violence, but thirty or forty years ago it was still semirural. I drove out there from Long Beach once a few years ago, using surface streets, tracing the old route to Compton Foundation Hospital, along Long Beach Boulevard. I remember there used to be truck farms and dairies, and wide stretches of nothing, just eucalyptus trees and sagebrush. I stopped at City Hall to find out where the hospital was, and they told me that it had been gone for many years, but they gave me the address anyway and said there was a condominium complex there now. All the streets around the old sanitarium were named for trees—laurel, almond, magnolia, poplar, palm—but now the streets were marginal neighborhoods. I found the condominium complex without much difficulty. It took up most of a block and had a high fence around it and a locked gate. Until I saw the trees, there was nothing to remind me of the old sanitarium. And then I saw them, waving high and old, on the fenced border of the complex, the old Royal Palms, the fig tree, and the eucalyptus.

There seemed to be trees everywhere at the sanitarium and it had beautiful grounds, manicured and green, and adobe-style buildings with bars over the windows. My mother took us first to the room she shared with another woman. How strange it was to hear my mother talking of a roommate. "I've told her about you," she said in one of the short sentences that were such labor for her to form and for me to understand. The room was narrow, with two white beds, monastic. On my mother's night stand were her familiar copies of *Science and Health* and the Bible. There was a photograph of me and my brother. The roommate came in. She was as thin as my mother, and smelled of medicine too. She was an older woman, with a faint smile and a tired look.

"What darling children," she said.

In the corridor we ran into more people that my mother seemed to know. A big woman in a wheelchair, an odd birdlike woman with dyed red hair and hundreds of wrinkles, who put her face right up into my brother's and said, over and over, "What a pretty, pretty, pretty boy."

She took us all around, from the cafeteria to the rec room. "This is where we do occupational therapy," she said. There were tables for crafts and painting and ceramics. More people greeted my mother; she introduced us to the workshop leader. It was like a kindergarten class somehow, but all the kindergartners were adults. "I think your mother might have something for you," said the occupational therapist. My mother gave me a bunny that she'd made. It had gray braided limbs and a Styrofoam ball for a head, that had been covered with strands of gray yarn. The ears and the eyes had been glued on, and so had the little mouth, which was pink and smiling.

"Thank you," I murmured. I was trying not to look at my mother when she looked at me; but when I could I stared from the corner of my eye. My father and brother seemed to be acting as if she looked normal, as if this was normal—to have her here, to have her look like this.

"Your mother is getting tired," my father said after a while. My mother didn't dispute him. When he'd told us that we were going to see her today, I had imagined that she would be coming home with us, and that everything would go back to being just as it always had been. But when she walked us to the parking lot and waved good-bye, with such a sad look, I knew that she didn't belong to us in the same way she used to. She belonged here now, with these people.

To my father, my mother's religion and her mental illness seem unrelated. He has talked about cancer metastasizing to the brain. Once he said, "It's so strange that your mother and uncle got sick around the same time." This isn't really true; my uncle's problems began when he was in his late teens, as many schizophrenics do. But the fact that my uncle had hallucinations and psychotic episodes can't help but raise the specter of a genetic link between brother and sister. Yet while my uncle seems to have manifested symptoms of schizophrenia early and often, my mother showed no signs of madness until the summer she was forty. Up until then she'd never done one thing that was inappropriate or abnormal. Indeed, it was the suddenness with which she cracked that took everyone by surprise. One week she was fine; the next she was trying to kill herself. No wonder my father sought for some organic or hereditary reason.

But was it so sudden? Did it come out of the blue? I asked my father about the months preceding her breakdown. Did anything unusual happen? "No," he said. "I was away for a week at a convention in July. And your mother went to San Francisco. She had decided to take some special classes so she could become a practitioner. Her teacher was a Mrs. Arborgast."

I didn't remember my mother having gone away to study that summer and, in any case, when my father told me in 1988, I knew so little about the organizational aspects of Christian Science that I didn't think about the significance of it. But now I understand that for most Christian Scientists, class instruction is a large step towards greater commitment to the principles of the religion. Anyone who follows Mrs. Eddy can become a healer, but only practitioners who have been through class instruction may be *Journal*-listed. Each Christian Science teacher is only allowed to give one class a year, and for a small number of students. The teachers themselves are church approved, and have been through the "Normal School" teachers' course, which takes place only once every three years in Boston at the Mother Church and admits only thirty students at a time. One of the main things that the teachers' course focuses on is how to handle the claims of Malicious Animal Magnetism, which is thought to increase the higher one moves in Christian Science and the closer one gets to the Truth.

My mother did not become a practitioner when she returned from San Francisco. Why not? She was eligible. She'd had ten days of intense study and she was under the direction of Mrs. Arborgast, the church-approved teacher. How could it be that a woman who was on the verge of entering more fully into the world of the church would, a few months later, dream that her teacher was dead, imagine that animal magnetism was out to get her, and hear voices that told her to go into the kitchen, pick up a can of Drano and swallow it?

In years to come my mother refused to talk to psychiatrists. My father told me once, "She would just sit there, silent. It was a waste of money." It's safe to say that no doctor ever asked her much about her religion or tried to get to the bottom of the conflict she was experiencing between her strict Christian Science upbringing and what seemed to be unarguable evidence of disease. It doesn't seem likely that she would have told my grandmother about the lump. My grandmother was devout, but she was enough of a pragmatist to send her straight to the doctor—I think so anyway. I know that my mother didn't tell her closest friends in church, not Viv Edyth or Georgina. What did she fear from telling them? That they would see her as a failure—someone who said she wanted to become a healer and instead developed cancer?

Denial of illness is not peculiar to Christian Science. In the early stages of any illness, most of us are tempted to pretend it doesn't exist, or could somehow go away without us having to acknowledge it. In her book *Informed Consent*, Jane Cowles writes: "Some psychologists have postulated an average time of four to six weeks before a woman can sufficiently marshal her weakened emotional resources to call her doctor. Even educated women have been known to live in a crisis state for five years or more—living with the lump—before they seek medical attention." The disease of cancer in particular has had a particular shame attached to it. It's invisible mostly, it grows like a fungus, it rots us from the inside. We are more to be blamed for having cancer than other diseases somehow. We're too repressed perhaps, or should have eaten more broccoli, or shouldn't have worked overtime so much. The situation is changing—so many people have cancer now—but the tendency has been to want to hide our cancers and pretend we're well. For my mother, schooled in Christian Science, which had told her since childhood that disease was unreal and a lie, hiding must have been second nature.

Somehow I imagine that she told Mrs. Arborgast about her fear that she had cancer. I know nothing more of this teacher than her name, and that she wasn't home the night my mother dreamed she was dead, but somehow I imagine that she knew about my mother's lump, my mother's fear. And that instead of telling her to go to a doctor, she planted in my mother's mind the notion that mesmerists were working on her and causing this disease. Which mesmerists? Her brother perhaps? Whom she'd thrown out of the house and who'd ended up on a mental ward out of his mind.

Again, I remember Viv's story of my mother's distress when talking about my uncle that summer. "She was very upset. She talked about those murders in the paper a couple of years before, and how she was afraid he might have had something to do with them. She blamed herself for sending him away and for the fact he was institutionalized. I talked to her for a long time. I was . . . worried . . . about how she was talking. I told her she was not to blame for anything."

Were there signs and portents that summer? Could anyone have helped, have seen what was happening and intervened? Didn't anyone notice she was heading for a breakdown? Did she keep it so well hidden, her mental torment, her struggle with her long-held religious beliefs, her fears that something was taking over her mind, some malevolent force that wasn't any part of God, yet still existed?

"She was very upset about running over the cat," Viv says, wracking her brain. "Of course it was an accident, but she took it terribly hard."

My father says, "I don't remember anything unusual. One day she was fine, and the next day she was . . . she was . . ."

But I remember something that happened earlier, something that disturbed me but that I had no words for at the time. It must have been late August. The summer was coming to an end. It was time to buy our back-to-school clothes and supplies. I was going into the fifth grade. I wanted a corduroy jumper and new shoes and I wondered why we didn't go shopping this year as always. I began to pester my mother, "Aren't we going to go shopping? Aren't we going to get any new clothes?"

She kept putting me off. But one hot afternoon she suddenly said we were going to the department store. It was more than hot that afternoon, it was one of those blazing Southern California days when it feels as if there's no air at all. We didn't have air conditioners then, only fans; my brother and I spent a lot of time in wading pools and under the hose. One thing I remember clearly: standing under the hose and getting completely wet, then lying down on the cement sidewalk and hearing the sizzle, watching how my body made a wet shape on the cement and how when I stood up the shape gradually vanished. The cement seemed to suck it right up.

That day I'd been playing with the hose, lying down and getting up and gradually getting bored the way you do at the end of summer when it feels like it's been going on forever. I was wearing a one-piece cotton sunsuit. I had two or three of them: they were printed with diamonds and dots and animal figures and tied at the shoulders while the bottom puffed out above the thigh. I had grown that summer and my sunsuits were too small for me; the elastic on the legs was too tight and I was always pulling the puffy part down over my bottom.

Bruce had been playing Indian all afternoon. He was wearing a two-piece costume of cheap tan cotton, and on his head he wore a feathered headdress. Usually he was happiest being a cowboy with a holster and Stetson, but someone, perhaps my grandmother, had given him this Indian costume. I don't know whether he'd gotten into my mother's lipstick, or whether she had helped him, but he had several broad red streaks across his cheeks and a couple on his forehead.

I don't remember how it started. Had I been bugging my mother all day about shopping? Had she promised to take us that day and just hadn't gotten around to it? But suddenly the three of us were standing in the driveway next to the car and my mother was trying to get us inside. "You wanted to go shopping, we're going to go shopping."

"I can't wear this sunsuit," I said, panicking. "It's too small."

"I thought you wanted to go shopping." My mother's freckled face was perspiring, she was clutching her handbag, and wore a frantic, irritated expression, more as if she were punishing than rewarding us. "It's getting late, you don't have time to change."

I stayed rooted to the driveway, acutely aware of my sunsuit, of my brother in his Indian costume.

"Bruce can't go, he's got warpaint on."

"There's no time to wash his face; if you want to go, get in the car, we're going."

She had gotten in the driver's seat, but she didn't start the engine. Bruce was going to climb in but I stopped him. I remember his stiff scared little face under the red lipstick. My mother got out of the car and came around to me; she took my upper arm and tried to push me in the car. I fought back, I jumped away from her. Everything in me was scared and offended. It was *wrong* to go shopping dressed like this. Shopping was a special occasion and we only went a few times a year. It wasn't even so much the clothes, but the whole outing, the trip downtown, the rides on the escalators, the possibility of going into the Buffums book department, the lime freeze or root beer float we might have at the counter of Woolworth's.

I was scared of my mother for the first time in my life. Once or twice she'd been mad at me; once she'd run after me with a hairbrush, but she didn't catch me and afterwards burst out laughing. If I was bad, if I lied or didn't clean up my room or teased my brother, I got a talking-to that made me ashamed.

This time it was different; this time I had the strangest sense that I knew what was right and she didn't. And that she was going to try to make me do something that wasn't right.

I repeated, "I'm not going."

"You're not getting any school clothes then." She had let go of me and was standing, vindictive but defeated, by the car. She could have gone without me, she could have just taken Bruce, but suddenly she was worn out.

"Can't we change our clothes and go?"

"You can go like this or not go at all."

I was silent, too scared and stubborn to cry.

My mother gave up; still holding her handbag closely to her chest, she went into the house and slammed the screen door. Bruce stood there in his warpaint, and said, "Aren't we going?" I pulled the puffy part of my sunsuit down over my bottom and went and got the hose. I had the urge to spray the water hard at him, and wash that stupid red lipstick off his face. Maybe we could have gone with me in my sunsuit, but not with him in his warpaint. But I only turned the hose on myself, the force pummeling into my head, shooting out over my shoulders and down my back. When I was completely cool and wet I went and lay back down on the sidewalk, placing my cheek to the burning hot cement so I could feel the sizzle.

Chapter 8

Eleven

It was the fiercest and most horrible face that ever was seen or imagined, and yet with a strange, fearful and savage kind of beauty in it.

—Hawthorne on Medusa in *The Tanglewood Tales*

 I t was a Sunday sometime in late spring when my mother came home for her first visit. We had been visiting her for a few months, driving out on weekends to wander around the grounds of the sanitarium for an hour or two. Bruce and I always climbed the low-bosomed fig tree; our parents sat on the veranda of the administration building. Every week we saw the thin roommate and sometimes my mother gave us things she'd made in occupational therapy, mosaic ashtrays mostly. But now she was judged well enough to come home for a visit. My father and my mother's friend Georgina had driven out to get her. I was excited and nervous that she was coming home, though I had been told she wouldn't stay. I remember how dazed she seemed as she came in the door, how fragile. She kept looking around the house, at the familiar furniture, the familiar views out the windows. She went out in the backyard for a while to look at her rose garden, which was neglected, though my father had hired someone to cut the grass regularly and do some weeding. My brother and I were supposed to water, but we often forgot.

It upset me to see her here at home in a way that seeing her at the sanitarium had not, for here there was a way of measuring the change in her. Once this had been *her* home and she had made the meals and vacuumed the rug and put roses in vases and hummed Christian Science hymns as she worked. Now she was a visitor. You never would have guessed, from the way she drifted from room to room, from the way she sat politely in the kitchen while Georgina heated up the food she'd brought with her, that she had watched this house being built from the ground up back in 1950, that she had moved in with her new husband a month before her baby daughter was born, that she had loved the picture window out the back and planned someday to remodel the kitchen. Now she looked at everything wonderingly, but slowly (I'm sure she was on tranquilizers that day) and only said, in her hard-to-understand mumble, "It's good to be here."

The Sunday dinner that Georgina had prepared was hard to sit through. My mother could not eat real food. She couldn't chew and couldn't swallow well either. She had to eat strained baby food. It had been warmed up and put on a plate for her. Georgina sat next to her and fed her. When she opened her mouth, not very wide and in obvious pain, her previously white teeth were yellowed and the tongue was short and shriveled. Sometimes a drip of green or brown dripped down her chin, but she must have had little sensation there, because she didn't notice and someone else had to wipe it away. Often she choked, and had to be pounded on the back and carefully given a glass of water to drink. It was no wonder she was so thin now, and that her hands were almost translucent.

After dinner she sat for a while in her old blue rocking chair. My brother crept up to her and climbed into her lap. She held him close and rocked him. It was where she had always rocked us and held us when we were hurt or in trouble, where she had read to us from the Bible and *Science and Health*, where she had told me, with absolute conviction, "God loves you, Barbara. He wouldn't want you to feel bad. That hurt is a bad dream. It will go away." And the hurt would go away, always, as my mother rocked and held me.

But on this visit, when my mother saw me standing in the doorway of the hall, watching her cuddle Bruce, and held out a hand to me, I didn't move. I was too horrified by the change in her, by seeing her in her rocking chair, by her face with its violently etched mask of pain and suffering. I stood there, feet rooted to the floor. *I want . . . I want . . . I want my mama back.* Not this dull gray stranger with the white and pink patched-together face. My mother saw me hesitate, saw me unable to come to her, saw my fear, and gradually her arm dropped. Without saying anything, I turned and went back to my room. I climbed on my bed and lay there and cried.

She did not try to hold out a hand to me again.

That summer my mother began to come home for weekends and for longer periods. We had to be quiet when she was there; we had to play outside or stay in our rooms and read. She spent a good deal of time lying down. The big double bed with the dark walnut headboard disappeared and two twin beds on rollers took its place. But eventually my mother began to do some cooking and cleaning and to get out a little. Edyth told mé of coming to get her occasionally and taking her out. "She was stir-crazy; she felt stuck in the house all the time. I'd drive up and she'd hop in the car. We'd go out for a milkshake. That was about all she could have at that time."

There were no explanations, not from my mother, nor from anyone else, not then, and not until years later. I knew a word—"crazy"—and that's the word I secretly applied to her, but if anyone else had said it, I would have killed them. I knew that most of the time she had to stay in a sanitarium, a place I knew was the same as a booby hatch, a loony bin. But I did not know anything about what she suffered from, either physically or mentally, did not know she'd had electroshock and was taking medication or what kind it was, did not know she'd had a breast removed and radiation therapy. Did not know what had caused her face to become like that.

I knew that I could not ask her questions, for Christian Science teaching, which she gave no indication of having abandoned, prohibited acknowledging disease as real. Thirty years later, I asked her friends Edyth and Viv if they ever asked my mother what had gone on in her mind the day she tried to kill herself. They shook their heads. "She never mentioned it," said Viv, "and neither did we." And so I imagine that my mother, long habituated to ignoring sin and sickness, sometimes was able to put what had happened out of her mind sometimes and resume some of her old habits of going to church and testimony meetings. But many other times, when she lay for hours in her room, soundless, she must have been tormented by continued spiritual suffering. Depressed or not, psychotic or not—I find those are never the questions that come to mind when I think of her during that time. What I wonder, over and over, and will never know the answer to, is, Did she continue to believe in God? Did she understand what she'd been through? Did she—how could she?—continue to believe in the religion of her childhood, in Christian Science?

Every week Georgina would pick my brother and me up for Sunday School. I don't remember a time in the next three years when she failed us. She was a plain-faced woman in her forties, married, with two tall sons. I have a photograph of my mother and the two sisters from Battle Creek, Harriet and Georgina, arriving in Los Angeles in 1946. They're all wearing sunglasses and carrying cardboard suitcases. But the Georgina I knew in those ten-minute drives back and forth to the church was a kind, mild woman who seemed more of my grandmother's generation than my mother's, though she was only a few years older. She made us feel that we were still safely enclosed within the loving arms of the church, however, and that was enough. And it was the same when my mother was well enough to be home and go along to church. Georgina pulled up in her dark blue sedan, and we all got in. On the way she would point out particular gardens that she liked, and if my mother was there, they might discuss roses or notice a big sunflower in someone's yard and say, "They grow so large!"

I don't know what my mother thought about Christian Science, and I don't know what her church friends thought about her. Georgina was long dead when I began to talk to people, and Viv and Edyth simply shook their heads. "It was a shock," Edyth finally admitted. "But we loved your mother as much as before. We tried to help her. She was"— and here tears came into her eyes, this stout woman with the expressive face—"one of the best creatures who ever lived, and I'm not just saying that."

And tears come to my own eyes and I think that perhaps denying my mother's illness, continuing to see her as a perfect child of God, had its benefits. The Christian Science friends who stayed close to my mother saw past her disfigured face and broken body to the struggling soul inside. Even if she couldn't talk about her despair with them, at least they didn't make her feel like a pariah. It's true; with my mother at church, or in Georgina's car, I never felt the shame and stigma that I almost always felt elsewhere in the world.

For I hated to go out with her usually. I could see everyone staring at us, could see them wondering, What *happened* to that woman? I wanted to have a mother to drive me to the place where the bus came to pick us all up to take us to the Camp Fire Girl Camp in the San Bernardino Mountains, I wanted to have a mother, like all the other girls with their suitcases and sleeping bags, to hug me good-bye and wave as the bus drove off. But I did not want to have *my* mother, the woman with the monster face, whom all the little girls looked at. "What happened to that girl's mother's *face?*" I heard them whisper, and then the "Shhh!". I didn't look out the window and wave at my mother as the bus drove away; I pretended to be reading a book. And for the next two weeks at Camp Fire Girl Camp I hardly spoke to anyone. It was my first time away from home by myself and I was horribly homesick, but when a counselor, seeing how withdrawn I was, tried to talk to me about my family and offered to let me speak to my mother by telephone, I said, "No, I'm fine."

I have wondered, in the years since, how awful did she look, really? Can I trust my memory, or have I made it worse in my mind? Was it partly the hypersensitiveness of children to the strange, especially the strangeness of their parents? I can never know. There are no photographs from that time. The last photograph I have of my mother was taken sometime in the late Fifties on a vacation. She's beaming that wide white smile, that smile that is in so many of her photographs from childhood through her thirties and that I loved so much and that always told me how much she loved me, how delightful she found me. I remember that smile, and then I remember the ragged lips that replaced it and that were painted with a bright peach or pink that kept smearing because there were no edges anymore. Women friends were always taking my mother off to the powder room to help her with her make-up. In the Fifties women used expressions like "fixing up my face," or "putting on my face" and so had my mother before the suicide attempt. Now those expressions were only too real. In the bathroom were bottles of Cover Girl make-up and tubes of something called Erase.

I could tell when my mother had her face on and when the lipstick was smeared or when the make-up dried in the tiny pockets and crevasses of her face. I was exquisitely attuned to my mother's face, even though I never ever looked at it directly. What did I fear? That I would be turned to stone, as if she were Medusa? I kept my eyes turned slightly, just in case, or looked at her through stranger's eyes, or reflected in the dark windows of shops we passed. Captured in a shop window, my mother's face was often almost beautiful, the ragged terrain of her chin and mouth softened, her eyes and strong nose prominent.

The day I left for Camp Fire Girl Camp, the summer I was still ten, I stared at her longingly through two sets of glass panes and a mirror. One glass pane was the bus window and the other was the window of the car in which she sat, doubly distant from me, and with a fragment of her forehead and eyes reflected in the rearview mirror above her head. She had been excited for me, going to camp for the first time, had helped me get my things together, had driven my father to work so that she could have the car, and had promised me that she would write and send me the Sunday funnies. The other mothers stood outside the bus, waving frantically; I bent over my book, but from a corner of my eye I watched my mother. She sat there so quietly, head lowered—was she crying? Would she miss me? She must have known I was ignoring her, the way I often did in public.

She couldn't have seen me looking. No one was supposed to see me at all. For I was wearing my helmet of darkness, like the one Athena had given Perseus. And this helmet, which I put on the first time I saw my mother coming towards me in the parking lot at the sanitarium, and that I kept near me almost all the time, ready to slip over my head at any moment, rendered me invisible and safe. It allowed me to go about my business, unseen, unremarked, and most of all, unrelated to the monster woman, who was my mother, beside me.

My mother had a friend who had moved to Fresno and that same summer we went for a weeklong visit. The family had a swimming pool in which we and their two girls, close to our ages, spent almost every minute. When we weren't in the pool we were playing Barbies (Bruce had to amuse himself otherwise), for the two girls had a huge wardrobe for their dolls and a little catalog that described even more clothes and accessories. I had a Barbie at home, but after my new kitten had chewed off her foot, I hadn't liked to play with her much. Now the full force of my imagination was given over to Barbie and her outfits: Barbie the beach bunny, Barbie the stewardess, Barbie in foreign countries. The three of us pored over that catalog of clothes and I spent hours contemplating how I would dress the new Barbie I would get to replace my footless Barbie at home.

There's a sweet eroticism in the memory of us little girls in our bathing suits sitting in the shade of the house out by the bright blue swimming pool, handling the Barbies, and speaking through them to each other in high doll voices. Since we changed their outfits frequently they were naked as often as clothed, and a naked Barbie is of course not the same as a baby doll without her diapers. I can still recall running my fingers proprietorially over Barbie's cool, impossibly proportioned limbs. Her long slender legs with tiny feet already arched for little scuffs and backless heels. Her narrow hips and waist blossoming into those missile-head, nippleless breasts. Barbie's pale skin was hardened plastic, but there was a way she could feel soft and silky and utterly manipulable. We stretched her legs out—"She's doing the splits"; or lifted one leg high, "She's a cancan dancer." Or we dressed both Barbies in lacy lingerie and see-through short nighties and pretended they were having a slumber party. In our high, artificial Barbie voices we expressed delight: "Barbie, I'm so glad you could spend the night!" "Me, too, Barbie!"

At night we three girls lay in sleeping bags in one bedroom with the air conditioning on and our nighties creeping up around our legs and they told me about Vanilla Dips—swimming nude during the daytime—and Chocolate Dips—swimming nude during the night. They had never done either, they said, only heard about such things at school. After those conversations, the next day a tingly languor would come over my body as I shot from one side of the pool to the other, and I felt the cool blue water slide against my skin and imagined what it would be like to be a water baby with nothing between me and the water. But it was nighttimes that the fantasies grew and flowered, like the perfumy hibiscus outside the window. We lay half in and half out of our sleeping bags, hot and restless in spite of the air conditioning, and daring each other to sneak through the house out to the pool.

We never dipped ourselves in chocolate or vanilla. The most we managed was tangerine sherbet perhaps—for it was sunset when the older girl, still in the pool with me while everyone else was inside, suddenly said to me, "Now," and we pulled our one-piece suits down to just below our thighs and shot underwater across the orange-red pool. Water bubbled deliciously between my legs and tickled my chest where my heart was beating all out of proportion to the effort. I saw the flash of her pale body and then we were hastily pulling our suits up again and speaking in artificial voices, "Well, guess it's time to go in now!" "Yes, I sure am hungry!"

In Fresno, after having mastered the art of not looking directly at my mother's face, I had to learn to see but not see her body as well. It meant being shocked but not showing it the first time I saw her in a bathing suit, and saw that there was a square scar on her upper thigh, where it looked as if all the skin had been removed. I understand now that was where they took the skin to graft on to her face, but at the time it was just one more thing that was wrong about her. Then, one afternoon in the pool, I couldn't help noticing that something new had appeared on her body. It was a brown wrinkled spot about the size of a silver dollar and it was located near her armpit at the edge of the bodice of her old yellow swimsuit, that now hung so awkwardly on her thin body. It was so ingrained in me not ever to comment on anything odd or ugly about my mother that it never would have occurred to me to say, "What's that?" I kept glancing uneasily at the spot and grew quiet in the pool.

Then my mother looked down and said naturally, "Oh, I'm falling out of my swimsuit," and tucked her nipple back under the bodice. I must have looked odd now, because she said, a little sharply, "Has it been like this the whole time?" I nodded dumbly. "Well, why didn't you *tell* me?"

I couldn't say, Your body has become so strange to me that I couldn't recognize what it was. Or, I thought it was more of your sickness breaking out. Or, I thought that if I didn't mention it, it might go away.

After all, that's what we learned in Sunday School.

I have another memory of Fresno, and that is of coming upon my mother and her friend in her friend's bedroom. My mother lay on the bed with her mouth open, while her friend gently moved my mother's tongue back and forth and around in some pattern, and my mother made vocal sounds. It must have been speech therapy exercises that my mother followed.

What's clear now is the love of this woman for my mother. She was a friend who didn't turn away in horror, but treated my mother like the complicated person she was, suffering but healing, and who helped her with recovering her speech.

It was I who turned away in horror then. I who could not bear my mother's flawed, diseased, imperfect body.

My grandmother and I stood on opposite sides of my bedroom door. She was in the hallway, trying to push it closed; I was in my bedroom, trying to keep it open. We were both determined, and very very angry. My father said we quarreled because we were two of a kind, stubborn and willful, but my grandmother knew it was because children were meant to obey their elders and I knew it was because she was a cantankerous old lady who wanted to break me somehow.

This was Grandma's second stay with us, the fall I started sixth grade. The first time my grandmother had come to stay with us, just after my mother's suicide attempt and hospitalization, she was somber and abstracted. She spent long hours with my father at the various hospitals and long hours studying Mrs. Eddy. She made midwestern meals of meat and potatoes and did all the washing and ironing. During that time she was not only preoccupied with my mother's illness, but with my uncle's. And then, over the Christmas holidays, there was a sudden freeze and thaw in Battle Creek that split the pipes in the old house and flooded the entire basement and kitchen. A younger friend of hers, Hazel, told me a few years ago how Grandma had had to deal with the problem by phone until Hazel and her husband Ed offered to supervise the plumbers and the contractor who came to repair the house.

"Of course, since it was your grandmother," Hazel said matter-of-factly, "we were worried that when she got back she'd find something wrong, but when we brought her home from the train station, she threw her arms around us and thanked us with tears in her eyes. She couldn't have been more grateful. 'It's absolutely perfect,' she said. We didn't really know at first," added Hazel, "why she'd had to go out to California so suddenly. Not when Andrew was so bad.

"Then she told us, Ellen had been in a car accident." She looked at me. It was clear she still didn't quite believe that story.

"No," I said. "It was . . . cancer."

My grandmother wasn't tall and she wasn't enormously fat; she was seventy years old and her skin was old-lady-wrinkled and soft as old fruit. But she was solid through and through, from her blocky white shoes to her imposing bosom. Her prominent nose had begun to meet her prominent chin and her dentures sat between them like a gate in the fortress of her face. There was no one so determined as my grandmother—except me, and I had not known that before.

Grandma managed to slam the door closed and to lean against it with her full, heavy weight. However I tugged, I couldn't get it open.

But we were at a standoff: the knob to my room had no lock inside or out. She could only keep me in if she stayed out there forever. I let go the knob abruptly and heard her relax slightly. There was a hint of conciliation in her tone as she said, "Stay in there for an hour and think about what you said. Then you can come out and watch TV with your brother."

I backed away from the door, as if in agreement, and heard her steps recede down the hall and into the living room. Then I flung open the window and jumped to the ground. I ran as fast as I could, for as long as I could. Until the anger was burned out and the resolve to resist was hardened in me like petrified wood that once was live and is now stone.

That evening at dinner Grandma told my father all about my rebellion and flight. "And she disobeyed me and jumped out the window."

My father looked at me soberly. "While your grandmother is here taking care of you, you'll do what she says. Do you understand? If she tells you to go to your room, you'll go. Do you understand?"

In a couple of years my father would be supporting my stepmother in the same way, and I'd be spending days and weeks grounded and behind the closed door of my bedroom. I could resist my grandmother, just as I would be able to resist my stepmother, but it was harder to resist him. He was the only adult I was sure still loved me.

"Yes, Dad," I mumbled.

My grandmother looked at me complacently.

I said, "What about when Mama is home?"

There was a pause, and then my grandmother said firmly, "We'll take each situation as it comes." By which I knew she meant that she, and not my mother, would decide.

My mother was getting better by the time my grandmother arrived that fall. She could speak in sentences that we could understand and she could participate a little more in family life. I imagine, looking back, that the reason my grandmother came was so that my mother could spend more time at home during the week, and so that she could gradually ease herself into being at home all the time.

How much had she recovered from her breakdown of the year before? How much of her fragility was due to her cancer and how much was due to her disfigurement and her consequent difficulties in eating enough to nourish herself? How much was due to her mental illness and how much was due to falling into the hands of the madness establishment? When she tried and failed to commit suicide, she lost most of her rights as a human being. She had surgery for the cancer and radiation therapy; she had plastic surgery; she had electroshock and forced medication. For someone who had been completely outside the medical establishment most of her life, she was now thoroughly inside it, and its prisoner. If she said, I don't want to take my pills, no one treated that as the comment of a sensible adult, but as the recalcitrance of a mental patient. Suddenly everyone was an expert on her life; everyone was her guardian. And no one more so than my grandmother.

My mother had never really had rights with her mother. That's probably why she had escaped Battle Creek after the war was over and why she'd moved so far away. "That's undoubtably the reason your mother came to California," my father says. "Aside from just wanting something new like the rest of us. Because your grandmother was such a strong personality—she was like a steamroller. She used to write your mother once a week and call her regularly, and sometimes your mother would be upset afterwards. It was worse after your grandfather died—he had always been so kind and I think he was a good influence on your grandmother. And then Andrew got sick, and your mother kept feeling partly responsible for that."

I remember from early childhood the letter coming once a week from Grandma. The printed label in the corner: Mrs. John J. Lane, 124 N. Broad St., Battle Creek, Mich., and the address in firm cursive: Mrs. Cecil W. Wilson, 3675 Fanwood Ave., Long Beach, Calif. Sometimes there would be money inside for my mother to buy something for me and Bruce. My grandmother was hardly a rich woman, but I think now that she didn't do badly in her Christian Science practice, and she was always generous. The addition out in back, one room for my father's office and the other for a guest room, was mostly paid for by Grandma, and I'm sure she helped with the medical bills for my mother too. But like much generosity it came at a price.

It was my grandmother's tendency to come in and take over wherever she turned up. So as soon as she arrived she immediately began doing the cooking and cleaning. She wanted my mother to rest on her visits home and to study Science. Since my mother had never particularly liked cooking and cleaning, I doubt it was a great hardship to sit by and see Grandma whip through a day's chores. But it was harder for her to see my grandmother impose her rules on me and Bruce, and hard for her to see my grandmother paint me as a headstrong, angry child.

"Barbara has always had a mind of her own," my mother tried to explain, "but I've never had a problem with her obeying me."

But then my grandmother would launch into one of her stories about me. For instance, just last week. . . .

I'd been coming home from school, horsing around with the neighbor kids and I'd pretended mid-scream to lose my voice. Gasping feebly, I was led to my grandmother. "Barbara's lost her voice," my little brother said. At first he hadn't believed it, but my tremendous acting powers had convinced him it was so. My grandmother pretended to go along with it. Unlike my mother, who would have instantly reached for *Science and Health*, my grandmother simply nodded wisely. "There's only one cure for laryngitis," she said. "And that's warm water." Very kindly she led me into the kitchen where she had been washing the dishes. "Once you get done with these, young lady, your throat should be back to normal."

"Where did she learn to pretend she was sick!" my grandmother demanded of my mother, and there was accusation in that. For Grandma truly did believe that most sickness was nothing but a con, and she had built her successful Christian Science practice on her impatience and bullying temperment. Her friends and clients in Battle Creek simply didn't dare persist in being ill around her. Although she knew that my mother had cancer, she didn't want to put up with any other mental shenanigans.

One afternoon I was standing out in the backyard and overheard the two of them in the guest room. My grandmother's voice took up almost all the space. She was lecturing my mother loudly in a tone that admitted no other side. "You've simply got to pull yourself together, Ellen," she kept saying. "How are you going to get better if you keep on seeing error everywhere?"

My mother's voice was tearful. "I can't. I can't. It hurts! It hurts!"

"We've got to do these exercises for your tongue."

"Leave me alone!"

I ran away then, down to the other end of the backyard where I couldn't hear them. I couldn't stand the thought of my grandmother's thick, soft, white hands inside my mother's mouth, pulling and pushing at her wounded tongue, manipulating it so that it hurt, saying it was for my mother's own good.

Before my grandmother came to stay that second time I had continued to long for my mother to be my mother again, to somehow step out from the enchantment she had been under and to smile her beautiful white smile and laugh her joyful laugh. But that fall I began to realize that the mother I had known was no more and that she would never return. The woman in her place was in some ways as young as I was, younger. For my grandmother at least treated me as a worthy adversary, and laughed when she outsmarted me. "Oh, you'll never get ahead of *me*, young lady," she would say. "I know every trick in the book."

But my grandmother treated my mother like an infant sometimes, alternately coaxing her and trying to force her to eat more, and to eat more solid food. It was painful to sit at the table together and hear my mother say, "No thank you. I'm full," and have my grandmother say, "You're *not* full, Ellen. How can you possibly be full on one scrambled egg? You need to eat some bananas, they're very good for you, and some toast too. See, I've soaked the toast in milk."

And depending on my mother's mood she would either dutifully eat some banana or she would get up from the table and run into the bathroom, crying.

I had always heard from my grandmother that I was like her, but it was during this visit that I realized she didn't like seeing that resemblance in someone else, especially a child. I also realized what a strength there could be in saying no—not in the way my mother said it, as if it were a last resort, and not firmly, because at ten, almost eleven, I was not allowed to be firm, and attempts at firmness always ended in punishment. But if I took my grandmother literally when she said, "I don't mind a good tussle with mortal mind," then two could play that game.

One afternoon after school I decided to go over to my old friend Connie's house, on the other side of Patrick Henry Elementary. Connie and I had been good friends in fourth and part of fifth grade. Now sixth grade had just started and we'd forgotten all about not liking each other last year and had just been happy to see each other. I had always liked to go to Connie's, and had missed all the people in her huge Italian Catholic family. Not that I think they ever really knew who I was. There were too many of them. When I used to visit Connie once or twice a week after school, we'd take care of the babies crawling around on the floor and play with her older sisters' make-up and rosaries. Connie's mother never cared what we did. A big bold woman with long black hair, she seemed always to be shoveling clothes in the washer or drier and folding them.

That afternoon Connie and I played for a long time, longer than usual. I'd told my grandmother that morning that I was going over to Connie's after school—that wasn't the lie. The lie was pretending that Connie lived close by and that if it was dark Connie's mother would give me a ride home. But Connie's mother didn't have a car; she hardly noticed my departure.

I was ten years old, out on streets I didn't know in the dark, with almost a mile to walk. I was a little scared, yes, as I started down the street, first retracing my steps to the school and then the known rest of the way home. But more than scared, I was excited. To be alone, walking at night, was an adventure. I swung my arms, whistled and sang songs, loudly, looked at the twilight sky. Independent, free, autonomous. My mother would have called Connie's by now and come to get me in the car.

I felt a little pang of guilt as I burst into the house, where my grandmother was finishing dinner and Bruce was watching the "Mickey Mouse Club" on TV. The house was warm and cozy; my grandmother looked old and unknowing as she moved around the kitchen making hot dogs and creamed corn for us.

"Did Connie's mother give you a ride?" she asked.

"Yes," I answered and went into the living room to watch television with my brother. My independence was my secret now, a secret to keep as long as possible.

The frequent arguments with my grandmother took their toll that September and my mother's condition, instead of continuing to improve, deteriorated. Ever since her suicide attempt she'd been marked as a risk. And, in fact, she had tried a few more times over the past year to do away with herself. But just as I hadn't known about the first attempt, so of course I didn't know about the others, which all took place at the sanitarium.

But one day she tried to commit suicide at home during one of her stays. And this time, I was there.

As soon as I woke up, I knew I didn't want to go to school. After the first month or so of classes, the excitement had worn off, and I longed back to summer days. It was October, but still very hot. This morning it was just nice to lie in bed and feel the sun on the sheets. Yesterday when I was running I fell on the playground blacktop and hurt my ankle a little. I decided I could use that as an excuse.

"Mama," I called, as pitifully as I could, out into the hall. "Mama, I hurt my ankle yesterday and now it hurts more. I don't think I can walk on it. Can I stay home?"

She came in to look at it. It wasn't swollen but it vibrated with all the vulnerability I could send down into it. For a moment it was like old times. Her warm gentle fingers were on my skin and she said, "We'll pray for it today. Yes, you can stay home."

My father had already gone off to work and my mother helped Bruce get ready for school. He left and for half an hour there was a delicious quiet in the house. Grandma was out in her room, where she always did her mental work in the mornings. She was still doing absent treatment for all her clients in Battle Creek, as well as for some new ones she'd picked up through the Long Beach church. I was lying in the sunlight with some fairy tales propped up in front of me when my grandmother stormed in, with my mother behind her.

"What's this?" she snapped. "Put that book down." She flipped back the sheet and grabbed my ankle firmly.

"Ow!"

"There's nothing wrong with that ankle," she said. "It's not even swollen! Get up and get your clothes on, young lady! You're going to school."

I pulled the covers back over my leg, which now truly throbbed.

"My ankle is so twisted," I claimed. "It's sprained or something."

"I told her she could stay home, Mother," said my mother, with more firmness in her voice than I'd heard for a long time. "It doesn't mean I believe it's sprained. But we can work on it," she added.

Grandma turned on her furiously.

"What's wrong with you, Ellen? It's the principle of the thing. If she gets the idea she can stay home for every little ailment, she will. Is that the kind of Christian Science you want to teach her?"

"I'm not pretending," I wailed.

"She's my daughter. This is my house," my mother said, but she was retreating. She began to cry. Grandma looked so large and overwhelming next to her frail daughter, whom she was edging out the door and into the hall. When my mother was out of my room, Grandma turned on me and said, "If your ankle is so bad you can't go to school, you can just stay in bed all day!"

She slammed my bedroom door, and I began to cry. I hadn't had any breakfast and I was suddenly hungry. I wished I'd never brought this up. I wasn't hurt, I was never hurt or sick. If only I were at school now. Miss Swanson was so nice; she thought I was smart and funny. But it was too late now. Now I was going to have to stay in bed all day. I wasn't going to get any breakfast and no lunch either probably. My grandmother would keep me here to show me a lesson. *The Red Fairy Book* didn't seem very interesting anymore.

I listened anxiously through the door. Their argument had gone into the living room and suddenly my mother was shrieking loudly, "I'm sick of being treated like a child. I'm sick of always being treated as if there's something wrong with me!"

Sobbing loudly, my mother ran into the bathroom.

"Ellen," said my grandmother, following her with heavy steps. "Ellen, come out of there." She rattled the knob, which was locked, and I heard panic in her voice. "Ellen, what are you doing?"

Did my mother unlock the door or did my grandmother force it open? I was petrified to get out of bed to see what was happening. The minutes went by: anger turning to fear on my grandmother's end; only silence on my mother's. And then I heard the door open, heard my grandmother's angry gasp. "Ellen, what have you done? Did you take the whole bottle of pills? How many were there? You're going to tell me!"

The next thing I knew my grandmother was on the phone in my parents' bedroom talking with a doctor or emergency room. She was telling them in a frightened, but professional tone what pills my mother took, and she repeated, "Cream of Tartar. Cream of Tartar will induce vomiting."

I opened my door, but I didn't dare go out into the hall to see what was happening. I went back to bed, huddled under the covers. I could hear everything. I heard my grandmother trying to force my mother to swallow something and throw up the pills. My mother was resisting in a garbled voice, saying, "I want to die, let me die."

Someone came to the door and banged hard and they took my mother away. Maybe it was my father or a friend, maybe it was an ambulance. My grandmother went with them and nobody returned for a long time. They had forgotten about me, the cause of everything, now curled up in a tiny ball, as small as a seahorse, trying to pretend that none of this had happened.

My mother didn't come back that night or for a while. She had been having a good period, a quiet summer, and now it was over. She wouldn't be at home for my eleventh birthday in October. The next morning Grandma wrote a note to Miss Swanson to excuse me because my ankle was sprained. She was not cruel enough to tell Miss Swanson I was fibbing. She was not cruel enough to say to me that what happened to my mother was all my fault. But she looked my guilt at me. Nobody said anything more about the incident, then or ever, and sometimes I managed to believe that I dreamed it. But there were times when I knew it really happened and I heard my mother saying, "I want to die, let me die."

And a locksmith came to the house to change the knobs on the bathroom door.

My mother wanted to die, but everyone else wanted her to live, or at least to prevent her from dying by her own hand, so that the cancer could kill her slowly and painfully.

There would be other suicide attempts, including one at a Christian Science nursing home in Palo Alto the next summer, where my grandmother paid to send my mother for a stay. One day a nurse called my father in a panic and asked what they should do: my mother had taken an overdose.

"It was just like that first time," my father railed to me years later. "The nurse hadn't even called an emergency room. What was wrong with these goddamn people?"

But I wonder, Why didn't anybody just let her go?

If my mother was a failed Christian Scientist, who couldn't heal herself from cancer in spite of everything she'd read and heard in church all her life, then my grandmother was even more of a failure, because she, after all, made her living as a Christian Scientist practitioner. Not only did she have a son diagnosed as schizophrenic living in an institution, but her dutiful daughter, her beloved first child Ellen, had gone crazy as well.

Hard as it may have been not to share her pain, my grandmother didn't tell a single soul in Battle Creek what had happened and what was happening to her daughter. In 1965, two years after my mother's death, Bruce and I visited Battle Creek for the summer. A meddling sort of woman from the church got me aside at a picnic and asked,

"Now dear, I'm just trying to remember, isn't your mother about my age now? Forty-five or so?"

I stared at her in horror. "My mother is *dead*."

"Oh, I know, dear. I'm so sorry. I only meant, how old *would* she have been?"

But I could see the woman hadn't known. And that shocked me deeply.

Years later I heard from a friend of my grandmother's that Grandma had told Andrew his sister died in a car accident. "There was always something mysterious about Ellen's death," she said delicately. "Your grandmother's next-door neighbor told me that right before your grandmother died of her stroke she came over as if she had something on her mind, and she started talking about Ellen. She said something about Ellen's mouth and throat, and then she started crying, and couldn't finish and left the house."

Words that stop in the throat.

My grandmother stayed on for a few weeks more, but my mother didn't come back to visit for a while. I'd been hoping somewhere in my heart that my mother would come home for my eleventh birthday. My father told me gently that she wouldn't be able to make it.

I still expected to have a birthday party, though.

I had always had birthday parties, some quite large. There were invitations, and paper streamers, and a big decorated cake from Rose's Bakery and Neapolitan or chocolate ice cream. If it was warm, and it usually was in California, the celebration would take place outdoors under the golden leaves of the apricot tree. We played games; we ran around wildly. Once there was a clown. And there were lots of presents. My grandmother had always sent something from Michigan, usually clothes, but once a huge doll, and another time a china tea set.

So I asked my grandmother what we would do the day I turned eleven.

"Nothing," she said. "Not while your mother's in the hospital."

So many holidays had been put on hold since my mother's illness. Last year there'd been no Christmas to speak of, and Easter had come and gone without new patent leather shoes and Easter baskets. But I couldn't quite believe that my birthday, my eleventh birthday, was going to pass without some sort of celebration. My brother had had a party in May, I told my grandmother.

"Your mother was here for that," she said. "No, I think we'll just skip it this year."

I still didn't believe it. The week before my birthday I poked my head in various closets and drawers looking for a present. I tried to talk to my father. "I'm sure your grandmother will do something," he said distractedly, for he was often distracted in those days.

Some neighbor kids asked me if I was having a party, and I said bravely, "No, not this year. Cause my mom's in the hospital. I wouldn't want a party."

On the day of my eleventh birthday I woke up and got dressed without anybody saying anything to me. I went to school. A couple of people said Happy Birthday after Miss Swanson announced it in class the way they always did. But instead of being pleased and excited the way I'd been before, I felt ashamed. No one should know that my family didn't care about me.

After school I went to my Bluebird troop meeting, and we made little log cabins from popsicle sticks. Every once in a while someone would say something about my birthday. "What do you think you're going to get?"

"Oh, nothing much," I said. " 'Cause my mom's in the hospital, you know."

"You going to have cake and everything tonight?"

"Oh sure. Yeah, and ice cream and everything."

I walked home very slowly from Bluebirds. I'll remember that walk all my life. The twilight came on less like dark than a strange sickly bleaching process. The sidewalk lost its color and became insubstantial, as if you could sink right through into the meaningless core of the earth. The cactus that neighbors liked to plant in clusters went transparently spiny and even the houses almost vanished like gray smoke into the invisible sky. There was nothing to hold on to and nowhere to be and even the familiarity of the walk was painful, because familiarity was so empty now.

I dragged my feet all the way and when I got to our house I sat out on the steps, so coldly cement they burned into my flesh. In the air was the scent of autumn, dry and burnt. The streetlights went on, fathers came home from work, the kids were called in, the evening began, and somehow those lights on in all those houses were even sadder to me than the bleak gray of the earlier twilight.

I had been sitting there a long time when my grandmother suddenly opened the door. She stood there a minute, worried, and then said in a different, more tentative voice than I'd ever heard her use, "Don't you want to come in, Barbara? You've got a surprise in here."

I went in and there was a cake on the dining room table and some presents.

"I thought you weren't going to do anything," I said dully. "You said."

"Oh that was just so it could be a surprise." My grandmother laughed, but with an edge of uncertainty. "If I'd told you about it, it wouldn't have been a surprise."

After dinner we ate the cake and I opened the presents. My grandmother gave me books and clothes, and the whole time she looked at me anxiously, so that I thanked her more than I wanted to. My father said after she died that she was an upright woman, but that she didn't know the meaning of the word apologize.

Childhood never vanishes overnight; it only seems to. The way I remember it, my childhood simply faded, from something vivid and real to something gray and insubstantial. A neighborhood I no longer recognized, even though I still lived in it.

Chapter 9

Writing an Autobiography

*P*atrick Henry Elementary School looks much the same now as it did thirty-five years ago—shabbier, yes, but still clean and serviceable. The stucco buildings have been painted recently, the same dull peach color, and the game circles on the asphalt newly brightened, though the asphalt itself is more gray than the burning black of my time. I didn't remember that there was so little grass. Only a small rectangle of green with two pine trees sits in the center, near the cafeteria—all the rest is asphalt. No wonder I was always skinning my knees. We hung a piñata in one of pine trees once in fourth grade and, blindfolded, banged at it with a baseball bat.

It's a February weekend when I return to the school, and the air is sweet. The playground is edged with soughing eucalyptus and locusts, and in the quiet streets around the school are purple-blue jacarandas in flower. On the school grounds the tetherball poles are empty and their chains rattle a little in the slight breeze. The windows of the class-rooms are filled with colored paper cutouts. I peek inside to see more of the students' work on the walls, along with the painstakingly cheer-ful and informative displays made by their teachers. A list of students' names is displayed in the window of my old first-grade classroom, where Mrs. Glover reigned; once the pupils here were all white, now the names include Garcia and Lee. The two temporary bungalows they put up in the Fifties for the older classes are still there; each one holds two classrooms, each with wooden floors and green blackboards. I see, as I stick my nose through the metal webbing over the tall windows, the same old wooden desks.

I've been walking around the school, letting myself remember and feel again emotions of the past. Excitement and fear as I stand outside the kindergarten door—after all those months of asking, "When do I get to go to school?" I was finally there. There for years and tedious years to come. Pleasure as I look through the window of my second-grade classroom where Mrs. Franken one day read us a picture book version of "How the First Letter Was Written" from Kipling's *The Just-So Stories:* "But a time will come, O Babe of Tegumai, when we shall make letters—all twenty-six of them—and when we shall be able to read as well as to write, and then we shall always say exactly what we mean without any mistakes." Afterwards, seeing me poring over the book, memorizing the pictures, she said, "Take it home tonight, Barbara. Read it. I know you can." It was with that book that I finally began to understand how to read, how I could train my brain to see a whole paragraph or page at once and absorb its meaning, rather than stumbling dyslexically over each disconnected word.

I press my nose against the bay window of the library—home to my years of special reading hours while everyone else studied science. It's the same too: the little blond tables and straight chairs, the shelves neatly marked. Fairy tales, says one sign. Ghost stories, says another. Third grade, fourth grade, I hardly remember them. Learning my timetables, which was fun, and learning to write cursive, which I found hard to master. "Your lines need to slant to the *right*, Barbara!" Miss Chicoletti kept telling me in third grade. "Why are they always slanting *left?*" But right from the beginning, I grasped my pencil awkwardly and my handwriting went backwards.

When I get to my fifth-grade classroom I have to sit down on one of the picnic benches. The door has such a cold hard look to it. Our teacher was going through a divorce, I remember; she left midterm to move to Alaska. In this room we studied American history: the girls made samplers for colonial times and bonnets for the pioneer days; the boys made slates and then miniature log cabins. My friend Connie was in this class with me, the last real friend I was to have for several years. "What happened at your house?" she kept asking me, until she got tired of me not answering, and told a group of girls one lunch period that I was stuck up.

I expect to feel just as bad when I get to the door of my sixth-grade bungalow, but instead it's happiness that wells up. Happiness? Was I ever happy during those years? I stand outside and peer through the window in the door. I can't help smiling. The chairs and desks are arranged much the same, in front of the green blackboard that lists countries of the world. They're studying geography, just as we did that year.

My sixth-grade teacher, Miss Swanson, had bright blond hair in a Dutch cut, and a long face with a smile that showed a lot of gum. She was interested in politics and world events and she was a great fan of President Kennedy. Within days of starting her class, she had told us all about Kennedy's plans for the Peace Corps. How Americans, young and old, with skills to teach, would fan out across the world and involve themselves in the lives of poor and uneducated people, and help them. She wanted to join up. Maybe we would be Peace Corps volunteers ourselves someday. In any case, we had to learn about the world.

I had always been interested in geography and travel. I was fascinated with an old cardboard globe we had at home and loved to spin it round and round. Its shape had early on gotten mixed up with the movie *Around the World in Eighty Days*, and with a trip a retired woman of my mother's acquaintance had once taken. She went to Europe and kept right on going until she arrived back in Long Beach by ship one day. And then for a year or two we belonged to something called the "Around the World Program," sponsored by the American Geographical Society and published by Nelson Doubleday. Every two months a stapled sixty-four-page booklet would arrive in the mail. Each booklet featured one country or region—England, Ghana, Indochina, Finland—and was full of maps and drawings and black-and-white photos, and full of informative and genial facts. Ghanaians lived in large extended families and wove kente cloth; the Finns owed their existence to an inner quality called *sisu*, which was a combination of inner moral strength and stubborn courage with a touch of fatalism in the face of adversity. And the Vietnamese, ominously, were split between north and south. But what I liked best about the little books was the colored photos in the form of stamps that you could stick into the books in the appropriate empty square with the caption underneath:

> The Royal Palace in Phnom Penh, within spacious grounds, is gayly Oriental. Prince Norodom loves Western culture, conveniences, modern plumbing but retains traditional luxuries, his ballet troupe of young girls, his stables of albino elephants.

And

> To the average Englishman, Piccadilly Circus is not only the heart of the theatrical and restaurant district, but the "crossroads of the world." It derives its name from the pickadils, or ornamental collars, worn by smart young men-about-London in the 17th century.

Miss Swanson liked in me the things that I liked about myself and that my mother had always praised. She often asked me to read aloud for the class and when I failed the scale-singing test to get into glee club, she said, "Never mind, you do the best rooster imitation I've ever heard." For she sometimes had us read plays aloud and would record them on a big old-fashioned tape recorder. When it came to sound effects, I was tops. It was in Miss Swanson's room, too, that I wrote my first real short story. It was about rescuing some people who'd been stuck on the wrong side of the Berlin Wall when it went up. The plot was creaky (a noiseless helicopter lifted them to safety), but the atmosphere was judged very evocative (lots of fog).

For a geographical project at the end of the year she had us write a paper on a country of our choosing. I picked Italy, but I asked Miss Swanson if I could write it in the form of letters from the traveling Marcie to her friend Betty at home. In time, my project came to be an elaborate notebook filled not only with the letters, but with cutout photographs of Marcie's travel wardrobe and of the places she visited: Naples and the Isle of Capri ("The Blue Grotto is the most magical place in the world!"); Rome ("When they call this the city of antiquity, they mean old!"); and Venice ("Here I am in St. Mark's Square at last!")

Marcie's breezy letters were stuffed with facts gleaned from the *World Book Encyclopedia* and travel books. My mother loved the idea of Marcie and took me to the library to do research. Mindful of the episode with the plagiarized duck poem, I was careful to rewrite all the travelogue sentences so they were in Marcie's voice, factual but wildly enthusiastic. My mother typed up Marcie's letters and told me I had a wonderful imagination, the same thing Miss Swanson said when she gave it an "Excellent" grade. She had me read some of the letters aloud to the class; it was my first experience of reading aloud what I had written myself. It was my first heady experience of having an audience listen intently and laugh.

I sit on the steps of my old sixth-grade classroom and something of the feeling of that year wraps around me and warms me. Dear Miss Swanson, did you ever join the Peace Corps? And then I think, wait, my *mother* helped me with the project? My *mother* took me to the library and typed up the letters? My crazy mother? But my memory puts her squarely in the Los Altos Library. I see her, her face healed though still disfigured, still a face that people look at twice and then turn slightly away from, her hair gray, her figure slender. With bright eyes and a smile she's coming over to the table where I sit with books around me, and she has a volume full of photographs of Rome in her hand. She sits beside me and I see us talking naturally about Italy, where neither of us have ever been, imagining it for each other.

A psychiatric diagnosis doesn't always mean much, for every mental illness takes its own course and plays itself out in its own way. That was why it was so confusing to live alongside, and is so hard for me to remember accurately. How crazy was my mother? Or was she sometimes not crazy at all? Would she have improved her way back to mental health had she not had cancer too? Would she have broken down if she hadn't had cancer? Did the cancer make her mental disease worse? For if her struggle was always with God over how she could be sick in a perfect world, what could resolve that tension except the healing that never came?

Looking back, all I have is contradictory snapshots: my mother beside herself with sobbing in the bedroom; my mother sitting quietly in a chair reading *Science and Health* as if none of this ever happened, as if her faith were as pristine as ever; my mother locked in the bathroom, swallowing pills to punish her mother, heedless that I am in the next room; my mother typing up my letters from Marcie to Betty, telling me, "Someday you'll go to Rome yourself. I know you will."

After her suicide attempt and falling out with Grandma sometime during the fall of my sixth-grade year, my mother seemed to improve. Not the cancer of course; it continued on its steady course, hidden for a time and then bursting out again, but in other ways she seemed to get better. She was able to speak more clearly and eat more solid foods; she was home more often and seemed more present when she was home. She spent more time with some of her old friends and she went to church on the Sundays when she was at home. She was far from well; sometimes she was weak and in great pain and, according to my father, the nurses at the sanitarium always kept sharp objects away from her. But she was not quite the shadowy creature she had been the first year after her breakdown. And when I saw her, if she was up to it, it was possible to talk with her, to have some kind of relationship, not the old, unquestioning, loving relationship, but something new, wary and ambiguous, but genuine.

My mother was the person I told, during the spring of the sixth grade, that I wanted to be a writer someday, and my mother was the one who encouraged me. She said that she had always known I was talented—I was talented in many ways, drawing, acting, writing—but that she was glad that I had chosen writing. I must work at it and take it seriously. And she told me that she had been on the staff of her high school newspaper, and that she had once dreamed of being published in the *Christian Science Monitor*. She said, "But I wasn't like you. I somehow didn't have a style of my own or a strong enough desire. I think you do."

Because of my mother and because of Miss Swanson, by the time I entered junior high I expected that I would continue to be praised and singled out for my writing talent. Now I would have a separate English class and a real English teacher. Miss Swanson had prepared me for the joys to come: "You're going to be in the accelerated track when you start junior high. You'll be reading and discussing books in a way we don't have time for here. I know you'll enjoy it."

My seventh-grade English teacher was a man, the first male teacher I'd ever had. Mr. Baldwin was young and tan, with streaked blond hair. Rumor had it that he was an ocean lifeguard during the summers, and that his name was Bob. All the girls had crushes on him, and used to crowd around his desk after class and after school. But I didn't care about that. I wanted to learn something from him—how to be a writer. And I was thrilled when he announced that we'd be doing a lot of writing in his class, and not just book reports and term papers, but creative writing. Then he announced our first assignment.

We were supposed to write our autobiography.

An autobiography, he said, is the story of your life and the life of your family. Tell me where they come from, what your father does, where you live and what you like to do. Tell me about your grandparents, your brothers and sisters, your dogs and cats. Tell me your favorite TV shows, your favorite books, your favorite hobbies and sports. Tell me a secret about yourself.

Some of the students looked puzzled, others excited. I thought I must be the only one in class who was plunged into shock by his use of the word "secret." I didn't know then about the prevalence of incest and abuse and alcoholism. I didn't suspect that there were others who had family secrets to guard with their lives. I imagined that I was the only one in class who couldn't tell her story, who couldn't tell her secret.

We had a week to write this piece. I thought about it all week without knowing what to do. I had two models of writing: one was the approved *Sentinel* story style—cheerful parables of reality and unreality—and the other was fairy tales and other works of the imagination. I'd never read an autobiography, had never heard of writing that was supposed to be about your real life, about your real family. Of writing that was supposed to be the truth. I thought that writing was meant to be *better* than the truth, meant to be *better* than reality. That's what I knew I was good at: making up things. "You're so imaginative," my teachers would say, encouragingly like Mrs. Franken and Miss Swanson, or irritably like Miss Chicoletti.

The only way I knew how to tell anything was by making a story around it. And so finally, the night before I had to turn my first paper in to Mr. Baldwin, I sat down and began to write, and everything I wrote about I exaggerated and changed. We had an older dog, a cat, and a parakeet: I made them into a Saint Bernard, a tame baby puma, and a talking parrot, and for good measure threw in a monkey. I liked this idea so much that I turned our backyard into a kind of wildlife refuge, and described stray animals that made their homes there. My vision of this backyard became increasingly real, even though at first it had been influenced by the Doctor Dolittle books, and by a program I'd seen on TV about a couple in Sherman Oaks who trained wild animals for Hollywood pictures.

I wrote three or four pages in this vein, all about our astounding animals, and I made it as funny and lighthearted as I could. How was Mr. Baldwin going to know if it was true or not? It *sounded* true. Better than true. He'd said that those who wrote the best papers could read them aloud. I knew mine would be the best.

The paper came back with a grade of B-minus, and the words, scrawled across the top, "Some good description. But what about your family?!?"

I was humiliated and angry. When my mother came home for a visit and asked me about school, especially English, I told her reluctantly, "We had to write our autobiography. It was stupid."

"Let's see," she asked. I dragged out my paper. "I don't have a very good teacher," I explained. "He's a lifeguard."

"A B-minus!" she said in surprise. Then she began to read it. She read it quickly and without a word. If I'd expected her to take my part and say that the teacher was an idiot who didn't know a sentence from a surf board, I was disappointed. My mother read over a couple of paragraphs again and then turned to me and said, "But this isn't true. None of this is true. Twinkie isn't a parrot! And a puma in our backyard? You make it sound like we live in a circus or something."

She gave it back. She didn't say, "Your teacher won't give you a good grade if you don't follow the assignment." She said, "You have to tell the truth when you write. I know you can do better than this."

I took the paper back and jammed it in my desk drawer. "I can not. I can't do any better. It was a stupid assignment anyway."

How could I do better if I couldn't write the truth about my family? What truth did she expect me to tell? What secret did she want me to reveal?

Visiting Long Beach this time to look at old neighborhoods and schools, I purposefully leave out Marshall Junior High, where I went in the seventh grade and the first half of the eighth. I know already what I would feel standing on the sidewalk and looking into any of the classrooms; I know what I would feel if I were to try to reexperience that six-month period before my mother died. Shame. Despair. Loneliness.

Like every child leaving elementary school for junior high, I had many preconceptions and expectations. Some of them came from older kids. The summer before I started seventh grade, I went with my father and brother to Santa Barbara for a few days, to my father's yearly accounting convention. There, on the university campus built on the bluff over the ocean, I shared a dorm room with a girl from Mill Valley. Susan was two years older than I, going into the ninth grade and very sophisticated. She filled my head with talk of necking parties and drive-ins and dirty books. She didn't have any of the books on her, but she told me about one, *Tropic of Cancer*, and how she and her boyfriend had read it and tried some of the things in it. I was still eleven then, plump and baby-faced with lank blond hair. I thought my eyes were pretty and sometimes I sucked in my cheeks to give myself cheekbones. I remember that week in Santa Barbara, the fog in the morning that burned off by afternoon, the buildings perched on a cliff overlooking the sea, the terrycloth short robe and sandals I wore when we walked down to the beach. I remember the night too, watching as the moon drew a gold streak across the dark waves and having a self-consciously poetic thought: "Midas is swimming to the moon." Later in our dormitory room, Susan would regale me with stories of girls who went too far (she implied that she had done everything but) and what you had to do to become a girl that boys liked.

I lay there in my bed listening to her and, without any basis at all, imagined the new and different me who would enter seventh grade, so different from the old me.

One of the things Susan told me is that I had to do something about my hair before seventh grade. She also told me I had to get a tight straight wool skirt and a big mohair sweater and that it was crucial to start shaving my legs so I could wear nylons and flats, but the most important thing was having a Hairstyle. At that time, 1962, there was a style called "the bubble," and its longer cousin, the "double-bubble." My hair was the right length for the double-bubble, but it lacked body and shape, so that even with a can of hairspray and a teasing comb, I couldn't seem to get anything like the height I saw on models in hair magazines borrowed from Terry next door. Terry suggested that I get a permanent at a beauty college; that way it wouldn't be expensive.

So a few days before seventh grade started I persuaded my father to drop me off at a local beauty college for a permanent and style. In a few hours, I was ecstatic. The double-bubble, rising high on my crown, bulging page-boy–like down to my neck, was an enormous lacquered miracle. I spent the next two days moving carefully, and sleeping with tissue paper carefully around my head. But I moved with a new kind of self-assurance; I didn't have to worry about the transition to junior high, out of childhood, into practically teenager-hood. My double-bubble, along with the tight straight skirt I couldn't walk fast in and the large mohair sweater that was stifling hot for a southern California summer, would be my passport to success.

The night before the first day of school I confidently washed my hair, and while it was wet, set it on small pink brush rollers, the only kind I had.

In the morning I couldn't get the rollers out of my hair. The permanent had bonded them in tight little packets to my head; the waving lotion and traction effect of the bristles on the rollers ensured that they would never unroll in this lifetime. I was in tears, and my father called Dolores next door. Dolores who could always be counted on to provide some womanly advice in an emergency, even though she made it clear she didn't really like it. It was she who had handed me a box of Kotex and a belt one day when I told her I was bleeding, and had said, "Read the directions." Now she had me come over to her house and, positioning me over the kitchen sink, poured vinegar on my head. She unwrapped the rollers, pulling hard at my roots as she did so, and complaining loudly, "What possessed you to use such small rollers just after you had a permanent? And rollers with brushes!"

The true answer—"How could I possibly have known? Who would have told me?"—was lost in my shamed mutter, "I don't know." I should have known. I should have known. Of course it was obvious now.

When the rollers were out, Dolores directed me to wash my hair in the sink, and then she tried to comb the tangles out. Finally she gave up and said, "It will relax in a few weeks, but for now you'll just have to live with it."

I was late for school. The girl down the street, who'd promised to wait for me at the corner at eight-thirty, was gone. I had to enter the grounds of Marshall Junior High school alone and to figure out where to go. I had to enter the gym where we were being given our class assignments and find my way to my right section. And all the while I was conscious of the large frizzy mass of hair which, drying, had gotten large as a basket of snakes sitting on top of my head.

My helmet of darkness was of no use. "What happened to your hair?" a girl from my sixth-grade class asked me, while two boys I used to know tittered behind her.

"Nothing," I said, and turned my back. If I could have walked out of that gym and never returned, I would have.

Seventh grade started badly, and it only got worse. There was little money for clothes and, worse than that, no assistance in choosing them. My father had allowed me to buy one outfit, but the straight skirt and mohair sweater looked all wrong on my awkward figure, and as for the nylons—I could forget it. My father wouldn't let me shave my legs; since I was blond the light hair was—to him—almost completely invisible.

In my music appreciation class the seats were arranged like a very small auditorium. Next to me sat a popular boy. Mill Valley Susan would have made the most of the situation and so would the girls in my gym class who gossiped about how to get boyfriends. They would have asked him his hobbies or they would have shared a laugh about Rimsky-Korsakov, and then he would have asked her to eat lunch with him. I had never said a word to this boy, nor he to me. One day he dropped a pencil by my feet; bending down to pick it up he noticed my legs. Suddenly I felt a hand on my leg. "Oooh, hairy, hairy!" he said loudly. Everyone looked, some kids laughed. I burned in shame and silence.

That day or another soon after I shaved my legs with my father's razor. I didn't know how—(I should have known how)—and cut myself badly, then had to lie at school about how I got the cuts.

A few weeks later we were told we had to get school pictures taken for the yearbook and we were allowed to buy extras. Somewhere in the back of my mind I couldn't get used to my ugliness. I believed secretly, away from school, away from the mirror, that I was still the cute little girl of my childhood, blond and blue-eyed and confident. So I filled out the form to get extra photos and smiled at the camera, as I had always smiled at cameras. The photos came back of a desperate-to-please round face with too many teeth and a barely tamed mass of hair, coiling out in all directions. I hastily stuffed the photos back into the envelope in which they came, and then into my notebook.

Later that day, in math class, I had to go up to the front of the class with my notebook to ask the teacher about our homework assignment. On the way back to my seat—and I always sat in the back because I was a W—the envelope with the photos fell out without my noticing. They fanned out on the floor between desks. A kind boy came back to me with several of them. "I think you dropped these, there are more on the floor if you want to get them."

It was shocking in the first place that he could recognize the photo as me (then I must really look like that!), and a nightmare that that face was spread out under everyone's feet. I had to go back and get down to pick them up, claim that face over and over. "Yes, thanks. Thank you, yes, that's mine. . . ."

I'd had no close friends in sixth grade, but I'd never felt excluded in Miss Swanson's classroom. I'd also had my Bluebird and then Camp Fire troop, and the neighbor kids I'd grown up with, as well as the girls I saw every week at Sunday School, Christine and Carrie. But everything changed in seventh grade. I dropped out of Camp Fire Girls because I'd heard that it was too weird to belong to things like that in junior high, and the girls I'd known all through elementary school formed cliques that had no room for me.

In seventh grade my only companion, for a few months, was a girl named Lou Anne Hastings.

Lou Anne had the kind of face that would later turn beautiful, but that looked odd on a child's body. These days she would probably be a Calvin Klein model, made up to look twenty-five. She had pale, almost white skin, an oddity itself in Southern California, blue-black hair, and dark blue eyes with long lashes. Her features were cold and classic; she rarely smiled, and then only mockingly. She was not at all popular. She was dressed as a child when the rest of us were trying desperately to look like cool teenagers. Most of us failed, but the ones who succeeded, with their teased hair and tight skirts, set the standard. Lou Anne wore dresses with puffed sleeves, or green and red plaid kilt skirts with blue Peter Pan blouses. Her shoes looked orthopedic and she wore short white socks. Black hair was growing in on her legs. I doubt she was really as indifferent about clothes as she appeared; it was her mother who made her dress like this.

She lived about two blocks away from us, but because she'd never been in my classes at Patrick Henry I hadn't gotten to know her. We started walking together to and from school a week or two after seventh grade started, and we discovered we shared English class.

It soon became clear that we were rivals for Mr. Baldwin's attention and approval. Lou Anne didn't want to be a writer, only his favorite pupil; but she knew that I had aspirations towards a literary career. She had read her autobiographical piece the second week of class, an excruciatingly detailed and dull family tree. Once after class we compared written exams. I had a B and she had an A-minus. I had never had an A in Mr. Baldwin's class; Lou Anne said she got all As and was surprised she'd received an A-minus. I asked to look at her paper and was amazed that we had answered two questions almost the exact same way. The only difference was that Mr. Baldwin had knocked off five points each from my answers while writing on the margin of Lou Anne's paper: "Very good!"

"But we answered this the same!" I said.

Lou Anne shrugged. "I guess he made a mistake," she said, but her dark blue eyes had a malicious look. "Maybe he just likes me or something."

I grabbed her paper and went back to Mr. Baldwin's classroom. It was after school and he was holding court, as he usually did, with some of the most attractive girls in his classes. Three or four of them, tall, blond, popular, stood around chatting as he leaned, muscular and tan, against his desk.

They all looked at me as I came in and I knew from their eyes that I was odd: my wild hair, my wool mohair skirt, tight, but not attractively so, only tight enough so that the zipper had already broken and the gap was safety-pinned together, so that I always had to keep my heavy mohair sweater on to cover the safety pins.

"Mr. Baldwin," I said, heedless. "I've been looking at Lou Anne's paper and you marked off points on mine and you said "Very good" on hers and we answered just the same way."

He took the two papers and studied them. "Well, I think Lou Anne expressed herself a little better," he said. He did not want to admit he was wrong.

"But you gave her an A-minus and me a B. You never give me an A." My face was hot and I wanted to cry.

Mr. Baldwin began to laugh, and the girls around him, catching his cue, began to giggle as well. He wasn't cruel, only embarrassed. He shrugged his broad shoulders and turned slightly away, and saw Lou Anne leaning in the doorway with her beautiful, adult-woman-in-children's-clothes look. "Why does it matter so much to you?" he asked, flushing like a boy. "After all, it's only a paper. You have plenty of chances left this year."

There was nothing to do but leave. All the way home Lou Ann gloated. "When you said you wanted to be a writer, I thought you must be pretty good at writing."

As seventh grade progressed, it seemed that everyone drew away from me or took delight in tormenting me and pointing out my weaknesses. I remember that one day after school I was walking home and a high school girl I didn't know came up behind me and began to lecture me about my appearance and my attitude.

"You look like a mess," she said. "I watch you sometimes slumping home from school and I think, doesn't that girl have any pride in herself? Her skirt's hiked up in the back and her sweater is pulled down nearly to her hem—have you ever thought what you look like?"

"My zipper's broken," I whispered. "I don't know how to fix it."

"Oh, for goodness sake," she said. "Wear another skirt!" and she walked quickly past me, disgusted.

But I didn't have another skirt, and no one to take me shopping. My mother no longer cared about things like that and she never came home anymore. Since Thanksgiving she hadn't even been home for a visit. My father said, "You have all those perfectly good clothes from sixth grade. Why don't you wear them?" As if anybody but stupid Lou Anne Hastings wore corduroy jumpers with white blouses anymore.

One day on the way to school, Lou Anne said, "You are so weird. What makes you so weird?"

I hesitated. If I gave a reason did that mean I was accepting being weird? I finally said, "My mother's in the hospital. She's been in hospitals since I was ten."

"You are so melodramatic," Lou Anne said contemptuously. "People go into hospitals all the time. My grandmother is always in the hospital. You make such a big deal out of everything."

I believed that. I believed that my fear and loneliness and grief, which I tried so hard to squash down and disguise, was nevertheless visible and revolting to everyone. And that that was what was making me as repulsive outwardly as I was inwardly. Death in movies was different. When people died in movies it was beautiful, but in real life there was something wrong with feeling sad to lose someone. My sadness, my apartness from the human race, was huge and embarrassing, enormous as my hair, growing and growing. It was permanent, it would not come out, not with vinegar or shampoo, not even with vigorous daily brushing.

I gave up on writing for a while in the seventh grade, though I didn't give up on reading. For hours after school that fall and winter I lay on my bed, ate sandwiches of grape jelly on white bread, and read my way steadily through every book in the Marshall Library. I wasn't discriminating; the main thing was to read, and every day after school I took home three books and read each one. They were trivial books mostly, neither the magically sustaining stories of childhood nor the adult novels I'd begin in another year. But they served their purpose, which was to numb if not console and strengthen. Nancy Drews, girls and horses, girls and boys, girls and dogs, girls and younger sisters—the jelly sandwiches of juvenile literature.

Reading was not only a way of not feeling, of blocking out reality, it was a means of pretending I was someone else. And sometimes I didn't just lie on my bed; I flew around the house in dress-up clothes, acting, singing, and pretending I was the star of a musical comedy.

We'd had among our few records at home the boxed set of 78 rpm *Oklahoma!* records, one song to a side, which I had sung along to for years. After my twelfth birthday I used the ten dollars my grandmother sent to buy LPs of *Carousel*, *South Pacific*, and *The Sound of Music*. I had never seen any of these performed; I think I learned about them from the *Ed Sullivan Show* and from poring through the small music section at the local Woolworth's. Within a short period of time I knew every song on all the albums by heart. I sang them all, and loved them all, especially the Mary Martin songs. Mary Martin was so spunky. She was going to wash that man right out of her hair, and send him on his way. She taught children their do-re-mi's and led them over the Alps to safety. Sure, she had her bad times and had to go to the hills when her heart was sore, because the other nuns thought she was a flibbertigibbit with curlers beneath her wimple. But mostly she was a cockeyed optimist who didn't believe the human race was falling on its face.

I always felt better when I was being Mary Martin. I'd crank up the volume on the record player that was part of the old Magnavox TV in the living room and dance wildly through the house, jumping on the beds and the two small sofas, careening from living room to hall to bedroom and back again. Bruce was usually outside playing with his friends and I had the whole house to myself. Sometimes I dressed up in my mother's clothes and put her jewelry on, the yellow chiffon going-out-to-dinner dress that she used to wear and the big rhinestone necklace, bracelet, and earrings. I'd put powder on my nose and red lipstick on my lips and I would look in the mirror and be amazed how beautiful I was.

It didn't matter that I'd always been told I couldn't keep a tune or that in square dance lessons I'd never quite been able to remember which was my right foot and which was my left. With the LP orchestra backing me up, the audience whispering to each other, "She's so amazingly beautiful and talented," I could do anything, from snapping my fingers and kicking my legs high or mooning longingly over the sofa back. I did comedy tunes and sad ballads with tears rolling down my face. For though Mary Martin made me feel better, I got the emotional release I craved from the wrenchingly sad songs of *South Pacific* and *Carousel*. Even the bouncy songs in *Carousel* foreshadowed the losses to come, from the opening, "You're a queer one, Julie Jordan." to the lyrical "When I Marry Mr. Snow." You knew that Julie Jordan was never going to have the happy, normal life of her best friend Carrie Pipperidge, who even before marriage was imagining with Mr. Snow blissful domestic life. But Julie was different and fell for the barker Billy Bigelow, who was bound to cause her unhappiness. It was my first experience of the romantic concept of fated love, a myth that was to cause me problems later in life. But when I sobbed over this song when I was twelve, I wasn't crying about a boy.

> *What's the use of wond'rin'*
> *If he's good or if he's bad?*
> *. . . He's your feller and you love him—*
> *That's all there is to that.*
>
> *Common sense may tell you*
> *That the endin' will be sad*
> *And now's the time to break and run away.*
> *But what's the use of wond'rin'*
> *If the endin' will be sad?*
> *He's your feller and you love him—*
> *There's nothing more to say.*

Yet even if I'd wanted to I couldn't break and run away, and soon I'd be back on my feet again, energetically romping from sofa to sofa, yodeling a Mary Martin anthem of hope.

But after my frantic activity I usually went back to my torpor. Sometimes I sat in the backyard or played with the dog, but mostly I remember lying on my bed after school. The bed was maple with little pineapple posts, and a white chenille bedspread. I knew the texture of that bedspread well, knew the bumps the raised chenille made against my cheek, knew the taste of the cotton on my tongue. I knew the pattern of the curtains, the way the light moved in and out of the small room.

It was after Christmas that my father told me and my brother that our mother was going to die in a matter of weeks. Now I think, But of course I must have known that she was going to die eventually. I must have seen her getting more and more ill. I must have realized. . . . And yet I believe, before he told us, I *didn't* know. Judging by the signs I could see, the two signs I always looked for, her face and her behavior, she had been getting better. For I had always believed that she was in the hospital for her face and her "problems."

So when my father said, "She's very close to the end," at first I didn't know what he was talking about. He had to be more explicit. "The doctors say she'll be dead within a few weeks."

"Dead of what?"

He stared at me uneasily, as if it had just occurred to him that no one, himself included, might have mentioned it before. "Cancer," he said. But he never said what kind, nor explained exactly what cancer was.

And then he said, "It will be the best thing." He bent his head and cried.

We were in the living room, the three of us, and my father gathered Bruce and me in his arms and he cried and we cried too, but neither Bruce nor I said much. My mind was spinning, trying to understand this. Dead? So soon? Secretly I had known since the incident with the pills last year that my mother wanted to die. But I'd kept that knowledge to myself, had never told anyone. And no one had ever talked with me about what I'd heard that morning, not my grandmother, mother, or father. I was left with the echo of my mother's shriek, "I want to die, let me die," and the feeling of my own responsibility.

In Christian Science they never spoke of people dying; they used the term "passed on," which evoked only thoughts of a car traveling towards and then over a horizon in the countryside: smaller and smaller and then vanishing. My grandfather was said to have passed on. Years later I learned he had died of cancer of the colon. I had unclear memories of the summer we visited Battle Creek when I was very young of standing by his bedside. The frame was dark walnut and the sheets were white. Grandpa's hair was white too and everyone said he was tired.

No one else I knew had ever passed on, and though I had heard from my father about the deaths of his family members, they were not real people to me, for I had never known them. In Christian Science the error of sickness was often discussed, but not the error of death. There would be no choirs of angels, nor welcoming bands of historical figures and friends, but there was some notion of perfection, some idea of "heaven"—though as usual with the Scientists, there were no pictures, only abstract ideas. The word "death" was linked more for sound than meaning in "death and disease."

It was natural that I brood over the Christian Science attitude towards death when I thought of what was happening to my mother, for through everything that had gone on over the past two years I had maintained my faith in Christian Science. This was partly out of familiarity, partly out of loyalty to my mother, and partly because I genuinely believed in its teachings, knowing no other. You often cling hardest to a faith that has let you down, precisely because you can't face the possibility that without this faith there is nothing.

At ten I was still reciting Mrs. Eddy's phrases almost rotely, conjuring pictures that would make them more memorable. "Perfect love casteth out fear," I would think to myself when I looked at my mother's face. And I would remember the story of *Beauty and the Beast* and try to understand how to love what was frightening to me. But at eleven I began to struggle with doubts. That was when I remember reading the story for Job for the first time and understanding how it could apply to me, to my mother. I began to understand the notion that a loving God could still appear to try our faith. And that we must keep on believing anyway. But at twelve my struggle was more intense. Why, God, why my mother? I asked, after hearing she was going to die. What's going to happen to me without her?

When I lay on my bed after school and realized that death was coming to my mother, I was paralyzed. There was a palpable absence in the house. Everything became a little more ghostly. Sometimes I would get up from my bed and go into my parents' room. I would finger my mother's clothes in the closet. I would look at myself in the mirror and pretend I was in a play. I would recite lines and I would sing to my own reflection.

I sang one of the songs from *Carousel* over and over:

Longin' to tell you,
But afraid and shy,
I'd let my golden chances pass me by.
Soon you'd leave me,
Off you would go in the mist of day,
Never, never to know
How I loved you

One day, a week or two before my mother died, and with the same desperation, self-destructiveness and bizarre hopefulness that had compelled me to butcher my shins with my father's razor, I took a pair of dull scissors to my hair. By now the permanent had grown out and I was left with partly straight and partly wrinkled hair. I'd asked my father to take me to a beauty parlor, but he hadn't had time. So I decided to cut my hair myself after school. I started out confidently and viciously attacking my bangs. The trimming left one side higher than the other and I kept on: once I had demolished the bangs I began on the sides and back. Dark blond hair fell on the wood floor, on my shoulders, in little clumps, in feathery afterthoughts. My round face stared back at me with horrid fascination, as if it were a stranger asking me, how far are you prepared to go—are you going to make me completely bald?

Tears ran down my face: my hopeful frenzy suddenly turned to panic. I didn't look better without the waviness that started just above my ears—I looked worse! Now you could see my ears—and my neck. I was shorn in lumps and pockets. A cowlick stuck out above my forehead, a square little lump of hair dangled above one ear. Thirty years later, I might have looked punk and interesting, but this was early 1963, the years of smooth teases (if you were good) and ratty high teases (if you were bad).

Where before I had looked like Medusa, now I looked like a mental patient.

211

In hysterics I called my father and asked if he could come home and take me to a beauty shop.

"It's going to have to wait till this weekend, honey," he said.

"But Dad," I almost shrieked. "I can't wait. I can't wait. I tried cutting my hair myself. . . ."

I stayed home from school the next morning and my father took me to a beauty shop. My father always had a kind and jokey way with people, but even he looked a little embarrassed as he waited for me. The beautician took hold of my shoulders and stared at me in the mirror. "Never, never, never cut your hair yourself," she said. "You look horrible."

Was it the confirmation that I wanted? That I had made myself as wretched looking on the outside as I felt on the inside?

My father had murmured as he handed me over, "Her mother's been ill a long time." That was always his excuse. He used it over and over to explain my behavior, and it exonerated him. Women sighed sympathetically before they turned their mean and punishing eyes and hands on me. I had no excuse.

"You're old enough to know better!" I must have heard that a million times during the years of my mother's illness. But I was never old enough, I never knew better.

My new haircut was short and odd. It mostly made people think how much better I'd looked before.

"You're such a pretty girl," my father said. "I don't know why you would do a thing like that."

If not wildly pretty, I suppose now, looking back, I was not hideous. But I felt hideous. Hideous in my soul and hideous on my face.

I lay on my bed all afternoon and into the evening, thinking about death. The baby-sitter, Terry, a true child of her mother Dolores, did everything she could to make me feel worse.

She stood in the doorway of my bedroom, the TV humming in the background. "Come in and watch TV," she cajoled at first, then, as I resisted, "Stop feeling so sorry for yourself." And then, turning on her heel in disgust, "Nobody feels as sorry for themselves as you do."

I watched the light drain out of my yellow room with its maple bed and chest of drawers, its little rolltop desk that I had loved so much and now was too small for me. I watched the wall, or sometimes the bedspread, or sometimes my arm. I repeated prayers to myself. I prayed to God. I thought about death, and thought, How could it be different than my mother's absence now? But it was different, I knew. It meant I would never see my mother again. It meant I would have to stop looking for signs she was better. It meant I'd have to stop hoping that someday she would turn back into the mother of my childhood. I thought I'd gotten over that wish a long time ago, but here it was back again. A wish that wouldn't come true now, a chance that would be gone forever. Never again would my mother look at anything I wrote, never again would I hear her say, "That's wonderful." Never again would I see her in her rocking chair, never again would I curl up next to her, never again would I hear her say, "God loves you. There is nothing to be afraid of."

My mother died on March 15, at 2 P.M. in the afternoon. At four o'clock, just after I had gotten home from school, the phone rang in the kitchen. I remember answering it while looking out the kitchen window at my brother who was playing in the backyard. He looked up at me and I remember our eyes locked together, as the man from the funeral home asked about the arrangements. Bruce came inside and I put the phone down without answering the man. I said, "Mama has died." And Bruce and I cried.

Although we'd asked if we could see her, if she could come home one last time, my father had said no, she wasn't well enough. Now he says she was completely insane when she died, that she didn't recognize anyone. She had to be held down, strapped to the bed. I can't imagine it, and yes it would have been horrible to see. And yet I'll always still wish that I was there at the end. I wish I'd touched my mother's face, just once. I wish I had kissed her lips. I wish I had said good-bye.

It was an open-casket funeral, and the funeral home was full of people from the Christian Science church and the neighborhood. The only person who didn't come was my grandmother. Everyone cried very hard, including my brother and me in our new clothes. We held hands in our special pew. The organ music was lugubrious, the sickly scent of the flowers overwhelming; I don't remember a thing that was said. Afterwards, when everyone had gone out to their cars to drive to the cemetery, my father and Bruce and I stood by the casket a few moments.

My mother's face was not peaceful, but hard and waxy and remote; still, I would have given anything to have her back. My father took us in his arms and said, "I'll be your mother now too."

Within nine months he'd be married again and we'd be living in another house with another family in another neighborhood.

There were several months of school left. I went on living through the days just as I had done before. I got up, dressed and walked to school. I walked home with books from the library, made a jelly sandwich and lay on my bed. I bought *West Side Story* and *My Fair Lady*. And sometimes, just as before, I sang the saddest songs and cried.

The only difference was that now I couldn't dress up in my mother's clothes. One day after the funeral, Dolores Bear had come in and packed everything up of my mother's from my parents' closet and had taken it all to the Salvation Army.

I would have liked to shine in my English class, but I remained a B student and never wrote anything I didn't have to. I stopped walking to and from school with Lou Anne after she told me I was being melodramatic. I avoided looking at Mr. Baldwin and I never spoke up in class; I couldn't bear having any attention called to myself, and, in fact, Mr. Baldwin stopped calling on me.

Yet after my mother died Mr. Baldwin was the only teacher who commented on the words written on the pink excuse slip that I had to take around to all my classes the day after her funeral.

He asked me to stay after class and when everyone was gone, he said, looking straight at me with those impossible blue eyes that all the girls raved about, "I'm so sorry to hear this, Barbara. Would you like me to tell the class?"

"Oh, no," I said. "Oh, please don't."

I couldn't think of anything more embarrassing, of anything that would put the last nail in the coffin of my public humiliation in the seventh grade, than to tell the truth.

Chapter 10

Orphans

*G*rowing up in Christian Science had been like acting in a long-running play where all I had to do was repeat the lines that had already been written for me, a series of well-worn, comforting phrases—God loves you; God doesn't want you to hurt; there is no life in matter. But now with my mother, one of the main characters, gone—vanished right off the stage—the dialogue had lost its resonance. I kept repeating the lines, but there was no answering response. And one of the characters, my father, who up to now had spent a large part of his time offstage, was suddenly front and center, improvising lines that were not in the script I had learned, and reciting a lengthy monologue that told a different version of reality, a monologue with lines about tragedy, and about survival.

Before my mother's illness, I hardly knew my father. That is to say, I knew him in the usual way of children who spend most of their time with their mothers and only see their fathers in the evening and on weekends. He was a presence, a kind, loving, joking presence, but a slightly insubstantial one. He did not enter, as my mother had, as both audience and censor, into my world of books and artwork and play-acting. He was, passively at first and then adamantly, not part of the Christian Science society and belief system that had shaped so many of my thoughts and expectations. His world was work, and the way to spend time with him was in that world of work, whether that meant listening to stories of his accounting students, the cute and spunky little gals who were planning to become bookkeepers and the ex-GIs who were going to school in the evenings while supporting families during the day, or visiting him in one of his offices and being shown the adding machine and typewriter.

My father had worked all his life, since he was a boy on the farm in Wisconsin; it was at work that my father was most himself. He had no hobbies or amusements other than work. He never read a book and rarely saw a movie. He didn't play sports, though he kept up with college football. On Wednesday nights, when my mother would go to her Testimony meetings, he would make us a bowl of popcorn and we'd all watch *Wagon Train* together. Other than that, and dinnertime, and occasional car trips, the main place I saw him was at his desk, working on people's taxes or grading papers.

If my mother's life was her religion; my father's was his work. My father had appeared never to have a religion and we had accepted that as children accept all things. There were many Christian Science widows, including my mother's friends Georgina and Edyth. I didn't think of fathers as being religious, and I never asked my father why he didn't go with us or what part of Christian Science he didn't believe. That he had his own distinct philosophy of life was something I never realized, for it was a philosophy that on the surface fit very well with Christian Science: Look on the bright side, keep working as hard as you can and the future will always be better than the past.

This optimistic strain in my father's philosophy of life failed him as surely as my mother's belief in a world free of mortal error. But my father's view of the world had a deeper note, even a fatalistic one, which accounted for tragedy and could accept it. He didn't struggle with reality versus idealism as my mother did. He was not betrayed by an ideology. Nor did he stumble into the shadowy zone of physical and mental illness himself. For his role in life was never to be the victim, but the helpless bystander, in some ways a worse fate. The events surrounding my mother's illness and death simply confirmed for him the truth of an older myth: that he himself was marked in some way. He was singled out for a difficult life, a tragic life. Not because he would suffer directly, but because everyone around him would sicken and die, leaving him always the lonely survivor.

As my father tells it and has told it many times, most recently a few years ago, when I got it all on tape, his first memory is of being taken to a new home, with George and Melissa Wilson, who had adopted him. He was four then. For two years he had been in an orphanage in Freeport, Illinois, with his two brothers. He was the middle child. Leroy was oldest; he died in a diphtheria epidemic that swept through the orphanage. My father almost died, too, but doesn't remember that. He doesn't remember the orphanage, or Leroy or his younger brother Donald, who came into the world as their twenty-year-old mother, went out of it. He doesn't remember his mother, Edith, the Swedish girl who had immigrated from Stockholm with her parents and sister to Wyanet, Illinois, or his father, Walter Stewart, who had put them into the orphanage because he didn't know, at only twenty-four, how to deal with three children under the age of three.

It was 1922. George and Melissa Wilson were tenant farmers, on the move from Illinois to a farm in Wisconsin. They took the train from Rock Falls, Illinois, where they'd been living with Melissa's parents, to Madison, where they were to start their new life with their son. They had changed his name from Cecil Stewart to Cecil Woodrow Wilson. They did not tell him he was adopted. "We were on a train," says my father. "Everybody was singing 'Dinah, won't you blow your horn?' And the train whistle went off and I thought that was part of the song. That was my first remembrance."

George and Melissa Wilson were share tenants. The crops that George Wilson farmed for his percentage were corn and hay. They had about twenty-five cows and a few horses for the plowing. They had no electricity, only kerosene lanterns, and no indoor bathroom or running water. The family bathed once a week in a galvanized tub filled with water boiled on the wood stove. My father wore only overalls until he was twelve. He got a new pair each Christmas, along with a little bag of treats: an apple or an orange, a few pieces of hard candy, and two or three walnuts. "Did you know how poor you were?" I asked my father once and he laughed. "It never occurred to me how poor we were until I went to college and studied sociology."

George Wilson used to beat his wife, and my father. Not often, but regularly. He would go into Madison, to the Italian section, and buy a bottle of "White Lightening." When he was drunk he was brutal, "raging angry," my father says. "One time he grabbed me by the throat and tried to strangle me. He left marks that I had for a long time. Sometimes he was so drunk he couldn't milk the cows. I had to milk them myself, all twenty-two cows."

He adds, "What I couldn't forgive him for was how he beat my adoptive mother when she lay in bed dying of cancer. I used to hear them from the barn—her screams, the tables and chairs overturning—and knew I couldn't do anything about it."

Melissa Wilson died the year that my father was eight. "She went to Rochester, Minnesota, to the Mayo Clinic. I missed her so much. Once I tried to run away from home to see her. My adoptive father found me walking along the railroad tracks and took me home.

"After that, it was just me and him."

My father didn't start school until he was eight, because the school was two and a half miles away and he had to wait until he could walk that far, back and forth. "We were all in the one room, all the grades," he said. "The big boys liked to terrorize the young teachers they'd send us. We had a lot of fun. We put crayons on the wood stove, tacks on the teacher's seat, and once, we managed to get a cow onto the roof of the schoolroom. We used to like to embarrass them in front of their boyfriends. We ran a lot of teachers out of there. But then an older lady came along; she was married, with kids of her own, and she settled our hash pretty quickly."

One day when my father was about nine, after Melissa Wilson had died, he was called out of the schoolroom and told that someone wanted to see him. There in the road, standing by a car ("no one had them where we lived in those days"), was a well-dressed man, a woman, and a little girl. "Hello, Cecil," said the man. "I'm your father. Your real father." Walter Stewart had remarried and moved to Grand Rapids, Michigan. He had a little girl Dorothy, but hadn't forgotten Cecil and had managed to track him down. He promised that he would find a way to get my father back. "You'll come and live with us then," said the man.

"Then he was gone. It was out of the blue. I just saw him for maybe half an hour. I never saw him again."

Walter's efforts to reclaim this son were futile. He died unexpectedly soon after the meeting with his son. My father didn't know that for years, had no way of knowing what had happened to this man who appeared out of nowhere, claiming to be his father, and then disappeared again. It was not until his half-sister, Dorothy, contacted him ten or more years later, that he got the full story. At the time he had no one to ask. He never told George Wilson what had happened.

But he knew now that George Wilson was not his real father. His real father lived in Grand Rapids, Michigan.

My father had often talked about his childhood on the farm to me and my brother when we were growing up, but mostly the stories were jolly ones. We heard about our father horseback riding on the farm, we heard about how the traveling threshers came every August to help with the haying, about the 4-H Club, and the cow on the roof of Estes School. We heard how chocolate bars were a nickel each and as big as your hand.

But my father began to tell other stories, of less fun and more loss, beginning when I was eleven and twelve. He usually told them in the car, when we drove, all three of us or just me and him, to the sanitarium on Saturdays or Sundays. It was on our weekly visits to see my mother that my father told us about the deaths of his mother, his father, Melissa Wilson and, eventually, George Wilson.

Until my father was about nine, when Walter Stewart, his real father, died, he was not technically an orphan. Until he was thirteen and learned through the welfare department that Walter Stewart was dead, he did not know he was an orphan, either. As far as he knew there was always the chance that his real father might turn up again to claim him and take him away. But in my father's stories, the stories he told to us on the way to the sanitarium, only twenty miles away from Long Beach in Compton, but eternally long, the going taken up with a worried tightness in my stomach, and the returning taken up with a never-acknowledged sadness, my father was always an orphan, always had been, always would be.

Orphanhood, I realized from his stories, which were of loss but also possibility, was more than not having parents; it was a mythic state of belonging nowhere and to no one, of learning to be self-reliant and to get ahead on your own, while taking what advantage you could of other people's sympathy for your losses and your courage. In retrospect I see that my father was, perhaps subconsciously, preparing my brother and me for the loss of *our* mother. He was telling us that only some people died and the rest survived, and those who survived had to go on. And perhaps, also subconsciously, he was telling us too: "You think you have it bad, losing your mother. I lost *four* parents." We could never compete with our father's losses, and wouldn't want to.

But if being an orphan was a sad business, we also learned that orphanhood had compensations. One of them was the freedom to invent yourself and be other than who your parents would have brought you up to be, to follow your true nature and not feel guilty about it. Another was the possibility of being helped along the way, by people who never would have crossed your path had you had parents. My father had many stories of people who had helped him, but one of those he most liked telling was the story of his connection with Miss Bush. Miss Maybell Bush was the Superintendent of Public Instruction of the State of Wisconsin, and my father met her when he was twelve in the following manner:

At that time, because he had started school late, he was only in the fifth grade, with just one other student, a girl. All his friends, either the same age or older, were in the seventh grade. They were all in the same schoolroom, but my father could see the day when they would graduate from the Estes School, going on to high school or going to work on their farms, and leaving him alone with the girl. He decided that he wanted to skip a grade or two, but his teacher told him that this was outside her power; he would have to go to the State Capitol in Madison and talk to the Superintendent of Instruction. So, early one morning he set off, in his one pair of overalls, catching a ride with the milk truck that picked up milk from the local dairies and brought them into town. He took a streetcar to the State Capitol Building and marched up the broad, sweeping staircase until he came to a sign that said DEPARTMENT OF PUBLIC INSTRUCTION. The receptionist, Louise Ziske, referred him to the Superintendent, Miss Bush.

Like all legendary figures, the details about Miss Bush are blurred. Now when I ask questions, the answers are vague. How old was she? "Oh, I don't know—late forties maybe—maybe only thirty. You can't tell when you're young." What did she look like? "Oh, she was a good-looking lady." Well, what kind of a person was she? He can only shake his head. She was Miss Bush, that's all.

The main thing about Miss Bush is this: she changed my father's life. She saved him.

Miss Bush took a liking to my father, to the brashness of this blond-haired, blue-eyed farm boy in overalls turning up in her office, and arranged for him to take the sixth and seventh grades together. More, she kept in touch with him. She took him out to lunch that day and in months to come. She loaned him books, she took him to the movies. When he graduated from the eighth grade, she bought him his first suit, along with a new shirt, shoes, a tie, and even a hat. She decided that my father needed to be taken away from George Wilson, whose alcoholism and abuse were increasing. She also determined that my father should go to college and that therefore he needed to go to high school and take college prep courses.

At fourteen my father left George Wilson's tenant farm for good and moved into Madison into the foster home of a family named Webster. For a year he was idyllically happy. The Websters had, among other urban amenities, indoor plumbing and a real bathtub. He attended Madison East High, studied Latin and algebra, which he liked, and at the end of the year received the Daughters of the American Revolution award. "I was thoroughly, exceedingly happy," my father says, and to prove it, adds, "I remember the address of the Websters—321 Riverside Drive."

He only stayed with the Websters a year. When my father told Miss Bush that he thought he was adopted, the Welfare Agency of the State of Wisconsin began to search for his "real" family and for relatives who could take him in. They found dozens of relatives in Illinois, Stewarts and Swansons, uncles, aunts, first and second cousins, even grandparents. My father was forced to leave Madison and Miss Bush for the home of his father's brother, Robert Stewart, Uncle Bob, who lived with his wife and two daughters in La Moille, Illinois.

"If I hadn't met Miss Bush," my father says, "I don't know what would have become of me. She's the one who first saw something in me, who made me believe in myself, who challenged me intellectually. She's the reason I could never fit in with my relatives."

My father, with his new, proud image of himself as the self-reliant young orphan, was astounded to realize that he was only a tiny part of the vast Stewart clan. "When they had their family reunions in Princeton, hundreds of people came. I had more than fifty first cousins alone. They used to say you had to show up just to keep from being talked about." He was also introduced in this period to his Swedish grandparents, who still barely spoke English, in nearby Wyanet, and his two aunts, Hulda and Gladys.

He didn't take to his new relatives, not after Miss Bush had expanded his horizons with her lunches and books. Uncle Bob wanted to leave the farm to my father, if my father was willing to take on the responsibility; but my father insisted on continuing his studies. "I was the first Stewart in all that bunch to ever attend high school, much less college." He went to La Moille High School, where, doubtless to Uncle Bob's disgust, he played Archibald Throckmorton in the play *Blue Moon,* and was president of his junior class. But after two years of quarreling about education, the summer before my father's senior year, Uncle Bob dumped him off one day at his grandparents. That was when my father decided to say good-bye to all his newly found relatives. He packed his bags and set off on his own.

He hired himself out as a hand during threshing season, for room and board and thirty dollars a month. After the hay and corn were harvested, he ended up in Milledgeville, Illinois, breaking stone in the rock quarry. Determined to finish his senior year, however, he asked around and heard of the Bushman family, who owned a big farm across from Milledgeville Union High. The day before school started my father knocked at the Bushmans' door. Impressed with my father's earnest desire to improve himself, the Bushmans took the boy in for a year. And as my father always triumphantly ends this section of the story, "The next spring I graduated valedictorian of my class and received a four-year scholarship to Illinois State Normal University."

And the Stewarts and Swansons? "I never saw them again. I'd been brought up alone. I suppose I never really accepted the fact that I was somebody other than a Wilson," my father says.

"Wilson" in our reduced family after my mother's death was a code name for pride and self-reliance and tragedy that could be survived. In spite of the fact that it is a common and boring name, which doesn't reflect any ethnic heritage particularly and not my own heritage of Irish and Swedish, in spite of the fact that being a W has meant sitting in the back of the classroom, being near the end of a roll call and usually discovering my books on the bottom shelf at the bookstore, I have found myself unable to change my name. I thought about it once or twice, and then gave up. I knew I could never break my connection to the memory of my father holding us kids close over the coffin and saying, "I'll be your mother now," and "We Wilsons will always stick together."

In grade school my brother liked to draw, and his notebooks were scribbled with drawings of cars and rockets in blue pen. He also did cartoon-like figures and, for a time during our mother's illness and after her death, he produced an occasional comic strip called "Elmer the Snail."

The plot of "Elmer" was always pretty much the same. The first frame showed a sun in the sky and all well with the world. Elmer, very small, was at the center of that world, on a surfboard, or sunning himself on a towel; he might be having a picnic on a leaf or taking a stroll down the sidewalk; he might be doing any number of innocent things, preoccupied by his own happiness and slow snail purpose. His balloon message was always the same: "Gee, it's a nice day." In the second frame, however, something seemed awry, though what it was, was not yet visible. The sun still shone, though it was slightly behind a cloud now, and Elmer continued on with his day, pausing only to ask, "What's that funny noise?"

"Splat," "crash," "crunch" was the answer. The surfboard overturned in a huge wave; a foot came down on the sidewalk; the tree branch broke off. Elmer flew or smashed to bits then, his only balloon cry: "Aieee!"

My brother and I found this simple three-frame story hilarious and immensely satisfying, and we often quoted it to each other.

Barbara: Gee, it's a nice day.
Bruce: What's that funny noise?
Bruce and Barbara: Aieeeee!

The strip encapsulated something we both already knew about life. That it only seemed to be sunny and safe. That any minute, with only the slightest warning—an airplane buzzing overhead, a motor starting up nearby, even leaves rustling in the breeze—that security could be shattered.

Our lives had been devastated by a single, unexpected event and its consequences, but in the strip we could laugh at our fate. How hopeful Elmer the Snail was and how innocent. And yet his hopefulness and innocence couldn't save him from being destroyed, over and over. My brother never tired of drawing this strip and devising new ways for Elmer to meet his end, and I never tired of reading them, or of reciting the lines with my brother. Even saying, "Gee, it's a nice day!" could send me and Bruce into paroxysms of laughter, to our father's mystification.

There was something of the same fascination with unexpected disaster in the flexible, long-running stories I'd been telling my brother in the evenings as we washed dishes, those long, slow evenings that had been going on for years. In the earliest days, after our mother's abrupt departure from the house, we'd had Grandma and Terry next door to baby-sit. Later on we learned to fend for ourselves. That was a phrase that hadn't previously been part of our vocabulary, but our father had introduced it to us: "You'll have to fend for yourselves tonight," he would call and tell us. By twelve years old I was considered old enough to be the baby-sitter on the two nights of the week Dad taught and to make sure we ate dinner and washed the dishes. These dinners weren't exciting: on Mondays we had Swanson's frozen chicken pot pies; on Wednesdays we had fried minute steaks and tater tots, with a small can of peas. Even when Dad was home in the evenings, he was out in his office grading papers and doing taxes. He might make dinner, but he left us to do the dishes and to make our own entertainment for the evening: homework, reading, and TV. Doing the dishes always seemed an enormous project. My stories about the boy and girl who went down the drain to have adventures were meant to ease the boredom of the task, but usually they just ended up prolonging it.

The tale of Jack and Nancy Feeble had begun innocently, with voyages down the drain in their saucer boat, but over the years worse things had happened to them. They never knew what monster they would meet, what disaster would befall them. It was certain that they would meet up with terrible creatures or find themselves in scary circumstances, and they would usually barely escape with their lives. Down in the drain, hurricanes whirled up and sudden waterfalls and fierce waterspouts came from nowhere. Jack and Nancy had to do battle not only with the elements but also with slime devils and giant dragonflies and the dreaded Monkawheezos, their persistent enemy.

Jack and Nancy had no parents, though from time to time it appeared that they had younger siblings that they had to save and bring through danger. They were orphans and had to fend for themselves. Nancy was older, but only just barely. She didn't take advantage of it, however, any more than Jack thought he was better because he was a boy. They were in this together, and they often told each other this in the midst of the very worst that could happen. "Hang on tight, Jack, we're sinking." "Don't give up, Nancy! We can make it to the shore if we grab that branch." "Don't let go, Jack." "Nancy, I'm holding on to you. Make a reach."

One constant in our lives throughout those years was our swimming lessons at the Pacific Coast Club downtown. Every Saturday morning Dad would drop us off and we'd spend much of the day there. We always had strict instructions not to leave the club, or to venture out onto the beach outside the club's bamboo enclosure, but for a long time we had been ignoring that. There simply wasn't enough at the club to keep us busy. After our swimming lessons we'd bounce on the trampolines and climb the monkey bars in the gym, then we'd invariably head for the beach. In summer we'd swim in the ocean and in winter we'd walk on the shore, or dash over the dunes playing "Escape from the Mean Uncle."

But at some point—perhaps by the time I was eleven and had figured out that to be independent you had to lie about it—we began to explore the city of Long Beach that lay so enticingly outside the glass front door of the club. Down the red-carpeted stairs we'd go, under the awning. On either side of this fake Norman castle of a building were stone sentries with trumpets. Suddenly we would be standing right on Ocean Boulevard, where every summer during the Miss Universe contest, girls from every state and many countries would wave at us from floats that conjured up their native land.

The first or second time Bruce said, thrilled, "We're going to get in trouble," but I just shrugged that off. "Follow me. I know the way."

I had no map of the city, had never seen a map of it, but its grid was etched on my brain through years of observation, and I led Bruce confidently along Ocean to Pine Street, to Buffums Department Store, where we rode the elevators and looked at the children's books in the green baize and walnut-paneled little bookshop on the first floor. From there we went to Woolworth's and to the Kress 5-and-10 store, across the street from the beauty college where our mother used to have her hair done sometimes. It somehow brought her back a little to be walking the streets where she had walked in happier times.

A Saturday or two later we made our way to the Pike, the old amusement park on the shore. It had been a long time since we'd been there, for the Pike, once the glittering showpiece of the Pacific, had grown seedy. Since Disneyland had opened six or seven years ago, the Pike, which had never been just for children and families, had become more a grown-up sort of place than ever, filled with sideshows, blood banks, tattoo parlors. Sailors from all parts of the world strolled singly and in groups, sometimes accompanied by the girls they'd met or picked up.

Bruce and I shouldn't have been there, but, naturally, it made it even better that it was forbidden. We walked cautiously through the arcades full of shops selling shell-encrusted purses and ceramic hula girls with real grass skirts and coffee cups that said "Souvenir of Long Beach, Calif." and postcards that showed the skyline of the city, with the Villa Riviera and the Pacific Coast Club against a cloudless blue sky. We stood gape-mouthed under the Gondola rides and Cyclone Racer, waiting for people to be tossed off into the sea. We lingered at the Carousel to hear the oompah music and wished hard we had money to ride the Bumper Cars so we could smash into each other and total strangers. We wanted tattoos that said "MOM" inside a heart or that pictured a green dragon breathing red fire. We were careful and quick and said nothing if anyone talked to us; we were terrified and hopeful that the weary barker at one of the sideshows might hook us into the tent with his cane and feed us to the Cannibal-Man, or that some sailor in whites with a cigarette dangling from his lip might offer us some drugs. For an hour or two we wandered without the money to scare ourselves on the rides or to gorge ourselves on the salty, sweet food, on foot-long hot dogs in meltingly soft rolls, or popcorn yellow as poppies, or cinnamon-red candy apples that could break your teeth with their glass coating.

Of course, every other minute that we weren't intensely enjoying ourselves, we were worried about the time, and about being caught, about being lost and about people from the roller coasters flying off into the sea, and about being kidnapped by drug-crazed sailors from South America. It was like being in a foreign country without parents or adults to say no to everything. It was like being Nancy and Jack Feeble, the brave and adventurous orphans of the Kingdom of the Drain. But it was also not a story; it was real life, and so, much better, and much scarier.

It was Bettye's furniture I disliked first. During the last few weeks of seventh grade, in my obligatory Homemaking class, we had been studying interior decoration. I'd been a total failure at sewing (managing to put a zipper in upside down not once, but twice) and at cooking ("Why are your muffins so . . . watery, Barbara?" "I don't know, Mrs. Sawyer.

I did everything right. One cup of flour, four cups of water. . . ." "That's four *tablespoons* of water.") But during the two-week section on interior decoration, I came into my own. I drew house plans, apartment plans, plans for bedrooms and plans for kitchens. I checked out *House Beautiful* and *Sunset Magazine* from the library. I loved befores and afters and wandered around our house imagining valances and recessed nooks. I kept a notebook that I filled with sketches of Queen Anne and Chippendale chairs, but that was just to give myself an idea of the history of furniture. Actually, I preferred country pine, bold checks and stripes and the colors of mint green and cobalt blue. If I could have, I would have filled the house with branches of apple blossoms or stalks of orchids; on the walls hung some good reproductions—Matisse was a favorite, or Paul Klee; in the bath placed fresh thick towels on shining racks and soaps in different shapes in shell-shaped dishes; and in the country kitchen put copper saucepans on the walls and a big bowl of fruit on the heavy pine table. Of course we had no money for this kind of thing, but I still dreamed of it, for what I was really dreaming of was transforming the old unhappy life into something new and wonderful, freshening it and beautifying it. When I wandered through our plain little bungalow, I saw a different life ahead for us, and in my mind we already lived in the house that I had designed.

Bettye had teak Danish modern. The sofa and one of the chairs had square cushions, covered in a nubby orange material, an orange the color of lifejackets, not autumn leaves. The other chair was a swivel armchair upholstered in sky blue. There was also an astonishingly ugly gilt cupid attached to the wall from which a spray of plastic ferns surged out. That sofa and those chairs and especially the cupid told me, the moment I walked in, that I wouldn't like her.

We'd been invited to her house for a Sunday barbecue, and my father had said nothing more than that. For years we'd been invited around to other people's houses, to brunches and barbecues and picnics. We went. We ate off paper plates and drank sodas. We played with their children, if they had any. We came home.

But Bettye was different. She was not like the widow we had sometimes visited with my father, a woman who was kind and quiet and wore old-lady shoes and made sure our plates were filled. Bettye had short champagne-tinted blond hair, a pug nose, and light blue eyes with powder-blue shadow on the lids. She wore pedal-pushers and a sleeveless knit top with a scoop neck that showed her pale, rather thick skin.

227

She smoked Salems from a cigarette holder and walked around the orangey shag rug of her house in leather thong sandals with a fake jewel between the toes. She had a martini in her hand, and then she had another. She had a large, red-lipped smile that sent a slight shiver down my back, me, who wanted desperately for anyone to smile at me and like me. Who was she? How did he meet her? On the way there my father was offhand. An acquaintance from the world of work, he said. A bookkeeper. On the way home, though, he asked, "Did you have a good time? Did you like her?"

"Yes," we'd answered enthusiastically to the first question, and, "Yes, I guess," to the second. It didn't occur to us that our answer meant anything. We'd had a good time not because of Bettye but because there were some other kids there, Bettye's seventeen-year-old-son Mike and some of his friends. And even though they were in high school they'd been nice to us. We'd played a board game and Mike had made us laugh and laugh with his jokes.

And it was probably because we were thinking of Mike, that when my father asked, a little nervously, "Would you like to go over there again sometime?" Bruce and I said, "Sure."

Every morning that summer I got up and rode the bus over to the junior high where I was taking an art class. It was the first time I had taken a bus by myself, and it made me feel happy and adult do this one thing every day, this one thing that organized and gave coherence to my life. The sadness of the spring was giving way to a new hopefulness. My hair had grown out and looked normal now: I wore it behind a headband. My body was lengthening and shaping itself somehow. I seemed older in the mirror and felt older, too. I was the woman of the house now. I was growing up. At this junior high no one knew me or remembered my unhappiness, my strangeness in the seventh grade. Every day I lost myself in large amounts of construction paper, poster paint, and crayons. My teacher was a wild and crazy guy who used to play records of the Smothers Brothers singing and joking their way through songs like "I yelled fire when I fell into a vat of chocolate."

When we went over to Bettye's house, which we did frequently though not regularly that summer, Mike was often there. He and I would usually talk about books. He seemed to have read everything: Hemingway, Dostoyevsky, Norman Mailer, authors I'd heard about and wanted to read, but that so far I had been told were too old for me, and that were not available in the junior high library or in the public library without an adult card, which you had to be fourteen to get.

"That's just stupid!" said Mike. "I'll get you any book you want! When I was your age, why, I was reading Freud!"

I told him I wanted to be a writer, that I had started writing poetry.

"That's fantastic!" he said. "Have you read the Beats? No, oh, you've got to read the Beats!"

I had been reading Emily Dickinson and Sara Teasdale. "Oh those are the old-lady poets they teach in school," Mike said. "You need to read the great writers. Like Kerouac. The Beats."

"Is e.e. cummings a Beat?" I asked uncertainly.

"No. He's dead. But he's fantastic," said Mike.

"I *know*," I said. "He's my favorite." Actually, I had only recently discovered him, through a paperback of *100 Selected Poems* that I'd gotten at the library. For some reason, the librarians didn't class poetry as adult books, and I'd been checking out different authors all summer.

I had begun to see how poetry could bridge the gap between the trivial world of young adult literature and the world of true literature, which I had entered a few times through books like *David Copperfield* and *Wuthering Heights* but which I had not yet come to inhabit fully. I was still longing, and had been longing for over a year, for the richly absorbing stories of my childhood, which had spoken of life's great hopes and desires, and in which I'd dwelled as if they were second homes. Now poetry began to speak to me in the urgent way that fairy tales once had, setting free my imagination and making deep emotions—not just a few emotions but a range of emotions, existing right next to each other— seem natural and right. Poetry spoke of death, but it also spoke of joy.

I had understood perhaps a third of the e.e. cummings poems in the book I read. Many of his scoffing, jocose, antipatriotic poems were unintelligible to me, as was the substance of the erotic poems. But I skipped over lines I didn't understand and tried to grasp his essential meaning. And this was not as hard as I imagined, for some of what made e.e. cummings seem familiar to me was his Emerson-inspired approach to nature and his fractured syntax, which turned up in Mrs. Eddy's writing all the time.

nothing false and possible is love
(who's imagined, therefore limitless)

love's to giving as to keeping's give;
as yes is to if,love is to yes

So e.e. cummings wrote, but it's not impossible to imagine Mrs. Eddy, with ecstatic pen, scribbling similar lines in an early edition of *Science and Health* (before the professional editor got hold of it). Like Mrs. Eddy, cummings was fond of using nature as metaphor, not bothering with exact description. There are flowers galore scattered through his poems and fifteen of the *100 Selected Poems* exult in some way about spring (and April is the favorite month). Along with his diatribes against government and war are little paeans and awakenings, joyful evocations of love, dizzy flows of sap, newness, freshness, spiritual aliveness. All untitled, all artfully jumbled on the page in a medley of lowercase rhymes, imaginative syntax, and nonsensical punctuation.

Reading these poems awakened joy in me too, and joy was what I was after. I copied out lines, chanted them to myself and tried to imitate cummings's lightness of touch and playful tone. Like many beginning writers I believed that writing poetry was easier than writing fiction, simply because the lines were shorter and all you had to write was ten or twelve lines to have a finished poem.

I read cummings's poems about love, and something began to stir in me. My mother was dead and I was alone, but being alone could be good, being motherless could be romantic. I wanted to live. I wanted to write. I wanted to be in love. I wanted to be thirteen. I read e.e. cummings and began to put Mike in the picture.

At seventeen he was not tall, but he was very thin, even bony. His skin was thickly freckled and his face marked with acne scars. He had a reddish-brown crew cut and very white teeth. He was never still an instant; he jumped, he twirled, he danced around. He wore white T-shirts and a medallion around his neck. He smoked. He was grandiose and lively, a whirlwind, a life force. You couldn't help feeling more alive in his presence, and both my brother and I were drawn to him. We never paid the slightest bit of attention to Bettye when we visited. We were always with Mike, out in the backyard shooting baskets or playing catch, taking a spin down to the liquor store in his mother's car, cooking up something in the kitchen. "Oh, Mom," he'd say to Bettye when she told him not to do something. He cajoled and teased her and he wrapped his grandmother around his little finger too. Mrs. Michaelson was in her sixties; she still worked as a maid for a wealthy family in Beverly Hills, but was thinking of retiring. "Oh, Grandma," Mike would say. "Don't say no. Only five dollars. . . ." And she couldn't resist him; she'd go straight to her pocketbook. He was not to be resisted, he was irresistible.

In August my father took Bruce and me on a two-week vacation all the way up through California to Crater Lake in Oregon. We went in our used Chevy station wagon, which broke down twice. Once, on the way north, on a boiling hot day in Merced in California's Central Valley. And once on the way home, on an equally hot day in Paso Robles. In between we saw zebras running wild on the grounds of San Simeon and bought backscratchers and an abacus in San Francisco's Chinatown. We drove through redwood forests and walked along windswept beaches. We stayed in motels with names like Driftwood Inn and Sequoia Motel. We ate a lot of hamburgers and chocolate malts. We bought souvenirs from roadside stands and collected stones and shells we found on the beaches.

In the car we sang songs from *Oklahoma!* and other musicals, and songs my father knew: "From the Halls of Montezuma," and "I've Been Working on the Railroad." None of us could hold a tune, but that didn't matter. My father still told his stories about orphanhood, but the emphasis was now on the possibilities of life, not just the tragedies. When we were having an especially good time, he would say, "We're the Wilsons!" He had given us his orphan name and included us in his own category of survivor. We were like him. What was bad was in the past. We'd gotten through it, not unscathed, but alive. And from now on life could only be better.

Since my mother had died, my sense of God had been fleeting. I never said to myself that I didn't believe, and I continued to go most weeks to Christian Science Sunday School and to read the Bible aloud and even from time to time to dredge up a positive story to tell as an example of God's healing power. But my certainties had been shaken; not only my certainties, but the belief that I belonged somewhere in this marvelous universe. My sense of the numinous, the ineffable in all daily things, the spirituality that was different from, though consistent with, my religious teaching—all that was gone. Not all at once, but gradually, so gradually that I hardly noticed it, so that the absence of God in my world had become like the absence of sunlight. The world had gradually dimmed until it had a permanent sad blue cast.

But that had been changing in the last couple of months, since seventh grade ended, since my art class, since my discovery of poetry, since our new friend Mike had appeared.

The last day at Crater Lake I took a short walk by myself to an overlook near the hotel, and I sat on a sun-warmed stone bench. Because of the steep sides of the cone, the lake was already in shadow, and that made it—already deep, deeper than anyone knew—seem unearthly. Up here the sky was still bright blue, the air warm with the strong scent of pine needles. Something was juxtaposed and I felt that. The deep, almost frightening feeling of the dark blue lake, and the brilliant airiness of my fragrant, warm viewpoint. *That* was the poetic feeling. Both things at once.

I had e.e. cummings, my new sacred text, with me and I opened to one of my favorite poems:

> *i thank You God for most this amazing*
> *day:for the leaping greenly spirits of trees*
> *and a blue true dream of sky;and for everything*
> *which is natural which is infinite which is yes*
>
>   .   .   .
>
> *(now the ears of my ears awake and*
> *now the eyes of my eyes are opened)*

I read this poem and it seemed to me that for the first time in years I was truly, purely happy. It had begun earlier in the summer and had reached its peak today. I was happy, not with the old unconscious happiness of childhood when I had looked at the world and seen that it was good, but with a new consciousness of having lost something immensely important but having gained something as well. What I had gained was a knowledge of my own aliveness, my determination to be alive. There was joy in that feeling, a fragile tenderness and hope. Things would be better. They were already better. I had my father. I had my brother. My hair was normal. I was reading and writing poetry.

"Now the eyes of my eyes are opened," I chanted as I flung my arms wide to embrace the blue of lake and the warm pine smell of the trees. "Now the nose of my nose is smelling. Now the mouth of my mouth is tasting: Now the heart of my heart is opening."

It was the last time for many years I would feel as happy.

That evening, over dinner, my father told us he was going to marry Bettye. We were having a last meal at a nice restaurant and were dressed up. We'd been told we could have what we wanted and I had ordered duckling in orange sauce, the most unusual thing on the menu. But as soon as he told us, I couldn't eat it, and it got stickier and colder on the plate in front of me.

"You children need a mother," Dad was explaining while he ate. "You can't have a normal life without a mother. You need help, Barbara, to grow into a young lady, and Bruce too, he's still just a little boy; he needs a mother."

"We don't need anybody!" I protested. "We know how to fend for ourselves."

"It's too much for me," he said. "Being responsible for you kids and having to work."

"But we hate her!"

Dad looked taken aback. "I thought you liked to go over there?"

"We only like Mike."

For the first time Bruce spoke, "Is Mike going to be our brother?"

"Mike will live with us too," said my father. "At least for his last year of high school."

I could see that Bruce was thinking it might not be so bad if Mike was there.

"He won't be our brother!" I said. "She won't be our mother! She'll never be my mother. None of them are like us. They're not Wilsons."

But it had all been decided already. The two of them had arranged everything. Their two houses would be sold and we would move to a bigger house. Bettye's mother would come to live with us too and help with the housework, since Bettye would continue working.

"You kids need a mother," my father kept saying. And never said, "I need a wife."

One evening, a few years ago, right around the anniversary of my mother's death in March, I happened to turn on the television to the program *20/20*. Without warning I found myself in a room of a converted house in Portland, Oregon, where children sat around on pillows talking with each other and counselors about the death of a parent or sibling. Opened in the 1980s, this house, The Dougy Center, was the prototype for many other groups in the country. It was a place children could come to ask questions, share feelings, and grieve openly. They had counselors, but most of all they had each other and the possibility of telling the truth. Some of the children came immediately after the death, some years later. Some had been coming to the center for years and now participated in groups with more recently bereaved children as peer support.

In the course of the program several of the children were interviewed about how it felt to lose a parent. These were some of the things they said:

"I don't feel able to talk to friends, to kids at school."

"You feel awkward, like people would gossip about it."

"You have dreams about them."

"You feel like their death was your fault."

The children were often very angry, and the center held a "volcano room," where they could hit things and blow off steam. Many of the kids said their other grieving parent didn't want to talk about the death. Other adults, such as teachers, would say, "It's time to move on now." One pudgy-faced boy said passionately, "You don't forget. You don't stop grieving."

A little girl said, "Putting away the photographs, that's the worst thing you can do."

And a boy, when asked how often he thought of his mother, who had been dead for two years, said seriously, "About three times a day . . . and when anybody says the word 'Mother.' "

These children all said things I'd remembered feeling at the time of my mother's death, but that had remained locked in my heart for thirty years. It would have seemed unimaginable when I was a child for anyone to ask me what I felt.

My father, from his own grief as well as for our supposed benefit, never mentioned my mother after she died. We never visited the gravesite or looked at photographs of her. Some of this was of course due to the nature of my mother's illness and death. Her memory was disturbing and much of what had happened was unresolved and unexplained. The habit of silence had, in fact, begun right from the start, and had been as much my mother's choice as anyone. My mother never spoke to us about anything that had happened or would happen, not about her face, her illness, or her death. Whether or not she still believed in God, she still maintained the old rules of her faith. In my father's case it was both denial and superstition that kept him silent.

"It's always other people who fall by the wayside," my father once told me. "I go on." My father's stories of the dead did not teach us about mourning, only about *surviving*. He never mentioned the feelings he'd had for the people who died; he dwelt on what he had managed without relatives; he dwelt on his sense that he was special, that his being alive while others didn't make it meant he would continue, wonderingly, to survive. The dead belonged to the past. But, in fact, it only *seemed* that he had left them behind; their ghosts were with him always, and Bruce and I were aware of them, and carried the burden of them. Just as we'd had to carry our mother's unexpressed pain—her religious struggle, her disfigurement, her madness and death wish—so did we have to shoulder our father's reawakened anguish at losing yet another woman he had loved. All his unacknowledged pain was our pain too, and it left little room for what we might feel ourselves.

Although our father told us he was marrying so we could have a mother, in reality he was marrying to have another woman in his life. We didn't know it then, but this was not the first time this had happened. Once before, our father had been married, and once before he had seen his wife die of cancer, and once before he had short-circuited his grieving process by finding a new woman—our own mother—to help him get over the loss of the old.

Marion was a waitress he met during the war in Long Beach. She was nineteen when they married and twenty-three when she died of lymphoblastoma. She was ill for about two and a half years, the same length as my mother's illness. She was part of the reason that our father spent the war fighting "The Battle of Santa Ana," as he'd jokingly called it. We thought he had been teaching pilots how to identify enemy aircraft, and he had, but he had also often been on compassionate leave to help care for Marion and to watch her die. Within a year after her death he was seeing my mother. It wasn't for some years that I would hear about Marion. There were no pictures of her, no one went to her grave, and no one ever mentioned her name.

That November, a week or two before my father and Bettye were married, the president was killed. It was a sunny, windy day, and I was out

235

on the girls' playfield with my gym class playing soccer when the news reached us. No one believed it for a moment. It must be a joke, or a mistake. President Kennedy, that handsome life force in the White House, might have been shot, but he wasn't *killed*. Then someone said, Look at the flag. In the stiff breeze the Stars and Stripes was moving steadily down the flagpole.

We watched some of the funeral on TV at Bettye's, where we were gathered post-Thanksgiving. The house was in a tumult with her relatives and neighbors coming in and out, but the news was kept on all day and every so often someone would look over, see the cortège or the flag-draped coffin or a close-up of beautiful sad Jackie in her thin black veil, and say, "What a terrible tragedy," "What is this country coming to?" or "I never agreed with him, but assassination?" Bruce and I were running through the house once on our way to play a game of hide-and-seek with Mike and some of the neighbor kids, when I saw, from the corner of my eye, Caroline and John on screen, solemn and small next to their mother. They've lost their father, I thought, and it hurt me, with some unexpected, wrenching pain, to realize how young they were, how many years they were going to have to live through, without his presence, with only his memory.

Then I kept running, out of the house with the others. Mike had chosen me to be his team partner and we raced across lawns to a spot he knew behind a hibiscus bush. There my future stepbrother sat me on his knee and told me I was interesting and pretty. There Mike gave me my first kiss. There he assured me that the coming marriage wouldn't be such a bad thing. There, behind the sweet hibiscus, in the twilight of that sorrowful day, my own sorrow, my own work of mourning, was interrupted, in the arms of someone who held me on his knee and told me that he cared.

Chapter 11

Wicked

*A*fter the wedding in December we moved into a new house. It was two stories with four bedrooms and three baths. One of the bedrooms took up half the second story of the house. Bettye referred to it as the "Master Suite." It was a house beyond our means, given my father's medical debts and Bettye's extravagant habits, but, then, that whole first year they were married was beyond our means.

Before we moved in Bettye had the house done over by an interior decorator from a furniture store in a suburban shopping mall. She dumped the Danish modern and went French provincial. The living room furniture was upholstered in white brocade and then covered with plastic slipcovers. Mock Impressionist paintings of fiacres rolling through rainy Parisian streets hung about the walls in gilded baroque frames. She had brought her gilt cupid plant holder from the other house and it was attached to a wall in the dining room. Then she'd bought another gold cupid, free-standing and about three feet tall. Both of them spilled green plastic ferns and gathered dust. It was unclear what the point of the living room was, since we were not allowed to enter it except to vacuum and to dust.

The den off the kitchen, where we spent most of our family life, was a herd of Naugahyde, with three large vibrating recliners jostling for space with our old Magnavox TV and a card table for Bettye's nightly poker and fantan games. The card table was used for dinner as well, because the real dining room, with its heavy French provincial table and eight chairs, like the white-upholstered living room, was judged "too good" to actually use. That meant that the adults—Bettye, her mother, and my father—squeezed around the card table, while my brother and Mike and I sat at a black-and-white tile bar that was across the room and that faced the open kitchen.

The bedrooms had all been done up too: downstairs was where Bettye's mother would live when she was with us, and upstairs Bruce and Mike shared a room. The Master Suite had a bath of its own, a television, and a small refrigerator. With its brocade-spread-covered king-size bed, and two occasional chairs around a hexagonal table, it looked like a motel room, and smelled like one too, of stale cigarette smoke and air-conditioning. It was the only room in the house to have an air conditioner. It was also the only room to have a lock on the door, right from the beginning.

My new bedroom had been decorated in an orgy of pink and lavender. The walls were pink, the drapes were pale pink, even the carpet, though actually gray, seemed to reflect the rose color of the ceiling and walls. On either side of my familiar old bed were two chests of drawers, each dominated by a gigantic lavender and white ruffled lamp with a milk-glass base. There was a padded lavender rocking chair, and the gilt-framed reproduction over my desk was Renoir's "Girl with Watering Can."

"Pink!" I said to my father when I saw it. "And where's my bookcase?"

"Bettye had it put in the closet," he said. "She thought it was out of place here." Nervous at my stunned reaction, he went on, "Bettye put a lot of work into making this house nice for us. You can't tell her that you don't like it. She'd be hurt."

"But I *hate* it. I hate pink."

"You'll have to get used to it," he told me, not for the first time and certainly not for the last.

The pink room was only the beginning. Bettye had other plans for transforming me into a different type of girl. She took me shopping and to the beauty parlor with her. My clothes, which had been peculiar and few, soon smartened up, and my hair, grown out from its permanent and butchering of the year before, was cut in a pageboy. They took me to an orthodontist, who removed four teeth and put on braces. By January, Bettye had me enrolled in a six-week charm-school course. Her belief—now that they were married, she felt free to expound on it endlessly—was that my brother and me, and especially me, had been allowed to run wild. It wasn't our fault exactly (though she implied that someone had fallen down on the job long before my mother got sick), but now things were going to be different.

The charm school was located in a miniature ersatz chateau of the sort that were once common in the older sections of Long Beach and Los Angeles. Our ages in my evening class ranged from teenage to middle age. At thirteen I was the youngest in the group, and since I wasn't allowed to wear make-up, most of the lessons on "making the most of your features" were actually useless, as were the long discussions over whether one should "color" or not. Building a wardrobe of basic black evening dresses and accessories was a lesson also lost on me. I had never worn black, had no jewelry, and couldn't imagine putting on a scarf. The one thing I remember was the endless practice of sitting with knees and ankles together, and of walking back and forth in the model's sultry slink, hips forward, buttocks tucked well in, shoulders proudly back, chin lifted.

It was Bettye who drove me to my charm-school class and Bettye who picked me up. Our conversations were one-sided: me monosyllabic, Bettye voluble with stories of how she wished her mother had been able to send her to charm school, but how she had picked up her taste on her own anyway. Since her teenage years, she'd often been asked to model and had frequently been begged by her restaurant-owner friends to come work for them as a hostess. "Just by being myself," she bragged, "they said I'd increase their business fifty percent."

These weekly conversations with me in the car, along with the occasional visit to her beauty salon, were Bettye's way of initially trying to establish some sort of bond between us, a bond that was on her terms. She talked at me about her life and rarely asked me questions about school or friends. She never mentioned my mother, nor my religion; everything that had happened in my life before she came into it was of little interest to her. She wasn't a stupid woman by any means, but her intelligence ran in other directions.

She liked good times, drinking and cards, shopping and eating out. In her best moods she was vivacious and lively. Although I didn't understand it then, she was sexy in an overblown, starlet-past-her-prime sort of way, with her champagne hairdo, polished nails, cigarette holder and jeweled sandals, and men found her attractive. She liked to be in the company of men—her son, my father, her brothers. She had one woman friend; all the rest were male. She threw back her head when she laughed, a bubbling, throaty laugh, and had a hundred little whims and fancies and phrases that, like the "e" at the end of her name, she believed gave her personality. When I think of her in a good mood I see her in a restaurant, in one of the dim, meaty steak houses she favored, the kind with red-glass lanterns on the tables. She always asked for and a got a booth tucked away somewhere in back. Martinis were her drink in these restaurants, doubles and light on the vermouth. She didn't like the food to come too soon, but when it did she put aside her menthol cigarette and third drink and dug into her rare steak or roast beef *au jus* and her baked potato. She was happy then, and would discourse on anything, but mainly the good things of life: rare meat, well-made martinis, and how she would open a restaurant if she could, and it would be "a damn good one, the best." "I've got it in me to become an excellent businesswoman," she always said. "If I could just get the opportunity."

Although I felt uncomfortable when Bettye talked like this and when she waved her cigarette and drink around and smiled at my father, I preferred her to be in a good mood than otherwise. When Bettye was happy I didn't exist for her. In her bad moods I was all too visible, and too audible. She listened to how I ate my food at dinner and told me to stop clanking the fork against my braces. She watched how I washed the windows. She watched me walk across a room or down the stairs, and she had something to say about it. At first the admonitions were made in that overbearing, unctuous manner of hers. "Barbara, go back upstairs and run a comb through your hair. A lady never goes outdoors without every hair in place." She often invited me to compare myself with her: "Look at me, my blouse is tucked *neatly* into my skirt. You don't see *me* walking around with shirt tails." But within a few months, since I didn't seem to improve much, her advice was more brusque, "Get that hair out of your eyes." "Stand up straight." And her voice would become pinched and ugly. "You must be doing this just to annoy me!" she would say. And, "Do you think I spent all that money on you at charm school so you could slouch!"

Bettye was an alcoholic, and that was part of what fueled her moods. When we were out in public and she had a drink in her hand she was happy; but she could also be a mean drunk, and her mornings were sometimes raw with hangover anger. She didn't go to work on those days—her health was fragile, we often heard, and anything could upset it. I didn't understand anything about the effects of drinking and it was only simple observation that made me see that she changed when she drank, and that it was sometimes predictable and sometimes completely unpredictable. My mother, like most Scientists, had been a complete abstainer and I'd never seen alcohol in the house, for during those years my father drank rarely, and only away from home. Before I met Bettye, I had never seen a drunk person except in movies when the character, always amusing, wove down the street or became too confidential.

Now we had a liquor cabinet filled with vodka, gin, and vermouth, and there were soda bottles in the refrigerator. The first thing Bettye did when she got home from work was fix herself a dry martini, and then another. By the third one, and seven o'clock, she was ready to start her elaborate dinner preparations.

Bettye congratulated herself those first few months on how thin I was becoming, and told everyone it was due to her suggestions on how to diet, and her constant admonitions to stand up straight. But in fact my weight loss was due more to starvation than any diet. We got home from school at three-thirty or four, but we weren't allowed to have anything but a glass of milk before dinner. If we were lucky, dinner was served at eight; more often we didn't sit down till nine or later. Boeuf Bourguignon and Stroganoff, lamb curry with little side dishes of shredded coconut and chutneys, coq au vin and veal Parmesan—these were not diet dishes, but came from Bettye's gourmet cookbooks. They were the dishes she would have served at the restaurant she had wanted to open. They were dishes that had created a sensation when she'd served them to her restaurant-owner friends. And they were dishes, she increasingly pointed out, that were lost on most of us, particularly me and Bruce, who frequently hardly touched our plates.

For by the time we sat down to eat at nine, Bruce and I were usually past hunger. Once it had just been Bruce who played with his food, now it was me. Across the room Bettye kept a wary eye and ear on us: she was convinced that I clicked the silverware against my teeth just

241

to annoy her. Then, invariably, she'd start on how we didn't appreciate her and the fine meal she'd cooked for us. If we didn't compliment
her enough, she grew irritated, self-pitying, and then enraged.

"I don't know why I bother wearing myself to the bone for you all.
You'd be just as happy eating TV dinners. Well, you know what? That's
what you're going to get. Starting tomorrow, I'll be damned if I'm going
to cook you one more meal."

"Now, Bettye," my father always said.

"Oh, Mom!" Mike would say if he were home that evening. "Your
food's fantastic. You know that!"

Bruce and I remained silent. The fact was that TV dinners we could
prepare for ourselves at six o'clock and eat in front of the television
without Bettye were what we preferred.

Bettye's role at home was gourmet chef and head housekeeper, she who
kept the keys in her pocket and supervised the underservants, but did
not do the work herself. Bettye's mother Ida had been a real house-
maid for most of her life, so she was ideal for the new house at first,
but she and Bettye had a tendency to quarrel, and within a few months
Ida had gone back to the wealthy family she had worked for for years
in Beverly Hills ("Jewish, but such lovely people"). After Ida left, it became clear that housecleaning was going to be Bruce's and my task,
and that our Saturdays were to be given over to meeting Bettye's ex-
acting standards. In addition to the dishes, which were my responsibility, and the dusting and vacuuming, which Bruce and I shared, every
week there were special projects. One Saturday it might be washing
all the downstairs windows. Another week it might be kitchen cupboards or the refrigerator.

It wasn't that I'd never done housework before, though certainly in
the motherless days, things were lax around the house. It was that I'd
never done housework under the eye of someone so ready to find fault.
Over and over I remember wiping vainly at spots on the sliding glass
door out to the backyard, while Bettye stood behind me pointing out
smears and specks that only she could see. One time she had me wash
the kitchen floor, not with a mop, but down on my hands and knees
with a small hand sponge. Every time I thought I'd finished I had to
go get her and wait while she inspected the linoleum. "Do it again,"
she would say. "I want that floor to glisten."

Aside from my grandmother's visits, I hadn't been punished or even seriously reprimanded as a child. Suddenly I was in a new world where everything I did, conscious or not, had consequences, and the consequences were usually some form of what Bettye called restriction, or being grounded. There were two kinds of restriction—one was room restriction and the other generalized house restriction. The latter was usually weekends, which suited the marathon cleaning sessions pretty well. Room restriction was more intense—the result of Bettye's temper, her sense of being "pushed too far." What usually pushed her too far in my case was what she termed my "look." Something emanated from my eyes that she didn't like. I often wondered what that "look" was. When I stared into the mirror I didn't see it. But gradually I learned to put the "look" together with a kind of feeling of despair and defiance that I felt and with what that did to Bettye. It made her want to lock me up, and throw away the key.

At first room restriction seemed like the worst thing in the world. Even in my saddest days at the old house, when I no longer played with the neighbor kids and wanted only to be alone, I'd always had the big backyard where I ran and danced and played with the dog. Especially in summer, when room restrictions could last longer, with no school to break them up, being confined to that pink room could feel like interminable torture. But as the months wore on, being alone in my room seemed preferable to being anywhere in the vicinity of Bettye. My room became a protective shell for me to hide in, and for a while I took it even further by spending most of my time in the walk-in closet, with my bookcase.

The bookcase I was so proud of was a simple thing, two feet wide with three shelves. During a good period, my mother and I had bought it at one of those stores where they sell unfinished pine furniture, and I'd put on the stain myself. It had become important—essential—for me to have my own books, to begin the work, which has never stopped, of collecting my own library.

At the beginning this library was very small. It consisted of some of the books that we'd had in a bookcase in our old living room—a biography in letters of Helen Hayes, which I had read many times, and a battered red Metropolitan Opera guide, which must have been a gift to my parents and which never showed any sign of having been opened. The other books I owned were mainly the children's books that had been my mother's, *Little Women, Winnie the Pooh, Alice in Wonderland,*

The Wonderbook, and *Tanglewood Tales,* and that I painstakingly rededicated to myself from her. When I open them now, I see my upright penciled letters (I'd stopped myself from writing backhand, but could not get the hang of going forward). "To Barbara From Mama" they all say, next to the older inscriptions: "To Ellen From Her Loving Mother," and "For Margaret Ellen, Christmas, 1928." Added to these were a few small volumes of Dickens, bound in smooth leather, and printed on moth-wing-thin pages in tiny type, that had been my grandfather's a couple of volumes in the Modern Classics series and a few paperbacks, *Gigi, Pride and Prejudice,* that I had picked up somewhere. There was also my small poetry collection, which consisted of *Favorite Poems, Old and New,* and e.e. cummings. On top of the bookcase I had made an invisible shrine to my mother: carefully placed copies of her Bible and *Science and Health.* Nothing evoked the spirit of my mother better for me than these limp volumes covered in pebbly brown leather, with the metal reference tags still embedded where she had last left them.

I would go into the closet, which was carpeted, but which was not pink, and sit in front of my bookcase for hours at a time, taking the books out and looking at them, studying the titles of other books in the Modern Classic series and making plans to read them, reading poetry and tentatively writing it. I had hardly enough clothes to make a dent in the space, so that it felt spacious and yet cozy. My room within a room, my office within the pink tower prison.

It was only as I was typing up the first draft of this chapter, two years after I first scribbled it down, that I was struck by the lack of differentiation in my memories between my stepmother's trivial humiliations and her acts of greater sadism. How jumbled together everything was, how non-hierarchical my memories. Having to wash the kitchen floor for a third time with a hand sponge while she stood over me watching seemed, as I recalled it, no less shameful than having her tell me to pull down my bathing suit so she could see if I was using a tampon. And that puzzled me, for it seemed, at first, in the telling of this part of my life, that what I should be doing was constructing a kind of case against my stepmother, in which I would proceed methodically from incidents that could fall within the norm of most people's experience of early adolescence ("My parents don't understand me; they're always trying to make me do what *they* want!"), to those incidents that could be explained away as merely the result of strict discipline, excessive but still "normal" in many households, to those incidents that could only be described as cruel.

It was by recounting these definably cruel words and deeds that I wanted to prove that my stepmother had been truly wicked.

But, in fact, there was no continuum of abuse in my mind. It was all mixed up in a world where punishments rarely fit the crime, where there was no sure way of predicting what action might bring down which response. In fairy tales the young hero is set a series of insurmountable, meaningless tasks, such as picking out tiny seeds from mountains of grain or emptying a lake with a sieve. The witch who sets her the task doesn't need the work done; the point is to break the spirit. The point is the certain punishment that will come when the task is done wrongly or is incomplete by a certain time. In fairy tales, heros are helped by magic hands and elves. In real life I usually failed at my tasks, as I was meant to.

It was the very arbitrariness of Bettye's attention that gave me the feeling of never knowing where she might spring next. Sometimes the discovery of the crime and the punishment were contiguous. I was not chopping vegetables correctly and I had a "look" on my face when she told me so: I could go immediately to my room. I had a button missing from my sweater: I could go to my room, sew it on, and stay there for two hours. But often there was no direct chronology. She would knock on my door or call to me from her room. "May I see you for a moment?" she would ask in the icily controlled tone that presaged a scene. There, in the cold motel-like Master Suite, which smelled of cigarettes and alcohol, she would make me stand in front of her while she observed me through narrowed eyes. Neither of us ever sat: that would have destroyed the effect.

After several minutes she would ask, "You know what you've done, don't you?"

In the beginning I would wrack my brain to think of something I might have done or left undone. Perhaps I lit on something, perhaps I offered, "Forgot to scrub the bathtub after my bath?" But soon enough I learned to say nothing. She was going to tell me anyway, and it was usually going to be something I had never thought of.

Her eyes would fix on me, that cold light blue, and her voice, low and lilting, like a sinister bubble machine, would blow out each word separately, "You say you don't know? You really don't know? Or are you just *pretending* not to know? Answer me!"

"I don't know." I tried, as time went on, to keep my answers as brief as possible.

"Well I think you do know. Because this isn't the kind of thing someone forgets so easily."

The buildup to the final revelation of my crime was always so immense that I lost any sense of proportion. On the exterior I was shut-down, immobile, resistant, but on the inside my heart beat in a panic. What had I done? How serious was it? Had Mike told her something I'd said to him? Did she find something I'd written about her? Had she figured out a way to read my thoughts?

She came closer. I could see her slightly flushed skin underneath her very pale foundation, the blue eye shadow that was flaking just around the corners of her eyelids, the thick mouth that was blotted with red. Over on the night table I knew I would see an empty glass with a pair of red lips kissing its rim.

"Today is Sunday, yes?" She began, getting down to the interrogation.

"Yes."

"And yesterday was Saturday."

"Uh-huh."

"And what do we do on Saturday?"

Her part of the "we" went to the beauty salon and maybe did some shopping on Saturday. My part of the "we" stayed home with my brother and cleaned.

"We clean."

"And what was your job yesterday?"

"The kitchen."

"Does the kitchen include a refrigerator?"

"Yes." Now, in spite of myself, a defense burst out. "But I cleaned the refrigerator! I did!"

This is what she had been waiting for: some pathetic show of resistance, some attempt to defend myself. She turned her back on me and went deliberately to the dresser, where she picked something out of the clutter of jewelry and make-up and glasses. It seemed to be—yes, it was—a withered-up cucumber. Bettye held it up in front of me, the prosecutor with the gun found at the scene of the crime. "Do you recognize this?"

"It's a cucumber."

"And where do you think I found it?"

I shook my head. "I don't know."

"You. Don't. Know. I see. And yet you say you cleaned the refrigerator?"

"Well I. . . . Well I. . . ."

"For your information, young lady, I found this in one of the vegetable bins. What do you have to say to that?"

"I, I . . . I thought I. . . ."

The Wicked Stepmother is the persistent myth it is because there is some truth to it. It comes down to us through generations of storytellers who had seen, who knew firsthand the effects of women's mortality in childbearing, and the consequent remarriages, sometimes two or three, this engendered. Some psychologists theorize that the wicked stepmother of fairy tales represents the split between the "good" mother of childhood and the "bad" mother of adolescence. A few feminist writers claim that the wicked stepmother is part of the despised "crone" face of the Triple Goddess, or wonder if the wicked stepmother is another aspect of the feminine that was rejected when the Virgin Mary became the dominant image of womanhood. But beneath the understanding, beneath the theories, some old archetype remains and has a truth to it. The new wife does not want to live with the shadow of the old wife. The new mother wants things done her way, and no other.

I used to wonder, if I'd been more accommodating, less stubborn and loyal to my mother, more of a girly-girl, able to enjoy talking clothes and hair, whether Bettye and I might have gotten along better. There is evidence, in the room she had the interior decorator design for me, and in the early shopping trips we took, in the drives to and from charm school, that she initially sought in me the girl she'd longed to be. In giving me a suitably feminine environment, one that her mother, who had raised three children while working as a maid, had not been able for provide for her, Bettye was giving me her childhood dream. Her anger at me came from my thorough rejection of her and all she stood for. I didn't want her childhood dream. I didn't understand it. Of course I seemed ungrateful.

247

Once, in ninth grade, my homemaking class gave a tea to which we were supposed to ask our mothers. I would have given anything to get out of it, but there was no way, we had to bring back a signed slip from the mothers. I hoped Bettye would refuse, but instead she took off work to come and she sat through the tea with a smile on her face. At the time I was contemptuous. I was familiar with the unctuous expression she sometimes got in public when I was around, when she would say things like, "Barbara's come so far since last year, don't you think? She's thinner, and stands up straight, and she's much neater. She has such a pretty smile. Of course *we* don't get to see it very often." But I remember that she seemed pleased to be at the tea, to be around other mothers, to pretend that we were a mother and daughter pair like they were.

I try to imagine Bettye and my father talking over my situation before their marriage. Perhaps my father confided fears that I wasn't more of a girl, that I showed little interest in traditional feminine tasks. And perhaps Bettye made suggestions that sounded reasonable: We'll send her to charm school for a few months; we'll make sure she takes more homemaking classes in school; we'll set up a regular schedule for her to do housecleaning here; I'll teach her to cook. It must have sounded fine to my father. It must have sounded as if his double shifts, as worker and parent, were over and as if his daughter, in particular, was going to have someone watching over her, teaching her, encouraging her in the feminine arts. He may have been relieved that he could hand over responsibility for us, that he could abdicate his father-mother role.

For me, of course, it was not fine. I'd had a lot of freedom in our lonely household of three, and had felt myself growing into adulthood there, learning to be, however awkwardly, responsible for myself and for my brother. Now I was thrust back into childhood, a form of childhood, moreover, that I had never experienced, a strictly gendered childhood. And my father, who, like my mother, had never required me to be much of a typical girl, suddenly seemed to line up behind my stepmother and to echo all her admonitions.

Even if I am charitable, even if I believe, as I do believe, that he was sometimes unaware of the exact dimensions of my stepmother's punishments, I must acknowledge that he stood by and watched us suffer. He could only have managed that by disassociating himself from his own memories of punishment and abuse, and by identifying himself with a voice that said, "It's for your own good, you need to learn." At the time, however, I preferred to think that he didn't know about the "real" Bettye, and that if he knew, if only I could tell him, then the punishments would stop. But when I did try to tell him, his response was often, "Go along with what Bettye wants. It will be a lot easier for you, and for me too."

I know now that that my father was having difficulties of his own with Bettye. They had disagreements not only over me and Bruce, but over Mike and the amount of money they were spending and what it was spent on. Years later, he said, "That first year was so bad I didn't see how I could get through it." He eventually learned to get through it by teaching himself to bend to her wishes, or as he put it, "Don't rock the boat." He managed to convey some of that to my brother, who was less resistant than I by nature, as well as being younger and a boy. But I refused to learn to bend. I would not. I could not. And that was how I lost my father, too, less than a year after my mother's death. I couldn't afford to stop loving him, but it didn't do any good. He could not help me.

My father was gone and I never got back the man who had enlivened my childhood with stories and jokes and who had taken care of Bruce and me during my mother's illness. It was as if Bettye had made some agreement that as soon as they married, we children would fall into her power. Later on Bettye would often say, "I wash my hands of your daughter! I wash my hands of her!" By then I was stronger and knew not to back down. When I was thirteen or fourteen, those first two years, I didn't understand why she treated me so badly, why she seemed to dislike me beyond anything I said or did, why controlling me was so important to her.

Bettye's control of me may have started with the externals, but as the months went on, she reached deeper. Until now my menstrual periods had been my own business, but now they were hers too. She kept track of my periods and looked at my underwear and in the garbage for used Kotex. Once, the first day of my period, when I was taking a hot bath to soothe my cramps, she burst through the door and stood over me, saying, "You filthy, filthy girl. Bathing in your own blood. Don't you know we don't take baths when we have our periods?"

Before Bettye became my stepmother I had started to use tampons, preferring them over the belts and bulky pads. But Bettye put an end to that immediately. "You're not to put anything inside you!" she always threatened. Once when I was lying outside on a towel in the back-yard in my two piece bathing suit I heard a rapping on the window of her bedroom. Because of the air conditioner in her room, she didn't open the window. Bettye's angry face summoned me upstairs. Warily, despairingly, I went into the house, bracing myself for punishment. I was no use trying to remember what I'd done or trying to prepare an excuse. I could never be prepared. The bedroom, even in the heat of summer, was always chilly and white with clothes strewn about and the enormous closet open to reveal dozens of outfits and shoes, everything smelling strongly of cologne and scented powder. She was in her white terrycloth bathrobe, which she wore constantly on her "sick" days, and her face was flushed.

"Pull down your bathing suit!" she said, with that cold anger I found so terrifying.

"What? No!"

"You're using tampons, aren't you?"

"I'm not. I'm not."

"Yes, you are. I can't see the belt and the pad. I was looking at you down there. There's no bulge. If you don't tell me the truth, you're going to your room for the rest of the day."

So then I had to blurt it out: "I just put some toilet paper down there because I don't like the pad to bulge when I wear my bathing suit."

"I don't believe you. Pull down your suit and show me."

I went into the bathroom. I reached inside and pulled out the small wad of lightly bloodied toilet paper. Trembling I returned and held it out to her.

She stared at it disgusted and turned away.

"Go to your room anyway," she said. "For talking back."

Mike and his mother had terrible fights, real screamers, up and down the staircase. She slammed her bedroom door and locked it; he pounded on it, threatening to break it down. She grounded him and he crashed out of the house, carrying a suitcase and threatening never to return. She told him to turn the music down and he shattered her favorite record of Frank Sinatra over his knee. Bruce and I found such volatile behavior frightening, but sometimes thrilling. We could not stand up to Bettye, but Mike could.

Bettye and I never fought. I was too terrified of her. I'd seen Mike's flippant humor as a possible response, but although sarcasm would increasingly become one of my defenses, I rarely used it with Bettye. Instead I withdrew, and became stubborn. "If you'd only be nicer to Bettye," my father always said, "you'd make it easier for us all."

When I was growing up in Christian Science I never heard much about hatred except in an abstract way. The *Christian Science Monitor* made it a point not to cover murders or killings, and in spite of my family history, I had not blamed anyone for what had happened to my mother, I had not hated anyone. I was used to taking on an outer burden of shame, but my inner life was separate, was resilient, still believed in God and the goodness of the world. I knew that even when my grandmother had punished me, she still loved me; I knew that even when my mother had been in the terrible grip of her visions, she had never said one unkind word to me. Now that began to change. Now I was confronted by a way of being that I had no words for at first. I didn't know what to call the huge rage that began to boil in me and to demand some expression. I didn't recognize the power of my growing hatred, for outwardly I remained sullen and silent.

One evening I almost killed Bettye. It was a late spring evening perhaps six months after their marriage. Ida had recently moved out in a huff after quarreling with her daughter, and Mike had also left the house, furious with Bettye and vowing never to return. So it was just the three of us Wilsons, as she called us, and her, the misunderstood queen of the castle.

She had called me down from my room to help her with dinner. I could tell immediately, with the radar I'd developed, that she was in a tense mood. She moved with a kind of crisp, suppressed fury, her lip-sticked glass of milky fluid not far away. Recently she had found out that she was developing ulcers, which she blamed on all of us. The doctor had told her not to drink; she had switched from martinis to Scotch mixed with whole milk on the rocks. The smell of the two together was strong in the kitchen.

She handed me an onion, remarking, "I suppose you think I work hard all day for my health, and not to help support you and buy you the things you need. And then I see you walking around with that look on your face. I tell you, it makes me want to scream."

I said nothing. In the kitchen was a clock on the wall with the legend "Time for a Drink," and a wooden "Mood Barometer." For a long time the dial had been turned to "stormy." I chopped glumly, staring out the window, knowing that this was only the beginning, that an evening like this could go on forever. There would be the interminable cooking, then the eating, when we'd have to stop every second bite to tell Bettye how delicious the food was. Then, if we complimented her enough and she was in a good mood, out would come the games, the Yahtzee and the cards for fantan and gin rummy and poker. Bettye would be in her element then, laughing, teasing, crowing with glee: "Sorry 'bout that," as she won game after game. But if something went wrong, as it so easily could—it was going wrong already—there would be tears and shouting and my father saying, "Now, Bettye," and Bruce and me looking sideways at each other, wondering what to do, unable to eat our dinner, knowing we were going to be punished.

I was standing there thinking all this, with the look of outward stupor that was usual with me, brought on by hunger and despair, when she snapped at me, "If you're not capable of chopping up a simple onion, I don't want your help. You might as well go upstairs until dinner's ready."

It wasn't different than I'd expected, wasn't different than how she usually spoke to me, but for some reason, that evening, rage gushed up in me and surged through my arm, down to the fingers that held the sharp paring knife. I'm going to kill you, I thought, and I felt the blade sharp and hot as lightening in my hand, could feel it slicing, with such pleasure, through the mushy meanness of her heart. I'd stuff her in the oven afterwards.

"And I've had about enough of those looks of yours. You can forget dinner. Just don't bother to come back down."

I didn't kill her of course. I turned the violence against myself. That night, or one like it, after sobbing so long and so ferociously that it was as if my body were twisting on a torture rack, I got up and went into the bathroom. I could heard the sounds of laughter below—Bettye loudest of course, but also Bruce and my father. They were playing Yahtzee. The traitors. I was the only one who had really loved my mother. I was the only one who really missed her. I stared into the mirror at my face. I was thirteen now, and at the present moment it seemed like all I'd ever known was the pain that went through me in great spasms. I couldn't bear it anymore, couldn't bear it if life was really going to be like this.

I had been crouched in my closet in front of my bookcase, the only thing that felt like mine in this house, and I had been holding my mother's Bible and *Science and Health*. "Your sainted mother," Bettye had once called her in a sarcastic tone. "You and that sainted mother of yours." And, it's true, my complicated, suffering mother had become martyred in my mind. No one ever spoke of her but her spirit was all around me. I prayed to her for help. I cried aloud, "Mama, why did you die and leave me?" I asked my mother's own question, "Why me, God? Why me?" And I came to the same spiritual dead end. The same closed door to Heaven, the same deafening silence. No one cared. Nothing would ever get better. I was trapped and would be better off dead.

I found a packet of Mike's razors in the cabinet and took one out, and quickly, before I could think too much about it, made a small slash at my left wrist. It wasn't deep and missed the artery. But then I cut myself again, right on the artery, and the blood spurted out. And as it spurted—my old curiosity about my blood had been replaced by revulsion over the years—I looked in the mirror and realized I could never go through with it. For my eyes looked back at me and even reddened and tear-swollen as they were, they begged me not to do it.

I wanted to kill myself, but I didn't want to kill myself because of Bettye. I didn't want to give her the satisfaction. And at that moment something took deep root in my heart, something I would have a hard time dislodging: a violent, sustaining hatred for another human being. A hatred that would be the model for all lesser hatreds to come, that would strengthen me and tell me who I was, that would help me keep on living.

I let the tap water run over my wrist and bound it up as best I could with Band-Aids. I hadn't cut through any tendons, and the wounds healed quick and clean. My scars, though noticeable at first, would fade to the thin white lines I have today. I wore long sleeves for a month, but no one seemed to notice. That was the odd thing about that house: what was known and what was not. Known was everything I ate and everything I wore; known was the time of month I had my period, known were things I'd said to my friends that their mothers had overheard and reported back to Bettye. But unknown were huge things— the secret connection I'd had with Mike, the religious faith that I maintained in my closet like a Marrano Jew, my enormous ambition to be a writer someday. And the fact that one evening, while everyone else was playing cards, I tried to kill myself.

Hatred is a terrible friend. She seems to give you strength, a rock-hard shoulder to lean on, a tough-as-nails sneer and an upturned chin: *So make me!* But with the other hand hatred steals your wallet and most precious possessions, with the other foot she trips you and sends you sprawling. Fairy tales will tell you that no matter how much wickedness you encounter on your path you must not give in to wickedness yourself. You must hold fast to your courage, your wits, and what you love. But it had been a long time since I'd read a fairy tale, and I had forgotten this important truth. Bettye's wickedness had enchanted me and had turned me into a stone statue with a raging heart of anger that could only show itself through glittering metal-hot eyes. She had made me wicked, too, had made me forget what I loved and who I might have been.

There were other times in my adolescence that I wanted to kill myself and looked at my wrist and thought, "I won't let you kill me, you bitch. I won't give you the satisfaction. I hate you too much." And I didn't commit suicide and I kept on living.

But while hatred may be enough of a reason not to die, it's not enough of a reason to live.

Chapter 12

Jail Bait

*I*n the darkened room, humid with adolescence, the projector whirred from behind and up in front, on the slightly lopsided screen, filling that screen, was the picture of a draped body with surgeon's sharp knives hovering over it. Hands parted the sheets, revealing a pale and hairy chest. The other eighth-graders, who would usually have smirked and shrieked over the sight of a nipple, were absolutely still. The knife went up—slash! I quickly put my head down, but not quickly enough to avoid the sight of a blackened, bloody, spongy-gray *thing* inside the chest. "This man was a heavy smoker. Two packs of cigarettes a day for the last twenty years are what have given him this tumor in his lungs," a serious male voice explained over the projector whirring. My head was down, my eyes closed, but still the image burned like a cigarette butt into my brain, forcing me to see it, to see the inside of my mother's cancerous body.

A month earlier Bruce and I, without explanation or discussion, had been dragged to a doctor's office for a physical (Bettye telling the doctor in loud *sotto voce* that this was our first time and we needed a *complete* work-up) and had been poked and prodded from top to bottom and given a series of shots and tests. And now, for the first time in my life, I was enrolled in a science class, where ghostly embryos of rats and pigs floated eternally in formaldehyde glass jars on shelves up behind the teacher's head in front of the class, so you couldn't avoid looking at them unexpectedly. I didn't want to be a squeamish girl who squirmed at the sight of the dissected and dismembered parts of birds and frogs, but every time I contemplated *physicality* of any sort, my brain swam and my stomach heaved convulsively. My earlier fear of the mysterious illness that had consumed my mother now combined with the mingled revulsion and fascination I had for what was happening to my own body. It was changing, before my very eyes, to something hairy and smelly, but at the same time, it was awash in perfumy, delicate rushes of sensation I had never known before.

I knew, from covertly studying other girls in gym, that this was happening to them too, at least the hairy, smelly, breast part, and that some of them were far ahead of me. This excited as much as disgusted me. Every day I anticipated our forced showers in the locker room and every day I thought to myself, *I won't look*. What did it all mean and how were we supposed to get real information about these changes? We had had a brief course in "Hygiene," in which our severe teacher, Miss Arthur (she let girls she liked call her Chris), dressed for the week in street clothes instead of her gym costume, but still with the whistle around her stocky neck, told us that we had nothing to worry about if we continued to use deodorant three times a day. She also told us never to pierce our ears, and if we did, not to wear hoop earrings because she knew of a case where a girl's earlobes had been ripped off during basketball. She also warned us about leaving our hair in its ratted-up state too long, and told us the cautionary tale of a girl who never washed her hair, but just kept spraying the outside until the lacquer turned into a wood-like varnish. Suddenly this girl died, and when they did the autopsy they found that a family of black widow spiders had nested in her hair and that one of them had bitten her.

This was the extent of school sex education in 1964. Once, in fifth or sixth grade, I had seen the film about menstruation provided by Kotex, but there was no explanation what set in motion the busy, colorful horse race of sperm towards the egg. Of course I knew that I should not really be interested in things that had to do with the body. Physical education was an oxymoron: you couldn't learn about something that wasn't real. I kept my quandary to myself, however. I didn't want to carry that old sense of being different and ostracized with me into my new life.

But although I didn't believe in the body, I knew a lot of things about it that I couldn't say. At seven, for instance, I'd known that there was something so bad about what my uncle was doing that I should never tell anyone and just forget it, as he told me to. My mother had explained to me that I must never touch myself down there and that I must always use a washcloth in the bath. But by the time she thought to mention that it was bad to touch yourself, I'd been doing it for a year or two at least. And what was I to make of having been aroused for years by the sight of naked women's bodies in the ladies' locker room before and after my weekly swimming lesson, or of having fantasized about swimming naked with other girls? I already knew about the necessity of keeping secrets about what the body dreamed, what the body wanted, what the body did from my conscious mind. In Christian Science, as in incest, the body was not real, did not exist and sex was never mentioned.

And yet, like all those who are too pure, I was drawn through curiosity and rebellion, to purity's opposite, to what was ripe and physical and disturbing. Even before I met Mike I had some notion of the shame and excitement that attached to girls who "went too far," who "did it." Whatever "it" was exactly. In sixth grade the novel *Gidget* (much steamier than the later movie or TV series starring Sally Field), was passed around by some of the girls, with the pages turned down on the sexy parts. And there had been those late-night talks with Susan of Mill Valley the summer before. Already wise for her age at thirteen in the clear demarcations between good and bad girls, and where you had to draw the line, or at least make sure that others thought you had drawn the line, she recounted to me stories of parties when parents were away and couples went, turn by turn, into the bedrooms. It was through having read sections of *Gidget,* and through hearing about *The Tropic of Capricorn* and *The Tropic of Cancer,* that I had come to realize that reading might perform other functions than to entertain or enlighten. Certain books were seductive, not only in their style, but in their intent.

Education, in fact, is one of the abiding themes of sexual literature, which often depends for its thrill on the juxtaposition of innocence and decadence, of good and evil. Such literature explores the awakening of desire in innocence while insisting, paradoxically, that innocence was never as innocent as it appeared, that good always had in it the seed of evil, which is the desire for knowledge. The theme of virginal girls who are corrupted, spoiled, defiled is a constant in literature, not just pornography. The sad fate of Tess of the d'Urbervilles is the other side of the coin from the story of Fanny Hill, the innocent whose first se- duction leads to more and more perverse pleasures which she grows to welcome and indeed elaborate on. The virgin may initially resist, but in discovering pleasure or in being forced to acknowledge the sex- ual side of her nature, she is corrupted, and capable of corrupting oth- ers. Every disgusting old procuress was once a lovely, untouched maiden.

After that first kiss from Mike, I expected others, but that's all I ex- pected. I didn't expect that the bedroom he shared with my brother would be close enough so that I would pass it sometimes and see Mike in bed or half-dressed. I didn't expect that he would be constantly going by my bedroom room on his way to the bathroom. I didn't expect that the bathroom would fill with his male things, his shaving cream, his male deodorant, his cologne. I didn't expect that I would feel dis- turbed in some way by his nearness, or that when he sometimes talked about an article he'd read in *Playboy* or when he mentioned a book he and his friends had read that was "really hot," that I felt a warm flush of suppressed interest. I didn't understand that perhaps too much of Mike's conversation with me had begun to turn on sex, and that, in the guise of educating me, he was actually trying to seduce me. I lacked information; Mike seemed to have it. That his information came to him through the medium of *Playboy* magazines and conversations with other boys, and could quite possibly be mistaken if not outright false, was something that never occurred to me. He was older and a boy. He must know. And I was curious.

In the beginning, my brother and I both thought of Mike as a quasi godlike being, a high school senior, almost an adult, able to drive a car, on the verge of going out into the world. With his carrotty crew cut and hard pack of cigarettes stuck in the rolled-up sleeve of his white T-shirt, he seemed able to do anything. We felt he was firmly on our side, against the adults, particularly Bettye. "Oh, Mom, let them go to the store with me," he'd say. "Oh, Mom, give them a break." He knew how to handle her in ways that, if we had ever tried them, would have imprisoned us for life. He could talk his mother into things that she would never condone from us. They had an old unspoken history and even though he made her furious, she also forgave him more readily. They shared an impetuous nature, a yearning for finer things, and a self-deceit that made them believe they were telling the truth when, in fact, they only wanted to impress.

He was kind to Bruce and me and we adored him. In that household where everything seemed strange and chaotic, where our father seemed to have vanished and we were living under new and arbitrary rules, Mike was our protector, our buffer. When he was home in the evening for those long-drawn-out dinners and card games, Bettye went easier on us. He could intervene for us; he could advise us; he could teach us ways to distance ourselves from our parents and mock them, so they didn't hurt us. What we didn't see, of course, was how disturbed he was himself. How years of living with a capricious woman and being alternately indulged and screamed at had given him the same emotional volatility as his mother. We didn't see that the marriage and the move had disrupted his life as it had ours, that he suffered by not having a car and having to be driven to school and back (which since we'd moved was fifteen or twenty miles away) by his mother or a friend. We didn't see that at eighteen he had no real outside interests, that he neither played sports nor took part in any school activities, that he didn't have a girlfriend or go to school dances or out on significant dates. We didn't realize that he had no specific plans for the future, that he was doing badly in school and in fact would not graduate.

One evening Mike paused at my doorway on his way to the bathroom. I was doing my homework with my little transistor radio propped up next to me. We got talking, and he asked me how I liked the books he'd given me to read. He had gotten them from a trunk in the garage; they were his mother's, a mix of book club selections, *Reader's Digest* abridgments and paperbacks. The ones he had given me were *Mildred Pierce* by James Cain and *Roxana* by Daniel Defoe. *Mildred Pierce* I had raced through, entranced by the story of the waitress who built a restaurant empire up from baking pies in her kitchen, only to see happiness crash around her when her cruel and ambitious daughter stole away her husband. *Roxana* I was having a harder time understanding. Although Mike had said, significantly, "It explains a lot of things," the language was so ornate and old-fashioned that I barely realized that the people "lyeing" with each other were having intercourse.

Suddenly Mike said, "Why don't you come to my room tonight?" He had lowered his voice and was looking at me in a way that made my heart thump. I often dreamed he'd look at me more often like this, the way that Tony had looked at Maria in *West Side Story*, and the way Mike himself had looked at me that first time he kissed me a couple of months ago.

"Why? What do you mean?"

"So we can talk some more, without having to worry about some busybody overhearing us."

"But . . . what if they did hear us?"

"If you wait till they're asleep, no one will know."

Mike had a casual way of making things I'd never imagined sound normal and right, and of making me feel cowardly and dull if I didn't go along with them.

"But why can't we talk now?" I whispered.

"Do you think I'd talk about important things where anybody could hear?"

So he had important things to tell me?

But now he was turning away, as if he didn't care at all, as if he'd thought better of it. "No biggie," he said. "See you around."

"Wait! I'll come. What time?"

"After midnight should be fine." Mike grinned his white smile and winked; then he went on into the bathroom, where he began to run the shower.

But how could I stay up that late? I usually went to bed by ten at the latest. I took my little transistor radio to bed with me that night and placed it between my head and the pillow. My favorite station was playing one of my favorite songs, the masochistic "My Guy" by Mary Wells, once every thirty minutes. I listened to it several times, along with the new Beatles tunes, and songs by the Beach Boys and Gerry and the Pacemakers. I fell asleep anyway.

When I woke up I could see by my clock dial that it was almost one A.M. Heart pounding, I slipped out of bed and tiptoed the few steps to Mike and Bruce's bedroom. They were both asleep. There was no sound in the house, not from downstairs where Bettye's mother slept or, most importantly, from across the hall, in the Master Suite.

"Mike," I shook his arm. "Wake up, I'm here. What did you want to tell me?" I kept my voice very low and crouched on the floor, wondering if I could squeeze under the bed if anyone came suddenly. Across the room, I could hear Bruce snoring. I wasn't afraid of him waking up—he slept like a log. But what about the others?

Mike seemed befuddled at first, then he yawned and began to speak, almost as if he'd composed something to say earlier. "I feel worried about you."

"You do? Why?" But I felt a warmth around my heart. Although for years people had been announcing they were worried about me, this was the first time it didn't seem like the prelude to some form of punishment.

"You're very naive for the age you are. And things happen to naive girls." His voice took on an avuncular solemnity. "I've been trying to help you. Remember I drew you that picture and explained some things?"

"Uh-huh." A few weeks ago he had drawn me a crude, quick sketch of the female reproductive system. "And this area," I remembered him saying, "is called the Public Zone." I had been pondering that one ever since.

"And I gave you some books?"

"Uh-huh."

"But I'm still not sure you get what sex is about. You haven't asked me any questions. I doubt that means you really understand it. Maybe you're just shy."

I wracked my brain for something to say. I was torn by all kinds of conflicts, from Christian Science notions of matter's unreality, to memories of my mother's bodily suffering, from my resistance towards Bettye's efforts to make me into a feminine girl, to my own confused longings and revulsions about the changes in my body. "I'm not that shy," I said.

For answer he gave me a long kiss that turned me dizzy. Then he leaned back. I could see that he was wearing his white T-shirt and briefs under the thin covers. I crouched uncomfortably, half kneeling, beside him. "Well, I could teach you a lot, if I wanted," he said. "I learned a lot about sex and life in general when I was in prison."

"Prison!" I forgot to whisper. We both stopped breathing, and waited for someone to wake up, but there was absolute silence. "Why were you there?" I whispered.

"I tried to kill my mom's second husband. I came home one evening and they were having a fight. He was trying to strangle her. So I shot him in the leg. And for saving her life they put *me* in juvenile prison."

"Wow!" This confirmed everything I believed: that Bettye was awful and Mike very brave.

Mike propped himself up on the pillow. "Of course, prison wasn't so bad. They tested my I.Q. and found out it was 180—that's genius level—so they put me to work in the library. That's when I developed my taste for reading. I used to read all the time, I read all of Freud's collected works. That taught me a lot about sex. But I learned a lot of other things too, like how to do breaking and entering. Hey, you know how you break a window so it doesn't make a sound? You put masking tape all over the glass, so when you break it, the pieces stay stuck and you can peel them off. I can break into any room, any house. But what I'm saying is, you need to know stuff like that—and other stuff—because you've led too sheltered a life."

If a sheltered life is to be molested by your uncle and to witness your mother going crazy, then perhaps I had been sheltered. But I knew that Mike was talking about sex, and I knew that he was right. I didn't have a clue what Freud thought.

"Tell me a dream of yours," said Mike, reclining back on the bed as if he were the analysand not the psychoanalyst.

"I think I was dreaming . . ." I quickly made this up . . . "of playing Ping-Pong."

"Ah. That's an easy one. The handle of the paddle is the male organ in its rigid state, the Phallus. The round part of the paddle symbolizes the woman, because women are circular and interior. They are passive, while the male is active and thrusting. So when you dream of playing Ping-Pong, you're dreaming of sex."

Every dream or pseudo dream that I ever offered up to Dr. Mike turned out, strangely enough, to be about sex, but for now I was impressed, and made uneasy by his interpretation.

"What rigid state?" I finally ventured.

For answer, Mike took my hand and guided it under the covers. Something bone-hard but covered with flesh that moved was sticking out of his briefs. "That's the Phallus," said Mike calmly, but with a slight catch in his voice. "Don't rub it too hard or I might ejaculate."

Actually I wasn't moving it at all, I wanted to pull my hand away from the rather creepy, chicken-neck feeling of the thing, but Mike kept it there a minute longer, until he gasped and I felt something liquid on my hand.

"You'd better go now," he said, and I uncurled my needle-pricking legs and tiptoed back to bed, almost as mystified as when I had arrived.

After that, I began to visit Mike once or twice a week after midnight. I fell asleep listening to Mary Wells singing "My Guy," woke up and crept into the room to talk. He told me stories about his mother and some about my father. For instance that they'd gone off to get married in October, in Las Vegas, six weeks before the actual church wedding, so that they could buy the house together. He told me about his real father, whom Bettye had divorced when Mike was just a baby, and about his desire growing up to have a father he could admire. Mike didn't consider my father much to admire. He didn't call him Woody; he called him "Cec" as in "cease and desist" and talked about him as a straitlaced bumbler, someone to mock. I had never realized that my father might appear old-fashioned and dull to anyone, but now, in my own feelings of abandonment, I sometimes joined in making fun of him. Mike gave me a way of distancing myself from my need to be parented, yet he also became my new, albeit secret, father substitute.

Nevertheless, for all the talking, there was an escalation of sexual intimacy, for talking about sex almost always produces an atmosphere of physical familiarity. Perhaps Mike rationalized getting me to touch him as part of the older brother persona he tried on with me. Aside from French kissing and touching my breasts occasionally, he didn't try to do anything "down there." The Phallus was his focus, and he taught me what he knew about it. Sometimes he said that sex was natural and these were just repressive times. Sometimes he said that as a writer I needed to know everything about life in order to describe it. And sometimes he fell back on his particular form of older-brotherness. What he was telling me were things I needed to know about boys for the time when I eventually began to date. How to pleasure the boy, but how to contain that pleasuring. He seemed to envision my future as a sexual one and to rationalize that by being corrupted early rather than late, I had a head start on most other girls. All he could teach me was about his own pleasure, of course, not my own, but I didn't understand that then. My head was in the clouds. There was someone in the world who cared about me. Someone who thought enough of my intelligence and spirit to talk to me about my dreams, to open the world of psychoanalysis to me. Someone who treated me as an adult, and who believed that I had a future as a writer, and as a woman.

One day in March, after about four months of living in the new house, and shortly after his eighteen birthday, Mike took a few movables from the living room and his mother's car and gasoline credit card. Although they got the car back and one of the lamps, Mike never returned to live with us, though he did turn up "like a bad penny," as my father began to say. He stayed with friends, or with his grandmother. He sponged off her and off Bettye. He didn't get a job or finish high school. He tried to join the Army, but they said (he reported) that he was too skinny to enlist. Sometimes he dropped in for dinner and everything would be fine; then Bettye would begin to lecture him and he'd fly into a rage and slam out the door. Other times he stayed for a weekend or a week, talking big about girls he was seeing or jobs he planned to get.

Thus, one day in early summer after school had let out, he was around the house on a weekday. Everyone was gone except me and Mike. He had gotten a cold and was still somewhat feverish; that was his rationale for breaking into the Master Suite using a knife in the lock. He needed the air-conditioning. He had ensconced himself in the king-size bed, had slept for a while, and was now restlessly playing solitaire and reading a *Playboy* magazine. He called to me to come in the room. There he sat, wearing a white T-shirt and briefs. His St. Christopher medal hung around his neck. "Can you get me some orange juice?" he asked pathetically.

I was vaguely repulsed—by his sickness, first of all, for I didn't like people to be sick. It aroused in me a kind of nostril twitch of impatience. As if illness had a faint reek I could not accustom myself to. And then, I had become aware recently that I did not like him as much as I once did. He was too skinny and nervous; he smoked too much and didn't really do anything, and he was too out-of-control with his anger. Once I'd admired the way he stood up to Bettye, but since my suicide attempt I knew that I could stand up to her too and that my way would be to keep to my room and avoid her as much as possible. I was working on creating my own world to counteract hers, and had been in my room reading when he called. It was disturbing to find Mike in their bedroom. It was disturbing to me that he lay in the king-size bed. I could not imagine doing anything like that myself, not without the possibility of being discovered and murdered.

After I brought him the orange juice, he patted the side of the bed, in his most charming way, and said, "It's so boring being sick. How about staying and playing a game of cards?"

"Well, I was reading. . . ."

"Just a game or two."

Bettye was the card player in the family, and she had taught us all fantan, gin rummy, and poker. But I was always, intentionally, bad at cards. It seemed to me such a waste of time. Nevertheless I played a few rounds of rummy with Mike, and he told some funny stories and we laughed. And he seemed sympathetic. "It must be so hard living here with Mom and Cec, knowing you have years to go."

His sympathy made me remember how he had been my ally, and how I had adored him, and how, when he left last March, I'd felt so frightened and unprotected. I found myself wishing that I could just curl up next to him, or that he would hold me, and in some way comfort me. But he had other ideas.

"I've learned a new game since I left," he said rakishly. "It's strip poker."

"What's that?"

"It's a party game for guys and girls. Really fun. Every time you lose, you have to take off a piece of clothing. By the end, almost everybody is naked."

"Well, we're not at a party."

"Yes, but we could practice. So when you're at a party and someone says, Let's play strip poker, you'll know what they're talking about."

In spite of the air-conditioning, the atmosphere in the room seemed close and sultry. There was a feeling of coercion in the air, a feeling that I didn't like. It was in this room that Bettye had made me pull down my bathing suit to see if I had a tampon in.

"No," I said. "I think I'm just going to go back to my room and read."

"But you used to like to spend time with me. You know, during those nights." Mike tried to pull me close to him, and for a second I let him. I wanted something, but not this. Desire was mixed with repulsion and with shame. The *Playboy* magazine lay open on the disheveled sheets, and I caught a glimpse of a woman's huge pink breasts. It was a shameful thing to me that I had liked looking at *Playboy* pictures and that I had liked reading some of the books he gave me. But being held close by Mike in the daylight, smelling his feverish sweat and cigarette smoke and feeling his arms pressing on me awakened some kind of old panic. I know now it was part of having been molested as a much younger child, but at the time I thought the feeling of wanting to throw up was solely connected with Mike.

"Let me go!" I said, and jumped up. "You disgust me!"

"You didn't use to be disgusted," he said, and I knew that he would always have that over me, my old compliance and curiosity.

"Yeah, well, well . . . you should get a job!" I said, because that was the only thing that occurred to me. "You bum!" And I ran out of the Master Suite and slammed its door.

Joyce Padgett was in my social studies class in the new junior high I began to attend in February. Although it was for the "accelerated" students, it was like no class I'd ever been in before. Our teacher, the energetic and eccentric Mr. Herman, spent most of his time shouting at us to be quiet. There was a great deal of talking in this class, also a lot of laughing and joking, a lot of throwing of paper airplanes and balls of paper. I had noticed that this junior high, Bancroft, seemed to be run along more chaotic lines than Marshall, but my classes in particular seemed to be taught by outright maniacs, adults who had either given up on teaching and were content to ride the wild waves of puberty with us, or adults who somehow drew energy from us and found a way to turn it around so that we learned something. I remember most of my teachers from that junior high with affection: Mr. Garson, in English, who insisted we recite Dylan Thomas aloud in spite of our great embarrassment; Mr. Martinez, in French, who once threw a ruler at me and Janie Williams for talking in the back of the class, Mr. Jackson, the stand-up comedian of algebra, and Mr. Herman of eighth-grade social studies, who tried so heroically to teach us the history of World War I and II.

Joyce sat next to me in social studies. She had heavily acned skin, a beautifully cut mouth and straight nose, and warm, wise brown eyes. She wore her long hair in a very teased and hairsprayed beehive, more like a helmet, which rose about six inches from the top of her head and was decorated with a row of plastered-down bangs, thin and stiff as flat toothpicks, two spit curls over her ears, and a single long strand of hair hanging down her back. This Southern California version of the Gainsborough look was very popular in 1964, at least among girls who had the time and energy to devote to keeping it up. It went along with pale lavender or white lipstick and dark eyeliner and mascara, which Joyce also wore. She wasn't tall, but she had what my instructor at charm school had referred to as "a mature figure."

It took a few weeks for me to sort myself out at the new school and look around, but when I did, Joyce was there, ready to be the best friend I'd lacked since the fifth grade, when I'd lost Connie because I couldn't talk to her about my life. I believed that wouldn't be a problem with Joyce, who was quietly circumspect in her knowing sort of way, and who appeared to be a girl who knew how not to ask, as well as to keep a secret if she did. By late spring, after Mike's departure and my suicide attempt, I was going to Joyce's house after school occasionally and spending Sunday afternoons there, with her older brother and his friends and her mother, who ruled the house from her wheelchair.

Mrs. Padgett was a big gypsy-like woman with white skin and long, dyed-black hair that she wore in a braid or horsetail. She wore large cotton muumuus, square-necked, in floral patterns, and large fluffy bedroom slippers, the kind that look like tired stuffed animals. At bottom she was a slightly perverse and melancholic woman, who rarely went out in the world and who lived on disability, but she prided herself on her good humor and sociability. "My home is open day and night to my children's friends," she always said. "It's how I get my company." And, "Since I have to be here anyway, I want my children and their friends here with me." She was the kind of mother who believes herself to be in the perfect confidence of her children, who thinks she is an honorary teenager too, and is always disappointed when she finds there has been any attempt to keep her out of the know.

There was no false gentility at the Padgetts' house, as there was at mine. It wasn't only messy, it was downright dirty, with dust mice big as cats under the sofa and beds, a sink full of dishes and overflowing garbage. I loved it. The Padgetts rarely sat down to regular meals, but there were always cans of soda in the refrigerator and bags of potato chips and Doritos open on the counter, and occasionally Joyce or her mother would bake a batch of Toll House cookies or throw some hamburger patties on the grill, and break out the catsup and mustard. And there was always enough for everyone.

Only once had Bettye invited people over. They were her employers and their wives. The cooking had gone on all afternoon, and although Bruce and I didn't sit down with the guests at the rarely used dining table, I was enlisted to bring the platters in and remove the plates. At one point, as I staggered through the swinging door with a load of plates, I heard Bettye say in her lilting, false way, "It's so sweet of Barbara to help when our regular maid is ill."

As the weather grew warmer and school ended, I began to spend more and more time at Joyce's. Bettye and Mrs. Padgett seemed to have a good understanding between them (which at first did not concern me as it should have), and Bettye almost always said yes if I asked to go over there. They had a small swimming pool, for Mrs. Padgett's therapy, and we all spent a great deal of time throwing each other in, being pushed in, or just jumping in, usually with our clothes on. Often these pool parties would go on into the evening and the barbecue would come out and the music come on. They didn't have a record player, but we swam and danced to the top tunes on the radio. Joyce was a great dancer; she did the Twist, the Mashed Potato, the Locomotion, and I followed her. I had never danced like this before, and now I loved it, loved dancing side-by-side with Joyce as Mrs. Padgett sat and watched, to the Chiffons, the Ronettes, the Supremes, and Martha and the Vandellas. "Where Did Our Love Go" and "Heat Wave" were our favorites, and we refined our movements endlessly, turning sharply in unison and making circles and signs with our hands. Sometimes, in the evenings, when it was dark and Mrs. Padgett was inside, I watched Joyce dancing close with one of her brother's friends. She hardly moved, but threw her arms around the boy's neck and buried her face in his shoulder, so that her high hairdo stuck up like a hump. The first time a boy asked me to slow-dance, I imitated Joyce and hugged him close, the way I thought I should.

During the slow, hot afternoons, when her mother was napping and her brother was out with his friends, Joyce and I would sit in her room and read through copies of old *True Confessions, Secret Romance,* and *Silver Screen* that belonged to her mother. They sat in great piles under the bed with the dust mice, an apparently limitless supply. While Joyce preferred the Hollywood confessionals and knew everything there was to know about that endlessly wicked and flirtatious home-wrecker, Elizabeth Taylor, who had first stolen Eddie Fisher from Debbie Reynolds and then, in the midst of filming *Cleopatra,* had set her sights on Richard Burton, I preferred the melodramatic stories of forbidden love and terrible consequences.

"I Made Love With My Husband's Best Friend"; "I Said I'd Never Sleep With Him Again—But I Did"; "I Had My Boyfriend's Baby—Twice." In these stories, always told from the point of view of the woman who'd transgressed, the feeling of shame was thick and warm as peanut butter on toast. The double-standard was so well in place as to seem as fated as a Greek tragedy. Helplessly, the female narrator was drawn into situations that had tragic repercussions. She knew better than to respond to her brother-in-law, but then he came over on an errand, and no one else was around, and she couldn't say no, and now she was living a lie, telling her husband she loved him but secretly lusting after her sister's husband. These women seemed utterly mystified by the enormous forces that drew them (they never called it a sex drive); they only knew that they couldn't stop themselves and that they had to pay the consequences. And the consequences were usually pregnancy. How awful that sounded. In one story a fourteen-year-old girl had to admit to her parents that she was going to have a baby. She was shipped off to a maternity home and returned six months later (without the baby of course; they never kept the baby). And then—can you believe it?—she again started seeing the boy who had made her pregnant. And again they succumbed to obsessive love, and again she got pregnant. And again—at only fifteen!—she had to admit to her parents that she had been knocked up.

I read these stories lying in the heat of Joyce's dim bedroom, on her bed, while she sat on the floor, staring hard at photos of the heartless Elizabeth. I was sweating, sweating in desire, sweating in shame, sweating in fear. I hadn't known *any* of this when I had been going to Mike's room at night and having educational conversations that led to me touching and rubbing his penis. I hadn't realized that the crush I'd had on him could have had such drastic effects. What if he had been less responsible; what if he had really taken advantage of me? What if I had gotten knocked up? What if—oh, horrible, horrible thought—I had had to go to Bettye and tell her? Tell my dad! What if I'd had to miss eighth grade and part of ninth because I was in a maternity home for unmarried teenagers? What if people found out that I'd done it, and not just with any boy, but with my stepbrother, in the house, practically under the eye of Bettye? And what if they thought I was a slut, and I thought of myself as a slut, and then there was no other way to live than to keep being a slut, with everybody?

"There's a word for girls like you," said a male teacher who had succumbed to one of his high school students in one of the stories, "it's jail bait. You tempt a man past his control and then you threaten to expose him and take away his livelihood. You act so innocent, but everybody knows you'd spread your legs for anyone. You've done it before and you'll do it again."

Jail bait. I had heard that word before, a few months before, when Bettye and my father had gone away for the weekend and Bruce, Mike, and I had gone to stay with an old friend of Bettye's, a man who lived in a slovenly apartment and looked at me in a way that made me feel used and creepy. I don't know who he was—I never saw him before or after that time—but I know that his bathroom was full of *Playboys*, which I looked at, and that he made some jokes to Mike about "Getting any lately?" as he looked at me. I hadn't known what that meant, hadn't known why Mike blushed and winked, but all the same I'd felt uneasy and violated. Afterwards I'd asked Mike about it, and Mike had explained that the man thought I was a cute "piece," and that I was real jail bait material and to be careful. "Did you tell him about us?" I demanded. "Oh, no," said Mike, but I knew that he had, that he had wanted the man to think of me that way.

"Oh, poor Debbie Reynolds." Joyce sighed, but you could tell she was imagining herself as Elizabeth Taylor the way she was secretly smiling and touching her St. Christopher necklace as if it was made of emeralds.

"Joyce," I said. "Have you ever done it?"

"Oh, no," she said, and then paused. "There's nobody that I like enough. I would do it, though, if I liked a boy enough."

"You would?"

"Sure. Wouldn't you?"

"But what about getting pregnant?"

"Oh, you just have him wear a condom."

"But what if he doesn't?"

"You'd be wearing a diaphragm. You know, inside you. It stops the sperm."

I had never heard of this form of birth control before. Joyce seemed so matter of fact about it that I wondered why the girls in these magazines didn't know about how to protect themselves. But birth control sounded so . . . rational and hygienic.

"What about you?" She was casual. "Ever done it?"

"Me!"

She laughed. "Just kidding. You're about the most innocent girl I ever met. You don't even look like you're thirteen most of the time, much less fourteen like the rest of us."

"I do too!" It was a sore point with me that, because my birthday was in October, I was younger than most of my classmates. I had the impulse to tell Joyce about Mike. About the nights I'd rubbed his penis, about the day he wanted to play strip poker. I hadn't had actual sex, but I'd had more experience than she realized. But something stopped me. "Well, I'll try anything once." I shrugged, and sank back into the sordid, engrossing world of sexual secrets and shame.

"And what is that supposed to mean, what you said to Joyce: *I'll try anything once?*" Bettye demanded a few days later. She had brought me up to her room to have "a serious discussion."

I was too stunned by the realization that Joyce could have told her mother what I'd said and Mrs. Padgett could have told Bettye, to be able to respond at once. I simply stared.

"And don't give me that innocent look! You know what I'm talking about."

"I just meant, I just meant, I like to try things, I'm interested in. . . ."

"There are things a girl your age shouldn't be interested in and this is one of them. How do you want to be treated by boys? You want be treated with respect. And they won't respect you if you let them do what they want."

"I don't know any boys," I said, quite truthfully. I might dance with them. I might even kiss them. But I didn't *know* them.

"I know you don't, because if you did, I would know too. But I don't want you even thinking about such things."

"I just meant. . . ."

"I know exactly what you meant, and Joyce and her mother did too. And if I ever hear you say such a thing again, you'll stay in your room until you're eighteen."

As a child I'd run, roller-skated, biked, and swum. Now I didn't have a bike and no longer went to swimming lessons. All that was left to my energetic body—since walking, though we all had to do it, was considered not very cool, was dancing. And dancing was a wonderful discovery. You could wear yourself and your hormones out by gyrating to "Do Wah Diddy Diddy," by Manfred Mann and "The Way You Do the Things You Do," by the Temptations, and of course anything by the Supremes. The Supremes were at the top of the charts in 1964, with "Come See About Me." Like everybody else I loved the Beatles and the Beach Boys, our home-grown band, but it was the girl groups that really spoke to me: about love and loss and broken hearts, but also about independence and bravado. Between the often masochistic lines were images of strength and resilience.

All that summer I danced, and I felt myself turning into a new person. A girl who was brainy, but not stuck up about it, a girl who was funny, a smart mouth, a girl who could dance hard and sexily, a girl who was reckless and fun-loving, but not slutty. With boys I hovered on the edge of daring, but always pulled back. I might dance close, I might kiss briefly in the shadows, but that was all. And it wasn't just because I knew now that anything else would get back to Bettye; it was because I had learned my lesson from Mike and my reading of confession magazines. Bad girls got punished, always and inevitably. Their lives were ruined. So that even though I knew what they were talking about in those magazines and in the pop songs of the girl groups, about the undercurrent of helpless sexual fate pulling at teenage girls and women, I determined to resist it. I had found where I wanted to be on the good girl/bad girl scale, and there I was going to stay. I wasn't going to be a slut, but I wasn't going to be a moony-eyed doormat either.

Who was that new person I became by the end of my thirteenth summer, and what happened to the old one? I'd refused to let Bettye construct me into a feminine version of herself, but I went ahead and reconstructed myself anyway, at least on the surface, into a very recognizable type of teenage girl. The power to imagine and invent worlds in which I could do anything narrowed to the power to withhold, to manipulate and to enchant the opposite sex. In spite of Christian Science, my body had once been a source of pleasure to me. Now there was a split, as I began to feel sexual and to be sexualized. I wanted pleasure, but pleasure could only be in danger or near to danger, and I knew I must protect myself at all possible costs. Dancing let me do both, and dancing was what I did, intensely and persistently, for the next four or five years.

. . .

Tragedy and pain may ennoble adults, but they rarely ennoble children. The great lessons I learned from my losses were how to hate and how not to trust. I learned that nobody likes the look of a victim, and that adults who have no compassion for themselves will show no mercy to a child. The defenses I learned against sorrow mimicked those I had seen and saw around me: to distance myself from my true feelings, to clown instead of speak seriously, to use my humor both to make people like me and to punish them. To forget my sadness in sexuality while controlling what I could feel sexually.

Alice Miller has called it "soul murder," the construction, for protection, of a false self which masks the true or authentic self, which is then allowed to wither or be buried. But I don't know if the distinction between the true and the false self can ever be entirely clear. Like most children and adolescents, I was ingenious and adaptable, and who I truly was could not be easily crushed. It was not a false self that loved to dance and swim, to crack jokes and clown at school, to take my reading and writing absolutely seriously even though I kept my grand ambitions secret. No, this self was me. It was authentic enough. Nevertheless, as my tragedies piled up, something disappeared, and that was the ability to experience my feelings as real, and to know what they were. At twelve I was sad, lonely and ashamed, and it showed; by fourteen I was outwardly bouncy, flirtatious, and funny, and everyone liked me much better. But the full range of my emotions was increasingly lost to me. What I had left were pop songs, movies and literature, which evoked the emotions that other people had. Only when I listened to the Shangri-Las' "Remember" or Peter and Gordon's "A World Without Love," only when I saw films like *Dr. Zhivago* or *The Umbrellas of Cherbourg,* only when I read *Gone with the Wind* or reread *My Friend Flicka,* could I cry over the mysteries of fate, the sadness of being abandoned, and the loneliness of continuing to live on.

I didn't think, of course, that what I was losing or had lost, was the ability to feel truly and deeply about what happened to me and to confide those feelings to someone I knew and trusted.

I just thought of it as growing up.

Chapter 13

Fire and Brimstone

"They did not call themselves survivors, but hibakusha, *'explosion-affected persons.' "*

—*Hiroshima,* John Hersey

When I was fourteen my father suddenly got religion. Up to that time, he had been, as far as anybody could tell, an unbeliever. Even during the years of my mother's illness he had never looked anywhere for spiritual comfort or understanding, had never gone to church, had never prayed. If anything, he had turned against religion. Christian Science had failed him just as it did my mother.

But my father had been baptized and confirmed in the Evangelical Lutheran Church, and after he married Bettye, who was also Lutheran, they began to go to church together occasionally and to want us all to go. It seemed purely social, at first. My stepmother's primary interest in the church was commenting on other women's clothes and chatting after the service in the room where coffee and pastry were served. She had no religious life that I recognized and was content to simply attend a service once in a while and to keep a small but steady conventional faith in God going, like a pilot light in the oven. It didn't surprise me that Bettye thought Bruce and I could be easily converted to her beliefs, for she thought that way about everything she forced on us. But I was upset that my father followed her into her faith, where he had not followed my mother, and more upset still that he tried to make us follow, too.

Somehow, without anyone noticing, he had been saved.

Before my encounter with the Lutherans, I was a novice to the beliefs and practices of Protestants, and to me the various denominations were basically indistinguishable. Catholics I knew about from my old friend Connie. We had sometimes tried to explain to each other our religious beliefs, had nodded understandingly and had each privately judged the other's faith extremely bizarre, though I was more fascinated by the holy cards and rosaries in the bedroom Connie shared with her two sisters than Connie was intrigued by the blue chalk used to underline passages in *Science and Health.*

But Lutherans, Baptists, Episcopalians, Presbyterians—what was the difference? All I knew was that their congregations were more physically active than those in Christian Science—kneeling, genuflecting, promenading around the aisles—and that most churches had more *things:* chalices, incense, candles, stained glass, embroidered altar cloths and fancy tunics. They ate wafers and drank wine—in *church.* They had choirs and altar boys and pastors. This knowledge I had somehow picked up from photographs and television. But until I actually went to the Lutheran church for the first time, I didn't know the language or beliefs behind the rituals and objects. I knew that Lutheranism had Martin Luther, just as Christian Science had Mary Baker Eddy, and I naively thought that the Lutherans read from some book of Mr. Luther's just as we read from *Science and Health.*

All that changed after I heard my first sermon.

The beginning of the service was vaguely familiar to me: hymns, standing and sitting, a communal prayer. But then Pastor Jensen, brilliant in purple and yellow, came to his podium. He began, as he was to begin every week, with a genial welcome and a few announcements, then, in a quiet, measured voice, he introduced his topic of the week, which I'd seen posted in large letters on a board outside the church. "Love Your Neighbor," he began. "What does that really mean?" His examples of the difficulty of living next door to irritating people, much less loving them, came straight from suburban life and raised predictable chuckles in the audience. Maybe one family had a barking dog or another family had a son with a drum set, or the smoke from the next-door neighbor's barbecue drifted into your open windows. Was it possible to love a neighbor who dumped grass clippings into your yard late at night? Could you possibly love the *children* of your neighbors, especially if they were teenagers? But these homely anecdotes about everyday situations gave way to sterner questions, with biblical references. How would Jesus have responded to a barking dog? And what did St. Paul have to say on the subject of barbecue smoke? Then, as Pastor Jensen's voice began to rise in volume, the dogs and drums and barbecues were left behind. We were standing, naked and quivering, before God's throne. And this God was no pushover. This God was a stern God, a wrathful God.

Now red-faced, with thundering voice, Pastor Jensen painted a terrifying picture of us poor sinners on Judgment Day, standing before the Lord and St. Peter and having to explain ourselves. Only explaining was really no good, because the Lord knew exactly what we'd been doing and thinking every day of our lives. He could see right through us. He could see into our hearts, and He knew if we had accepted Jesus Christ as our personal savior or if we had just been pretending to be Christians, going to church, taking Holy Communion week after week, saying the words of the Nicene Creed, but not taking those words into our *hearts*, not really believing them at all.

Here came a searching pause, while Pastor Jensen looked out at his congregation, into our faces, as if *he* were the Lord and could see into our hearts. The first time I thought that this pause was the end of the sermon and that we were to be let off with a warning, but within a couple of weeks, I realized that the pause was purely a launching pad for the final description of what would happen to us if we were not saved. It was not so much a description as a threat, which Pastor Jensen delivered in magnified tones of doom. His face turned the color of his purple surplice and he told us in great detail about the hot flames and burning pitch that awaited us sinners in hell. He spent little time describing Heaven. Presumably if we were going there we'd know all about it soon enough.

"Now there's some old-time preaching," the nicely dressed people said afterwards as they filed out of the church and across the patio to the building where the donuts and coffee awaited. "That's some preaching to rattle your bones." Presumably they took some of Pastor Jensen's words into their hearts but you would not have known it from their conversations, which quickly turned to the concerns of ordinary life: weather, work, taxes. Nor would you have guessed, from the way that Pastor Jensen now circulated jovially through the crowd, shaking hands and making jokes, that he had minutes before been threatening these very same people with the hot, eternal flames of hell.

How many here were truly religious people? And what did it mean to be a religious Lutheran? These people didn't look scared of Judgment Day. But could their hearts be pure? How many here were going to hell? My eyes lit on Bettye, dressed in a pastel suit, with matching shoes and a handbag, with her deliberately ladylike voice and seductive laugh. Now *there* was an example of hypocrisy; now *there* was a real candidate for hell. And while she smoked a cigarette, chatting with the others about the weather, I imagined her standing in front of God and having to explain her every act of cruelty to me and my brother. But of course she wouldn't be able to explain in any way that would satisfy God, and anyway God already knew every mean thing she'd done, and he'd immediately consign her to hell, where she would roast forever. I pictured the flames licking at her lilac pumps and saw her champagne hair catch fire, as she shrieked, "Give me another chance! I'll be nice to Barbara."

"Too late, Bettye," said Satan. "You should have thought of that earlier."

It was a satisfying fantasy, the image of Bettye in flames, sobbing that she was sorry. I wished I could believe in it.

Janie Williams was another W; she sat directly in front of me, at the back of the room, in several classes. We also shared a home economics class. I'd been forced by Bettye to choose it as my only elective, instead of speech and drama, but Janie was there of her own free will. She actually liked to sew and cook, and fortunately liked it enough so that she helped me. More than once she put in a dart or the gathers in a skirt in one of my sad attempts to make wearable clothing.

I was still friends with Joyce Padgett and ate lunch with her and her friends out of habit, but she was drifting more and more into the lowrider crowd and their conversations about drag-racing on the weekends were of little interest to me. Instead I gravitated towards Janie, skinny, pugnacious Janie, with her thick glasses and ready laugh. In only a year Janie would reinvent herself when her family moved to another school district and she would suddenly get contact lenses and turn out to be beautiful and popular, but in the ninth grade she was still slightly awkward, with a coolly rebellious streak. Her father was a sociology professor at Long Beach State and she'd taken over his politics as I had taken over those of my father.

In the presidential race of 1964, she was for Johnson and I was for Goldwater.

"Goldwater!" she shrieked when she saw the bumper sticker I'd put up in my hall locker. *"How* can you possibly be for *Goldwater?"*

"Because he's the best man for the job," I said, though I had no actual idea of what he stood for or what his qualifications might be. All I knew was that my father, who'd been a Republican forever, was for Goldwater.

"But he's ready to drop the bomb on Vietnam. He's trigger-happy."

"The bomb?" I said uncertainly. We were standing in the hallway between classes. It was the same hallway where we had often crouched, heads bent, one hand over our eyes, the other protecting our necks, during bomb drills.

"The A-bomb, stupid. The H-bomb. The *nuclear* bomb. If Goldwater is elected it won't be just advisers going over to Vietnam; he'll wipe out their whole country, and then the Russians will bomb us. Boom!"

The corridor was emptying and just as Janie shouted "Boom," the bell rang as if it were a siren and suddenly we were as alone as if the rest of the planet had died or ceased to exist.

"I'll bring you some books to read," called Janie over her shoulder as she raced off to her next class. "So you'll know what *happens* to people who've had the bomb dropped on them."

One of the books was about Nagasaki and the other was *Hiroshima* by John Hersey. In precise, unaffected language Hersey told exactly what had happened to six people and their families at the moment the bomb dropped at eight-fifteen A.M. on August 6, 1945. One had been fixing her children's breakfast, another reading the paper. A blinding flash, whiter than white, a "sheet of sun," hit Hiroshima. People at the epicenter were instantly vaporized, thousands of others were flash-burned and thousands more, apparently untouched by burns, died of radiation sickness. And more died from the fires and floods that raged through the city and countryside in the days following. At least a hundred thousand lives were destroyed immediately, and another hundred thousand were injured. None of the victims knew what hit them; no one knew what kind of bomb it was. Four days later Nagasaki was struck with a bomb of even greater magnitude. The horror of the explosion, and the suffering that came afterwards—it was beyond anything I'd ever heard of.

I had been crouching down under desks and covering my head ever since I'd started school in 1955. But I had never thought about what it meant, just as I had never thought about fallout shelters. One man in our old neighborhood had built a bomb shelter; his son showed it to us once: a tiny cement room with folded cots and shelves of baked beans and peas. "We'll stay down here until after the blast and then, when it's safe, we'll come up." The rest of us had stood around uneasily. Our families didn't have bomb shelters—where would we be?

Reading *Hiroshima* I understood that entering a bomb shelter wouldn't help much, and that getting under your desk at school or filing out into the hall to duck and cover would be useless. At the center of the blast the temperature was 6,000 degrees Centigrade. In Hiroshima 95 percent of the people a half mile from the epicenter were incinerated. They hadn't told us that during the brief emergency review we had each year. They didn't tell us about the flash burns that left people with hollow eye sockets, their melted eyes running down their cheeks, or about people so burned that their skin fluttered off their bodies like tattered rags. They didn't tell us that when the burns healed, they healed with deep layers of pink, rubbery scar tissue called keloid tumors. They didn't tell us that thousands of people died without a burn or a scratch on them, from the radiation that destroyed their cells. They didn't talk about the long-term effects of radiation poisoning, the hair falling out, the diarrhea and vomiting.

Janie had the good sense not to look smug when I gave the books back to her.

"Didn't you know *any* of this?"

"No," I said weakly. I knew it wasn't only my Christian Science upbringing that had kept these horrors away from me, but some larger conspiracy. Last year in eighth grade when we'd studied the two world wars, Mr. Herman had told us about the concentration camps with tears in his eyes, but he and the school books had stinted on the Pacific War. I'd only known that the bombs dropped on Japan had ended the war. And I knew that because of those bombs we were now living in the Atomic Age, and that, because the Russians had come up with the bomb too, we in the U.S. needed to have the bomb to protect ourselves.

"It's because we did it," Janie said wisely. "If they'd done it to us, just imagine."

"How could the United States do such things to people?"

"Where have you *been*?" Janie asked. "The Indians? Slavery? How Negroes are treated now?"

But I was overwhelmed. Hiroshima was bad enough. Hiroshima was on my mind for weeks. Like a scab I had to keep opening up, I went back to its images over and over, trying to imagine what the blast could have been like. The terrible heat and absence of water. Being buried under collapsed buildings, unable to get out. Seeing the blackened bodies everywhere, looking for my family, losing them. How quickly it had happened. You were in your garden, you were reading the newspaper, you were making breakfast, when suddenly there was a bright flash and everything you'd ever known and cared about was gone.

And then, worse than the blast itself, was the life that came afterwards. When you looked for the house you'd lived in and couldn't find it again, when you looked out at the city and the city itself was gone. When all around was shock and death, and indifference from the rest of the world. When you were weak and sick for years with radiation disease or healed with mutilating scars.

I couldn't bear to look directly at the burned and scarred faces of the victims in another of the books about the blast that I found at the library, but I would snatch glimpses and feel recognition and fear. My mother had looked like an atomic war survivor. My mother had looked like that at first. And the people who helped the Hiroshima victims had had to keep reminding themselves, "These are human beings."

It was through the library that I discovered the case of the Hiroshima Maidens. They were young women those thick keloid scars and deformed hands and faces had made them unable to work, marry, or have children. Most of them hid themselves away in their houses or in groups in refuges. Somehow Norman Cousins, the editor of the *Saturday Review,* had got it into his head to bring a number of the women over to the U.S. for plastic surgery, so that they could live normal lives. In 1956, twenty-five Hiroshima Maidens arrived in New York for a prolonged series of treatments involving tissue reconstruction and grafting. What I read about them stayed in my mind a long time, both for the horror they had undergone, as well as for the kindness of strangers who did not deny what had happened, but who worked to help the women heal, who worked to make them feel human again. What was unstated, but understood, was that it was worse for a woman to be scarred. For her face was who she was; it was what could be loved or unloved about her. It was her job, her happiness, her future.

In 1517, Luther tacked his Ninety-five Theses on the main door of the church in Wittenburg and the Reformation was born. The Protestant movement began as a revolt against the indulgence system of the Catholic church, a system that was used to raise money for salaries and building projects. Luther said that for a man to try to erase his sins one by one, through confession and absolution, was like trying to cure smallpox by picking off the scabs.

"The whole man is sick," my father said. "The only cure is acknowledgment of our sinfulness and acceptance of Jesus Christ into our hearts."

We were in the car, going to church. Bettye wasn't with us because she didn't feel well. We took it for granted by now that she often didn't feel well in the mornings. I had wanted to stay home too, but was never allowed to anymore. In fact, now my father was pressuring us to be baptized and to be confirmed. He, who had been so indifferent about our religious education all through our childhood, now had the fiery enthusiasm of the convert in his voice.

"Why can't I go back to Christian Science?"

"Because I want us to go to church as a family."

"I don't believe anything Pastor Jensen says."

"You just need to give it time. You need to study religion like you study anything else. The Bible is more interesting than you give it credit."

He was trying to get me to join the Sunday School class he'd begun to teach, a class of nerdy Lutheran teenagers. "The Bible is real history," he went on enthusiastically. "The Dead Sea Scrolls prove it's all true."

Once I'd enjoyed it when my father talked to me about history, but now it bored me stiff. He was always going on about the Dead Sea

Scrolls. Whatever they were. I pictured a few urns in caves by a waterless lake.

Besides I knew that half the things in the Bible were made up, were just metaphors to illustrate some deeper truth.

"Your brother has agreed to be baptized."

I looked at Bruce in the back seat in disbelief. "What for?" I said.

He shrugged and looked out the window. "It's no big deal. Everybody gets baptized."

"Not in Christian Science."

"I'm not a Christian Scientist anymore. It's too weird."

"Oh, so what are you now—a Lutheran?"

"Yes."

"You lying traitor."

Away from Bettye, in front of our father, we could still argue without getting punished. "Kids!" he said. "It's Sunday."

"Well, I'm *never* getting baptized," I said.

My father said, "If you're not baptized, you'll go to hell."

"You don't really believe that, do you?"

"You'll see when you get there if I was right."

"You just calmly sit there and tell me I'm going to hell?"

"Why are you always so stubborn?"

"I'm not stubborn. I just don't think the way you do. I don't believe that man is sick. I don't believe in sickness."

But it was no use disagreeing. My stubbornness had became legendary. "She is the stubbornest girl I ever met," I heard Bettye tell someone, loudly, on the phone. My father said, "You must take after your grandmother. She was the stubbornest woman alive."

I didn't care what they said. I didn't believe everything they told me, and if that was being stubborn, fine. I even I liked thinking it was something I might have in my genes, a heritage passed onto me from my grandmother. Stubbornness might have bypassed my mother, who was half-crushed by the steamroller that was my grandmother, but it would not bypass me. I might not be a steamroller, but I would be a stone in the road of whoever tried to crush me.

Janie meant for the books on the atomic bombings to awaken me to political reality, and they did. After reading them I took down my

Goldwater bumper sticker and became a pacifist. I bought a Peter, Paul, and Mary album and one by Joan Baez and soon knew all the words to "Where Have All the Flowers Gone?"

Late 1964 and 1965 were the years when I woke up to the world I lived in, the years when civil rights began to have meaning to me, when I understood that white people in the South were beating up and killing black children out of pure hatred. I woke up and saw that the United States, the country I had so mindlessly saluted every morning, was rapacious and ill-intentioned toward the rest of the world. Under the guise of democracy it had tolerated and encouraged racism at home and oppression abroad.

Most adolescents come to the age when they ask, furiously, "Is this the world you've left me? It's so fucked-up." Most adolescents understand then that their formerly all-powerful parents are weak and hypocritical. And of course I felt this too. But in my case it was complicated by a Christian Science upbringing that had deliberately kept out news of the world and its violent, greedy, cruel, and indifferent history. I'd been protected from history as a child, had been told that reality was unreality so many times, that good was all and evil did not exist, that when I woke up, I woke up angry.

Reading about Hiroshima and Nagasaki gave me a hunger for more stories of horror and destruction. I moved on to books about the Holocaust, and not just the *Diary of Anne Frank*, but *Mila 18*, the Leon Uris novel about the Warsaw Ghetto Uprising, and memoirs of Auschwitz and Treblinka. But reading about the concentration camps was a fundamentally different experience than reading about the atomic bombings. When I read about the latter I was angry at the U.S. government, was horrified at what I called "man's inhumanity to man," was full of pity and sorrow for the dead and more for the living. But when I read about Auschwitz or Treblinka, my horror and sadness mingled with a sense of identification that was missing with the victims of the mushroom cloud. I too had felt ordered about and treated badly, I too had the sense of not being able to escape the fickle wrath of a sadistic guard. I could imagine myself in wooden shoes that didn't fit, vainly holding on to my bowl of broth, standing knee-deep in mud, trying only to survive and to hold on to some tiny remnant of my humanity. I could imagine Bettye as Eichmann, giving the order to send me to the showers, while my father, the capo, averted his eyes and pushed me into the gas chamber. All the time talking about God and salvation.

I became politicized in part through my own suffering and through the injustices done me. But my specific distrust of the adults who ordered me around and whose hypocrisy I could plainly see, fed into a growing anti-authoritarianism that was mirrored in the youth culture around me. It could be as cheeky as the Beatles, as accusing as Bob Dylan, or as rude as Frank Zappa, but definitely gave the finger to adult values, which were not only square and old-fashioned but also were harmful to children and other living things.

Like many in my generation it became easier for me to feel outraged on behalf of populations of people whom I didn't know than to feel compassion for one individual, especially myself (self-pity yes, but not compassion). Outrage at injustice gave me a sense of community and power. It didn't bother me to be in the minority—I was used to that from childhood—because I felt in the minority that had right on its side. My shame and anger about my own sad little life, its loneliness, losses, and humiliations, was projected out, and made righteous. I couldn't speak out on behalf of myself (because I couldn't talk about my life, and who would listen anyway?), but I could speak out on behalf of all other oppressed people. And I did.

My poetry, which for the last year had mainly been abstract descriptions of sunrises that, not being a morning person, I had never seen, now veered into the political. When I went to the beach I no longer saw the bright blue waves crashing on the shore, but the craters left by the building of sandcastles which I found very reminiscent of Hiroshima.

I wrote:

> The pock-marked shore
> Remnants of a child's play
> The pock-marked world
> Remnants of a child's war.

And I showed this to Janie and other friends, along with many other poems like it that were equally deeply felt. I now scorned writing that was merely entertaining and I turned my back decisively on the magical fairy tales and novels of my childhood in favor of books that offered social commentary like *The Grapes of Wrath*, *Of Mice and Men*, *A Farewell to Arms*, and *All Quiet on the Western Front*. I read my first novel by a black writer, James Baldwin's *Go Tell It on the Mountain*, and was moved to indignation that I had never known his world existed. Although I had yet to meet a single black person, I talked knowingly and angrily with Janie about prejudice and that summer, when Watts burned, I told my speechless father that I hoped they would destroy every building in Los Angeles, *and* Long Beach, because we deserved it.

Literature had to grapple with the difficult things in life, I thought, ignoring the fact that most writers wrote about the difficult things in *their* lives. Literature must take on great themes: love and death and tragedy. Literature must grapple with the notions of Good and Evil.

But here I faltered, here I came up against a lifetime of Christian Science indoctrination. I found it hard to name that which was not good. I might close myself in my room, with Bob Dylan on the record player singing "A Hard Rain's Gonna Fall," and sit there reading Steinbeck or writing protest poetry, working myself into a state about "man's inhumanity to man." But to actually go further, to label what was done to man by man, never mind by man to woman, evil—that was a step I could not quite take. For it meant, once and for all, acknowledging that the God, the all-loving, all-knowing, all-powerful, all-good God I had known as a child, did not exist. And I knew that once I let go of this God, this god of my childhood, I would not be able to believe in another one. And that meant I would cease to believe.

I'd been edging closer to this position for some time, and it had been fueled by my father's rabid conversion to Lutheranism. In church I would sit listening to Pastor Jensen give one of his fire-and-brimstone sermons and I would think of the Hiroshima survivors walking speechlessly away from the blast like blackened ghosts. I would think of the crematoria at Auschwitz and Buchenwald and hear the screams of children locked in the shower room. If I believed in any hell, it was the hell that humanity had made for itself. Once I had prayed regularly, and though my prayers had been laced with uncomprehending pain, still they had been prayers. "Please God," I had prayed. "My mother is a perfect child of the universe. Let that perfection be reflected in her face." But now I could not pray at all.

No adult Christian Scientist had ever tried to sit down with me and help me understand the meaning of what had happened. To acknowledge that anything *had* happened would be to give in to mortal mind, would be to believe a lie. So I was left to struggle on alone in a theological wilderness, asking Job-like questions. If God was so good, how could He have let my mother suffer so much? If God really cared, why had He given me a stepmother like Bettye? Like many better theologians, for a while I came to a temporary solution. God may not love us quite as much as we would like Him to, but He still loves us. And any God, even an indifferent one, was better than no God.

The last time I'd gone to the old Christian Science Sunday School was on Easter when I was thirteen. I was supposed to go to the Lutheran church with the rest of them; instead I'd called up Georgina and asked her to come get me. As the rest of the family was preparing to leave for the church service, I ran out of the house to Georgina's car and jumped in. But that Sunday was the last time I saw Georgina or any of the Christian Science friends and families I'd grown up with. As Edyth was to tell me years later, "It was like you all just dropped off the face of the earth."

Being openly Christian Scientist was out of the question at a time when I was trying to reshape my identity and to fit in with my new classmates. What a relief to say, when asked about my religion, "Nothing much." What a relief not to have to say, "I can't study science," or "I can't go to the school nurse." I no longer had to explain anything, or to consciously keep it a secret. No one in my life now had seen my mother or knew what had happened, and I wanted to keep it that way. But I had still kept up the belief system in my mind out of loyalty and habit. I didn't know another way to believe. Once I had come across an article in *Writer's Digest* called "The Problem of Evil for the Novelist," by Erskine Caldwell, and I had closed the magazine quickly, without reading it, out of sheer nervousness. Does a novelist have to write about evil? Shouldn't writing be about truth and beauty? Shouldn't I continue to write the way my mother would have wanted me to, forgetting about mortal error and telling stories of healing and love?

But my encounter with the magazine article was before I threw myself into the Holocaust and Hiroshima and civil rights and Vietnam. Knowing about all those things, how could anyone believe that man's nature was essentially good? The Lutherans, of course, had presented a way out. Although man was sinful, man could be saved by God. But I struggled with the notion of an arbitrary God who only saved certain people. For if people could only be saved by God and yet most people were not saved (which is why there were churches and missionaries) then what did that say about the nature of God?

I could more easily believe in the all-good God of the Christian Scientists than in the God of the Lutherans who played favorites. And although I could see that there were many bad people in the world, starting with Bettye and going right up to President Johnson—who was hardly better than Goldwater, even Janie had to admit, when it came to stopping the Vietnam War from escalating—I balked at the idea that my own nature was essentially sinful, and that *I* needed to be saved as much as anyone else. Because I was not to blame.

Most people I know who lost their faith in their teens treat it as a joke or a necessary rite of passage. Some friends tell stories of becoming extra-religious in an effort to stave off disbelief, of going to Christian fellowship meetings or revivals, of dreaming of going to Israel to work on a kibbutz or to Africa to become a missionary. But hardly anyone spoke of their religion or their struggles at school. No one ever spoke of their struggle to me, and I never spoke to them. It wasn't cool to have a spiritual crisis, so whatever happened with people I knew to make them stop believing in God happened in private. My own spiritual battle took place over months and came to an end one evening after Bettye had been particularly spiteful to me and had sent me up to my room.

I put Dylan on the record player and played "Subterranean Homesick Blues" about five times in a row. I rocked back and forth with tears and made my usual secret threats: "If she ever hits me, I'm running away." I cried out once or twice, in the old way, for my mother. I asked why my life had to be like this, and reminded myself that prisoners in Auschwitz had it worse. I thought about the terrible sight of a mushroom cloud over Hiroshima. And then, when I was worn out and lying on my back on the floor, the simple thought crossed my mind, "There is no God."

And that was that.

In July, at the very height of summer, my brother and I flew to Battle Creek to visit our grandmother for six weeks by ourselves. On the way there I played at being sophisticated; I smoked a cigarette (from a complimentary pack that was on my lunch tray on the plane) at O'Hare, where we changed planes and where I made my brother walk a few feet behind me, for fear someone would think he was attached to me. But once we arrived in Battle Creek, I seemed to shed years, and gladly, and to become younger and younger.

For Battle Creek, compared to Southern California, seemed as plain as apple cobbler, and the house on North Broad Street, with its simple horsehair furniture covered with doilies, was a haven compared to the overdecorated one where we lived in Long Beach. Next to my stepmother, the grandmother I had remembered as fierce and controlling seemed the essence of mild rationality. She never made us do housework and rarely asked us to do anything we didn't want to. There was no talk of punishment and generally it was easy to do what she asked. We were so grateful to be out of Bettye's jurisdiction and so much more conscious of our grandmother's kindness than her severity that we rushed to please her. Her stubborn morality now seemed a thing to be trusted and relied upon, not battled. How reassuring it was that her world, this world, still went on in the same old way.

Every morning Grandma got up from the carved walnut bed across the room from where I slept. She put in her teeth and braided her thin, snowy white hair before putting it up. She eased herself into her slip (she never wore a bra, but laced herself into a corset before she went to church on Sundays), and then into one of the patterned rayon dresses that buttoned up the front. She always pinned a small cameo above the top button, so that the V was less pronounced under the cascade of wrinkles that was her neck and throat. She put on her stockings last, some kind of support hose, and then her slippers. Sometimes I slept through this, for it was only five A.M. with the first birds barely up, and sometimes I watched her from the comfort of her old marriage bed with its soft mattress and well-bleached soft white sheets.

I knew that she was going downstairs and into her study, the glassed-in sun porch, to do her mental work. She would read and study the Weekly Lesson and then begin to pray for her clients, whoever and wherever they were. By the time I finally made it downstairs, at ten or eleven, she was finished with giving absent treatments, and had finished doing the housework as well. She might be baking a cherry pie or ironing in front of the TV, for she loved to watch soap operas, especially *As the World Turns* with its gloomy organ music. Sometimes I would come down the stairs, still groggy from our late-night TV watching, and I'd hear, "And that's the real reason I can't marry you, Matthew," punctuated by a fatalistic chord. Grandma never felt the need to justify her love of the soaps, or explain how their drama-laden world view was compatible with Christian Science.

We never went to the movies in Battle Creek and there was no mall.

My brother found friends in the neighborhood to play with; I took an art class at a local school and often walked downtown to the old-fashioned Willard Library. The days were slow and hot and the sidewalks shaded by huge old Dutch elms. When I reached the library I'd sit awhile on the steps before going in the square old brick building. I was reading Dickens that summer and trying to read *War and Peace*. I checked it out twice and spent many hours trying to get through the first chapter, where seemingly dozens of people with patronymics are introduced, all throwing around French phrases. Eventually I found a friend too, a girl one grade older named Lisa. Lisa was not the first girl I had yearned towards for her sweet normalness, but she was the first one who saw me as normal. And in the context of Battle Creek and my grandmother's house and community, I did seem normal. As long as I didn't talk about anything that had happened to me, I could be an innocent young girl again, swimming and canoeing with Lisa on the lake, where her parents, who attended the Christian Science church and were friends of my grandmother, had a house. Though I had begun the summer bragging to a few girls I met about the exciting and dangerous life I lived in California, what with my surfboard and boyfriend with a motorcycle, within a week or two I'd forgotten that life ever existed. The surfboard had just been on loan from Joyce's brother, and the boyfriend had been Joyce's too.

Sometimes I tried to explain to my grandmother what things were really like in the House of Bettye and once I suggested that maybe I could just stay with my grandmother through high school. She looked more uneasy than thrilled by the idea. "But Bettye can't be that bad."

"She *is*. She's, she's"—I knew any real details, from Bettye's drinking and childish sadism to my suicide attempt, would shock her—"she's a *Lutheran*. She made Bruce get baptized."

But my grandmother just sighed. "Water means nothing one way or the other."

In Battle Creek we went to Sunday School and church. The congregation's decline had not yet begun and the wooden pews of the large church were packed. The familiarity of the service comforted me. What a relief not to have a red-faced man shouting about going to hell. The Sunday School was full of bright-faced, sober Midwestern children, attentive and saying all the things I had once believed, had once believed so very deeply. Instead of acting the cool California teenager with them, I sat quietly and read from the Bible in my turn and felt something of their reflected faith beam mildly and kindly in my direction.

I didn't tell anyone, not my grandmother of course, and not my Sunday School teacher or even my new friend Lisa, that I no longer believed in Christian Science and no longer even believed in God. I could not bring myself to quarrel with Christian Science as I had with Lutheranism. I didn't sit in church on Sunday and say to myself, *Well, what about Hiroshima? Where were you, oh all-powerful, all-loving, all-knowing God, when the bomb was dropped on children who blistered and blackened?* I didn't bring up the Holocaust to my kindly Sunday School teacher, a graying man about the same age as my father. I didn't demand to know the church's position on civil rights or Vietnam. I simply sat there in class, loving the language of the King James Version, and feeling very safe and very much at home.

The one disturbing thing about that summer was Uncle Andrew. One day we visited him at the big redbrick V.A. Hospital outside town. We walked through seeming miles of corridors with a medicinal smell that I thought I had forgotten, and saw old men without legs and wearing bathrobes in wheelchairs everywhere. When we came to the section where Andrew lived, we encountered slobbering grown infants and vacant-faced giants in blue work overalls. Next to these people Andrew seemed normal; when we arrived at the laundry where he worked, he seemed to be completely at ease and relaxed. Still it was sobering to see him in an institution that was so similar to the sanitarium where we used to visit our mother. She hadn't seemed crazy some of the time, and yet she was. How could it be that a brother and sister could both go crazy, for no good reason? Bruce and I didn't say much during the visit to the V.A. Hospital. I know now from talking to him that he also feared sudden madness as much as I did.

A few times Andrew came for Sunday dinner and once or twice friends took us all to Howard Johnson's. I generally avoided looking at him or talking to him as much as possible. I didn't know why. Was his craziness a reminder of my mother's, or was it something more? One hot afternoon I was lying on my grandmother's bed, once again trying to read *War and Peace,* and he came up the stairs—I heard his slow, deliberate footsteps—and stood in the doorway close by the bed. His brown hair was roughly cut, beginning to gray, above his craggy, still handsome features. Now he wore glasses, and his speech was slow and labored.

"What are you reading?"

"*War and Peace.*" My heart was pounding. Why was it so frightening to have him standing there by the side of the bed?

"That's a big book."

"Yeah."

He waited a while and then, shoulders sagging, turned and walked back downstairs. I felt terribly cruel and guilty. He had just been trying to make contact! But underneath that was relief he was gone, that he was not looking at me, standing so close like that. It had given me some feeling of—well, I didn't know what.

My grandmother treated him normally, that is, with some irritation and with great love. But she never spoke of his condition to us. She never mentioned our mother, not in Andrew's presence certainly, but not otherwise either. I would not have known how to ask her how she felt about what had happened. Being back in this house again reminded me every day of my mother, just in the smells, the cellar, the kitchen, the little parlor with the piano and horsehair furniture. But I didn't know how to say it. It was part of the reason, though, I slipped back to childhood there and that I wanted to stay.

"You wouldn't be happy here," said my grandmother. "And I'm getting too old to struggle with you. I have Andrew to worry about. That's enough."

We were sitting on the front lawn, as we often did after dinner. Bruce was still playing, though it was dusk, with friends down the street. Occasionally neighbors wandered by and stopped to chat. In humid dark evening, with mosquitoes nipping at my legs, and the stars overhead, a glass of lemonade by my side, fireflies sparkling by, I felt at home. If I lived here, I could go to the high school where my mother went, and to the same college. And I wouldn't have to struggle to be in the cool crowd and not be seen as enough of a girl or too smart. I would stay friends with Lisa and be a bookworm and go to the Christian Science church, not telling anyone I didn't believe; everything that had happened in the past would fade away, as if it had never happened.

"But I wouldn't struggle, Grandma! They say I'm stubborn, but I'm not stubborn. I just don't . . . I don't agree with them."

She sighed and shook her head, which was so white in the dark evening. I never thought of her as being seventy-five or of having lost her husband and her two children, of the price she had to pay to keep their memories out of her mind. I saw her as the powerful woman of my childhood, who could protect me and keep me safe. I didn't see she might have cause to be afraid of me and the questions I would have. That that was partly why she pushed me away. That night she only said, "It's your nature to get your back up and refuse to be pushed around. But in the end, that will help you. It has always helped me. It will get you through."

My grandmother always went to bed early, by nine-thirty, and she believed that Bruce and I followed her not too much later. In reality Bruce and I usually stayed up till one or two, playing cards and watching old movies on TV. The old television was upstairs, in the small room where my brother slept, in what used to be Andrew's room. It was piled with boxes of clothes and books, and had a closetlike feel, with a slanted roof. It was always very hot up there, even at midnight. The heat was the reason we couldn't get to sleep in the first place, for it was a humid, heavy Midwestern heat, not the kind we were used to. But we liked spending time together; it was the closest we'd been for years. At home there was always so much separating us. Now we could talk about Bettye and just how horrible she was. Now we could both say, "If only Grandma would let us stay here forever." Now I could ask him about his baptism: "Why?"

"Because . . . if I die, then who knows what happens? If you're baptized, then at least you *know*."

"Know what?" I demanded. "And besides, you're not going to *die*."

"Jamie did," Bruce said. "Jamie died. And *he* was baptized, 'cause he was a Baptist."

Earlier this spring we'd received an invitation to the funeral of Bruce's best friend from the old neighborhood, Jamie Krebs. Johnnie and Jamie had gone hiking in the Sierras, which were still snowy, and had gotten separated from the rest of the group. Although Johnnie had tried to cover Jamie with his body, by the time they were found in the morning, Jamie was blue and stiff.

At the funeral we'd seen our old friends from the neighborhood. All the black snap had gone out of Keith Krebs's eyes, and Dot, more white-faced than I remembered, could not stop weeping. Her face was soft and broken at the same time. My father went up and touched them on the shoulders. Keith grabbed his hand and shook it hard. They all knew now what it was like to lose someone. The three of them stood there, sorry for the past.

Johnnie was wearing a suit, standing by the open coffin of his brother as we filed by. He was handsome now, big and blond, his cowlicks neatly Brylcreamed down, the boy I once would have liked to be, or have lived next door to always. I wanted him to notice that I had changed too, that I was better-looking than I used to be, that I was older. Between us, Jamie lay in the coffin, in a suit, but just as freckled as ever, as if he were simply sleeping. My brother sobbed next to me as we stopped— to die in the snow after all those fires of their childhood, how could that have ever happened?—and Johnnie looked up as if in a dream. It was the old face I had known since I was a baby, brown eyes, scrunched-up face, a little goofy.

"Johnnie," I said, holding out my hands.

"My name is John now," he said automatically. "Thanks for coming."

Now I said to my brother, giving him permission, "You can get baptized. Water doesn't mean anything one way or the other. But never get confirmed. Because then you'll be a Lutheran forever, even when you're dead."

At midnight every night there was a movie on TV; for reasons I never understood the station ran the same movie all week. My brother and I had gotten in the habit of staying up late to watch some of these movies, sometimes once, sometimes several times. One week we watched *Titanic* five times in a row. We didn't say we were going to, or discuss it during the day, but at midnight all that week we gravitated to the hot little dormer room and turned the set on once again.

This film about the sinking of the *Titanic* was a 1953 rerun with Barbara Stanwyck and Clifton Webb. Most of the film was taken up with the drama of a failed marriage and the revelations and recriminations between the husband and wife ("He's not your son!"), with a secondary plot involving a romance between the daughter and a Purdue college boy. But there were just enough ironies (which were even more apparent once you'd seen the film more than once) to keep the tension up. People talked about how lucky they were to find a seat on this maiden voyage, and they talked about what they were going to do once they disembarked in New York. Mr. Astor had waiting for him in New York not just a railway car, but a whole train. Everyone mentioned the unsinkability of the ship at the same time as the officers noticed that there were not enough binoculars to go around. "Those in the crow's nest will just have to do without," said the captain. The first-class passengers were absorbed in their elegant, vacuous lives, dining, dancing, playing bridge, while those in steerage huddled in their shawls, muttering in foreign languages and making their own music. Meanwhile warnings from nearby ships about ice floes in the Labrador Current went ignored. "This is our second-in-command," the captain said to some wealthy passengers, introducing an anxious mate who had come to ask if the *Titanic* should perhaps proceed more cautiously. "He's the worried type."

Darkness fell and most people were in their cabins, sleeping or getting ready for sleep, when—straight ahead—the fatal iceberg loomed up. In this film version the sky was gray rather than jet black and the iceberg had a menacing, sculptured look. Orders were quickly given for the ship to bear hard aft, and at first it looked as if the ship had narrowly missed the iceberg. Up top anyway; we viewers saw the underwater view: a sharp blade of ice slicing the hull like a can opener.

And then inexorably (even more inexorably by the time you'd seen the film two or three times), the countdown to tragedy began. The realization that there were only nineteen lifeboats for more than two thousand people, the deliberate calmness with which the passengers, especially those in first class, were enjoined by the stewards and officers to dress warmly, put on their lifejackets and proceed to the boats. The realization when they got to the boats that only the women and children were getting on. The irritation of some elegant ladies with the whole tiresome affair, the reluctance of many ladies to leave their husbands, the steadfast courage of most of the men at seeing their families depart, and the abysmal cowardice of a few in dressing up in bonnets and shawls. The hysteria of the steerage passengers at being kept from the boats until the first-class passengers had boarded; the luck of a few, the misfortune of many. The heroism of most of the officers and the great discipline they showed in the face of certain knowledge of death.

And through all this wound the story of the family we'd been watching, the caddish father suddenly revealed to be strong under pressure and capable of great, almost offhand gallantry. The wife suddenly realizing how much she loved him, now that this was it. The little son, wanting to be like his father, jumping off the lifeboat at the last minute to give his seat to an old immigrant woman. The mother's anguish when she sees him gone. The father's despair and pride when he understands his son will go down with him.

The first night our tears were unexpected, and came upon us near the end, when the little boy stood with his father on the deck, and when, still singing the Welsh hymn, "Nearer My God to Thee," on the tilted deck of the ship, the passengers and crew realized they were lost. But by the second night we had quietly begun to weep at the second the iceberg first appeared, knowing that while the passengers on the upper decks continued to play bridge, soon the icy waters of the Atlantic would begin to pour in.

We cried, as we shifted viewpoints, from doomed passenger in the seconds before the ship sank into the icy sea with mighty roar, to shocked survivor staring back at the disaster that a few hours before seemed unimaginable. We didn't talk about what we felt, or why the story of the *Titanic* so riveted us, just as we had never talked much about what happened to our mother and why our lives had gone the way they had. We only cried in that little hot room that smelled of mildew and heat and the long ago past, and we understood through that movie that to be a survivor of such a tragedy is hardly to be a survivor at all.

It doesn't matter that you lived through it. You will never be the same, because you will always, even though you try so very hard not to, you will always remember the sight of the ship going down, with the person you loved best in the world going down with it.

Part Three

Testimony

Chapter 14

Stand Porter at the Door of Thought

*"Mother-love—isn't it awful. I long for an Arctic climate where
no emotions of any sort can possibly grow . . ."*

—Elizabeth Bishop, letter

"Refrigeration is our only preservative."

—Marie's Salad Dressing bottle

*H*e was looking hard into my eyes in his little soundproof
room at the back of the drama classroom. "You're very deep, Barbara,"
said Mr. McMenamin, and I was flattered. But then he went on, "I don't
know what we're going to do with you. I don't know what parts I can
give you that would suit you." He shook his full head of black hair with
the dramatic white streak and waggled his black and white overhang-
ing brows. After my promising start in the tenth grade directing and
starring in a one-act, he had invited me to join his Advanced Drama
class, a rarefied group of the beautiful, the talented, and the misfit. But
all through my junior year he had insisted on casting me in boy's roles
and marginal ones at that, a soldier in *Abraham Lincoln* and Tom
Sawyer's friend in a gender-bending production of *Tom Sawyer*. I didn't
mind wearing boy's clothes, or even a beard, but I wanted something
I could sink my teeth into. A leading part in *The Crucible* had turned
my head and now, in my senior year, I longed to really let loose and
emote. Whenever we got to choose something to present to the class,
I picked something like Ophelia's mad scene or Medea's speech after
she'd killed her children.

"When I look at you, I think, O'Neill," he said in that cryptic, intense way of his, with his big head tilted to the side. "O'Neill, I think. A woman going crazy, yes. There's a one-act, I remember. Just the thing for that competition that's coming up. Your husband is the captain of a whaling ship. And you've persuaded him to bring you along. You've been trapped in the ice for months now and are begging to go home. He's agreed and you're just about to return to Nantucket when the first mate calls, 'Whales!' "

"Whales?" I said.

"He's seen a school of them. Your husband is a whaler. He leaves you to go on deck. You can't take it. You go to your piano and begin to play. Your mind has snapped."

"Am I supposed to play the piano?"

"Just a few deranged chords, don't worry. We'll get some portable thing. You'll be great."

Drama, always written and pronounced with a capital *D*, was more than a class in high school. It was way of life, and a world. Though I also took art and creative writing, they remained classes. The Drama crowd was my crowd and the Drama schedule provided a haven for me as it did many of my friends. It provided not only a focus at school, but something to do most afternoons, many evenings and weekends. Even if I wasn't rehearsing, I could always go into the darkened auditorium and watch the rehearsals. In the chummy dimness of the auditorium or in the wings, I felt myself safe and protected. Being in theater was like being in a religious sect: you felt special, chosen, and unable to explain its attraction when out of its confines.

At home things had gone downhill. Sometime during my first year of high school, Bettye had stopped speaking to me. It began in a kind of huff one day, and then just continued, until it became part of the way life was. If she had a message for me she would make my father deliver it, but as the months went on, there were fewer and fewer messages. She glared at me if she saw me in her vicinity, but the lectures about my clothes and hair and posture were over. So were dinners together. She stopped cooking and ate her special ulcer diet—egg dishes, puddings and Jell-O. She did not stop drinking, but it was hidden from us. She'd installed a Yale lock on the door to the Master Suite after realizing that Mike had been in and had taken various objects (she would have liked to have blamed the thefts on me, but must have realized I was hardly enterprising enough to fence a jewelry box, much less a lamp), and spent most of her time there. She worked full-time, but always for different companies, since she was always quarreling with her employers and quitting. She continued to take many sick days and to visit doctors. Her ulcers worsened and during my senior year she went into the hospital. After she'd been there a month, the billing department noticed that she didn't have any insurance. Either she or my father had forgotten or neglected to pay the premium.

Forgetting to pay bills was a habit at our house. I wore my braces for almost two years, but only went to the orthodontist for the first six months. Eventually I begged just to have them *off*. It was the same with many things that started out in a more prosperous time. Most of the clothes I had, Bettye had bought me during a single day's shopping spree in the eighth grade. I wore them all through high school. Still, we'd staggered along. I worked occasionally and Bruce had a paper route: we were no worse off really than many of our classmates. It was only that we looked as if we should be doing better, in that big house, with all that plastic-covered white brocade furniture that no one ever sat on. At least that's what I told myself, we were no worse off, for I was already adept at secrecy and denial. If life seemed easier, it was because I had resources now besides my own imagination and reading that I hadn't had before: friends whose houses were open to me, activities at high school, the college classes I had begun to take at Long Beach City when I was sixteen, and, of course, Drama.

I still have my copy of *The Long Voyage Home: Seven Plays of the Sea* by Eugene O'Neill. My penciled notes in the margin of "Ile" (the New England word for oil) are there too. Even though O'Neill had given me, Mrs. Keeney, plenty of stage direction himself—[Dully], [Intensely], [Wildly]—I have written in things like "low crooning voice" and "rock back and forth." I took my descent into madness seriously. I had seen someone pacing the hall, I had seen wild, unseeing eyes, I had heard repetitious muttering. I knew how it was done. It felt like my last chance, this one-act, to show what I could do. To get it out of my system.

For though I had loved to act since I was a child, I'd never thought of making acting my profession, any more than I'd thought of trying to become a professional artist because I'd always enjoyed my art classes. It wasn't a matter of not feeling sufficiently attractive or talented, or even of realizing how difficult it was to make a life in the theater; it was that I continued to believe in myself as a writer. Yet in high school I threw myself into Drama the way I never could in my creative writing class, where sweet, prematurely white-haired Miss Peel labored to help us understand the difference between metaphor and simile. The reason I loved the theater and felt at home there while I struggled with my assignments in creative writing were the same as in my childhood when I play-acted with Johnnie. Play-acting was make-believe. You could be anything or anyone. You didn't have to be just *you*. You weren't bounded by your own limitations, or own experience. You could be an old lady, a boy, or the rear end of a horse in a costume. When I played Dulcinea I was beautiful; when I was Tom Sawyer's friend I was a somersaulting scene-stealer. Writing fiction, writing from the imagination was make-believe, too, but I never found it far enough removed from my reality. "Start from something you know and change it," Miss Peel was always suggesting when we looked at her blank-faced. But for a long time I didn't want to know what I knew. Didn't want to admit it was me who knew it.

Drama offered me a solution for dealing with my fear of and my desire for attention. From being a bold little girl who had once wanted every eye on her, I'd become nervous and shy about being stared at. Even with my mother dead, the effect still lingered, and sometimes I felt her ghost behind me, over my shoulder. I still imagined I could hear someone whisper, "What's wrong with that woman's face?" Acting solved the problem. I could wear my helmet of darkness yet not be invisible. I could be on stage, the focus of everyone's interest, but I could be up there as someone else besides me, expressing or venting emotion without anyone imagining it was my emotion. Even in class, without make-up or costume, I could transform myself into another character. A character, for instance, who went mad. I could draw on my own experience of having seen someone career into madness, cross the line from health to sickness, without having to acknowledge that I myself had seen such a thing. I could explore the state of being mad without going crazy myself.

Mr. Mac had told us about the origin of theater, as a Greek ritual of Dionysus. "It was an opportunity for the Greeks to get all that emotion out in public," he said. "To get rid of it. The Greeks called it *cathar-*

sis." I both craved and hated the part of me that needed to perform my catharsis in public, and often. Ultimately I didn't want to just confine it to the stage. I wanted to master it, and to eradicate it if I could. The Greeks had obviously thought long and hard about this whole problem of excess and moderation, and I turned to them for help.

The summer before my senior year I'd begun taking morning classes at Long Beach City College and was now enrolled in Ancient Greek Philosophy. The questions the Greeks posed were essential; they were the ones I'd been asking myself. What was the world composed of? Why were we here? What should our behavior be? Philosophy asked the questions that Science did, but without all the icky mess of dissection, and went deeply into Religion without requiring belief in God. The early Greeks lived in a new, fresh world and their pronouncements had a cool clarity that I relished. Heraclitis, who believed that Fire was the main element of life, wrote, "The dry soul is wisest and best," and "It is death to soul to become water." I clung to such statements, for I was in a life and death struggle with my own personality to see which side would predominate—the immature, loud, to-hell-with-the-consequences drama queen or the withdrawn, solitary intellectual and writer. My struggle would go on for many years, until the drama queen finally expired for lack of oxygen and people praised me for my thoughtful calm, but it was in my senior year that the struggle began. Every morning I'd get up and read selections from the Greek philosophers before going to class, and every afternoon I'd rehearse one of my mad scenes for Drama. No one in my philosophy class, hearing me carefully elucidate the main points of Plato's *Republic*, could have imagined me compulsively rolling my eyes and pacing back and forth as Mrs. Keeney on the deck of the icebound boat. At seventeen I could only manage to be calm and rational for about an hour every day; still, I strove for this. What I thought I wanted was a life where I felt nothing, and never did an untoward or unexpected thing, a life where I never felt anyone looking at me, thinking, Lock *her* up.

One evening my father asked me what I was doing up in my room, muttering so loudly and pacing back and forth.

"I'm acting in a play. The woman goes mad in a boat that's stuck in the ice."

"Oh," he said, and hesitated at the door.

My father himself had acted in high school. He had been on the school newspaper, and had written term papers by the dozen to put himself through college. Still, he reminded me, often, that you couldn't make a living doing any of that "creative stuff." He urged me to think of the future, to settle for classes in business so I could become a secretary or bookkeeper, or if I really wanted to major in English, then to get a teaching certificate. Once he came for a meeting at my high school with my counselor after we had taken some tests. "You have a very high I.Q.," he said afterwards. "I'm not supposed to tell you how high." He seemed mystified and pleased. "You could do anything you want to," he added. "They say."

"I want to be a writer," I said with my usual bravado, though so far I never written a single thing that I liked a week later.

"You can't make a living that way."

I suspected he was right (and the years have proved him more or less correct), but it didn't mean anything. Writing I had always known to be my vocation. It wasn't about making a living; it was about accepting what I had been placed on earth to do.

"I *will* be a writer. Somehow."

He just sighed. "You'll see," he said. For not only was he an orphan and child of the Depression, he was a man for whom little had turned out the way he expected. Life had dealt him one series of blows after the next, and he had no reason to believe that it would be any different for me. In fact, life *had* already dealt me some terrible blows, some of which, like my uncle's abuse, my father didn't even know about. Still, my father was an example, just as he always had been, of a dogged survivor. And he recognized and fostered that quality in me. He believed I would be eventually be disappointed in my desire to become a writer, and yet he always said, "Be persistent in what you do." Mostly he instructed by the example of his own persistence, the old stories of the Orphan Triumphant who would always go on no matter what.

That evening he stood watching me in the doorway as I acted out some of my lines for him. "I won't stand it, I can't stand it, pent up by these walls like a prisoner. . . . Take me away from here, David! If I don't get away from here, out of this terrible ship, I'll go mad!"

On a chair sat the portable organ Mr. Mac had loaned me. I crashed out a few dirge-like chords that shook the house.

Bettye came to her door and shouted, "Is a little quiet when I'm sick too much to ask for?" and my father backed out into the hall, muttering, "Very convincing, Barb, very convincing."

My father and I had begun to talk more frequently and more deeply over the summer, after my grandmother died, when I was a senior. Sometimes when I came home late I would find him sitting in one of the recliners downstairs, smoking his pipe and reading *U.S. News and World Report*. We had political discussions sometimes, for I was strongly under the influence of my best friend Sandy's parents, the Freemans, liberal, antiwar Democrats. I challenged my father about the Vietnam War and sometimes he made me happy by saying, "Maybe you're right. I've been wrong about a lot of things." He told me about his own wartime experiences, generally a positive time in his life. And that led to his telling me about his first wife, Marion, and her death. He talked a little about my mother sometimes, very carefully, about the early days, the happy days. And we found ourselves talking about my uncle Andrew and my grandmother too.

The summer before my senior year I was supposed to visit Grandma Lane in Battle Creek. I'd been working on her for some time about such a trip, for two years, in fact, ever since I'd visited her last. My primary motivation was to get out of the house, of course, but that was not all. No, I actually wanted to see my grandmother. Over the past couple of years we'd become closer. She'd call from time to time and I'd tell her what I was doing, what I was reading. She'd send me books I asked for and sometimes a ten-dollar bill or a blouse or a sweater. More important than the presents were the notes that came with them. They told me that my grandmother cared for me, that she wished me well, that I was not alone in the world.

I have often wondered, if I'd gone that summer to see her, whether I could have prevailed upon her to let me stay, as was my Midwestern fantasy. I've wondered if I could have talked to her about my mother. I've wondered if the two of us, so alike in some ways, could have sat down and made peace and found a way to give each other the love we each so badly needed.

I'll never know. A week before I was to fly to Michigan, she had a stroke and was taken to the hospital. She lingered on a day or two and then she died. "It was a blessing," said my father. "Andrew wouldn't have been able to nurse her at home." For he was still in and out of the V.A. Hospital then.

I want there to be more success and happiness in my family's history. I want them all to have suffered less. I want them not to have died with so many hopes unfilled, so many words still locked in their throats. I want some kind of reparation for their silent pain, their broken hearts. But there is no reparation other than remembrance. I remember my grandmother for her stories of a headstrong girlhood; I remember her for her cherry pies and cameo pins; I remember her for her being, as her friend Verna said, "the kind of person who made you want to be well." I remember her for her laugh and her fierceness and for her rock-bottom belief in Mrs. Eddy and God, her stubborn allegiance to a religion that caused her, in the end, as much pain as happiness.

It turned out that my grandmother had remembered me as well. She left me and my brother each $4,000 in trust to use for "educational purposes." Only part of the money ended up going for college tuition. Most of it I used for travel to Europe to live, work, and study for three years, years that gave me connections with other cultures and helped make me a translator and a writer. Although I sometimes thought that my grandmother would be turning in her grave to see me wandering around Andalusia with my guitar, drinking sherry in dark bars and talking knowledgeably about *duende,* or washing dishes on a Norwegian ship sailing up around the North Cape, sometimes I thought she might have admired my spirit, the spirit I had inherited from her.

I missed my grandmother when she died, but it was nothing like the pain I'd suffered when my mother died. It was more an empty feeling, a further sense of abandonment, of connection and meaning shut off. During this time I turned to my father in a way I hadn't been able to for a long time. We sat late nights in recliners facing each other in the family room that had rarely seen any family life. Mike was long gone, Bruce was asleep. Upstairs in the cold Master Suite was Bettye, but my father seemed to prefer to be downstairs with me, contemplating his childhood and his later struggles and losses, giving me, seventeen and about to go my own way, some cautionary lessons.

I had two parents. One had too many feelings and went crazy. The other was closed off and damped down—he survived, though not intact. There was the example of my stepmother, too, of course, whose anger turned in on itself in alcoholism and ulcers, but I didn't see her way as a choice. I saw only feeling or not feeling, acting or philosophy. Evenings when I used to sit talking with my father late and he related once again the stories of his boyhood to me were evenings when I learned his lesson, that the death of the feeling self was the price of survival.

One day, just after I'd graduated from high school, my stepmother slapped my face. This was a surprise to both of us, I think. In the early years of our acquaintance, I'd lived in daily fear of being beaten by her, and I knew that it was only my father's presence that prevented her from knocking the living daylights out of me. For she used to say, "If you were my daughter, I'd put you over my knee, pull down your pants, and paddle you till you couldn't stand up." The few times my father had hit me were at her urging.

Her rage that day was illogical, but that was nothing new. She'd given Bruce some money to buy our father a shirt for Father's Day. I'd gone with him and we'd picked out a blue, short-sleeved one. Now she was at my bedroom door claiming that we were supposed to buy him a white one. I said, "Bruce didn't say it had to be white. We thought blue was okay."

Thwack, my head snapped back, and a burning sting went across my cheek. Furiously, but unsteadily, Bettye turned away. "That will show you not to talk back to me," she said, going down the hall into the Master Suite and slamming the door.

I walked out of the house and didn't come back. The old promise I'd made myself years ago, "If she ever hits me, I'm running away," still held. I walked around for hours and then I went to a friend's house and stayed there.

The life that had begun in such a flurry of interior decorating and gourmet meals, of hopes on both Bettye's and my father's side for a new start, had been crumbling for at least six months. Bettye's uninsured hospitalization had guaranteed that they would never climb out of debt now. My father left his beloved teaching job so he could collect his pension early, but that still wasn't enough to keep up with the mortgage payments. About a week before Bettye slapped me, I'd been sitting with a friend in the kitchen when there was a hammering at the front door. We went out to see what was happening and found an official-looking document nailed to the door. I tried to rip it off before my friend could read it. BANK AUCTION, it read. The ice was breaking up around the frozen sea that had held our unhappy family boat, and we were all moving into dangerous waters.

My father and Bettye decided to separate for a while, and part of the reason was that my father was angry she'd hit me. Bettye took most of the furniture, including everything that had been my mother's, and moved into a two-story town house. We got the three Naugahyde recliners and squeezed into a small two-bedroom apartment. My brother slept on a cot in the living room. He would get my room when I went away to college in the fall.

Sometimes my brother has said to me, "Where were you when I needed you, when I was in high school? It's like you just vanished." And I feel a terrible guilt at abandoning him. After I left things got worse for Bruce, especially after Bettye and my father reunited. Bruce ran away from home, didn't finish high school, joined the Army young. Eventually he found his feet, married well and happily, and has raised three wonderful children, but all that has been through his own effort, not from any help he received from us. In Bruce's eyes I did vanish; more or less, it's true. I left the city, the state, and, eventually, the country. I couldn't get far enough away from everything that had gone before. I stopped taking Drama and appearing on stage, but I still hoped that if I tried hard enough, I could become someone else.

Perhaps it was inevitable that I drifted into health care work to pay the bills while I began my other careers of writer and publisher. That I looked for balance, that I tried to remedy my entrenched ignorance about the ways of the body. But at the time I took it up at twenty-five, newly moved to Seattle after years of restless travel, working as a hospital ward clerk seemed just a job with flexible hours, reasonable pay, and medical benefits. I liked the work, too, for its camaraderie, and because when it was busy I worked intensely and when it was slow I could sit around reading books or waiting room magazines. I never had to pretend to be occupied or that I was doing the work more than temporarily, until Seal Press and my writing could support me. Most of my nine years as a ward clerk were spent evenings and weekends on a pediatric unit, though I also worked on the orthopedic, rehab, and kidney wards, and for an eerie six months on a coronary care unit in a Catholic hospital where, after calling the code when someone had a heart attack, I also had to phone the resident priest to come administer last rites.

It was a strange job for a girl raised as a Christian Scientist, who didn't know an aorta from an aneurysm when she started. My job, of course, was not to know, only to carry out the orders of those who had been to medical school and did know. Still, I couldn't transcribe orders from the patient's chart to the nurses' cards and make up requisition slips for lab work and X-rays, and I couldn't write out the names of medications and the results of blood tests and procedures without picking up some medical knowledge. I couldn't overhear the doctors talking to the nurses, the doctors explaining things to the patients or their relatives, or the nurses talking to each other without learning how specific illnesses were diagnosed and how they were treated. I picked up so much over the years that I, who'd never had a biology class or been more than half a dozen times to the doctor in my own life, found myself saying things like, "Take a look at these lab results. The electrolytes look off," or soothing the parents of sick children by explaining hospital routines and procedures. My friends began to ask me medical questions about themselves and their families, assuming that if I worked in hospital I must know something.

The particular smell of a hospital, once so nauseating to me, became familiar, as did the sight of half-naked people in hospital gowns being wheeled by on stretchers or wheelchairs. Blood in vials sat on the counter in front of me, and samples of stool and urine. More than once, because I worked off-hours, I found myself helping a nurse hold down a wriggly child so she could insert an IV. More than once I changed a putrid diaper or held a baby who was dying on my lap. All this grew to seem quite ordinary, as if the way of the world was to be sick, not well. I remember, long into my years on the pediatric ward, noticing some children on the way home, running and shrieking. "But they seem so *healthy*," I thought, puzzled.

Once health had been my norm in life; now sickness was. As I grew desensitized to the sight of blood and gore, my language about health and illness changed too and I mimicked the offhand professionalism of the doctors and nurses and techs around me, talking of cancers and amputations and chronic diseases with detachment. I never got to the point of referring to people by their disease as some did ("What room is the little brain tumor in?" a social services worker once asked me), but I grew matter-of-fact. The body, especially in its infirmities, was no longer strange to me, no longer such a mystery.

My new straight-forward, no-nonsense attitude towards the mechanics of the body, my very acceptance that there definitely was such a thing as disease and that it could be cured through surgery, radiation, pills, and frequent liquids paralleled my journey away from spiritual explanations to material ones. I had started out in college majoring in philosophy and reading Rilke and Jung, and had later lived in Scandanavia and Spain, studying languages and literature. But when I moved back to the States I found myself embroiled with mildly leftist politics and the feminist movement. My romance with travel, with language and poetry, took a backseat as I began to live what I thought I had been longing for, an engaged and committed life, all day, every day. I wrote for a collective newspaper, helped start a women's publishing company, demonstrated against racism and nuclear power and for abortion and gay rights, and wrote fiction in the evenings after I got off work at the hospital. My personal life became merged with my political life, exactly the way I thought it should be. I reinvented myself as an activist, a feminist, someone who could make things happen, someone who had strong opinions, on art, on society, on who was to blame for the state of things, and on what needed to be changed, and fast.

At some point in my twenties I stopped reading books on Zen and Jungian psychology and turned to Angela Davis and Shulamith Firestone instead. I looked to economics to explain society and to race and gender to explain why economics wasn't the whole story. Now I moved in circles (though over the years those circles grew and shrank and overlapped and stopped speaking to each other and did abrupt about-faces) where we argued about anarchism versus socialism and about civil disobedience versus armed struggle. About ends versus means. About blowing up a nuclear power plant as opposed to merely occupying its site. About voting Democratic or not voting at all. About running a business as a collective or a hierarchy. About racism in the women's movement. About the hidden injuries of class. About international solidarity. About the purpose of art and the responsibilities of the artist.

About religion we never spoke at all.

I fancied myself grown hardheaded in those years. Although, when I look back through rose windows, I'm amazed at the exuberance and confidence I brought to all my endeavors in my restless twenties and ambitious thirties, I see that in spite of my joy in finding a sense of community and a role to play in changing the world, in spite of my great, unflagging idealism, I seemed to grow, as the years passed, increasingly cynical. I saw the potential of the movements I was involved with; I also saw the hypocrisy, the authoritarianism, the cruelty. The discrepancy I felt between the stated goals of some of these political groups, goals in which I believed, and often still believe passionately, and the motivations that brought people into them and directed their behavior, was often jarring. I had been antiauthoritarian for years; it was my generation's attitude to life as well as my own response to the strictly hierarchical church I'd grown up in. Although I wanted to believe in a movement for social change, I felt increasingly skeptical about the people in this movement, and this growing unease emerged in my writing as satire and a tone of ironic detachment. Satire can be passionate, but skepticism is more often the refuge of those who have lost their faith.

If I look back through blue windows, though, instead of the rosy ones, I see that in spite of my commitment to social change, my inner life was somehow frozen. I see, through an ice-blue window that flickers like an old TV screen with disturbed and interrupted signals, a woman who drinks a little too much, and who was highly charged but brief affairs because of a fear of getting close (she calls it keeping her independence). I see a woman who, in the guise of changing the world, increasingly finds her weekends and evenings taken up with work and meetings. I see a woman with a photograph of her mother buried somewhere in a box in her closet, a woman who hates to have her picture taken, and who sometimes disappears in public situations under her comforting old helmet of darkness. I see a woman who never says much about her childhood and nothing about her mother. I see a woman who, although she is a writer now, has struggled hard to become one, is rarely able to give her vocation the time or attention it deserves, and who seems less and less able, as the years pass, to write about anything that would let anyone catch a true glimpse of her heart.

For many years I lived what I thought of as an engaged life. A longing for justice and reparation led to an identification with those who had been wronged, and this led in turn to an anxious, though invigorating, self-righteousness. My interest in social change didn't come out of compassion or a desire to mend the torn fabric of the world, as the beautiful Hebrew words *tikkun olam* have it. No, I wanted change because I was angry and indignant. Because my side was right. I did not recognize or refused to understand that by cutting out whole chunks of who I was and how I was raised, I made it impossible for myself to be very present, much less deeply engaged. In reality I was not engaged, I was deeply disengaged, cut off from memories of my past, unable to integrate what I had experienced as a young child with what had come later, much less with what I had become as an adult.

What I didn't want to remember, what was the hardest thing to bear, was not the damage done to me; no, the hardest thing to bear remembering was that I had been loved once, and that I had grown up in an atmosphere of loving-kindness. I had no idea how to get back to that feeling of safety, peace, and joy. If I sneered at the soft, touchy-feel side of some of our alternative groups, or ignored the fact that, as the Eighties progressed, people I knew were increasingly turning away from hard-edged politics to women's spirituality, Buddhism and 12-Step meetings, it was in part because deep inside I longed for what those groups promised: love and compassion, a reawakening of the sacred, a reverence for life.

Promises I knew to be a crock of shit, a disappointment, a big fat lie.

As a child I'd been directed to "stand porter at the door of thought," and to keep all thoughts of disease, death, and evil outside the fortress that was my mind. Although I had given up on Christian Science long ago, that teaching, much distorted, was still with me. I grew adept at shutting out everything painful as I moved into my thirties. Sometimes I wondered why I was so anxious when people close to me showed violent emotion; sometimes I wondered why getting up in front of people and being looked at made me so nervous. But mostly I didn't think. I certainly didn't think about religion in those years. I stopped every thought of sacredness and spirituality before it could enter my mind, and refused to acknowledge any of it had to do with me. And yet, as the Eighties progressed, I could see that all my worthy causes seemed helpless to avert many kinds of suffering. Not every pain or sorrow in life was the result of injustice. Not every ill could be solved by meetings and demonstrations.

This discovery was not mine alone. All around me people were discovering some of the limits of working for social change. Some were burned-out; some were disgusted; some were frustrated. And some began to gravitate towards a spiritual path. I didn't know anyone who took up with a guru, but I knew plenty who began attending Quaker meetings or alternative Jewish synagogues. Some women I knew became eco-feminists and talked about goddesses and Gaia; others went off to sit with *vipassana* mediation teachers in Northern California, or put up Tibetan altars in a corner of their bedrooms. Some went to AA or other 12-Step groups. Others did spiritual weekends out in the woods or joined drumming or chanting groups. And one or two just started going to a Protestant or Catholic church again.

None of this was for me. I mocked all spirituality, especially anything that had to do with New Age jargon about creating your own reality and healing yourself. Yeah, right, I knew all about that. Good luck, sucker. And yet I understood my friends' spiritual searches, even as I kept my distance and honed my sarcasm. I couldn't imagine myself going to church, praying or even meditating. I didn't want anything to do with any of that, ever again. But cynicism only masked my despair. It prevented me from telling anyone I'd had an intensely religious life once as a child. It prevented me from acknowledging that I might have any need for a spiritual life now. And it certainly prevented me, until I had to, from setting out on a journey to find what shape that spiritual life might take.

Chapter 15

Meeting Medusa

"When people prayed to Hecate, they put on a black veil over their heads, so as not to see her—in order not to become like her."

—Maria-Lusia Von Franz, *The Feminine in Fairy Tales*

*T*here were two things that struck me when I traveled to Greece for the first time in the spring of 1993. One was the number of classical statues with battered faces, faces that seemed familiar to me, and the other was the Medusa head, reduced to the size of an apple and pinned like a large brooch on Athena's breastplate.

The faces of the Greek statues were chinless, mouthless, sometimes noseless. The lips were gone and sometimes whole sections of a cheek. But most of the damage had been done long ago, and now the marble faces looked more worn than broken, the edges softened to a polished grain. These were the statues I liked best, the broken ones. I often reached out, when I found them solitary in gardens or outdoor museums, to touch their faces. And I put my own hand to my face, my mouth, surprised to feel myself intact. For often enough in the last years I'd had the sensation that when I tried to speak, everything that could have helped me was gone.

It had been in London, five years before this trip to Greece, that I first began to see a therapist, and it had been in Deborah's small flat that I first began to experience the sensation that the lower half of my face was paralyzed. All she had asked was for me to tell her about my childhood and my family. What was so hard about that? I told her a few superficial, basic things—my mother was dead, my father had remarried, I didn't get on with my stepmother—but began to have increasing difficulty forming the words. My jaw seemed locked tight and my tongue alternately felt like it had shrunk down to a stump or was something huge and heavy pressing against my teeth and down my throat.

I didn't experience this consistently. Whenever I spoke about the ostensible reason for some of my problems—trying to maintain a two-year-old transatlantic relationship—I was articulate and clear. Whenever Deborah asked anything about my childhood, however, I was literally tongue-tied. Sometimes trying to get the words out felt like carving a bar of soap with my tongue. I felt as if I had stones in my mouth. I felt as if I had a plaster cast on my face. Once I told her that I felt as if I had an iron bar across my jaw. Another time I felt as if I had a medieval knight's helmet jammed down over my face, so tightly that the visor wouldn't open.

"It sounds like you had a gag order," said Deborah one time. Another time she noticed, "You put your hand in front of your face sometimes when you speak."

I did it to hold my face together, for sometimes it felt as if it were going to fly apart when I opened my mouth. Other times I held my hand there for shame, because all I had was a gaping hole where my mouth had been. And yet, the words came spilling out anyway. The memories burst like blood blisters in my throat and spattered me and, across from me, Deborah, who did not turn away, but kept steadily regarding me with interest and concern, who kept listening, who said, "Go on," and "What did that feel like?"

About six months after I had first begun to talk to Deborah about some of the things I remembered from my childhood, my mother's breakdown and suicide attempt, and how it was to live through her illness and death, a close friend came to London to visit me. I decided she would be the first person I told about some of these memories. Although I found myself crying uncontrollably, I still got the words out. That night I dreamed my friend and I were swimming in the sea and about to be dashed on a sharp coral reef, when we were suddenly lifted up and over by an enormous wave. The dream seemed to say, in large letters, "Finally." Now that I'd told one person I could begin to tell others. But the next day, and the day after, my friend was careful not to mention my story, and seemed, at least to my increasingly anxious eyes, more distant than usual. Finally I asked her timidly if my telling her had made a difference in our friendship.

She chose her words. "It was hard to hear . . . about your mother's . . . about your mother. But it doesn't change my feelings for you." The tone underneath said, "And don't ever mention it again." I never did.

At the time I felt rebuffed and shamed, forgetting that I too had sometimes turned away from friends with stories of abuse and unbearable misfortune. It is not easy to feel another's pain, to know what to say or do. Sometimes our silence is a superstitious fear—we do not want to be touched, contaminated, by knowledge of uglier realities, of deeper evils than we've known ourselves.

I had reached out and the answer was silence. And this perceived rebuff was heavy on my heart as I contemplated telling other friends. After I returned to Seattle, I used to hold long internal debates with myself, about who to tell, how much to tell, who definitely not to tell. What would they say, what would they do? I imagined their responses before I opened my mouth. "Oh, by the way, did I ever tell you about the time my mother drank Drano? Yeah, it was a real drag." I imagined my friends looking shocked and turning away nervously, or almost worse, treating my story as gossip and passing it on to friends who might tell strangers. I saw myself once again as the Christian Science kid who had to leave Science class and refuse polio shots, who always had the disfigured mother, about whom they said, "What's wrong with her?"

Though I didn't know it then, Christian Science was the main obstacle to my telling my story with any coherence. Without explaining what Mrs. Eddy's teachings had said and what they'd meant to my family, my mother could only appear the sad victim of a mysterious and virulent mental disease. I knew the story was more complicated than that, but without a real, adult understanding of the religion myself, I had no idea how to convey the seriousness with which Christian Science notions of health and the absence of pain or evil were taken. No idea at all how to explain how the world had exploded back then when those notions did not hold up to reality.

In the Mysteries of Eleusis, which the Greeks performed in memory of Demeter and her lost daughter, part of the ritual included placing a key on the tongue, a key that represented the key questions and revelations that were part of the Mysteries. My work with Deborah had given me a key, but it had not enabled me to speak, not yet. One of the problems is that friends who say they care about us are not always up to hearing the details of our lives or knowing what response to make. But another, perhaps greater problem for me was that I didn't understand enough to make my story a coherent one. I knew that Christian Science was one of the key revelations, but I was far from understanding how to explain its importance to me and to my mother.

If the missing chins and lips of the Greek statues reminded me of my mother's ravaged face, and my own difficulties in speaking about the past, the little Medusa heads pinned to Athena's tunic—gorgonians, I learned they were called—were reminders of the myths I'd read as a child and the games I used to play with Johnnie. With their wild bulging eyes and teeth bared in a fierce grimace below a crown of writhing snakes, they were also reminders of everything I'd once tried to run away from and push away in my life: memories of abuse, craziness, alcoholism, cruelty. Especially craziness.

Two years before my trip to Greece, my life had started to unravel. I could pinpoint the moment almost exactly—the warm February day in 1991 when I stood by my mother's gravesite, weeping for her death and my life without her, and most of all for the fact that no one from our family had been to the cemetery since the day she was buried.

It had taken me three years to get to the cemetery from the time I first began to talk about my childhood with Deborah in London, and it seemed such a feat, such a triumph, that it was inevitable that I see my standing on the grassy hillside with its view of the blue Pacific as proof of my healing, as a kind of ending. Instead, it was only the beginning. I thought I'd dealt with the demons of my past; in reality they had been lying comparatively quiet, and now rose up to surround me with the force of a whirlwind. They rose up when I thought my healing was complete, that February day when I drove back from the cemetery to Long Beach and took a walk along the ocean and thought: *I'm ready to write something about this now.*

Within weeks I was forced to realize that nothing in my life was structured to allow me to explore my memories in depth, much less find time to write them down. For years I'd carried on a balancing act between writing and translating, editing and helping manage first one growing publishing house and then another smaller one that focused on translations and survived on grants. It was a balancing act that was precarious at the best of times. Now, in my increasingly fragile, overworked, frustrated state of mind, the balance didn't work at all. I had too much responsibility and not enough support. Women in Translation was having trouble fund-raising; Seal was in the midst of staff problems that were not easily sorted out. My love life was difficult, too. Each of us wanted to help the other; neither of us seemed to know the right way. In spite of some wonderful times and a shared commitment to literature, I'd come to find the relationship, after two years of ups and downs, more demanding than supportive.

I felt as if I were drowning, as if I were falling. I felt as if I were sliding into a huge black hole in the universe. I felt as if the people around me didn't notice that I was slipping off the edge of the known world and that when I waved my hands for help (but not wildly, for I didn't want anyone to imagine that anything was seriously wrong) they simply handed me a list of new assignments or pointed out that I was not meeting expectations.

And so I slid, and slid, and slid. Until I couldn't slide any further, any deeper.

The only myth of Medusa that I knew when I noticed the gorgonians in Greece was the traditional one, from Hawthorne's *Tanglewood Tales*. In this myth and the variations on it that I've read since, Medusa was one of three Gorgon sisters who lived at the edge of the world. Once they had been beautiful. Once Medusa was human and lovely and desired by Poseidon. But in a struggle for power Athena turned Medusa into a monster and banished her. The Gorgon sisters were all monsters, with wings and talons and hideous faces and snaky locks, but Medusa was the most fearsome. It was Medusa who had the power to turn men to stone with just one glance, and it was Medusa whom Perseus had to decapitate.

But Barbara Walker, in *The Women's Encyclopedia of Myths and Secrets*, suggests that the Perseus story was invented long after, in order to explain the appearance of Medusa's face on Athena's aegis. In fact, she says, the goddess and the serpent had been linked for millennia with female wisdom and power, and the face of a woman surrounded by snakes had in previous times been a symbol of the divine, not of the

319

bestial. Medusa, Walker says, was the queen of the Amazons who was killed by the pre-Hellenic Greeks during their wars in North Africa. These tribes in Morocco were called Gorgons, and they wore magic belts and goatskin tunics and fierce masks. It may also be that the Gorgon mask is something that all goddesses wore at some point, as a function rather than an identity. Walker brings up the possibility that Athena and Medusa were actually the same goddess. Before the Greeks reinvented Athena as the patroness of their city Athens, giving her a royal birth straight from Zeus's head (and in the process changing an earlier myth that had Athena being born from the head of her mother Métis), Athena had originally come from North Africa, where she was the Libyan Triple Goddess, Neith. The Gorgon Medusa was her Destroyer aspect. It is the same Destroyer imagery that the Indian goddess Kali represents. Woman as both creator and destroyer, birth and death. That frozen face with the staring eyes and lolling tongue, decapitated and surrounded by snakes, was once not an image of fear, but one of power.

For hundreds of years since the time of the Greeks, the only power Medusa has had is that of evoking fear, or perhaps sexual excitement (Freud saw the Medusa head as the *vagina dentata*). The Romantics of the nineteenth century wrote about her and re-created her in art as the symbol of uncontrolled female rage and hatred, her head cut off from her body, her mouth screaming, her head a mass of serpents. In the lower foyer of the Musée d'Orsay in Paris is an enormous Medusa head, half a story high, fierce, hideous, and compelling all at once. More recently, women have tried to reclaim some of Medusa's power and she has appeared in literature and psychology alike. But in many cases Medusa's rage is taken for granted, something we either need to either embrace or reject. Only the poet May Sarton seems to have captured some of the contradictions of the Medusa image in her poem "Muse as Medusa":

> I saw you once, Medusa; we were alone.
> I looked you straight in the cold eye, cold.
> I was not punished, was not turned to stone.
> How to believe the legends I am told.
>
> .   .   .
>
> I turned your face around! It is my face.
> That frozen rage is what I must explore—

Oh secret, self-enclosed and ravaged place!
This is the gift I thank Medusa for.

I'd had low times before 1991 of course, but they'd been mostly the dull and frozen sort. Paralysis rather than hysteria; bleakness rather than rage. Something always came along to pull me out of them—a trip, a new romance, a little success. I'd always had work that I loved and that was meaningful to me, and much of my life was as enjoyable as it was busy. I was a survivor and one of the ways I had survived had always been through nourishing my imagination and claiming my right to take art seriously. I was proud that my self-sufficiency, my sense of humor, my optimism, and my stubbornness could see me through most situations. I had other moods, moods of despair and self-loathing, and I'd had them more frequently since beginning to remember my childhood, but I tried to think of them as transitory, tried to believe that they would pass without my needing to deal with them.

But this low time went on all that year, like a train going downhill, gaining momentum with every turn. I was forty, the same age my mother had been when she broke down. I knew I didn't want the same thing to happen to me. In September of that year I ended my relationship, and in late October I jumped at the chance to sublet a friend's small flat in Mexico for a few weeks. I wouldn't give into despair, I wouldn't let go. In Mexico, far away from the phone and the mail, away from all my responsibilities, I would finally sit down and seriously begin the work of writing down the past.

In Mexico I had nightmares almost every night. They only reproduced the images I saw during the day of skeletons and skulls, for I'd come to this town just before the Days of the Dead, and the markets were full of sugar coffins and dancing skeletons. I had come to be alone, and I was alone. Terribly alone. But I did write; all day I wrote. I had no idea where to start, no idea what was important yet. I only knew I had to start somewhere, had to pour it out on paper. So I wrote. And I remembered. I wandered around the dusty little town and the skulls grinned menacingly at me. One night I woke up and knew another piece of my history. I had seen my uncle Andrew standing in a green river with his bathing trunks down.

I left Mexico early, afraid to be alone for one day longer, afraid to see anything more, to have one more nightmare. Back in Seattle I heard that I'd been awarded a literary prize in England, and the news acted temporarily to bolster my spirits. I flew to London for the banquet, saw friends, went to museums and the theater. That I could enjoy myself so thoroughly was proof I was over my depression, I told myself sternly. But with the Christmas season I began to slide again, towards the edge of the universe, further and further away from the warmth of human contact. I was losing the ability to pretend to myself or anyone else that I didn't feel absolutely wretched most of the time.

Then, one evening just before Christmas, I saw the face of madness.

I'd been using the holidays to write and had spent the past couple of days describing how it was to be twelve years old, in the seventh grade, knowing my mother was going to die. It was wet and dark outside, and I was home that evening, reading, trying to ignore a kind of paralysis that was creeping over me, a feeling of horror in the pit of my stomach. I was afraid. Afraid as if this might be my last evening on earth, as if I might not live through this evening. I thought of going out—anywhere—but it was ten o'clock, dark and pouring with rain, and I was petrified to leave the house. I thought of calling someone, but I couldn't seem to walk over to the phone. I knew my fingers wouldn't work to dial the number, I knew my mouth wouldn't work to call for help, and in my terrified state I couldn't remember the name of a single friend whom I thought would listen to me or save me.

Thirty years of being emotionally self-sufficient, of being a survivor, of dealing creatively with my pain had brought me to this point: an inert lump in a corner of the sofa, surrounded by threatening silence and demonic figures that came closer and closer. I was going crazy, I was close to the edge. No, I was just talking myself into that. I *wasn't* crazy. I refused to be crazy. That's one thing I would never be, crazy. A month or so earlier I'd had coffee with a friend, who told me she'd been prescribed antidepressants. I'd been sympathetic but slightly skeptical: Could her deep-seated problems really be cured by a pill? She said the Zoloft had taken the edge off her intensity and was making everything more tolerable. More and more people I knew were on Zoloft or Prozac. Was that what I needed too? My own therapist had never suggested antidepressants; she was the old-fashioned kind, the kind who believed in talking. Earlier in the fall, in the midst of overwork and the breakup, when I'd tentatively suggested that maybe I was having a nervous breakdown, she'd said, "With your history, you should be careful of how you phrase these things to yourself."

With my history. With my history.

My history was to have witnessed madness but to have carefully stayed away from it myself. My history was to be more afraid of losing my mind suddenly than of anything else. My history was to connect strong feelings with being mentally ill. My history was not helping me, but I didn't know what else to do, other than to go on trying to live in the way I always had. I kept going to my office, even though sometimes I found myself staring at the wall or resisting the urge to hide under my desk when staff members came in with daunting problems. In therapy I seemed to be stuck at age twelve. All I could think about was how strange I probably looked, how everybody thought I was weird, and how bereft I felt.

That December evening in my cozy little house, I suppressed the urge to start screaming. No one must know I felt like this. I must hide my craziness at all costs. I must hide my fears, no matter what. I must go on acting as normal as I could so that no one would suspect how disturbed I was. No, I wasn't disturbed! There was nothing wrong with me. A good night's sleep and everything would look better in the morning.

Breathing deeply I got up and went into the kitchen. I would make myself a cup of soothing tea. Inside my head an insistent voice was whispering, "What it is that you're afraid of? What are you really afraid of?"

The box of chamomile tea in my hand, I found myself pressed against one of the walls, muttering, "I don't want to. I don't want to. I'm afraid."

"Afraid of what?" that small insistent voice asked. "What don't you want to?"

"I don't want to *feel*," I gasped. I had no breath to shriek. "If I feel I'll be killed. My feelings will kill me!"

And then it came. How can I describe it? It was like a beast ripping my body into shreds, it was like an atomic bomb burning me to a cinder, it was like a wall collapsing in on itself, it was a wave flooding through every pore. I was being eaten alive by a monster with a gaping mouth and bloody tongue, my head was torn off and every limb was broken and mangled. My heart stopped, my blood poured out everywhere, and as I dissolved, I became part of the monster herself, fanged and howling and flying through the air with talons outspread. She had devoured me and made me part of her.

It was no one feeling. It was feeling itself. Unleashed and fiery, bloody and white-hot at once, scorching every protesting, fearful thought in its path. The old me disappeared in less than a second, and there was no new me, for I was her.

My knees buckled under me and I found myself on the floor, still clutching the box of Celestial Seasonings tea bags. Millennia passed before my old heart began beating again and my legs renewed their connection to my body. But when I cautiously opened my eyes, I found I was still in my kitchen. The tea kettle wasn't even boiling yet. My cat had come over to look at me, but she didn't seem alarmed. She sniffed my head and pronounced me still alive. I had seen the face of madness. I had felt her devouring breath. I had felt her breath burn through me. I had become her for just a millisecond. But afterwards I had returned to being me. I was still here. Still alive.

More alive, in fact, that I had been in months, or perhaps in years. My feelings had not killed me. There was no reason any longer to be afraid that they would.

What does the myth of Medusa tell us? What is the meaning of the snake-coiled face with the grinning mouth and lolling tongue? Why the myth of decapitation and then containment? What is Medusa's place on Athena's aegis? Does it mean that wise Athena has conquered her emotions and reduced her to mere decoration, to a trophy brooch, to a medallion that signals a warning to supernatural forces to stay away? Or does Athena wear her Gorgon mask proudly, to show a face that is part of her? On many statues the gorgonian is small, but on others the snakes themselves circle Athena's brow or wind their way around her shield, her aegis, or her ankles. They are more integral, and less contained. They are movement and change.

In India, where the Goddess has never ceased to be worshipped in one form or another, Kali is venerated, especially in Bengal, as the goddess of destruction. Her parallels with the Athena-Medusa myth are striking. Like the original story of Athena emerging from her mother Métis's forehead, Kali sprang full-grown from the goddess Durga's head. She emerged as Durga's helper in the battle with the Buffalo Demon, a battle that ended when Durga decapitated him. Kali has wild hair, a gaping mouth, and an extended tongue. She wears a necklace of skulls and often holds a severed head in one of her hands. Most interestingly, some stories and illustrations show Kali astride Shiva. The blood of death and destruction flows from Kali's head, and from Shiva's comes health and creativity. In the Medusa myth, after Perseus beheaded her, he saved two vials of her blood, one containing blood from the veins of Medusa's left side and one containing blood from the right. These vials were given to Asklepios, the Greek healer, who had ties to the snake goddess, the Great Mother. With blood from the left vial, Asklepios slayed, and with blood from the right, he healed. The symbol of healing, the caduceus, is two snakes wound around a tree, a symbol of the Great Mother.

Medusa may have been decapitated, her face frozen in a mask of rage, her only power that of turning others to stone, but Kali is worshipped not only as the force of destruction but also one of creation. The Hindu Shakti movement venerates the feminine principle as one of energy and sees Kali as embodying the active, creative force at the heart of the ever-changing world. Medusa's face illustrates the moment when the energy stalled and froze; but Kali is always in movement, dancing from life to death and back again. She makes possible the dying that proceeds change, so that life can arise anew.

I first noticed the gorgonians on my trip to Greece, at the museum at Epidauros, a couple hours outside Athens, where the guidebook said that they represented control of the forces of nature, that they were talismans against illness, mental and physical. Epidauros had been the sanctuary of Asklepios, the god of healing. It was a center for not only physical healing, but spiritual, for the Greeks believed that they were connected. I read in *The Traveler's Key to Ancient Greece:* "The cause of illness lay in the psyche, and the manifestations were both physical and spiritual. If a man was not 'thinking straight,' he was not capable of relieving the physical symptoms of illness. First the mind had to be aligned to the mind of Apollo, then the body might recover its balance and health."

The familiarity of the idea struck me, for hadn't I been taught as a child that the way to be healed was to correct my thinking and align my mind with the divine Mind? Here at Epidaurus, under the Greek spring sun, were the ruins of a place where people had flocked in ancient times to be healed and to heal themselves. One method was drama, and the amphitheater at Epidaurus is still considered the finest remaining example of a Greek theater, with acoustics still so perfect that even sitting up on the fiftieth row you can hear a coin drop on the stage below. Here the Greeks acted out the catharsis of illness and madness. But the heart of Epidauros was the Abaton, where, whatever your physical illness, you came to sleep and be cured through your dreams. "Therapy at the Asclepeion relied mainly on the patients' shattering psychical experience, the shock of having come into direct contact with the supernatural—an experience which, in psychogenic and nervous disorders especially, must have given immediate and impressive results."

Only ruins are left now, of course. I walked through them and thought about my mother. Had she really been crazy and what was craziness anyway? I still had no way of judging. Whenever I tried to talk to my father, the person who had lived through that time by her side, he proved resistant to my hypotheses. "The cancer must have metastasized to her brain," he said, or, more obscurely, "You know, your uncle Andrew got sick around the same time . . . strange how two kids in the same family could have the same problem. . . ."

Now at Epidauros, it struck me, perhaps for the first time, how it had been my father who spoke of my mother's mental illness most forcefully. "She was like an animal in a cage"; "She was completely insane when she died." They were the only words he had to explain what was happening to her. The medical model. The model that said it was her genes at fault. The model that kept her sedated and controlled. The model that had no room for other explanations or other treatments. Once I'd asked him what he knew about Malicious Animal Magnetism.

"Nothing really," he'd said. "It was just part of your mother's religion. It was something she was screaming that night, that night it all started."

The December evening I saw the face of madness was the evening I began my first hesitant steps toward acknowledging my grief and sadness and moving on, toward leaving the ship stuck in the frozen sea, toward stepping out from behind the frozen mask. It is a process I have tried to keep up in the years since, this learning to acknowledge whatever feeling is troubling me, seeing it fully, and hearing what it has to say to me. Sometimes I'm able to let it go. Other times I must struggle with it, or make a real place for it in my life.

I used to fear the idea of being moody, as if it were a moral flaw, as if by continued vigilance I could keep my moods docile and within safe parameters. I especially feared, and tried to control, any violent swings between two distinctly different emotions—anger and joy, for instance. At first letting go of that control left me feeling powerless and immature, but eventually I got used to having a greater range of emotion. I stopped calling myself moody and simply noticed that in the course of a day I was capable of many moods. I paid more attention to their flow, less to their content. I also acknowledged that I was not manic-depressive or depressive. I had not inherited a mental illness from my relatives. I had been terrified that I would go crazy once I truly felt what I felt, remembered what I remembered. That hadn't happened. I moved away from using words like depression to describe my frozen grief, from the clinical terminology I had sometimes used to scare myself and simply said, "I'm sad. It hurts to feel sometimes."

I sat with my grief and I learned to befriend it. The more I remembered, the more I wrote down, the more I was able to share my memories with close friends, the more my old grief became part of me, part of my life, the less threatening and overwhelming it became. Much of its intensity had come from pushing it away for so many years.

The more I remembered, the more I wanted to remember. I asked questions of my father and women who had known my mother; I went back to Battle Creek and found people who had known my grandparents. For years I had never looked at the one photograph of my mother I'd had; now I began to pester my father to give me all the photographs of my mother and her family and our family that he still held on to. It took a year or two for him to find them, and another few months for me to arrange to come to Los Angeles to retrieve them. When he came out of his apartment he handed me a large brown bag of unsorted pictures, some in folders and some loose. "Here." He sighed. "I had to pretend to Bettye that I was taking out some garbage."

Over the years I had come to accept my father's relationship with Bettye as inevitable, as a mutual dependence that both found irritating but inescapable. She treated him badly but he remained attached to her. He had lost so many people in his life—was it it a surprise that he would cling to the one person who, although she often threatened it, would probably never leave him? Bettye kept drinking and her health stayed bad enough to cause frequent dramatic crises, but no real diagnosis of disease. "She'll outlive us all," my father joked gloomily. "Only the good die young." But her longevity was a source of pride to him. In a peculiar way, her scrappy working-class resilience mirrored his own fierce attachment to survival.

I had rarely seen Bettye since the day she slapped my face and usually I visited my father alone. Bettye never understood my desire to investigate my history. "She asks me, Why are you always coming down here asking questions about your mother?" my father reported. "I told her, 'Bettye, it's her mother.' She just says, 'Oh that girl and her sainted mother.' " My father shook his head. "She never understood about your mother."

My stubborn anger at Bettye was frozen into my own Medusa mask. It had been a way of holding on to something that had once protected me. For a long time I thought I could never and would never forgive my wicked stepmother. You can forgive someone who has unintentionally wronged you, but not someone who has humiliated you, I believed and still believe. All the same, holding on to anger is a means of remaining powerless. Emotionally I was still thirteen when I thought of my stepmother. She still had me under her thumb.

The fact was, I had two Medusas in my life. One was my mother, wild-eyed and spitting blood, and the other was Bettye, whose anger had turned into alcoholism and ulcers, and whose need to protect herself had made her stare icy and paralyzing. Although I have never wanted to admit this: I had not one mother, but two, and I learned from both of them. My personality was partly formed in opposition to Bettye, and my frozen rage against her has been part of my life for longer than I care to recall. Only very recently have I come to understand that I am not at her mercy any longer. My anger is a choice I make. It is one I once made too often.

The changes I went through after hitting bottom hardly took place overnight. Sometimes it was hard to tell the difference between sitting with my grief and wallowing in it. Just as it had taken a long time to bury these feelings, so it took a long time to resurrect them, and I wasn't always sure that resurrecting them wasn't an act of morbidity and self-pity. Only when I had begun to come to terms with my mother's death did the pain of being abused by my uncle begin to surface, and only when that anger and sadness had diminished was I able to really face my loneliness and shame at having to hide the story of my mother's breakdown and disfigurement. At times I wondered if the peeling-away process would ever be over.

But of course my life went on and got better in many small and large ways. I had always loved nature, had always loved being outside and watching the seasons change. Now I set myself the task of naming the world in a way I'd never learned as a child. I watched the ducks on Lake Union where I lived on a houseboat, and soon they were not just "ducks" to me, but Buffleheads, Barrows' Goldeneyes, Mergansers. I went out into the forest with my tree identification book and learned to distinguish firs from cedars, spruces from pines. During a period when I lived in Northern California I spent hours watching hawks and blue jays soar above the scrub oaks and ceanothus in the U.C. Botanical Gardens above Berkeley. I sat in the sage-scented, sunny gardens and read natural history books. I wrote down in my notebooks the names of flowers and shrubs—chaparral honeysuckle, common soap plant, western wake-robin—and sometimes made drawings. Back in Seattle I started my first real garden and finally understood the difference between an annual and a perennial.

As I learned the names of things in the world, often for the first time, I also began to repair other connections to my childhood and adolescence. I played more, worked less. I read poetry with delight, started making art again, listened to all kinds of music, spent pleasurable hours with children. Tentatively I dipped my toes back into the spiritual stream, reading among the wealth of religious literature, finding myself more and more drawn to Buddhist thought, challenged and yet at home.

If I was healed by attention to my deepest feelings and by a renewed sense of wonder and gratitude toward the natural world, I was also healed by love. My partner Tere has an ardent, generous spirit, one that embraces life and celebrates it. Over the years I've marveled at her kindness, her honesty, her intuitiveness, and most of all, her buoyancy. From the beginning I have felt more alive around her, the way I remember being as a child.

One morning last year, Tere came home unexpectedly, her right cheek hidden by a large gauze bandage. At the construction site, where she worked as a union carpenter, someone had dropped a hammer from sixteen feet above and it had ripped a gash next to her mouth. Now a line of twenty-seven black stitches decorated her face, like a Berber woman's tattoo. There would be a scar. An impressive one. Perhaps a frightening one.

I think I was more upset than she was that day. Like most women in the trades, she had to act macho on the jobsite, so it had not quite sunk in what had happened. I was, however, in tears at seeing the face of someone I loved behind bandages, knowing there was a possibility she would be disfigured for life. I sobbed and shook with fear and pity, all the old demons come back instantly to haunt me. My response was so extreme that the following week Tere called before she came home. "I wanted to warn you," she said, "I've had another accident on the job—to my face." This time something had snapped back and struck her cheekbone, just missing her eye. Although she had only a small cut, her face was swollen, and she had two black eyes.

For days afterwards when we went out in public everyone stared at her, and covertly, at me. I recognized that feeling all too well. More unnerving to me were the conversations that came up with other people, about facial disfigurement and scarring. Everybody had a story about a scar. I had one too, of course, but I found myself as close-mouthed, as dumbstruck as I had ever been. It had been an emotional relief to cry out when I saw Tere, the way I hadn't been able to do as a child when I first saw my mother at the sanitarium, but how would it be to live again with someone who was disfigured and who caused us both to be stared at?

But as the months passed, the scar, angry red and raised, retreated and grew pale. Tere's own mother, seeing her six months after the accident, didn't notice it at first. Especially when Tere's mobile face is laughing or talking, it blends into the other lines around her mouth; it becomes a deeper laugh line.

I notice it only rarely now, just as I hardly see my own facial scar, the one under my eyebrow, the one I got years ago playing with my brother in the backyard. Perhaps it should have been stitched up, but of course a visit to the doctor was out of the question then. I'm sure my mother held me on her lap and hugged me and told me that God loved me. In the enthusiasm of my religious convictions I prayed with her for it to heal, and believed I saw, with my own eyes, how it disappeared. That it was gone. It was not gone. I just didn't see it. Not until

I was being made-up for a play in high school one day and someone remarked, "That's quite a scar you've got there."

And then I saw, quite suddenly, what had been there all along.

Healing is not accomplished by ignoring a wound, but by tending it. A wound will never disappear, but it will fade and become part of a beloved body, a laugh line perhaps or a visible reminder of pain long gone. Scars are memories of healing and we all have them. These days I have photographs of my mother in my room. I look up often to see her beautiful smile and her happy eyes. But I have found myself wishing that I also had photographs of her face after the suicide attempt. Not only so that I could remember if it was as bad as I believed as a child, but so that I could get familiar with her scars, and learn to love them too. The way I have learned to see and accept and even love Tere's scar and the two white lines on my own wrist.

That day in Greece, in Epidauros, was a turning point for me. That sunny day in spring, I sat up in the amphitheater listening to my fellow human beings delightedly check out the acoustics ("Okay, now I'm going to drop a coin!"). I would have adored acting on this stage as an adolescent, and Mr. Mac would have been in seventh heaven directing us. I remembered myself as Mrs. Keeney pacing wildly across the stage, on the ice-bound ship my husband the whaler had consigned me to. And I imagined my mother coming to Epidauros with her cancer and it being taken for granted that her disease was not just physical and could not be cared for by medical means alone. I allowed myself to feel my mother's anguish and her rage and fear, allowed myself to see them not as craziness, but as a true response to her world turning upside down. In my imagination I greeted her at the Abaton and led her to a sleeping room, and there I sat with her all night, acknowledging the power of her demons, of M.A.M., of Kali, of Medusa. I imagined her learning to see her illness as a beginning, not an ending, not as a failure, but an opening. I imagined her reinventing the language of Christian Science to serve her more deeply and wisely, not forsaking her spiritual training and practice, but adapting it, enlarging its scope so that disease could be something to learn from, not ignore.

I imagined her coming to understand, as I was understanding now, that the answer to our prayers is not always the healing that we hope for. But it may be the healing that we need.

Chapter 16

Testimony

The method of averting one's attention from evil and living sim-
ply in the light of good is splendid as long as it will work. It will
work with many persons; it will work far more generally than most
of us are ready to suppose, and within the sphere of its successful
operation there is nothing to be said against it as a religious so-
lution. But it breaks down impotently as soon as melancholy
comes . . . the evil facts which it refuses positively to account for
are a genuine portion of reality; and they may be after all the best
key to life's significance and possibly the only openers of our eyes
to the deepest levels of truth.

—William James, *The Varieties of Religious Experience*

In Crete a few years ago I picked up four small blocks of glass. One
is rose-colored and three are shades of blue, from ice to cerulean to
cobalt. The cobalt is so dark you can hardly see anything through it,
and yet of all the squares it's the one I am always drawn to. When I
hold it up to the light I don't see a world full of suffering and pain, but
one of mystery and magic. Blue is the sound of a train whistle at night
passing through a small Midwestern town, is the long-held note of a
saxophone, is a Mozart violin concerto; blue is twilight, is autumn, is
a lake in the woods, is rain in the city, is a sad movie about lovers part-
ing or dying. Blue doesn't make the world less beautiful; it only con-
jures up what I once called at twelve "the poetic feeling": rapture
tinged with yearning, sadness made pleasurable through art. Joy mixed
with sorrow. Both things at once.

Sometimes I wonder if I have always loved blue notes, blue shadows, and blue tears, or if I grew to love them because they mirror back
to me the sense of loss I've had since I was young. I wonder if I love
blue things more now because I claim them more readily, if making

melancholy a friend of mine instead of an enemy has made me friends with melancholy's pleasures. I wonder if I love blue things more because of my upbringing as a Christian Scientist or in spite of it. Was I a happy child whose temperament changed unalterably into one overlaid by melancholy, or did I always have this streak of sadness? It's an idle wonder, one of many I entertain as I look back on my life and think, *What would have happened* if? I'll never know the answer. I only know that I have come to see my own blue times as valuable, and as necessary. Although I remember a time when I was happy and beloved and safe, a time when my mother and I drew pictures together and I sat on her lap listening to the Bible, I would not want to go back to a time when the only windows I was supposed to look through were rose-colored. I do not want to live in a country where there are only cheerful people wearing smiling faces. The world is an achingly beautiful and awful place. There is meaning and even pleasure sometimes in melancholy and in wrenching, reverent grief.

The Dalai Lama, a man of great wisdom, is said to begin every speech with the comment that the purpose of life is to be happy. But in my as yet unenlightened state I will settle for what Alice Miller asserts instead, that "the true opposite of depression is not gaiety or absence of pain, but vitality, the freedom to experience spontaneous feelings." I don't always like to feel my true feelings—in fact, I sometimes hate it—but the joy that is the other side of misery is my reward. Anything is worth not staying frozen, not being stuck, keeping moving, letting the energy of Kali, goddess of creation and destruction, move through me, letting Medusa's blood run in my veins, both healing and slaying. It may be, in the end, that the windows of the house I want to live in are neither blue nor rose, but clear, both transparent and reflective, revealing only a constantly shifting skies, from sun to rain to night to fog, ice storms followed by balmy afternoons, hurricanes giving way to tropical breezes. Night and day, and night again.

Testimony is a vital part of the religion I grew up in. The word comes from the Latin *testare,* which means "to witness." In Christian Science Wednesday is Testimony night, the evening when members of the congregation come together to tell the stories of their healing. As I have worked on this book over the years I have come to see this memoir not only as an act of witness, but of mending, a chance to explore the religion that formed my early years, a chance to see where it came from, a chance to acknowledge my admiration and respect for some aspects of it.

Christian Science is a nineteenth-century church created by a woman and as such will have enduring interest as a part of our cultural and spiritual history in this country. But of what value is its historical importance to me, this religion that turned my early life upside down? Without Christian Science my mother might still be alive or, if not, she might not have broken down or suffered such mental torment. How can I, so harmed by this church, still find it the source of so much meaning in my life? I was raised like Candide to believe that all was for the best in this best of all possible worlds, but like Job, I found out differently. My education in fear and suffering was thorough. I was often ashamed and lonely and frightened inside as I grew up, cut off from my feelings, worried about going crazy. I was also cut off from a spirituality that had once given me solace and joy. My shame and anger prevented me from looking at that spirituality or any other, for fear of being duped again.

Yet my memories told me other stories too, stories of empowerment and love. From the beginning I was taught that God was our Father-Mother and that women had an equal right to divine attention. I knew that the founder of our church was a woman and every Sunday I saw women in positions of power, a sight that affected me profoundly and that made it possible for me to help create a feminist workplace and to wield power myself. I saw women like my grandmother engaged in moving mountains and I saw women like my mother engaged in a daily spiritual practice that sustained them through many of their troubles. I may have been taught a lot of metaphysical claptrap, but I was also taught the importance of love as a healing force. Although I later rejected that teaching, because of the way healing was defined, I have come back to it. I may define love differently and healing differently, but the concept of loving-kindness is one I learned early on and have tried to relearn.

Fairy tales helped me prepare for the wickedness and suffering that came my way, but I was still stunned when my life changed, and when things that were supposed not to exist turned out to be such a large part of life. Yet as I grew up, I continued to see evil as outside me, as out there, in political-economic systems that denied justice and equality, that polluted the world and kept so many down in order that so few could prosper. Now that evil feels closer to home: it's also my own anger and lack of compassion, my own judgments and denial that contribute to the world I live in. I work on acknowledging my shadow side even as I continue to believe in social change and to work for it.

When I was young my father usually preferred, in spite of what had happened to him, to look at his life through rose-colored windows. It must have seemed to him, by the time he was in his thirties, that life had tried him enough and that his struggles were far behind him. He had suffered so much, as a child, as an adolescent, as a young adult, with sickness, loss, and death, that it must have seemed that nothing more could happen to him, that he had used up his allotment of bad luck, that he had used up several lifetimes of misfortune in fact. My early years were full of stories that traced his rags-to-riches biography. Obstacles existed only to be overcome, pain could be surmounted, loss could be forgotten. I did not expect life to be easy, but I grew up expecting, in that strange, cockeyed way of my father, to be lucky. Often I've felt that I've been extremely fortunate, and just as often I've been made to realize, humbly, that things don't always go the way I would like. That's especially true in the literary world. A grant or award one year can presage a string of rejections the next; good reviews can be followed by indifferent ones.

But this notion of luck and success and putting together a résumé that underlines my persistence and ambition means less than it used to. Writing is my vocation; it is, as it has always been, what I have been placed on earth to do. I don't judge myself so much any longer on what I have accomplished or not accomplished. I don't judge my father on the basis of his success or failure either. There are ways in which I've tried to rescue him, ways in which I still yearn for his attention, for the praise I longed for and never received. But mostly, these days, as he slides toward eighty, I find myself struck by the tenacity with which he enjoys small things in life and the mindfulness with which he can invest the present. Once he questioned his life and was bitter. Now he does not blame, but often rejoices.

A few years ago I took him to the Ballard Locks in Seattle. The locks raise and lower the water level from Lake Union to Puget Sound, so that boats and ships can pass from one to the other. It's a process that is absorbing to watch, and we stood there for a long time that sunny autumn day, smelling the mingling of salt and fresh air, watching the seagulls dive and the water rush in and out of the locks. Then we walked across to the fish ladder that has been constructed so that the salmon can return from the ocean to the streams where they were hatched. The ladder is actually a series of weirs that climb up the side of the dam, and that have water rushing downwards through them. Alongside several of the weirs a viewing room has been built, with aquarium-style plateglass windows that show small bubbling water rooms bursting at certain times of the year with Coho or Chinook struggling to swim upstream against a fierce current that keeps pulling them down.

We looked at the fish quite a while, and then I left my father so that I could read about the life cycle of the salmon. When I returned, he was still there, absorbed in the progress of one particular fish, a big battered silvery Chinook salmon that seemed to be making no progress in the strong current.

"I've been watching this fish," my father said. "I've been watching him for half an hour. He gets a little ways, and then he goes backward. Once he got sucked back into the tunnel. Then he came out again.

"I think he's tired," my father said, and I could see his reflection in the glass, softened, so that his strong features stood out through the wrinkles. He still had the bright blue eyes of a Midwestern Swedish farm boy, brighter than the dreamy blue-green of the water. "I don't know if he's going to make it. But every time I think, No he's going backwards, he goes forward. He doesn't give up. Is he making headway? I don't know. It looks very hard. But he just keeps going. He doesn't know why."

I always thought my father's gift to me was persistence, but now I wonder if his legacy is more complicated: a lack of bitterness, an acceptance of fate's twists and turns, a reverent awe at the mystery of life, a mystery that lets some of us die and some of us keep struggling.

I once cast my life as one sort of fairy tale: the story of a motherless girl who sets off to find her fortune and, after many setbacks, achieves success. That was the myth I told myself, and that I lived by. But now I wonder if the fairy tale I have lived through did not have an entirely different meaning and focus. If it was not the story of an enchantment that must be lifted, a silence that must be broken in order for the healing to begin. In their introduction to *The Classic Fairy Tales*, Iona and Peter Opie write: "The wonderful happens, the love is recognized, the spell of misfortune is broken, when the situation that already exists is utterly accepted, when additional tasks or disappointments are boldly faced, when poverty is seen to be of no consequence, when an unfairness is borne without indignation, when the loathsome is loved."

"Ye shall know the Truth, and the Truth shall make you free." Each time I sit in a Christian Science church, I see these words on the wall. I've been sitting through services at Christian Science churches since I began to write this memoir, not frequently, but consistently. As I listen to the service, tears often come to my eyes. It is so familiar and so reassuring. I still love the hymns and I still love hearing the Bible read aloud. I love seeing two women up in front on the dais, reading to us and to each other in measured voices. My childhood always comes back to me, and I weep for what I once loved and what I once believed. But at some point during the service I find that I grow restive and skeptical. My ears will catch some line from Mrs. Eddy about false sense impressions or about the nature of reality, and I will realize that I am longing for the hour to be over, so that I can get outside and back to the world of the senses that sustains me.

Still I notice that, over the last years, my resistance to religion has vanished, and instead of scorn I've become possessed by a large curiosity. Many books I've thrown down on the floor in disgust, and I'll probably never lose my irritation with simplistic statements about God being Love, and Love being All, and All being One. My sense of humor is still a healthy part of my personality. I don't like mush and I don't like metaphysics and I don't like authorities who deal in either. Yet the surprise to me is how many books I did not throw down in disgust. Books by Thomas Moore and James Hillman on the mysteries of the soul and the necessity of reclaiming the foolish and shameful and shadow sides of our selves. Books on the goddesses of ancient times and on women's religions today. Histories of God and works on snake-handlers and those who speak in tongues. Books on Buddhism, especially the lively and compassionate works of the Tibetan Buddhist nun Pema Chödrön. Memoirs about religion and spirituality by Catholic feminists and journals of travels and awakenings by those who felt the urgent need for a spiritual life. Stories of Jews who became Buddhists; Lutherans who joined Zen monasteries; Catholics who became followers of the Great Goddess.

I'm not a candidate for conversion, nor will I ever return to the religion of my childhood as some of my Jewish and Christian friends have done. Christian Science is too airy and meager for me, too narrow and poverty-stricken a faith. Its Neo-Platonism has also made it difficult for me to take up polytheism, however much I enjoy reading about devas and goddesses. I am still hostage in some manner to the beliefs instilled in me in childhood, suspicious of pomp and ritual, loud preaching, extravagant devotions. I am more able to imagine a practice that involves attentive study and quiet prayer than one with music and calling out and letting the spirit come. The concept of an extremely personal God is hard to accept, which makes Buddhism a more congenial place for me than any Protestant faith, however liberal. I stay away from sects and feelings of being special, and the antiauthoritarianism I still carry in response to Mrs. Eddy's iron grip on her church makes it unlikely I could ever follow a leader or a guru. And yet in spite of all these reservations, my sense of the sacred is stronger than before, as is my conviction that private and communal spiritual practices are as essential as community service and political action. I have stopped turning my back on what was once so important in my life, and embraced it. Spirituality seems to me full of richness and contradiction, of answers that I do not want, and questions that I want to keep asking.

In the summer of 1995 I went back to Ireland with Tere. It had been eight years since I'd looked up my cousin Dan. In the meantime he'd married Kathleen and had three young children, Anne-Marie, Noel, and Fiona. I loved the idea of being related to a little child called Fiona Lane. I met other relatives too, cousin David and his family, and old Sean Lane, whose West Cork accent we could barely understand, but who remembered the name Jeremiah Lane, and the story of the children who had left for America long ago.

One night David and Dan decided to take Tere and me and most of the children to see where some of the Lanes were buried. It was in a little, out-of-the-way cemetery near Ballynacarriga, a cemetery where so many victims of the Famine had been buried that it was called the Famine Graveyard. We arrived at sunset. It was an old strange hummocky landscape, full of tilted stone Celtic crosses and cracked slabs, and the broken gravestones were barely legible. Many graves didn't have stones at all; the families were buried all together, and only metal crosses with initials scratched on them marked the graves. Four-year-old Anne-Marie, wearing my sunglasses and watch, held my hand and we stumbled with the others over the lumpy ground. There was solemnity there in that green and gold place, and gaiety too. We found ourselves laughing as we fell and picked ourselves up, as if the place had a funhouse floor and we couldn't keep our footing. Still we helped each other, still we made our way, and still we laughed, although choked up too, some of us, with an emotion we couldn't speak: reverence for the dead, and sorrow at their passing.

I thought of how a few days before Tere and I had visited some gypsy fortune-tellers and had had our palms read. My gypsy said that I had many lines that showed early sorrow, but that the sorrow was over now. "It's in the past," she said. "Put it behind you now, my dear. You must believe me, my dear, your sorrows are over." And she predicted happiness and love and friendship for me, and a long life.

Outside her caravan, afterwards, I peered closely at my palm and showed the deep lines of early sorrow to Tere. They were not far from the two thin white lines of sorrow and rage that I had once made myself. I wondered if the gypsy had seen those two pale scars over my wrist, if that was why she held my hand tight at the end and looked into my eyes and said, so urgently, "You must believe me, my dear, your sorrows are over."

I wished I could believe her. Some days I wanted nothing more than for my sorrows to be over forever. But what would that mean? That I wouldn't remember and miss my mother? That I wouldn't grieve for my father when he died? That I hadn't been and wouldn't be desolated when friends and family sickened or disappeared? Sorrow comes from living, and while I still lived, I would know sorrow. Someday I would lose Tere and everybody else I loved. Or I would get sick, I would know what it was to die slowly or suddenly. So many things were wrong in the world, so many people were suffering. The natural world itself was suffering terribly. Anything could happen—look at the Famine, the *Titanic*, Hiroshima. Sudden disaster and death were never far, at any time, from my thoughts.

But there in the Famine Graveyard with the bones of some of my ancestors below me, I felt at peace with death as much as with life, with whatever it had brought me and would bring me. I had been well loved as a child, I had known loving-kindness, and I could finally, after many false starts, give that love wholeheartedly back. My life had become complicated and contradictory and I had learned to appreciate contradiction and to accept sadness, to value seeing through blue windows as a gift rather than a penance. I will never know the true story of my mother's life, or indeed my own, but I can still tell it, and find meaning in its many mysteries.

I held out my palms, crisscrossed with lines of great sorrow and of great happiness, to Anne-Marie, and together we helped each other stumble back through the Famine Graveyard to the open gate.

Some Notes on Further Reading About Christian Science

*I*n the course of working this memoir I had the pleasure of roaming through many volumes on everything from nineteenth-century medicine to twentieth-century research on the mind/body connection, from theological texts to nature history, from studies of madness to fairy tales. Some of these books are cited in my memoir. I would particularly like to acknowledge the work of Maria-Luisa von Franz, especially in *The Shadow and Evil in Fairy Tales,* and of William James in his classic, *The Varieties of Religious Experience.*

In telling the story of a childhood steeped in Christian Science I relied on my memories of what I was taught when young. For this reason I particularly emphasized *A Child's Life of Mary Baker Eddy* by Ella Hay (Boston: Christian Publishing Company, 1942) and the stories in *The Christian Science Sentinel* from the fifties. However I also needed to inform myself about the historical and theological context of this religion and for that I turned to a number of titles, some of which may be of further interest to the reader.

A good basic biography of Mrs. Eddy is the recent (rather oddly named, I think, given our founder's lack of interest in gore), *"With Bleeding Footsteps"* by Robert David Thomas (New York: Knopf, 1994), while *The Emergence of Christian Science in American Religious Life* by Stephen Gottchalk (Berkeley: University of California Press, 1973) still remains one of the most approachable academic studies of this religion. For a welcome new perspective on Christian Science as a women's faith, I relied on Susan Starr Sered's excellent study, *Priestess, Mother, Sacred Sister: Religions Dominated by Women* (New York: Oxford University Press, 1994), and on a fascinating article by Margery Fox, "The Socioreligious Role of the Christian Science Practitioner," in *Women as Healers: Cross-cultural Perspectives,* edited by Carol Shepherd Mc-

Clain (New Brunswick, New Jersey: Rutgers University Press, 1989).

In general, books on Christian Science and Mrs. Eddy fall into two categories: the adulatory and the caustic. Among the former is the methodical and praiseworthy three-volume biography of Mary Baker Eddy by Robert Peel, *Years of Discovery, Years of Trial, Years of Authority* (Boston: Christian Science Publishing Company, 1966; 1971; 1977). Peel, a Christian Scientist, is one of the few scholars ever to be trusted with access to the Mother Church's archives of Mrs. Eddy's papers. He has also written a couple of other interesting books, including *Christian Science and Its Encounter with American Culture* (New York: Henry Holt, 1958), which discusses the influence the New England Transcendentalists may have had on Mrs. Eddy.

The critical books at this point outnumber the positive and in general make for more fascinating reading. The best of them is still Willa Cather and Georgina Milmine's biography, now in print again from the University of Nebraska Press. Julius Silberger Jr.'s book, *Mary Baker Eddy: An Interpretive Biography of the Founder of Christian Science* (Boston: Little Brown, 1980), a speculative book by a psychoanalyst into Mrs. Eddy's suppressed emotional world, is worth reading for insights into the nature of Malicious Animal Magnetism in the church, as is *Deadly Blessings: Faith Healing on Trial* (Buffalo, NY: Prometheus Books, 1990) by Richard J. Brenneman, which investigates some of the court cases involving children of Christian Science parents.

Although not strictly about Christian Science, Cynthia Grant Tucker's study of the life of Mary Collson, *Healer in Harm's Way* (Knoxville: University of Tennessee Press, 1994, second edition, issued originally as *A Women's Ministry* by Temple University Press in 1984) provides a very valuable glimpse of the inner struggle of a woman who wanted to believe in good and was continually faced with evil. I am indebted to Tucker for her original research on this subject.

When I first saw Thomas Simmons's memoir about growing up Christian Scientist, *The Unseen Shore* (Boston: Beacon Press, 1991), I experienced the shock probably common to all writers who discover that someone else seems to have gotten there first—"He's written my book!" Thomas Simmons's story is, of course, his own very moving memoir of struggling with this complex faith. Reading it made my loneliness a little less and helped convince me that my own experiences as a Christian Science child could be told, and that they could also mean something to a stranger.